# OXFORD STUDIES IN EUROPEAN LAW

*Series Editors:*
Paul Craig, Professor of English Law at St John's College, Oxford and
Gráinne de Búrca, Professor of Law at New York University School of Law

The aim of this series is to publish important and original research on EU law. The focus is on scholarly monographs, with a particular emphasis on those which are interdisciplinary in nature. Edited collections of essays will also be included where they are appropriate. The series is wide in scope and aims to cover studies of particular areas of substantive and of institutional law, historical works, theoretical studies, and analyses of current debates, as well as questions of perennial interest such as the relationship between national and EU law and the novel forms of governance emerging in and beyond Europe. The fact that many of the works are interdisciplinary will make the series of interest to all those concerned with the governance and operation of the EU.

OTHER TITLES IN THIS SERIES

**Official Secrets and Oversight in the EU**
*Law and Practices of Classified Information*
Vigjilenca Abazi

**Risk Regulation in the Internal Market**
*Lessons from Agricultural Biotechnology*
Maria Weimer

**EU Health Law & Policy**
*The Expansion of EU Power in Public Health and Health Care*
Anniek de Ruijter

**The Horizontal Effect of Fundamental Rights in the European Union**
*A Constitutional Analysis*
Eleni Frantziou

**EU Powers Under External Pressure**
*How the EU's External Actions Alter its Internal Structures*
Christina Eckes

**Frontex and Human Rights**
*Responsibility in 'Multi-Actor Situations' under the ECHR and EU Public Liability Law*
Melanie Fink

**EU Equality Law**
*The First Fundamental Rights Policy of the EU*
Elise Muir

**Subnational Authorities in EU Law**
Michèle Finck

**Accessing Asylum in Europe**
Violeta Moreno-Lax

**National Parliaments after the Lisbon Treaty & the Euro Crisis**
Davor Jančić

**Environmental Integration in Competition and Free-Movement Laws**
Julian Nowag

**EU Agencies**
*Legal and Political Limits to the Transformation of the EU Administration*
Merijn Chamon

**Coherence in EU Competition law**
Wolf Sauter

**Foreign Policy Objectives in European Constitutional Law**
Joris Larik

**Economic Governance in Europe**
*Comparative Paradoxes and Constitutional Challenges*
Federico Fabbrini

**Private Regulation and the Internal Market**
*Sports, Legal Services, and Standard Setting in EU Economic Law*
Mislav Mataija

OXFORD STUDIES IN EUROPEAN LAW



# Accountability in EU Security and Defence

# Accountability in EU Security and Defence

## *The Law and Practice of Peacebuilding*

CAROLYN MOSER

*Senior Research Fellow and Head of Research Group,*
*Max Planck Institute for Comparative Public Law*
*and International Law, Heidelberg*

OXFORD
UNIVERSITY PRESS

OXFORD
UNIVERSITY PRESS

Great Clarendon Street, Oxford, OX2 6DP,
United Kingdom

Oxford University Press is a department of the University of Oxford.
It furthers the University's objective of excellence in research, scholarship,
and education by publishing worldwide. Oxford is a registered trade mark of
Oxford University Press in the UK and in certain other countries



First Edition published in 2020

Impression: 1



Published in the United States of America by Oxford University Press
198 Madison Avenue, New York, NY 10016, United States of America

British Library Cataloguing in Publication Data
Data available

Library of Congress Control Number: 2019957832

ISBN 978–0–19–884481–5

Printed and bound by
CPI Group (UK) Ltd, Croydon, CR0 4YY

*To my family*

# Series Editor's Preface

This book deals with two intersecting topics, each of which is of considerable interest for scholars of EU law and politics. The first is a particular dimension of EU security and defence policy, namely peacebuilding or civil crisis management, and the second is the question of accountability for EU policies and activities.

As the author points out, relatively little is known about the security and defence aspects of EU law and policy, not least because these are governed by intergovernmental rather than supranational structures and processes, and hence they tend to be relatively less transparent and visible than many other areas of EU policy. And yet peacebuilding is an important part of the EU's external activities, with at least ten EU missions existing at present in different countries of Europe, Africa, and the Middle East. This book fills some of the existing gap in the literature.

Moser's interest is less in the detail of EU peacebuilding policy as in the structures, processes, and mechanisms of accountability—including political, administrative, and judicial—for this complex policy which is shared between the EU and its Member States. Her findings are very interesting, and do not necessarily match the assumptions the reader might begin with as to the likely lack of accountability in this intergovernmental field of EU external security and defence policy. What the author finds in her study is that although the field is in theory intergovernmental and hence subject to accountability scrutiny at the Member State rather than at the EU level, in practice EU peacebuilding is run by a small and apparently efficient EU bureaucracy which is not formally subject to national level accountability or to supranational EU processes of accountability. Nevertheless, and equally importantly, she finds that although de jure accountability is therefore weak, the de facto accountability supplied in practice by institutions such as the Ombudsman, the Court of Justice, the European Parliament, and the Court of Auditors, arising from processes initiated and complaints made, is quite significant. Further, she finds that the degree and quality of accountability at EU level for peacebuilding exceeds that at Member State level in the vast majority of Member States, where she notes that the dominance of the executive in security and defence—and particularly civilian crisis management—is hardly ever challenged.

The book is based on desk research as well as on interviews and case studies, and it integrates legal and political science insights and approaches in its assessment of the de jure and de facto accountability mechanisms and practices of EU peacebuilding. It is thoroughly researched and carefully argued, and should be of considerable interest to lawyers and political science scholars alike, as well as all of those interested in EU foreign and security policy and questions of accountability more generally.

Paul Craig
Gráinne de Búrca

# Acknowledgements

This book marks the culmination of an exciting academic journey that made me discover the law, practice, and politics of EU security and defence. It is based on my doctoral thesis, defended at Utrecht University in March 2018, which I revised and updated to include developments until September 2019.

Many people have made a difference to my research on accountability in EU peacebuilding presented in this monograph and I want the seize the opportunity to warmly thank them. First, I would like to express my deep gratitude to my PhD supervisors Mark Bovens, Gijs Jan Brandsma, and Anne Peters. My work has greatly benefitted from their complementary disciplinary expertise and valuable research knowhow. Their thoughtful guidance and precious advice has been a continuous source of inspiration and encouragement, as has been the great deal of trust they have placed in me and my project from the very start. Stimulating exchanges with various interlocutors, who generously shared their time and insights with me, have also been a great source of inspiration. Significant credit is due to my respondents from different EU and national institutions whose open-mindedness and outspokenness has been of tremendous help when unravelling the intricate realities of EU peacebuilding. Likewise, I would like to thankfully acknowledge the diligent handling of my various access-to-document requests by the staff of the European Ombudsman. Moreover, this book has considerably profited from enlightening and enjoyable discussions with a number of scholars. I would particularly like to thank Iris Canor, Marise Cremona, Deirdre Curtin, Hylke Dijkstra, Morten Egeberg, David Kosar, Albert Meijer, and Achilles Skordas, whose erudite feedback has contributed to fine-tuning my conceptualization(s) and advance my investigation. In addition, my work (in progress) has been significantly improved thanks to the sharp scrutiny, constructive critique, and considerate suggestions of many of my colleagues. I was indeed very fortunate to conduct research at two splendid academic institutions full of remarkably skilled and experienced scholars, namely the Max Planck Institute for Comparative Public Law and International Law in Heidelberg and the Utrecht School of Governance. In particular, I wish to express my sincere appreciation to Jelena von Achenbach, Anuscheh Farahat, Jochen A. Frowein, Michalis Ioannidis, Isabelle Ley, Davide Paris, Thomas Schillemans, Mira Scholten, and Nele Yang for reading and knowledgeably commenting on different bits of this book at various stages. Furthermore, I would like to thank the members of my PhD committee as well as the two anonymous OUP reviewers for their helpful observations and learned comments. I am also grateful to Matthew Milbourne for carefully proofreading the final manuscript. Likewise,

I am indebted to my research assistants Rabia Ferahkaya and Lukas Märtin for diligently checking bibliographic references. Finally, it is a pleasure to acknowledge at this juncture that, during the final phase of writing this book, I received funding from the Max Planck Society under the Minerva Fast Track scheme.

The last words of gratitude are for my family. It takes a village to raise a child, says an African proverb. Similarly, it takes a loving and understanding family to finish a PhD and to endure the painstaking exercise of turning it into a book. I definitely owe much gratitude to my parents and to my sister for their unwavering support. Lastly, I am most indebted to my husband, Samuel, for his heartfelt encouragement and admirable patience throughout this journey.

Carolyn Moser

# Contents

# List of Figures

# List of Tables

# Table of Cases

## CJEU

## EUROPEAN OMBUDSMAN

# List of Abbreviations

| | |
|---|---|
| $A_{(c)}$ | Accountability for conduct |
| $A_{(i)}$ | Accountability for information |
| *AFET* | (EP) Committee on Foreign Affairs |
| *AFSJ* | Area of Freedom, Security and Justice (see also JHA) |
| *AG* | Advocate General (at the CJEU) |
| *AMIS* | African Union Mission in Sudan |
| *BIH* | Bosnia and Herzegovina |
| *BUDG* | (EP) Committee on Budgets |
| *CCDP* | Civilian Capability Development Plan |
| *CEOS* | Conditions of Employment of Other Servants of the EU |
| *CFSP* | Common Foreign and Security Policy |
| *CIVCOM* | Committee for Civilian Aspects of Crisis Management |
| *CivOpsCdr* | Civilian Operations Commander |
| *CJEU* | Court of Justice of the EU |
| *CMC* | Crisis Management Concept |
| *CMCO* | Civil–Military Coordination (concept for) |
| *CIMIC* | Civil–Military Co-operation (concept for) |
| *CMPD* | Crisis Management Planning Directorate |
| *CONOPS* | Concept of Operations |
| *COPPS* | Coordination Office for Palestinian Police Support |
| *COREPER* | Committee of Permanent Representatives |
| *COSAC* | Conference of Parliamentary Committees for Union Affairs of Parliaments of the European Union |
| *CPCC* | Civilian Planning and Conduct Capability |
| *CSDP* | Common Security and Defence Policy |
| *CST* | Civil Service Tribunal |
| *DHoM* | Deputy Head of Mission |
| *EC* | European Communities |
| *ECA* | European Court of Auditors |
| *ECGAB* | European Code of Good Administrative Behaviour |
| *ECHR* | European Convention on Human Rights |
| *ECtHR* | European Court of Human Rights |
| *ECJ* | European Court of Justice (see also CJEU) |
| *EDC* | European Defence Community |
| *EEAS* | European External Action Service |
| *EP* | European Parliament |
| *EPC* | European Political Cooperation |
| *ESDP* | European Security and Defence Policy |
| *ESS* | European Security Strategy |

| | |
|---|---|
| *EU* | European Union |
| *EUAM* | EU Advisory Mission; or European Union Administration of Mostar |
| *EUBAM* | EU Border Assistance Mission |
| *EUCAP* | EU Capacity Building Mission |
| *EUCI* | EU classified information |
| *EUFOR* | EU Force (terrestrial) |
| *EUGS* | European Union Global Strategy |
| *EULEX* | EU Rule of Law Mission |
| *EUMC* | EU Military Committee |
| *EUMM* | EU Monitoring Mission |
| *EUMS* | EU Military Staff |
| *EUPM* | EU Police Mission (see also EUPOL) |
| *EUPOL* | EU Police Mission (see also EUPM) |
| *EUTM* | EU Training Mission |
| *FAC* | Foreign Affairs Council |
| *FPI* | Service for Foreign Policy Instruments (European Commission) |
| *HoM* | Head of Mission |
| *HR* | High Representative of the Union for Foreign Affairs and Security Policy (see also SG/HR) |
| *IIA* | Interinstitutional agreement |
| *IntCen* | EU Intelligence Analysis Centre (EEAS) |
| *ISP* | Integrated Approach for Security and Peace |
| *JHA* | Justice and Home Affairs (see also AFSJ) |
| *JSCC* | Joint Support Coordination Cell |
| *MEP* | Member of the European Parliament |
| *MS* | Member State (of the EU) |
| *MPCC* | Military Planning and Conduct Capability |
| *NATO* | North Atlantic Treaty Organization |
| *NGO* | non-governmental organization |
| *OLAF* | European Anti-fraud Office |
| *OPLAN* | Operational Plan |
| *orcon* | originator consent |
| *OSCE* | Organization for Security and Co-operation in Europe |
| *PESCO* | Permanent Structured Cooperation |
| *PRISM* | Prevention of Conflicts, Rule of law/SSR, Integrated Approach, Stabilisation and Mediation (EEAS) |
| *PSC* | Political and Security Committee |
| *RELEX* | (Council)Working Party of Foreign Relations Counsellors |
| *SALWs* | Small Arms and Light Weapons |
| *SEA* | Single European Act |
| *SECDEFPOL* | Security and Defence Policy (EEAS) |
| *SEDE* | (AFET) sub-committee on Security and Defence (EP) |
| *SG/HR* | Secretary-General of the Council/High Representative of the Union for the CSFP (see also HR) |
| *SGUA* | Support Group for Ukraine (Neighbourhood Policy) |

| | |
|---|---|
| *SOMA* | Status of Mission Agreement |
| *SOP* | Standard Operating Procedures |
| *SSR* | Security Sector Reform |
| *TEU* | Treaty on European Union |
| *TFEU* | Treaty on the Functioning of the European Union |
| *TTIP* | Transatlantic Trade and Investment Partnership |
| *UN* | United Nations |
| *UNC* | UN Charter |
| *UNSC* | UN Security Council |
| *VCDR* | Vienna Convention on Diplomatic Relations |
| *VP* | Vice-President of the European Commission |
| *WEU* | Western European Union |

# 1
# Accountability for EU Peacebuilding Missions

Though largely unnoticed, the European Union (EU) has for almost two decades conducted peace operations in conflict-torn regions around the globe. Roughly 2,000 civilian experts currently serve in ten ongoing civilian missions deployed to Eastern Europe, the Balkan region, sub-Saharan Africa, and the Middle East. While reading these lines, Scandinavian police officers provide strategic advice and training to their Ukrainian homologues to build up community policing—that is direct interaction and dialogue with (local) communities—with the aim of fostering and maintaining trust. In Bamako, police officers attend a seminar on professional ethics taught by a Spanish law enforcement officer, while local authorities together with a French security sector expert elaborate a new curriculum for Malian law enforcement staff. More than four thousand kilometres away, a Kosovar magistrate is about to close a joint investigation with her Italian counterpart in a civil claim related to a property dispute. Simultaneously, EU observers from Denmark and Poland help Georgian schoolchildren attend school across the administrative boundary line. In the West Bank, Palestinian participants interact with a Swedish police trainer with a view to raising human rights awareness. And at the same time, Iraqi authorities receive assistance by a German security expert for the implementation of the country's national security strategy.

These snapshots from the field illustrate the wide thematic and geographic scope of the EU's extraterritorial peacebuilding activities carried out under its Common Security and Defence Policy (CSDP).[1] The aim of these manifold civilian missions is to contribute to the restoration of stability and security in areas shaken by crises or conflicts, and to prevent future tensions or hostilities. Accordingly, mission mandates cover a broad range of multidimensional tasks: activities include border monitoring, rule of law support, police training, law enforcement capacity building, and security sector reform. Their operational diversity notwithstanding, a common thread underpins all of these missions: the aspiration to enhance the capacity of institutions key to the rule of law (ie police, judiciary, and the armed forces), all of which fulfil core State functions.

[1] Prior to the latest Treaty revision, the CSDP was called *European* Security and Defence Policy (ESDP). For the sake of consistency, this book uses the term CSDP to refer to the policy prior to and after the entry into force of the Treaty of Lisbon in 2009.

*Accountability in EU Security and Defence.* Carolyn Moser, Oxford University Press (2020). © Carolyn Moser.
DOI: 10.1093/oso/9780198844815.001.0001

Considering the extensive mandates of EU peacebuilding missions, who is holding the various actors to account? Insights from practice underscore the salience of this question. Indeed, a number of incidents revealed both institutional and procedural weaknesses and irregularities tied to accountability across EU peacebuilding activities. Despite these alarming realities, no evaluation has to date been undertaken to understand who can be held to account, by whom, and how, for the wide array of civilian CSDP action types. With an operational track record of more than twenty civilian missions of varying types and sizes set up so far, civilian crisis management accounts for two-thirds of the EU's peace operations. But regardless of this obvious operational tilt to civilian missions, civilian CSDP activities go largely unnoticed by the general public, and scholars show significantly more interest in the EU's military operations. This book, therefore, offers the first comprehensive legal analysis and empirical study of the law and practice of the civilian dimension of the CSDP and, more specifically, of accountability in the context of EU peacebuilding, which constitutes an important instrument in the EU's foreign policy and security toolbox.[2] Next to providing an innovative account of the integration trajectory and operational realities of civilian crisis management, the ensuing study disentangles the complex web of political, legal, and administrative de jure and de facto accountability arrangements at work.

## 1. The CSDP and Its Civilian Dimension

Civilian crisis management—as peacebuilding activities under the CSDP are termed in EU jargon—became operational in 2003 when the first police mission was deployed to Bosnia and Herzegovina. Since then, the EU has launched twenty-two missions across Europe, Africa, the Middle East, and Asia, as can be seen in Figure 1.1. Among them were seven police missions, three rule of law missions, two monitoring missions, two border assistance missions, four security sector reform missions, and four missions with both civilian and military components.[3]

Only resolute optimists would have thought one or two decades ago that, by the year 2020, the EU would be an international security provider deploying civilian experts as well as military staff to conflict-torn regions. Constructing a European

[2] In 2018 civilian crisis management received a significant politico-strategic stimulus with the adoption of specific Council Conclusions on the matter, followed by the endorsement of a dedicated capabilities development plan. See Council Conclusions on strengthening civilian CSDP, adopted by the Foreign Affairs Council on 28 May 2018, Council Doc 9288/18; Council Doc 11807/18 of 4 September 2018, 'Civilian Capabilities Development Plan'.

[3] To date (October 2019), twenty-two civilian missions (and twelve military operations) have been launched. They have been deployed to (in alphabetical order): Afghanistan, Bosnia and Herzegovina, Burkina Faso, Chad, Congo (Democratic Republic of Congo), the Former Yugoslav Republic of Macedonia (today North Macedonia), Georgia, Guinea-Bissau, Indonesia (province of Aceh), Iraq, Kenya, Kosovo, Libya, Mali, Niger, the Palestinian Territories, Tanzania, the Seychelles, Somalia, (South-)Soudan, and Ukraine—and, for military operations, additionally the Central African Republic.

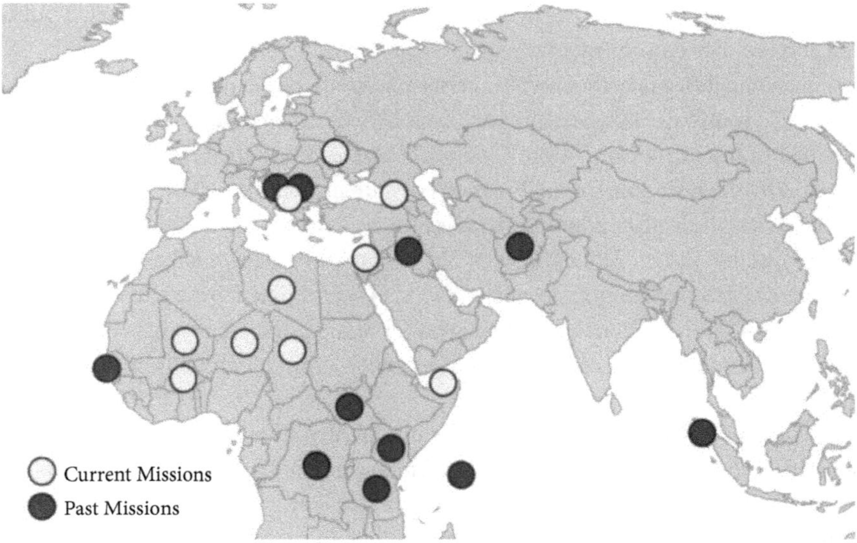


**Figure 1.1** Map of EU civilian CSDP missions (2003–19)

security and defence policy has undeniably been a tricky undertaking: the genesis of the CSDP, which is an integral part of the Common Foreign and Security Policy (CFSP), has been a story marked by the interplay of great aspirations and severe setbacks, as well as deeply rooted concerns and persistent hesitation. Only in light of the geopolitical transformations of the post-Cold War era did Member States finally decide to enlarge the EU's foreign policy portfolio of trade and development to include peace operations, which are open to the participation of third States (eg Switzerland, Norway, and Canada). The EU's efforts are obviously part of a broader peace operations scheme implemented under the United Nations (UN) umbrella. Regarding civilian missions, the EU budget allocates some EUR 300 million per annum to the ten ongoing peacebuilding missions (payments are generally a little lower). An additional funding stream comes from national budgets: contributing Members States share the missions' financial burden by bearing all expenditure related to seconded personnel, which includes salaries, medical coverage, and travel expenses.[4] Although the EU's contribution to global peacekeeping efforts is comparatively modest in numbers,[5] it carries a significant political weight: many

[4] Council Doc 7291/09 of 10 March 2009, 'Guidelines for allowances for seconded staff participating in EU civilian crisis management missions'.

[5] In roughly the same period (July 2018 to June 2019), the UN disbursed USD 6.7 billion for peacekeeping as indicated in Approved resources for peacekeeping operations for the period from 1 July 2018 to 30 June 2019, note by the Secretary-General, A/C.5/72/2 (1 July 2018). The EU deployed some 5,000 staff (both civilian and military), while the UN dispatched over 100,000 staff, including civilians, police officers, and armed personnel. However, the UN numbers paint a distorted picture, as they include both civilian *and* military activities and, therefore, cover peacekeeping as much as peacebuilding. 'Civilians' and police officers together account for some 25,000 personnel in UN missions.

stakeholders view them as particularly 'high profile' expressions of the EU's political and security commitments.[6]

Regarding its legal anchorage, EU crisis management is embedded in both international law and EU law. Missions are established on the basis of a decision of the Council of the European Union (Council),[7] and additionally rest either on an invitation by the host State or a UN Security Council resolution.[8] EU peacebuilding activities are indeed conducted in accordance with the international law principles contained in the UN Charter (UNC): apart from the fundamental principles protecting State sovereignty (Article 2(1) UNC) and prohibiting the use of force (Article 2(4) UNC), Chapter VI through VIII of the UNC are essential in the context of peace operations, albeit peace operations are not explicitly mentioned in the UNC.

At the EU level, the legal rules governing the deployment of civilian missions are laid down in Title V of the Treaty on European Union (TEU), as last modified by the Treaty of Lisbon (2007).[9] Chapter 1 of said Title, dealing with the EU's action on the international scene in general, sets out principles and objectives to be pursued in EU external action, including in the field of foreign affairs, security, and defence. Chapter 2 specifically deals with the CFSP (Section 1) and the CSDP (Section 2). It establishes the institutional and procedural set-up of the policies at stake. While the terms civilian crisis management or peacebuilding, which are used interchangeably in this book, cannot be found in primary law, they are alluded to twice: first in Article 42(1) TEU, allowing for the use of civilian and military assets outside the EU for peacekeeping, conflict prevention, and strengthening international security; and secondly in Article 43 TEU, where tasks referred to in Article 42(1) TEU are enumerated in a non-exhaustive manner.

Primary law provisions stipulate that EU peacebuilding activities take place in a fundamentally intergovernmental institutional and procedural framework, in which Member States call the shots: representatives of national governments act unanimously at high-level meetings—Heads of State and Government for the European Council, and national representatives at ministerial level for the Council.[10] According to Treaty law (Article 38 TEU), this decision-making

[6] Michael E Smith, *Europe's Common Security and Defence Policy. Capacity-Building, Experiential Learning, and Institutional Change* (Cambridge University Press 2017) 211.

[7] Art 26 and Art 31 TEU.

[8] Except for the European Union Rule of Law Mission in Kosovo (EULEX Kosovo), which is based on Security Council resolution 1244 adopted in 1999, all civilian missions were established upon invitation of the host State, as highlighted by Thierry Tardy, *CSDP in Action—What Contribution to International Security?* (European Union Institute for Security Studies 2015) 26.

[9] Throughout this book, the dates of the European Treaties (mostly displayed in brackets) indicate the year in which the respective Treaty was *signed* and not the year in which it entered into force. This is because in European security and defence matters, numerous developments took place between the signature of a treaty and its coming into force, so that Treaty law does or did not necessarily reflect the latest state of (integration) affairs.

[10] Taken in a literal sense, the adjective intergovernmental denominates an environment or situation determined by governments of different countries via national representatives. In the EU context,

activity is supported by *one* Brussels-based body, namely the Political and Security Committee (PSC), which is composed of one ambassadorial-level representative per Member State. Yet, these primary law provisions regulate the apex of the civilian crisis management pyramid only and say nothing about the bureaucratic substructure. But beneath the Council/PSC surface, there is a web of specialized Brussels-based administrative structures that autonomously handle civilian crisis management, including the preparation and implementation of Council decisions, strategic as well as operational planning of missions, and steering operational conduct. These far-reaching powers wielded de facto by the Brussels-based administrative structures raise an important, multi-layered question: are the involved actors actually held to account for their action (or omission), how might this be achieved, and by whom? Insights from practice emphasize the relevance of this governance question: numerous cases and incidents from field missions—some of which have ended up at the Court of Justice of the EU (CJEU) or the European Ombudsman, while others have led to investigations by OLAF, the European Anti-fraud Office—underscore that there are serious institutional as well as procedural weaknesses and irregularities tied to accountability.

## 2. Accountability Under Hard Governance Conditions

As a matter of fact, EU peacebuilding realities no longer correspond to the codified intergovernmental blueprint. Instead of national capitals exclusively pulling the strings in civilian CSDP, the centre of strategic and operational gravity is located in Brussels. At the core of this development is the web of specialized administrative structures located in Brussels referred to in section 1, which since the early 2000s Member States have progressively put in place to operate—initially within the Council and, since 2010—as part of the European External Action Service (EEAS). Almost two decades later, these Brussels-based structures have undeniably outgrown their 'support job'. Due to an incremental process of institutionalization and professionalization, the entire policy cycle of civilian crisis management—from agenda-setting, strategic planning, decision-making, steering to implementation and evaluation of civilian missions—is in the hands of some seventy dedicated Eurocrats.[11]

intergovernmental has come to have an additional, somehow broader meaning. As for the different elements making up an intergovernmental setting in the EU context, see Helene Sjursen, 'Not so Intergovernmental after All? On Democracy and Integration in European Foreign and Security Policy' (2011) 18 Journal of European Public Policy 1078.

[11] Ana E Juncos and Karolina Pomorska, 'Invisible and Unaccountable? National Representatives and Council Officials in EU Foreign Policy' (2011) 18 Journal of European Public Policy 1096; Hylke Dijkstra, *Policy-Making in EU Security and Defence: An Institutional Perspective* (Palgrave Macmillan 2013) 195–99; Daniel Thym, 'The Intergovernmental Constitution of the EU's Foreign, Security &

In the real world of EU peacebuilding activities, an influential and efficient Brussels-based bureaucracy runs the show, while high-level government representatives of Member States play a subsidiary role in merely formalizing or endorsing the work of the bureaucratic machinery. Treaty law, though, remains largely silent as to what happens in structures at the sub-Council level where the bulk of crisis management work is delivered. In other words, the de jure institutional and procedural framework of civilian missions remains fundamentally intergovernmental, whereas the administrative and operational realities have de facto been subject to Europeanization, 'a process in which powers are transferred vertically (from the national to the EU level) rather than horizontally (from [EU] institutions to specialized agencies)'.[12]

To capture this idiosyncratic setting, this book introduces the novel concept of *Europeanized intergovernmentalism*. The concept encapsulates the schizophrenic governance state of EU civilian crisis management, which is intergovernmental in conception but Europeanized in practice. Importantly, this Europeanization is not limited to the steady enhancement of decision-making in Brussels—a phenomenon referred to by the literature as the 'Brusselization' of EU foreign policy.[13] On the contrary, the Europeanization we witness in the context of peacebuilding also entails a substantial reconfiguration of the working level as capacities were shifted from national ministries to vertically specialized Brussels-based structures. This development, in turn, resembles the pattern of agencification.[14] But the agencification of EU peacebuilding has had a momentum of its own, as the autonomous bureaucratic crisis management structures have never explicitly been established under EU law as a body, office, or agency of the EU. Europeanized intergovernmentalism is thus the effect of *concealed* agencification, which is defined here as an informal vertical transfer of both governmental decision-making and action capacity from national ministerial departments to a specialized Brussels-based bureaucracy. As a result of this move beyond intergovernmentalism—not in law, but in practice—the powerful Europeanized peacebuilding structures remain invisible and potentially unaccountable.[15]

Defence Executive' (2011) 7 European Constitutional Law Review 453, 464; Hylke Dijkstra, 'The Influence of EU Officials in European Security and Defence' (2012) 21 European Security 311, 314, 323.

[12] Renaud Dehousse, 'Misfits: EU Law and the Transformation of European Governance' in Christian Joerges and Renaud Dehousse (eds), *Good Governance in Europe's Integrated Market* (Oxford University Press 2002) 221.

[13] David Allen, '"Who Speaks for Europe?" The Search for an Effective and Coherent External Policy' in John Peterson and Helene Sjursen (eds), *A Common Foreign Policy for Europe? Competing Visions of the CFSP* (Routledge 1998) 42.

[14] Jarle Tondral, 'Agencification' (2014) 74 Public Administration Review 545, 545, 546.

[15] The de facto transfer of power to de jure unaccountable public servants is not a new phenomenon in EU integration, as shown in the early 2000s by Carol Harlow, *Accountability in the European Union* (Oxford University Press 2002) 34. For the CFSP context, similar tendencies exist, as demonstrated by Juncos and Pomorska (n 11).

This discrepancy between law and practice in EU civilian crisis management is intriguing, not least because the de facto shift in power is likely to hamper or even harm accountability.

According to the prevailing contemporary conception of public institutions, public authorities in liberal democracies are expected to account for the exercise of power conferred to them.[16] In line with the definition provided by Mark Bovens, accountability is understood as 'a relationship between an actor and a forum, in which the actor has an obligation to explain and to justify his or her conduct, the forum can pose questions and pass judgement, and the actor may face consequences'.[17] Accountability is thus conceived as an institutional mechanism that aims at holding those entrusted with power to account for the use of that power.[18] This conception of accountability as the corollary to wielding public power[19] reflects a constitutional perspective on accountability that places much attention on checks and balances.[20] This implies that institutional as well as procedural arrangements allowing for countervailing powers play a crucial role in ensuring effective accountability.

The quest for accountability is not limited to the national sphere, whose constitutional systems traditionally provide checks and balances. The conceptual power–accountability nexus inherent to the constitutional perspective on accountability extends to the exercise of power at the international realm and in international institutions.[21] In other words, the exercise of public power should not go unchecked at the international level either. It follows from this that the process of delegating power from the national to the European plane needs to go hand in hand with the establishment of accountability arrangements if the exercise of power above the nation-state is to fulfil democratic requirements. As the European integration process is no exception to this rule, this prompts the question of who (actually) wields power in EU security and defence matters and, therefore, is under the obligation to account for the power exercised.

In a typical intergovernmental setting, decision-making and action power rests with the executive of the respective Member State. There is neither a transfer of power nor a delegation of functions to an entity above the nation-state. Therefore,

[16] Harlow (n 15) 8.

[17] Mark Bovens, 'Analysing and Assessing Accountability: A Conceptual Framework' (2007) 13 European Law Journal 447, 450.

[18] Mark Bovens, 'Two Concepts of Accountability: Accountability as a Virtue and as a Mechanism' (2010) 33 West European Politics 946, 946–67. The crucial question is thus whether public agents can be held accountable for their (in)action and not whether their action has been taken in a virtuous way.

[19] Public power is understood as the power vested in an individual or entity performing functions of the state—be they legislative, judicial, or executive in nature.

[20] Mark Bovens, Deidre Curtin, and Paul 't Hart, 'Studying the Real World of EU Accountability: Framework and Design' in Mark Bovens, Deidre Curtin, and Paul 't Hart (eds), *The Real World of EU Accountability* (Oxford University Press 2010) 51–52.

[21] International Law Association, Final Report on the Accountability of International Organisations, 2004, 5.

the existing chains of delegation and accountability remain within the national realm: power is exercised by national actors at the international level. This traditional intergovernmental conception finds its expression in the primary law provisions on EU security and defence, including peacebuilding activities. According to Treaty provisions, Member States retain their decision-making and action prerogatives, which they exercise at the EU level in meetings of two, in composition distinctively intergovernmental, institutions, namely the Council (ministerial level cooperation) and the European Council (meeting of Heads of State and Government). In addition, procedures mirror traditional intergovernmental patterns: unanimity prevails, giving Member States in principle a veto option. The usual supranational suspects—the European Commission (Commission) and the European Parliament (EP)—are excluded from decision-making and control, as is the CJEU.

This is in stark contrast to most other EU policies. In supranationalized EU policy fields, decision-making and action capacity has been transferred to the EU's institutional triangle composed of the Commission, the Council, and the EP. The function of steering, deciding on, and reviewing policy developments and measures is in the hands of supranational institutions, which can impose binding rules and decisions upon Member States.[22] In this constellation, power is no longer exercised by national actors on the national or international plane, but rests with supranational actors at the supranational level. As a result, national (governmental) actors who are not embedded in a structure at the supranational level (eg the Council) have only a residual role to play in supranationalized matters. Importantly, the shift in governance from the national to the supranational level has been followed by a shift in accountability. Hence, in the supranational EU setting, accountability processes primarily involve supranational actors and fora, such as the EP, the CJEU, the European Ombudsman, or the European Court of Auditors (ECA).

But what happens with the interrelated elements of power and accountability when the conferral of powers occurs in a context that is no longer (purely) intergovernmental but not supranational either? As described above, the administrative and operational realities of EU peacebuilding have undergone a process of concealed agencification and thus no longer correspond to the intergovernmental institutional and procedural blueprint set out in primary law: the strategic and operational centre of EU peacebuilding is incontestably in Brussels—and not in Member State capitals, as primary law suggests. But how does accountability

[22] The adjective *supranational* describes '*une autorité institutionnelle à laquelle, dans des domaines spécifiquement circonscrits, ses États membres ont librement consenti la faculté de produire des règles de droit qui leur sont directement applicables*'. See Frank Attar, 'Supranational', *Dictionnaire des relations internationales de 1945 à nos jours* (Éditions du Seuil 2009) 912.

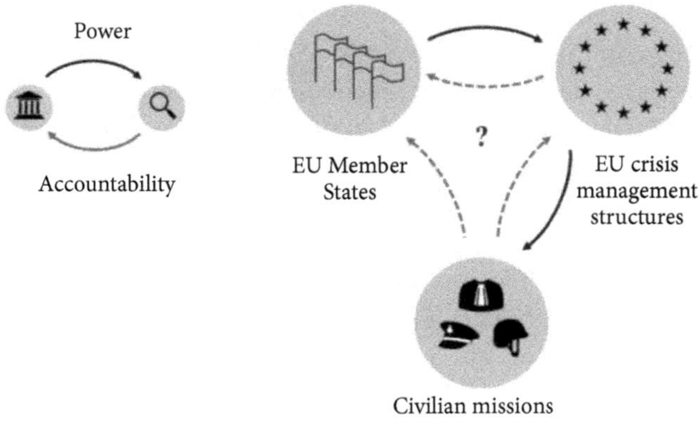


**Figure 1.2** Accountability and power: theory and practice

unfold in the distinctive setting of Europeanized intergovernmentalism? How do actors entrusted with decisional or operational powers carry out their tasks once a mission mandate has been adopted?[23]

A glimpse at the operational phase of civilian missions—that is everything that happens after the adoption of a mission mandate—reveals that it is difficult to clearly ascribe responsibilities and competences in the multilevel and multi-actor sphere of EU peacebuilding activities. Europeanized intergovernmentalism, therefore, seems to be a recipe for chaotic and at times impeded accountability, as Figure 1.2 on accountability in theory and peacebuilding practice illustrates.

This finding holds for all three dimensions of accountability, namely political, legal, and administrative accountability. It is prima facie unclear who is politically accountable for choices made in the context of civilian crisis management, or for the problems arising from civilian missions. Likely candidates for political accountability on the actor side are the European Council, the Council, Member State executives, and the Brussels-based bureaucracy, while, on the forum side, we count the EP and Member State parliaments. Furthermore, it is uncertain which judicial institution(s) can exercise legal accountability—potential fora include the EU judicature, the national jurisdictions of the sending and host States, and the European Court of Human Rights (ECtHR)—and whether jurisdictional

[23] It is judicious to specify at this juncture that the focus of this inquiry is on process accountability (who does what and how) rather than on output accountability (what the result of the action is). In other words, whether EU peacebuilding achieves its ambitious goal of building public sector capacities that allow for long-lasting peace, or whether the deployed means are appropriate is not the focus of attention. A comprehensive description of *process* accountability compared to *outcome* accountability can be found in Shefali V Patil, Ferdinand Vieider, and Philip E Tetlock, 'Process versus Outcome Accountability' in Mark Bovens, Robert E Goodin, and Thomas Schillemans (eds), *The Oxford Handbook of Public Accountability* (Oxford University Press 2014) 69–89.

competences are exclusive or complementary. Moreover, there are uncertainties regarding administrative matters. Does administrative accountability unfold between seconded personnel (in Brussels or missions) and the respective seconding Member State institution, within crisis management structures, or both? And is the sending organization (the EU) or the sending Member State, or both, in charge of holding actors to account if a deployed civilian expert is accused of corruption or other misconduct? These are only some unanswered accountability-related questions, all of which deserve more attention, not least because insights from practice illustrate that accountability issues have become highly salient.

## 3. A Salient Research Endeavour: Alarming Real-world Accountability

Indeed, evidence from the field underscores that dysfunctional accountability arrangements constitute a common thread across EU civilian crisis management. It is therefore not an exaggeration to state that the intricate Europeanized governance set-up of civilian CSDP facilitates an 'accountability deficit'.[24] Exemplary of the dysfunctional accountability scheme in EU peacebuilding activities is the emblematic case related to the Rule of Law Mission to Kosovo (EULEX Kosovo),[25] which brought to light patterns of deficient accountability arrangements regarding the specific mission and the overarching governance framework, and will thus serve as an analytical starting point for further scrutiny.

In November 2014, EULEX Kosovo—for a long time the EU's peacebuilding flagship mission—was hit by a corruption scandal that made it to the front pages of several leading newspapers across Europe. The origin of the scandal was allegedly traced back to Maria Bamieh, a seconded prosecutor from the United Kingdom, who was suspected by the mission to have leaked information to the press. Bamieh, denying this claim, publicly explained that some of her EULEX colleagues had been involved in unlawful actions, that her demands that these irregularities be internally investigated had been disregarded by EULEX, and that her secondment had not been prolonged for discriminatory reasons. The initial allegations concerned corruption—bribe taking by a seconded judge—and were exacerbated by secondary allegations regarding the handling of the issue—unfair treatment and obstruction of investigations. The incident was

[24] Carol Harlow and Richard Rawlings, 'Promoting Accountability in Multilevel Governance: A Network Approach' (2007) 13 European Law Journal 542, 542.

[25] The mandate of EULEX Kosovo is two-fold: it contains a strengthening objective (provision of advice, training, etc) and an executive dimension (prosecution, investigation, adjudication of war crimes, terrorism, corruption cases, etc). The mission was launched in 2008 by Council Joint Action 2008/124/CFSP of 4 February 2008 on the European Union Rule of Law Mission in Kosovo, EULEX KOSOVO [2008] OJ L42/92.

then subject to scrutiny by both the European Ombudsman,[26] and an external expert (Jean-Paul Jacqué).[27]

Although external scrutiny did not confirm the corruption allegations against the mission and its staff, the events did much reputational harm to the mission and EU peacebuilding in general because the incident uncovered serious accountability issues. First, the assessments of the European Ombudsman and the external expert showed that EULEX authorities had repeatedly decided together with high-ranking Brussels-based officials to deviate from existing procedures, in particular regarding sensitive recruitment cases.[28] The recurrent recourse to exceptional and highly opaque procedures generated administrative uncertainty and raised questions of legality. Secondly, there were shortcomings with reporting and information processing. The major issue here was the striking absence of crucial information (for instance on ongoing procedures) being handed over when senior personnel both at the Operational Headquarters in Brussels (ie the Civilian Planning and Conduct Capability, CPCC) and on the ground departed/took up their functions.[29] Other sources of concern were untraceable complaints by mission members,[30] as well as the fact that communication channels between the mission and the Operational Headquarters were believed by mission members to be insecure.[31] Thirdly, the handling of the allegations in terms of information disclosure was problematic. Not only did EULEX condition its responses to media requests (journalists were to hand in the documents in their possession to EULEX before the mission would reply to their questions),[32] but the disclosure regime applied to the external expert's report raised serious transparency concerns. Instead of redacting those parts of the report containing sensitive information (eg case material and names of alleged criminals) to comply with confidentiality requirements, *all* names—including those of (high-ranking) EULEX and Brussels-based officials, whose names were publicly known—were systematically erased together with sensitive or classified information. This peculiar disclosure regime, which is hardly compatible with the Draft Terms of Reference requiring a public report and adequate arrangements for classified information,[33]

[26] Own-initiative inquiry OI/15/2014/PMC of the European Ombudsman into the European External Action Service's (EEAS) investigation into the allegation of serious irregularities involving the EU Rule of Law Mission (EULEX) in Kosovo (14 November 2014); Decision of the European Ombudsman closing the own-initiative inquiry OI/15/2014/PMC into the way in which the European External Action Service (EEAS) handles allegations of serious irregularities involving the EU Rule of Law Mission (EULEX) in Kosovo (4 December 2014).

[27] Jean-Paul Jacqué, 'Review of the EULEX Kosovo Mission's Implementation of the Mandate with a Particular Focus on the Handling of the Recent Allegations' Report commissioned by the High Representatives and released (with annexes) on 31 March 2015 <https://eulex-kosovo.eu/eul/repository/docs/150331_jacque-report_en.pdf> and <https://eulex-kosovo.eu/eul/repository/docs/150331_jacque-report-annexes_en.pdf> both accessed 18 February 2020.

[28] ibid 30, 34; Decision closing the own-initiative inquiry OI/15/2014/PMC paras 11, 13, 29, 33.

[29] Jacqué report (n 27) 32, 36–37.

[30] Decision closing the own-initiative inquiry OI/15/2014/PMC paras 8, 28.

[31] Jacqué report (n 27) 28.

[32] ibid 35.

[33] Draft Terms of Reference, Ref.Ares(2014)3899224 (24 November 2014).

rendered the report difficult to read for informed civil-society members and almost impossible for the wider public to understand.

In sum, the EULEX Kosovo case revealed serious shortcomings, some of which pertained to procedural matters (ie deviation from codified procedures), while others were indicative of organizational deficiencies (ie lack of institutional handover and memory), and again others related to information disclosure and transparency matters (ie extensive redaction of the supposedly public report by the external expert). It is true that, when confronted with a major problem, several European actors proactively took steps to cast light on the alleged irregularities, including the High Representative of the EU for Foreign Affairs and Security Policy, the EP, and the European Ombudsman. But it needs to be stressed that this proactive stance became necessary to substitute weak or deficient internal procedures and mechanisms (ie internal/administrative oversight) for (stronger) external mechanisms, which indicates that the general governance framework related to accountability is fairly underdeveloped.

As mentioned above, the incongruences revealed by the EULEX corruption scandal are no isolated phenomena. Civil society reports indicate that since the Bamieh case of 2014, the Brussels-based bureaucracy has started several internal investigations regarding (human resources) management issues, inter alia, with regard to EULEX Kosovo, the EU Police and Rule of Law Mission for the Palestinian Territory (EUPOL COPPS, COPPS standing for Co-ordinating Office for Palestinian Police Support), the EU Capacity Building Mission in Niger (EUCAP Sahel Niger), and the EU Police Mission in Afghanistan (EUPOL Afghanistan).[34] At the same time, external scrutiny has increased with problematic dossiers piling up in Luxembourg, Strasbourg, and Brussels. The famous *H v Council* case before the CJEU, which concerned the redeployment and demotion of a seconded national expert after having internally reported on irregularities, illustrated that staff management in peacebuilding missions was a rather opaque and contentious issue.[35] In a similar vein, another CJEU case pertained to allegations of harassment that were not properly dealt with by the mission or the Brussels-based structures.[36] A number of complaints lodged with the European Ombudsman show significant parallels with the Bamieh incident and the *H* case as regards both the treatment of personnel reporting on irregularities as well as procedural shortcomings.[37]

[34] Nicolas Gros-Verheyde, 'Y-a-t-il un problème de commandement dans les missions civiles de l'UE ?' [2017] Bruxelles2 <https://club.bruxelles2.eu/2017/06/y-a-t-il-un-probleme-de-commandement-dans-les-missions-civiles-de-lue/> accessed 18 February 2020; Nicolas Gros-Verheyde, 'Les limiers de l'OLAF enquêtent sur un Britannique, ancien numéro 2 de la PSDC. Des dérives graves en cause' [2019] Bruxelles2 <https://club.bruxelles2.eu/2019/03/les-limiers-de-lolaf-enquetent-sur-un-britannique-ancien-numero-2-de-la-psdc-derives-graves-en-cause/> accessed 18 February 2020; 'Eulex, une mission qui enchaîne les scandales' *Le Monde* (Paris, 16 November 2017); 'Le chef des juges européens au Kosovo démissionne' *Le Monde* (Paris, 17 June 2017).

[35] The case *H v Council and others* is discussed in detail in Chapter 6.

[36] Case T–763/16 *PY v EUCAP Sahel Niger* [2018] EU:T:2018:181.

[37] See Chapter 7.

Other Ombudsman case files cast light on organizational and managerial deficiencies regarding missions and the Brussels-based bureaucracy. What is more, OLAF has reportedly opened a preliminary inquiry for serious misconduct against Kenneth Deane, who as Civilian Operations Commander (2014–17) formerly exercised operational and disciplinary control over all deployed personnel.[38]

All of these cases and incidents, dealing with different aspects of institutional as well as procedural weaknesses and irregularities tied to accountability, underline that accountability in EU civilian crisis management deserves scholarly attention. It is important to stress that the current fragile accountability environment of EU peacebuilding activities is far from being a hypothetical problem. In fact, the lack of accountability regarding civilian missions bears serious operational and reputational risks for the EU: if the EU does not live up to its own normative standards when acting abroad, it is likely to lose the credibility and legitimacy necessary for gaining support at the EU level and for having an impact on the ground.[39]

Set against this backdrop, this book seeks to answer the following fundamental question: *to what extent has the transfer of powers by Member States to Brussels-based EU civilian crisis management structures been matched with the establishment of appropriate accountability mechanisms at the European level?* The objective is to disentangle accountability matters with regard to civilian CSDP by investigating both de jure and de facto accountability arrangements. This will then allow to identify who is accountable to whom, for what, and on what basis, which will in turn enable a number of informed suggestions about how to cope with potential accountability challenges or shortcomings.

## 4. Contribution to the Literature

In the growing collection of legal and political science literature on the EU's governance credentials, EU security and defence activities have so far been underexplored. This holds particularly for EU peacebuilding missions, which have sparked only limited academic interest with scholars of both disciplines.[40]

[38] Nicolas Gros-Verheyde, 'Le SEAE dans la tourmente. L'OLAF pourrait saisir le parquet dans une affaire impliquant les missions civiles de crises' [2019] Bruxelles2 <https://club.bruxelles2.eu/2019/08/le-seae-dans-la-tourmente-lolaf-pourrait-saisir-le-parquet-dans-laffaire-k-d/> accessed 18 February 2020; Gros-Verheyde, 'Les limiers de l'OLAF enquêtent sur un Britannique, ancien numéro 2 de la PSDC. Des dérives graves en cause' (n 34).

[39] In this book, civilian missions are regarded as a 'soft power' EU instrument, whose success chiefly depends on the EU's reputation, not least because reputation is a form of soft power. See further Ruth W Grant and Robert O Keohane, 'Accountability and Abuses of Power in World Politics' (2005) 99 American Political Science Review 29, 37.

[40] The same conclusion was reached by Ana Juncos in Ana E Juncos, 'Civilian CSDP Missions: "The Good, the Bad and the Ugly"' in Steven Blockmans and Panos Koutrakos (eds), *Research Handbook on the EU's Common Foreign and Security Policy* (Edward Elgar 2018) 89.

Lawyers, for their part, have for a long time not paid much attention to the EU's foreign policy (CFSP), or its security and defence dimension (CSDP)—there was simply too little law to explore. However, legal scholars have been catching up, accompanying the incremental codification of EU foreign affairs, security, and defence through Treaty law with a vigilant eye. A considerable part of legal analyses pertains to EU law. Some writings elucidate general legal–institutional questions (eg separation of competences or delimitation of policy strands),[41] others carefully examine questions of international responsibility and liability,[42] in particular in relation to military activities, and again others clarify complex jurisdictional questions primarily related to the imposition of sanctions (legal remedies, etc).[43] A second thread of legal publications sheds light on general policy aspects and legal questions related to the EU's role as an international actor.[44] But only a few of these writings specifically address EU security and defence or crisis management matters,[45] and even fewer deal in-depth with (aspects of) civilian CSDP.[46] Thirdly, there are insightful reflections on legal redress options for (human rights)

[41] See, inter alia, Peter van Elsuwege, 'The Potential for Inter-Institutional Conflicts before the Court of Justice: Impact of the Lisbon Treaty' in Marise Cremona and Anne Thies (eds), *The European Court of Justice and External Relations Law. Constitutional Challenges* (Hart Publishing 2014); Marise Cremona, 'The Two (or Three) Treaty Solution: The New Treaty Structure of the EU' in Andrea Biondi, Piet Eeckhout, and Stefanie Ripley (eds), *EU Law After Lisbon* (Oxford University Press 2012); Piet Eeckhout, 'The EU's Common Foreign and Security Policy After Lisbon: From Pillar Talk to Constitutionalism' in Andrea Biondi, Piet Eeckhout, and Stefanie Ripley (eds), *EU Law After Lisbon* (Oxford University Press 2012); Alan Dashwood, 'Article 47 TEU and the Relationship between First and Second Pillar Competences' in Alan Dashwood and Marc Maresceau (eds), *Law and Practice of EU External Relations. Salient Features of a Changing Landscape* (Cambridge University Press 2008).

[42] See, inter alia, Joni Heliskoski, 'Responsibility and Liability for CSDP Operations' in Steven Blockmans and Panos Koutrakos (eds), *Research Handbook on the EU's Common Foreign and Security Policy* (Edward Elgar 2018); Frederik Naert, 'The International Responsibility of the Union in the Context of Its CSDP Operations' in Malcolm Evans and Panos Koutrakos (eds), *The International Responsibility of the European Union—European and International Perspectives* (Hart Publishing 2013); Ramses A Wessel and Leonhard Den Hertog, 'EU Foreign, Security and Defence Policy: A Competence-Responsibility Gap' in Malcolm Evans and Panos Koutrakos (eds), *The International Responsibility of the European Union: European and International Perspectives* (Hart Publishing 2013).

[43] See, inter alia, Christophe Hillion, 'A Powerless Court? The European Court of Justice and the Common Foreign and Security Policy' in Marise Cremona and Anne Thies (eds), *The European Court of Justice and External Relations Law. Constitutional Challenges* (Hart Publishing 2014); Ramses A Wessel, 'Lex Imperfecta: Law and Integration in European Foreign and Security Policy' (2016) 1 European Papers 439.

[44] Bart van Vooren, Steven Blockmans, and Jan Wouters (eds), *The EU's Role in Global Governance—The Legal Dimension* (Oxford University Press 2013); Malcolm Evan and Panos Koutrakos (eds), *Beyond the Established Legal Orders. Policy Interconnections between the EU and the Rest of the World* (Hart Publishing 2011); Panos Koutrakos (ed), *European Foreign Policy: Legal and Political Perspectives* (Edward Elgar 2011).

[45] Steven Blockmans and Panos Koutrakos (eds), *Research Handbook of the EU's Common Foreign and Security Policy* (Edward Elgar 2018); Steven Blockmans, Jan Wouters, and Tim Ruys (eds), *The European Union and Peacebuilding: Policy and Legal Aspects* (TMC Asser Press/Cambridge University Press 2010); Steven Blockmans (ed), *The European Union and Crisis Management: Policy and Legal Aspects* (TMC Asser Press/Cambridge University Press 2008).

[46] Martina Spernbauer, *EU Peacebuilding in Kosovo and Afghanistan. Legality and Accountability* (Martinus Nijhoff Publishers 2014); Panos Koutrakos, *The EU Common Security and Defence Policy* (Oxford University Press 2013) 133–82.

violations incurred in the course of CSDP activities.[47] However, the biggest part of the existing legal literature that deals with civilian missions occupies the analytical margins only, not least because many authors still see them as ancillary activities to military operations. As a result, many writings touch upon different transversal legal questions regarding EU security and defence only cursorily, without exploring the distinctive legal, institutional, procedural, and administrative features of EU peacebuilding, which have a great impact on competences and, thus, on accountability.[48] Hence, despite the richness of the academic legal debate, current legal scholarship falls short of the 'real world' of EU civilian crisis management, namely the Europeanized realities of EU peacebuilding.

In contrast to legal scholars, political scientists have from the outset shown a considerable interest in the development and implementation of EU foreign affairs, security, and defence. Next to the inspiring works of international relation scholars dealing with general matters of international cooperation and governance (eg Joseph Nye, Robert O Keohane, and James Rosenau), the most salient studies have been produced under the heading of European (administrative) governance.[49] Many authors carefully disentangle organizational and procedural matters relating to EU foreign affairs, security, and defence mostly with the aim of theorizing the institutional or operational output that has materialized in practice.[50] There are several thought-provoking writings on the development and current state of civilian crisis management,[51] but again those studies in general do not address the specificities of civilian CSDP. Even though several authors have

[47] Carolyn Moser, 'Loin de l'Union, loin des juges?—Sur les voies de recours juridictionnelles dans le cadre des activités de sécurité et de défense extraterritoriales de l'Union européenne' in Layla Kristina Jaber, Stefanie Lüer, and Anne-Marie Thévenot-Werner (eds), *Wechselseitige Einflüsse zwischen Rechtsordnungen am Beispiel des Zugangs zum Gericht gegen das Handeln der Exekutive* (Springer forthcoming 2020); Stian Øby Johansen, 'Accountability Mechanisms for Human Rights Violations by CSDP Missions: Available and Sufficient?' (2017) 66 International and Comparative Law Quarterly 181.

[48] The de facto Europeanization of the de jure intergovernmental civilian dimension of the CSDP is mentioned only by a few authors in one or two sentences, namely Koutrakos (n 46) 67–68; Thym (n 11) 464.

[49] Key publications for disentangling the (administrative) governance of CSDP include Dijkstra, *Policy-Making in EU Security and Defence* (n 11); Sjursen (n 10); Juncos and Pomorska (n 11); Per M Norheim-Martinsen, 'Beyond Intergovernmentalism: European Security and Defence Policy and the Governance Approach' (2010) 48 Journal of Common Market Studies 1351; Ana E Juncos and Christopher Reynolds, 'The Political and Security Committee: Governing in the Shadow' (2007) 12 European Foreign Affairs Review 127.

[50] This literature includes, inter alia, writings of Fabien Breuer, Hylke Dijkstra, Simon Duke, Giovanni Grevi, Eva Gross, Jolyon Howorth, Ana Juncos, Xymena Kurowska, Anand Menon, Michael Merlingen, Per Norheim-Martisen, Agnieszka Nowak, and Rasa Otrauskaite, and Richard G. Whitman. For a concise overview of this literature, see Giovanni Faleg, *The EU's Common Security and Defence Policy—Learning Communities in International Organizations* (Palgrave Macmillan 2017) 17–19.

[51] Juncos (n 40); Smith (n 6) 128–211; Thierry Tardy, *Recasting EU Civilian Crisis Management* (European Union Institute for Security Studies 2017); Raphael Bossong, 'EU Civilian Crisis Management and Organizational Learning' (2013) 22 European Security 94; Christopher S Chivvis, *EU Civilian Crisis Management—The Record So Far* (RAND Corporation 2010); Agnieszka Nowak (ed), *Civilian Crisis Management—The EU Way* (European Union Institute for Security Studies 2006).

described the move beyond intergovernmentalism of the CFSP/CSDP,[52] they have so far refrained from decorticating the broader governance implications of this development, in particular for the accountability (and potentially the legitimacy) of crisis management actors. Similarly, the appropriateness of the policy and law framework, within which extraterritorial peacebuilding activities are conducted, is generally not subject to scrutiny. The overall set-up is taken as a given variable in the output equation or as a fixed component of the codified environment. Consequently, a thorough political science study of civilian CSDP and accountability in this context is lacking.

It is worth adding here that the interdisciplinary corpus of accountability studies has so far remained astonishingly silent on EU security and defence matters. In the EU context, accountability is indeed primarily discussed with regard to supranational policies,[53] whereas intergovernmental policy fields tend to fall outside the analytical scope.[54] What is more, accountability analyses into security and defence issues (at the EU level) have hitherto mostly tackled military activities and have focused on legal issues (ie justiciable wrongdoings). Those very rare but illuminating analyses covering aspects of accountability in civilian missions have had a constrained analytical focus: they addressed only one type of accountability (political or legal) and/or one governance level (EU or Member State).[55] The administrative accountability dimension has to date been neglected.[56]

This book provides the first comprehensive study of the law and practice of civilian CSDP with a specific focus on accountability. By combining legal analysis with insights from political science (governance studies, agency literature, international relations scholarship, etc) and empirical material, this study adds a

[52] See, inter alia, Juncos and Pomorska (n 11) 1098–110; Norheim-Martinsen (n 49) 1356–58; Dijkstra, *Policy-Making in EU Security and Defence* (n 11) 195–97.

[53] See Mario Costas, *The Accountability Gap in EU Law* (Routledge 2017); Mark Bovens, Deidre Curtin, and Paul 't Hart (eds), *The Real World of EU Accountability* (Oxford University Press 2010); Harlow (n 15).

[54] Valuable exceptions to this trend are Daniel Thym, *Holding Europe's CFSP/CSDP Executive to Account in the Age of the Lisbon Treaty* (CEU Ediciones 2011); Adrian Hyde-Price, 'Decision-Making under the Second Pillar' in Anthony Arnull and Daniel Wincott (eds), *Accountability and Legitimacy in the European Union* (Oxford University Press 2002).

[55] As for *legal accountability*, Martina Spernbauer (see n 46), for instance, in her book on the legality and accountability in EU peacebuilding restricts accountability to justiciable matters; her inquiry mainly revolves around immunity and liability (ie legal remedies for external accountability demanders). Regarding *political accountability*, only a handful of thematically relatively confined journal articles exist. In her journal article, Guri Rosén, for example, limits her study of political accountability to the negotiation process of an interinstitutional agreement between the EP and the Council on access to sensitive information; see Guri Rosén, 'EU Confidential: The European Parliament's Involvement in EU Security and Defence Policy' (2015) 53 Journal of Common Market Studies 383.

[56] Exemplary of this gap in the literature is the 2017 Special Section of the online journal *European Papers* on 'The New Frontiers of EU Administrative Law: Is There an Accountability Gap in EU External Relations?' (edited by Marise Cremona and Päivi Leino). Whereas contributions cover a broad range of external activities (development, environment, migration, neighbourhood, accession, or sanctions), the CSDP is not subject to scrutiny. In the Special Section, security and defence matters are dealt with under the heading of judicial review only.

distinctive element to the existing literature. It offers a nuanced interdisciplinary scrutiny of the phenomenon of Europeanized intergovernmentalism and its manifold (accountability) repercussions, which has so far been missing. The empirical evidence of a move beyond intergovernmentalism serves as the point of departure for an in-depth analysis of whether the considerable decision-making and action capacity at the EU level is mirrored by a sufficient accountability capacity. This accountability inquiry is unprecedented in breadth and depth: it covers (i) both de jure *and* de facto mechanisms of (ii) a political, legal, and administrative nature at (iii) the domestic level, the EU plane, and across levels; and furthermore evaluates (iv) the strengths and weaknesses of existing accountability arrangements. In other words, *all* facets of accountability in civilian CSDP are scrutinized in detail based on a combination of quantitative and qualitative criteria—which constitutes a long overdue investigation given that these missions account for the major share of the EU's extraterritorial CSDP activities and, furthermore, that insights from practice underscore evident accountability shortcomings.

## 5. Structure of the Book

The investigation of accountability in the context of civilian CSDP will proceed as follows. It starts in Chapter 2 with an introduction to the policy context (international security architecture) and the policy area (EU foreign affairs, security, and defence), before studying in-depth the policy tool (civilian crisis management). The chapter explores in particular the delegation dynamics at work, which have produced the distinctive legal, institutional, and operational environment of the CFSP and CSDP. The analysis demonstrates that civilian CSDP is intergovernmental in conception but Europeanized through practice. Next to unravelling the idiosyncratic governance features, the chapter provides a detailed overview of the main actors in EU civilian crisis management. Moreover, peacebuilding activities are demarcated from other external activities of the EU. The chapter closes with legal arguments and pragmatic considerations that highlight the importance of accountability in EU civilian crisis management.

Building on these insights, Chapter 3 unpacks the conceptual and analytical framework of the study. Accountability is first delineated as a corollary to holding (public) power and conceptualized as a three-stage mechanism. In a further step, accountability is contextualized in the particular setting of international relations, which is the habitat of EU peacebuilding activities. The discussion then turns to accountability catalysts and inhibitors, namely institutional design, the accountability architecture, and information-sharing modes. Subsequently, the chapter offers a taxonomy of accountability in civilian CSDP by mapping actors and potential fora, both at the strategic and operational level. Prior to outlining the overall research agenda, the chapter addresses analytical and practical challenges for (studying) accountability in the subject area, notably the restrictive information disclosure policy regarding EU security and defence matters.

Chapter 4 explains the methodological choices made in this book that tackles a multilevel and multi-actor environment. The inquiry stretches across governance levels, while the focus lies on accountability arrangements involving the Brussels-based crisis management bureaucracy. Rooted in a constitutional perspective on accountability, which establishes a link between accountability and key concepts of constitutional law (eg the rule of law) and thus puts an emphasis on countervailing powers, the analysis covers both law and practice. The sources, hence, include legal and empirical material. The chapter also presents the criteria, according to which the appropriateness of accountability arrangements in the context of civilian crisis management is evaluated.

Chapters 5 through 7 thoroughly assess different types of de jure and de facto accountability arrangements in the context of EU peacebuilding activities. Political accountability is at the core of Chapter 5; legal accountability constitutes the analytical focus of Chapter 6; and Chapter 7 is dedicated to administrative accountability. The structure of each of the accountability chapters is identical: after a contextualization of the respective type of accountability in the distinctive framework of EU security and defence, the study moves on to explore accountability arrangements at (i) the national level, (ii) the EU level, and (iii) in their wider (cross-level) setting. As this book adopts a constitutional perspective on accountability, accountability-demanders play a vital role. Therefore, the nature of the forum is the core categorizing parameter. Accordingly, the analysis of political accountability focuses on parliamentary bodies—that is, Member State parliaments and the EP, as well as interparliamentary cooperation activities. Under the heading of judicial accountability, the role of national courts, the function of the ECtHR, and the jurisdiction of the CJEU are explored, with a concentration on the latter. The activity of the European Ombudsman and of the ECA constitutes the main subject of study in the context of administrative accountability, which also discusses the role of national administrative bodies in civilian crisis management.

Finally, Chapter 8 brings all the findings together. It provides a concluding overview of existing accountability arrangements—political, legal, and administrative in nature—from both a de jure and a de facto perspective. The conclusions further sketch out lessons learned, both for theory and practice, and provide an outlook on accountability in (civilian) CSDP.

# 2
# Unpacking the Civilian Dimension of EU Security and Defence

European Union (EU) civilian missions aim at consolidating the conditions necessary for sustainable peace in a post-conflict environment through a panoply of activities. Mandates therefore cover a broad range of multidimensional tasks, targeting public institutions key to the rule of law (ie the police, the judiciary, and the armed forces), such as rule of law support, police training and police capacity building, border assistance and monitoring, assistance for reforming the security sector, and military capacity building. In the wider spectrum of peace operations, civilian missions thus fit into the category of peacebuilding given their capacity-oriented focus.[1]

In operational terms, civilian crisis management accounts for a major share of the EU's extraterritorial security and defence activities. The EU has so far launched twenty-two civilian missions (compared to twelve military operations) in conflict-torn regions in Eastern Europe, the Western Balkan, the Middle East, sub-Saharan Africa, and South East Asia under the framework of the Common Security and Defence Policy (CSDP), which forms an integral part of the Common Foreign and Security Policy (CFSP).[2] At the time of writing, ten civilian missions are operational in Burkina Faso, Chad, Georgia, Iraq, Kosovo, Libya, Mali, Niger, the Palestine Territories, Somalia/Somaliland, and Ukraine. Some 2,000 civilians work in these missions, roughly half of whom are internationals—both seconded and contracted—and the other half hired local contractual staff.[3] Among the currently

[1] The notion peacebuilding, coined by the United Nations, was introduced in the international 'peace operations vocabulary' by the Agenda for Peace (1992), and was refined by subsequent UN policy documents. See An Agenda for Peace. Preventive diplomacy, peacemaking and peace-keeping, A/47/277-S/24111 (17 June 1992), Report of the UN Secretary-General pursuant to the statement, adopted by the Summit Meeting of the Security Council on 31 January 1992 para 21; United Nations Peacekeeping Operations Principles and Guidelines (Capstone Doctrine, 2008), internal publication of the United Nations Department of Peacekeeping Operations and the Department of Field Support 2008 s 2.1.

[2] To date (October 2019), twenty-two civilian missions (and twelve military operations) have been launched. They have been deployed to (in alphabetical order): Afghanistan, Bosnia and Herzegovina, Burkina Faso, Chad, Congo (Democratic Republic of Congo), the Former Yugoslav Republic of Macedonia (today North Macedonia), Georgia, Guinea-Bissau, Indonesia (province of Aceh), Iraq, Kenya, Kosovo, Libya, Mali, Niger, the Palestinian Territories, Tanzania, the Seychelles, Somalia, (South-)Soudan, and Ukraine—and, for military operations, additionally the Central African Republic.

[3] These numbers were retrieved from the European External Action Service (EEAS) website and enriched by information contained in Annalisa Creta and others, 'Civilian and Military Personnel in CSDP Missions and Operations', *EP/EXPO/B/SEDE/2016/02* (European Parliament 2017) 14.

*Accountability in EU Security and Defence.* Carolyn Moser, Oxford University Press (2020). © Carolyn Moser.
DOI: 10.1093/oso/9780198844815.001.0001

deployed missions, the EU Rule of Law Mission in Kosovo (EULEX Kosovo) counts the highest number of personnel with some 500 staff (at its peak, the mission had more than 3,000 staff), and the EU Border Assistance Mission in the Palestinian Territories (EUBAM Rafah) is the oldest, having been in place since 2005.

In conceptual terms, civilian crisis management can best be described as a box within a box within a box, as Figure 2.1 shows. It is an operational policy *tool* with a sui generis bureaucratic edifice (smallest box), belonging to the broader policy *area* of EU foreign and security affairs (middle-sized box), which in turn is embedded in the EU's international (security) policy *context* (largest box).

The chapter at hand sets out to unpack these boxes consecutively so as to provide answers to four questions: (i) Where did civilian crisis management come from? (ii) How has it become what it currently is? (iii) Why is accountability a salient feature of civilian CSDP activities? (iv) And which developments and (accountability) challenges lie ahead? The chapter starts in section 1 by outlining the broader political context of CSDP activities (largest box). It discusses the evolving perception of international security, the envisaged political and operational response to the identified security threats, and the politico-strategic rationale behind EU peacebuilding activities. In section 2, the chapter then explicates the middle-sized box, comprising EU foreign affairs, security, and defence. It elucidates the dynamics underlying (non-)delegation and, against this backdrop, provides an overview of the particular integration and institutionalization trajectory of EU foreign affairs, security, and defence. Section 3 thereafter explores the current de jure institutional framework of the CFSP/CSDP, which features legal, procedural, and institutional particularities. Subsequently, the analysis moves from the policy area to the policy tool, namely the realities of civilian crisis management, which constitutes the smallest box. The discussion in section 4 first covers the unexpected institutional and operational rise of civilian missions, which implies a reconfiguration of the civil–military nexus in the CSDP, and then outlines the problems arising from the overlap between CSDP peacebuilding measures and other policy strands of EU external action, such as development activities or the external dimension of the Area of Freedom, Security and Justice. Thereafter, the chapter disentangles the structures and modes of interaction of civilian crisis management (who, what, how) and outlines the idiosyncratic governance features of this policy tool

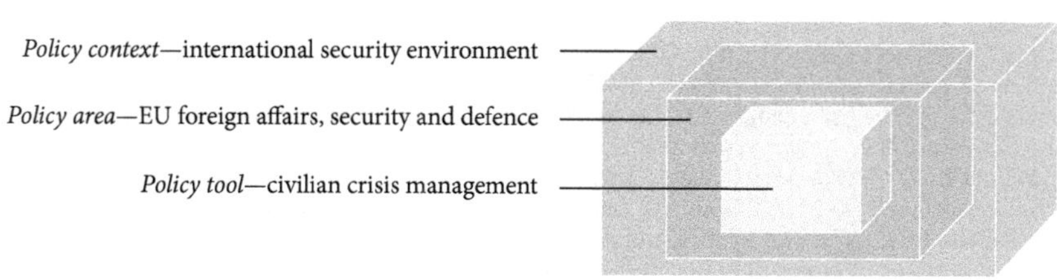


**Figure 2.1** Unpacking civilian CSDP

(section 5). The analysis demonstrates that civilian CSDP is intergovernmental in conception, but Europeanized through practice. The chapter closes in section 6 with legal arguments and pragmatic considerations that highlight the salience of accountability in EU peacebuilding.

## 1. Peacebuilding *à l'européenne*

Although EU peacebuilding is a child of the post-Cold War era, we begin our exploration of the largest box—the European security landscape—in the 1950s and the early days of the European integration process. This is because the quest for security and peace was at the very origin of the European construction and has constituted a fundamental thread throughout the incremental integration of the EU's internal and external facet. As the Schuman Declaration of May 1950 underscores, the leading rationale driving the first steps of European integration, namely the pooling of the coal and steel productions of the formerly hostile France and Germany, was indeed not an economic one. On the contrary, the European project has, from its inception, above all been about ensuring security and, eventually, peace in Europe and the rest of the world.[4] And Robert Schuman has been proved right: European integration has indeed made a considerable contribution to realizing the dream of peace among European States. As the following analysis demonstrates, Schuman's primarily introverted perspective on security (and peace) within the European polity has developed into a more extroverted conception, especially in the post-Cold War period. Back then, Europe's previously existing geopolitical context was profoundly altered, not least because the binary logic underpinning world politics ceased to exist. This new security environment incited Europeans to reconsider their system of security coordinates. The (potential) impact of external insecurity and instability on the EU, which became increasingly evident after the fall of the Iron Curtain and the subsequent wars in the Balkans that precipitated many of the region's citizens fleeing to European nations, prompted the incremental development of the EU security and defence policy, including civilian crisis management.

### 1.1 The rationale: embracing a new security environment

When Schuman made his famous Declaration in 1950, European nations perceived themselves as the biggest threat to peace in Europe and the rest of the world, with the age-old tensions between France and Germany causing particularly great

[4] The Schuman Declaration (9 May 1950) para 6.

concern. In the aftermath of Second World War, political action was therefore primarily directed at preventing warfare between European neighbours through diverse measures. The central idea of the Schuman Declaration (also referred to as Schuman Plan) was therefore to create a strong net of economic and political ties between European nations that, by increasing mutual interdependence, would then put an end to belligerent dynamics within Europe.

This vision comes close to what Karl Deutsch in 1954 labelled a security community;[5] that is, a community characterized by the absence of preparations for war or large-scale violence between territories or between groups within its borders.[6] In Europe's post-Second World War context, the primary security rationale was, of course, supplemented by another shared aspiration, namely the prospect of spurred economic prosperity through integration.[7] So the desired *effect* of a security community—that is the prospect of security, peace, and prosperity—explained the *cause*, namely European (economic) integration. There was thus an inverse (temporal) relation between effect and cause based on the rationality assumption of the anticipated benefits.[8] This hope of peace among European nations accompanied by a progressive merger of institutions through supranationalization precisely constitutes the premise on which the Schuman Declaration of 1950 was built and on which the ensuing European integration process would rest.[9] Indicative hereof are several paragraphs of the preamble of the 1951 Treaty establishing the European Coal and Steel Community, drafted along the lines of the Schuman Plan: based on the consideration that 'world peace can be safeguarded only by creative efforts equal to the dangers which menace it', the signatory States declare their resolve

[5] The term security community used by Karl Deutsch had initially been defined by Richard W van Wangen as 'a group which has become integrated, where *integration* is defined as the attainment of a sense of community, accompanied by formal or informal institutions or practices, sufficiently strong and widespread to assure peaceful change among members of a group with "reasonable" certainty over a "long" period of time'. The notion 'sense of community' has been defined by the same author 'as a feeling on the part of an individual or individuals inhabiting a given territory that consensus has been attained to the effect that common social problems *must* and *can* be solved or adjusted by processes of peaceful change'. Richard W van Wagenen, *Research in the International Organization Field: Some Notes on a Possible Focus* (Princeton University Press 1952) 10–11.

[6] Karl W Deutsch, *Political Community at the International Level—Problems of Definition and Measurement* (Doubleday & Company Inc 1954) 34.

[7] According to Deutsch, four considerations were crucial for engaging in the project to unify Western Europe, namely (i) security, (ii) prosperity, (iii) mobility, and (iv) power. Karl W Deutsch, *The Analysis of International Relations* (3rd edition, Prentice-Hall 1988) 250–51.

[8] This statement is made in reference to Robert O Keohane, *After Hegemony: Cooperation and Discord in the World Political Economy* (Princeton University Press 1984) 80. Mark A Pollack equally referred to Keohane in his seminal article of 1997. Mark A Pollack, 'Delegation, Agency, and Agenda Setting in the European Community' (1997) 51 International Organization 99, 102. This inverse cause–effect relation is mirrored in the writings of Deutsch on 'stable expectation of peace'. See Deutsch (n 6) 33.

[9] The adjective supranational describes '*une autorité institutionnelle à laquelle, dans des domaines spécifiquement circonscrits, ses États membres ont librement consenti la faculté de produire des règles de droit qui leur sont directement applicables*'. See Frank Attar, 'Supranational', *Dictionnaire des relations internationales de 1945 à nos jours* (Éditions du Seuil 2009) 912. 'Supranationalization' defines the process in which Member States have freely consented to render policy fields supranational, implying the establishment of supranational institutional structures.

'to substitute for age-old rivalries the merging of their essential interests', and to thereby pave the way for a 'broader and deeper community among peoples long divided by bloody conflicts'.[10]

The European integration process has made the EU a security community in which Member States share the assurance and belief that disputes among them will not be resolved with physical force, but by peaceful means. *Within* the EU, peace is taken for granted, while war has become unthinkable. It is precisely for this great achievement that the EU was awarded the Nobel Prize for Peace in 2012.[11] Thus, several decades of European integration have contributed to changing the initial (in)security scenery: whereas formerly Europe needed to be protected from European nations, EU Member States today want to shield themselves from external threats, which are understood to be linked to internal security challenges. This change of perspective, for a long time not explicitly acknowledged in official political discourse,[12] began in the early 1990s when the interlinkage of internal and external policy issues became evident.

In the post-Cold War period, Europe's previously existing geopolitical context was profoundly altered, leaving space for unprecedented security challenges: the Soviet Union collapsed, as did a number of communist regimes in Central and Eastern Europe; the Berlin Wall fell and Germany was reunited; and the role of the North Atlantic Treaty Organization (NATO) became somewhat unclear. In addition, the Balkan region was struck by war and European nations were incapable of adequately reacting to this crisis. These mainly external circumstances prompted Member States to reconsider and redefine the EU's international role—as well in relation to internal dynamics—and thus provided a crucial momentum for European integration in foreign policy, security, and defence matters. Again, the prospect of future benefits—peace and stability—drove European nations to further propel integration. The interplay of internal and external factors of the 1990s has indeed left its mark on successive European Treaties, corroborating and progressively enlarging the external political, institutional, and operational dimension of the European security community.

A new vision of conflict resolution materialized after the end of the Cold War in light of the changed understanding of security (ie conceptualizing internal and external security as interrelated variables) and the emergence of new

[10] The original version (in French) of the cited paragraphs of the preamble read as follows: *'Considérant que la paix mondiale ne peut être sauvegardée que par des efforts créateurs à la mesure des dangers qui la menacent'* (first paragraph) and *'Résolus à substituer aux rivalités séculaires une fusion de leurs intérêts essentiels, à fonder par l'instauration d'une communauté économique les premières assises d'une communauté plus large et plus profonde entre des peuples longtemps opposés par des divisions sanglantes . . .'* (fifth paragraph).

[11] The Nobel Peace Prize for 2012—Press Release 2012.

[12] Sarah Wolff, Nicole Wichmann, and Gregory Mounier, 'The External Dimension of Justice and Home Affairs: A Different Security Agenda for the EU?' in Sarah Wolff, Nicole Wichmann, and Gregory Mounier (eds), *The External Dimension of Justice and Home Affairs: A Different Security Agenda for the European Union?* (Routledge 2010) 9, 11.

conflicts (*inter*state wars decreased, whereas *intra*state conflicts increased). This is when *peacebuilding* made its appearance on the scene alongside external action instruments: to cope with the new security realities, military solutions to end belligerent conflicts were replaced by multidimensional missions intended to transform conflicts in order to achieve sustainable peace.[13] In the EU context, the peacebuilding concept found its expression, inter alia, in civilian crisis management carried out under the CSDP framework,[14] whose capacity-oriented tasks primarily aim at conflict prevention.[15]

## 1.2 A politico-strategic frame of reference between ideals and interests

The post-Cold War period has also been pivotal in shaping the politico-strategic frame of reference for civilian CSDP. Against the backdrop of the changing international security context, both in terms of threat perception and conflict resolution techniques, two paradigms emerged that simultaneously provided (i) direction for and justification of the EU's action on the international scene, and (ii) a reference point for the internal dimension of the European construction.[16] Common to both paradigms is the projection of EU values and norms beyond the borders of the EU. However, there are different rationales behind this projection: one is *ideational*, whereas the other one is *instrumental* in nature. These two paradigms, both of which eventually found their way into EU law and programmatic policy documents, have an impact on how the external facet of the European polity is construed. Moreover, the two paradigms are not mutually exclusive but co-exist with varying degrees of significance over time as regards the formulation and implementation of foreign policies, including civilian missions.

The first—ideational—paradigm draws a parallel between what the EU *is within* its borders (a peaceful polity) and what it *does outside* its borders (a polity promoting peace). Differently put, the international role of the EU is a projection of its internal norms and achievements. It is crucial to comprehend that the external promotion

[13] Giovanni Faleg, *The EU's Common Security and Defence Policy—Learning Communities in International Organizations* (Palgrave Macmillan 2017) 44–49.

[14] The civilian crisis management of the EU comprises, next to the CSDP (i), also activities undertaken by the Commission (ii), and actors of the Area of Freedom, Security and Justice (iii), as outlined in Thierry Tardy, 'The New Forms of Civilian Crisis Management' in Thierry Tardy (ed), *Recasting EU Civilian Crisis Management* (European Union Institute for Security Studies 2017) 15–16.

[15] For peacebuilding in the EU context, see Simon Duke and Aurélie Courtier, 'EU Peacebuilding: Concepts, Players and Instruments', *The European Union and Peacebuilding: Policy and Legal Aspects* (TMC Asser Press 2008); Martina Spernbauer, *EU Peacebuilding in Kosovo and Afghanistan. Legality and Accountability* (Martinus Nijhoff Publishers 2014) 15–45; Faleg (n 13) 41–49.

[16] This is, obviously, a vision of reality with reduced complexity; in the 'real world', economic, social, and other aspects are non-negligible parameters of the overall equation regarding policy preferences and choices.

and protection of EU values and norms can be understood as a window or wishful thinking on the EU's internal character. The Laeken Declaration of 2001, which depicted the EU as a 'force for good', is a case in point.[17] What is more, the projection of values satisfies the longing—in particular by European policy-makers—to construe an identity for the EU as an international political actor that is mindful of (and impacting on global) governance.[18] The projection of norms outside the EU is, however, also about hegemonic struggles within the EU, as the norms imposed on the outside can be a means to resolve internal norms-related disagreements.[19] The ideational paradigm is, hence, an expression of the *internal–external identity nexus* of the EU. In its White Paper on Governance (2001), the European Commission (the Commission) explicitly spelled out this nexus when stating that '[s]uccessful international action [striving for good governance at the global level] reinforces European identity and the importance of shared values within the Union'.[20]

The second—instrumental—paradigm emphasizes the interlinkage of internal and external security. This new perspective was induced by the post-Cold War impression that the clear distinction between external and internal security threats had become blurred, leading to an *internal–external security nexus*.[21] Interestingly, it was also the moment in time when reference to peace started to decline while allusions to security increased. In dealing with the internal–external security nexus, the external reproduction of EU internal norms and values is a crucial preventive tool: it is an instrument by which stability and security within the EU's territory can be safeguarded. Capacity building through police training, security sector reforms, or justice cooperation plays a vital role in this regard as it allows the EU to shield itself from external insecurity 'by exporting internal security instruments'.[22] The underpinning idea is to create a buffer zone, or a 'protective "glacis"',[23] to keep security threats potentially impacting the EU as far away from the EU and its external borders as possible. Phrased differently, the extra-territorialization of internal security mechanisms to third States is a way of pushing back the external borders of the EU.[24] This conception of fostering internal security through external

[17] Presidency Conclusions of the Laeken European Council (14–15 December 2001), Annex I: Laeken Declaration on the Future of the European Union.

[18] Michael E Smith, *Europe's Common Security and Defence Policy. Capacity-Building, Experiential Learning, and Institutional Change* (Cambridge University Press 2017) 12.

[19] Thomas Diez, 'Normative Power as Hegemony' (2013) 48 Cooperation and Conflict 194, 203.

[20] COM(2001) 428 final, 'European Governance—a White Paper' OJ [2001] C287/1 pt 3.3.

[21] Wolff, Wichmann, and Mounier (n 12) 11.

[22] Gregory Mounier, 'Civilian Crisis Management and the External Dimension of JHA: Inceptive, Functional and Institutional Similarities' in Sarah Wolff, Nicole Wichmann, and Gregory Mounier (eds), *The External Dimension of Justice and Home Affairs: A Different Security Agenda for the European Union?* (Routledge 2010) 46.

[23] See, on this point, Jörg Monar, 'Expending Experimentalist Governance: The External Dimension of the EU's Area of Freedom, Security and Justice' in Jonathan Zeitlin (ed), *Extending Experimentalist Governance? The European Union and Transnational Regulation* (Oxford University Press 2015) 250.

[24] Violetta Moreno-Lax, *Accessing Asylum in Europe* (Oxford University Press 2017) 39–41; Jorrit J Rijpma and Marise Cremona, 'The Extra-Territorialisation of EU Migration Policies and the Rule

capacity building also played a crucial role in the context of enlargement: strengthening the administrative structures of the police forces or the judiciary of candidate countries was a means to reduce potential factors of 'external' instability and insecurity.[25]

Civilian crisis management, which emerged at the same time that the two aforementioned paradigms were forged, embodies both paradigms. On the one hand, the capacity-oriented tasks undertaken in the context of civilian missions foster precisely the values and public institutions as well as functions that are core to the EU's identity (eg democracy, rule of law, and the protection of human rights). On the other hand, peacebuilding helps to contain insecurity, and therefore contributes to the preservation of the buffer zone. Hence, civilian missions are Janus-faced: according to the prevailing understanding of the international policy environment and the specific context of deployment, peacebuilding activities can have either an ideational or instrumental preponderance.

Since 9/11, the instrumental paradigm has progressively gained weight. As the terrorist attacks of September 2001 (New York; Washington DC) and March 2004 (Madrid) exacerbated the perception of an internal–external security nexus, they gave new impetus to security-oriented policies. Emblematic of this 'security turn' was the 2003 European Security Strategy (ESS), entitled 'A secure Europe in a better world'.[26] The ESS had a double motivation: it served as guidance for future policy developments and, at the same time, as a narrative intended to reconstruct a rationale for the security and defence dimension of the EU (namely the CSDP) progressively put in place after 1999.[27] The document encapsulated three central features of a security-centred discourse on external action. First, internal and external security challenges are interconnected. Therefore, the EU must act on the international scene to prevent external security threats from spilling over into or impacting on the EU in parallel to maintaining internal security. Secondly, the definition of security is broad, covering a wide range of actors, sources, and types of threats. Identified key threats, for instance, include terrorism, proliferation of weapons of mass destruction, regional conflicts, State failure, and organized crime.[28] Thirdly, to face the various security challenges, the EU follows a

of Law', *EUI Working Papers* (European University Institute, Department of Law 2007) 10; Mounier (n 22) 50.

[25] Ana E Juncos, 'The European Union and the Western Balkans: Enlargement as a Security Strategy' in Spyros Economides and James Sperling (eds), *EU Security Strategies—Expanding the EU System of Security Governance* (Routledge 2018); Wolff, Wichmann, and Mounier (n 12) 11.

[26] A Secure Europe in a Better World: European Security Strategy (ESS), endorsed by the European Council, Brussels, 11–12 December 2004 1–14.

[27] Per M Norheim-Martinsen, *The European Union and Military Force: Governance and Strategy* (Cambridge University Press 2013) 35–40; Panos Koutrakos, *The EU Common Security and Defence Policy* (Oxford University Press 2013) 80.

[28] For a detailed analysis of the 'old' and 'new' threats covered by the ESS, see Jean-Yves Haine, 'The European Security Strategy Coping with Threats. Is Europe Secure?' in Sven Biscop and Jan Joel Andersson (eds), *The EU and the European Security Strategy. Forging a Global Europe* (Routledge 2008).

comprehensive approach that combines all elements of foreign policy (diplomacy, trade, aid, military, and non-military instruments) and articulates a preference for conflict prevention over armed intervention.[29]

The latest European strategy document—the European Union Global Strategy (EUGS)—puts much emphasis on the necessity of combining different foreign policy tools to effectively deal with international crises. Released in June 2016 after the upsurge of migratory pressure, the EUGS calls for an integrated approach based on 'principled pragmatism'. This novel credo combines a 'realistic assessment of the current strategic environment [and an] idealistic aspiration to advance a better world'.[30] Again, the realization of eroded borders plays a crucial role in forging European strategic thought, as security at home is understood to depend on peace beyond the EU's borders.[31] The EUGS therefore does not represent a fundamental paradigm shift, but rather makes the hitherto implicit pragmatism or *realpolitik* underpinning European foreign policy apparent.[32] This interest-based policy rationale with an ideational twist is wonderfully encapsulated by a passage in the EUGS stating that '[EU] interest and values go hand in hand'.[33] As a side note, one might wonder whether this move implies that the EU has replaced 'milieu goals'—that aim at shaping conditions beyond national boundaries to allow for international peace—with 'possession goals' according to which nations/entities compete for a share in values of limited supply—namely security and stability.[34] What is certain, however, is that the EUGS labels civilian missions as 'a trademark of CSDP',[35] and thus underlines the salience of extraterritorial peacebuilding activities in the EU's integrated approach to conflicts and crises.

The revisited and more security-oriented politico-strategic frame of reference for EU external action has obvious repercussions on EU peacebuilding. The more recent civilian missions deployed to the Horn of Africa, the Sahel region, Libya, Ukraine, and Iraq indeed all focus on security-related matters, in particular security sector reform, law enforcement training, and military capacity building.[36] What is more, the mandates of some ongoing missions (in sub-Saharan Africa)

[29] Norheim-Martinsen (n 27) 47.

[30] Shared Vision, Common Action: A Stronger Europe. A Global Strategy for the European Union's Foreign and Security Policy (EUGS), presented by the High Representative Federica Mogherini on 28 June 2016 8.

[31] ibid 7.

[32] ibid 13. On the EUGS as an expression of European *realpolitik*, see Achilles Skordas, 'The European Union as a Post-National Realist Power' in Steven Blockmans and Panos Koutrakos (eds), *Research Handbook on the EU's Common Foreign and Security Policy* (Edward Elgar 2018) 403–10; Sven Biscop, *European Strategy in the 21st Century. New Future for Old Power* (Routledge 2019) 30–32.

[33] EUGS 13.

[34] On *milieu goals* and *possession goals*, see Arnold Wolfers, *Discord and Collaboration* (The Johns Hopkins Press 1962) 73–74.

[35] EUGS 48.

[36] Ana E Juncos, 'Civilian CSDP Missions: "The Good, the Bad and the Ugly"' in Steven Blockmans and Panos Koutrakos (eds), *Research Handbook on the EU's Common Foreign and Security Policy* (Edward Elgar 2018) 97.

have been reviewed with a view to contributing to the fight against terrorism and, importantly, to ease migratory pressures by improved border control.[37] In contrast, rule-of-law-oriented activities (eg justice sector reform, trainings for members of the judiciary) have become less prominent.[38] This development reveals aspects of the political climate within the EU: given that the orientation of CSDP activities depends on consensus among Member States, the decline of external rule of law activities under the CSDP framework originates at least in part from the internal struggle over rule of law principles (in particular with Poland and Hungary).

The operational reorientation of civilian CSDP has not happened out of the blue, but is the result of an extended debate about the purpose of the policy tool. After the release of the EUGS in 2016, which was calling for an integrated approach, the Implementation Plan on Security and Defence mentioned a possible enlargement of traditional civilian CSDP tasks to new functions.[39] The topic was again on the agenda when the latest politico-strategic documents on civilian CSDP—the Civilian CSDP Compact and the Council Conclusions on the development of civilian CSDP, both published in 2018—were drafted. While some States advocated that civilian missions should concentrate on conflict prevention and thus stick to traditional tasks—that is, rule of law, police capacity building, civil administration, and security-sector reform—others purported that new functions and objectives should be included in the mandates, in particular migration management (tied to border control) and the fight against terrorism.[40] As no final decision on the (future) orientation of civilian crisis management could be reached, the two aforementioned documents underscore the adherence to traditional EU peacebuilding priorities, while at the same time leaving the door open for the prospective integration of new tasks to combat threats such as 'irregular migration, hybrid threats, cyber security, terrorism and radicalisation, organised crime, border management and maritime security, as well as ... violent extremisms [and the preservation and protection of] cultural heritage'.[41] In particular, these broader crisis management tasks are intended to be carried out in coordination and cooperation with actors

[37] Carina Böttcher, 'The Compact Roadmap: Towards a New Level or Professionalization in Civilian CSDP', *DGAPkompakt n°11/2019* (Deutsche Gesellschaft für Auswärtige Politik 2019) 2; Nicoletta Pirozzi, 'The Civilian CSDP Compact—A Success Story for the EU's Crisis Management Cinderella?', *EUISS Brief 9/2018* (European Union Institute for Security Studies 2018) 4.

[38] For an overview of all civilian missions deployed from 2003 to 2019, see Table 2.2. A detailed description of most civilian CSDP missions deployed so far can be found in Koutrakos (n 27) 113–80; Jean-Claude Piris, *The Lisbon Treaty: A Legal and Political Analysis* (Cambridge University Press 2010) 269–73.

[39] Council Doc 14392/16 of 14 November 2016, 'Implementation Plan on Security and Defence', Annex 9.

[40] Böttcher (n 37) 2.

[41] Conclusions of the Council and of the Representatives of the Governments of the Member States, meeting within the Council, on the establishment of a Civilian CSDP Compact, as adopted by the Foreign Affairs Council at its meeting held on 19 November 2018, Council Doc 14305/18 4; Council Conclusions on strengthening civilian CSDP, adopted by the Foreign Affairs Council on 28 May 2018, Council Doc 9288/18 para 3.

from the Area of Freedom, Security and Justice (AFSJ).[42] This change, though, will obviously impact strategic planning and operational implementation. The underlying issue regarding current and future tasks is therefore intertwined, on the one hand, with recalibrating mandates on the conflict prevention–threat repression scale, and with repositioning EU peacebuilding between internal security concerns and external stabilization efforts on the other. Indeed, the ongoing discussions on the purpose and operational scope of civilian crisis management underscore that the policy tool is standing at a conceptual and operational crossroads: one sign points to traditional peacebuilding aimed at conflict prevention, whereas the other sign leads to externalized threat repression with a view to protecting the EU. It is worth stressing, however, that civilian crisis management has—despite its ambiguous positioning between ideals and interest, and despite recent security-oriented recalibrations of mandates—so far followed a *preventive* foreign policy *topos*. It formed part of the EU's toolkit of preventive diplomacy.[43] Accordingly, missions have in the past only exceptionally comprised a 'repressive' facet, namely in the rare event that the mandate entailed executive functions (ie EULEX Kosovo). The discreet shift to more 'repressive' mandates recently witnessed could change the nature and purpose of EU peacebuilding.

To conclude this section, the above analysis brings to the fore the following key elements regarding the security policy *context* of civilian crisis management—the largest box. Civilian missions, fitting into the category of peacebuilding, are a rather recent phenomenon. They materialized after the end of the Cold War because of a changed understanding of security, emphasizing the interdependence of internal and external security, and in reaction to the emergence of new types of conflicts and threats. In other words, civilian activities are a means to cope with a new international security environment that was (and still is) characterized by a diversification of security threats and actors. The rationale behind increased exterritorial civilian activities is both ideational (norm-focused) and instrumental (security-driven). In the last decade, security concerns have been on the rise, leading to an increase in security-oriented peacebuilding activities. This securitization tendency is likely to intensify not least because of the envisaged better coordination and cooperation with AFSJ actors.

## 2. The Incremental Development of EU Foreign Affairs, Security, and Defence

After having unpacked the first box—the international and European security context—we now turn to the second box—that is security and defence at the EU

[42] Implementation Plan on Security and Defence 10.
[43] Smith (n 18) 176.

level. This section looks at past developments, namely the incremental integration of EU foreign affairs, security, and defence, while the next section (3) specifically deals with the current legal framework of the CSDP.

EU security and defence has a particular integration history. Before being 'one of the most dynamic fields of European integration',[44] security and defence had for many decades lagged behind the achievements in other policy areas. Situated at the very core of national sovereignty, the issues at stake form part of high politics.[45] As such, they belong to the realm of prerogatives granted to the executive power, the *domaine réservé*.[46] It is not surprising, then, that governments have been and still are particularly reluctant to give up their decision-making power and operational leeway through integration, including in the EU context. Therefore, governments have integrated strategic and operational functions only on a small scale, in small bits, and with small risks. As a result, the CFSP and the CSDP have taken a long time to materialize in practice—and it has taken even more time to incorporate this practice into Treaty law.

Prior to engaging in a longitudinal analysis of this intricate integration process in sections 2.2 and 2.3, the next section (2.1) will outline the underlying dynamics causing hesitation or reinforcing Member States' fears of losing sovereignty in exchange for gaining efficiency through integration. That is because these dynamics have significantly shaped the past and current policy framework of EU security and defence.

## 2.1 Understanding delegation and institutional design dynamics

Integration, including in the European context, implies the delegation of functions from a principal to an agent in order to render cooperation fruitful. Phrased in the terms of rational choice institutionalism, delegation is primarily undertaken for efficiency considerations and is likely to occur 'when the expected benefits outweigh the expected costs'.[47] For the principal, however, this delegation comes with the risk of undesired or unpredicted ramifications, such as the loss of control over the delegated functions. Principals are therefore wary about an agency or bureaucratic drift taking place and need to make a trade-off.[48] In constellations where

[44] Hylke Dijkstra, *Policy-Making in EU Security and Defence: An Institutional Perspective* (Palgrave Macmillan 2013) 1. See also Daniel Thym, 'Auswärtige Gewalt' in Armin von Bogdandy and Jürgen Bast (eds), *Europäisches Verfassungsrecht: Theoretische und dogmatische Grundzüge* (2nd edn, Springer 2009) 475.

[45] *High* politics are concerned with questions of foreign policy and military security, whereas *low* politics deal with economic and social affairs. For a definition, see Robert O Keohane and Joseph S Nye, *Power and Independence: World Politics in Transition* (Little, Brown and Company 1977) 24.

[46] Also known as *royal prerogative* (United Kingdom) or *executive privilege* (USA).

[47] Jonas Tallberg, 'Delegation to Supranational Institutions: Why, How, and with What Consequences?' (2002) 25 West European Politics 3, 25.

[48] Agency loss has been identified by the literature to be primarily caused by 'shirking' or bureaucratic drift and constitutes thus the core aspect of principal–agent analysis. On shirking and on the

the principal is not satisfied with the delegation previously undertaken because of unanticipated and unintended consequences, re-contracting might take place at a later stage of delegation.[49] That occurs because delegating functions is a dynamic and incremental process with different stages, including positive and negative feedback loops. These feedback loops are crucial for the principals to better comprehend the ramifications of (non-)delegation and to shape institutional design accordingly. There is indeed a close link between (non-)delegation and institutional design: the degree of delegation impacts on the institutions that need to be put in place (or not), while institutional design is a factor taken into consideration when (further) delegation is discussed.[50] Hence, neither delegation nor institutional design are necessarily automatic or linear processes. The *fil rouge* of delegation and institutional design is going back and forth while balancing ideas and interests to find a (momentarily) viable solution.

Applying these findings from rational choice institutionalism to the CSDP context offers valuable insights. As Hylke Dijkstra convincingly argued, the development of the CSDP was a process in which Member States (principals) delegated—or not—functions and decision-making powers to bureaucratic structures in Brussels (agents) based on their conscientious weighing of anticipated efficiency gains against anticipated sovereignty costs.[51] In general, the fear of undesired consequences of delegation has resulted in Member States eventually passing on fewer functions than functionally optimal.[52] Whereas in the other EU areas, integration and thus the conferral of powers to Brussels-based structures took place precisely to prevent Member States from being too dominant, the rationale with regard to foreign affairs, security, and defence points in the opposite direction: Member States delegated functions only very reluctantly out of fear that

potential means of attenuating or reducing bureaucratic drift in general and with regard to the European institutions, see Pollack (n 8) 108–21.

[49] It has been argued by Tallberg that there is a four-stage causal chain regarding delegation, constituting of: (i) the expected consequences of delegation motivate EU government to delegation certain functions to [Union] institutions; (ii) the nature of these functions influences the design of mechanisms for controlling these institutions; (iii) the institutional design shapes the consequences of delegation by facilitating or obstructing attempts by the institutions to implement private agendas; and (iv) the consequences of previous rounds of delegation affect future delegation, institutional design, and interaction, through positive and negative feed-back loops. Tallberg (n 47) 24. On the matter of revising the agent's mandate in the European integration context, see likewise Pollack (n 8) 118–19.

[50] On this point, see as well Tallberg (n 47) 24.

[51] Dijkstra (n 44) 46–77. Sovereignty costs have been defined by David Epstein and Sharyn O'Halloran 'as the distance between the policy that a country would implement if it were not a member of the international organisation and the policy that it enacts once it has joined' as cited in ibid 31. The original quote can be found in David Epstein and Sharyn O'Halloran, *Delegating Powers: A Transaction Cost Politics Approach to Policy Making under Separate Powers* (Cambridge University Press 1999) 82.

[52] Dijkstra (n 44) 32.

Brussels-based structures could become too influential and too independent—to the detriment of Member States.[53] In other words, States tended to 'eschew delegation in order to reduce the political risks associated with a loss of formal decision-making control'.[54]

This cost–benefit calculation was exacerbated by the institutional design specificities of European integration, namely the tendency to (incrementally) supranationalize policies. Creating a supranational policy means that Member States consent to confer power and influence in explicitly determined areas to an institutionalized authority, which can then produce rules and decisions directly applicable to them.[55] And whereas a supranational setting privileges supranational over (inter)governmental actors when it comes to decision-making (and sometimes implementation), an intergovernmental environment gives (inter)governmental actors a better standing.[56] The key concern with regard to a supranational or intergovernmental institutional design is thus related to the question of 'who gets to cast the vote', or more precisely 'who holds (decision-making) power according to the institutional setting in place'. As foreign, security, and defence matters belong to the 'realm of sovereign wills and national interests par excellence',[57] the inclination of Member States to confer their *domaine réservé* powers to Brussels-based institutions was (and still is) far from exuberant. National governments, anxious to shield their foreign policy prerogatives, are therefore not keen to foster juridification in this policy field as more law implies (or is thought to imply, or to eventually lead to) supranational institutions and, eventually, supranational entrapment.

This spins the above line of argumentation on the interlinkage of delegation and institutional design further. It is reasoned here that the loss of formal decision-making control is indeed particularly high when functions are delegated to supranational structures because the prospect of controlling the behaviour of the agent or the outcomes shrinks compared to an intergovernmental setting. Therefore, the cost–benefit calculation that can be found throughout the development of the CSDP has not only been decisive in instances of (non-)delegation but has moreover clearly impacted on the institutional design of the policy at stake, the choice being between supranational or intergovernmental structures (with some hybrid

[53] Anand Menon and Stephen Weatherill have convincingly argued with regard to the EU and, more generally, the European integration process that 'delegation was rooted in a need to prevent "principal drift"'—in contrast to 'agency drift' or 'bureaucratic drift'. See Anand Menon and Stephen Weatherill, 'Legitimacy, Accountability, and Delegation in the European Union' in Anthony Arnull and Daniel Wincott (eds), *Accountability and Legitimacy in the European Union* (Oxford University Press 2002) 119.

[54] ibid 117.

[55] Attar (n 9) 912.

[56] The different components of an intergovernmental policy environment were described by Helen Sjursen. See Helene Sjursen, 'Not so Intergovernmental after All? On Democracy and Integration in European Foreign and Security Policy' (2011) 18 Journal of European Public Policy 1078.

[57] Martti Koskenniemi, 'International Law Aspects of the Common Foreign and Security Policy' in Martti Koskenniemi (ed), *International Law Aspects of the European Union* (Martinus Nijhoff Publishers, Kluwer Law International 1998) 27.

elements). Depending on the extent of delegation, certain structures had to be established; the nature of these structures—characterized by supranational or intergovernmental features—was, in turn, a key factor for Member States' propensity to proceed (or not) to further delegation. In addition, the legal rules transposing the conferral of powers to an institutional and procedural framework are negotiated by (inter)governmental actors who fear losing their impact and room for manoeuvre through supranational institutional design.[58] As a result, legal provisions on foreign policy, security, and defence were not only introduced comparatively late and on a small scale, but were in addition intentionally kept apart from the supranational branches of EU law.[59]

In view of the underlying delegation patterns and institutional design dynamics, national governments were initially reluctant to (in)formally pass on functions to Brussels-based structures, but once their resistance had been overcome, powers have progressively been conferred along intergovernmental lines, both regarding institutional design and agents selected. More precisely, the development of EU security and defence—both in terms of the normative framework and institutional set-up—took place in four phases.[60] While in the first phase (1950s–1997), no delegation and thus only marginal codification occurred, the second phase (1997–2007) was characterized by small steps regarding delegation and juridification. In the third phase (2007–16), some delegation arrangements have been revisited and modified by Member States to counter undesired ramifications of previous delegations and to ensure their influence.[61] One can suppose that a novel, fourth phase started after the annexation of Crimea in 2014 and the Brexit referendum in June 2016. Since then, an unprecedented cooperation and integration thrust has materialized, especially in the creation of new (military) CSDP structures in Brussels[62] and the launch of Permanent Structured Cooperation (PESCO) in late 2017.[63] What is more, the Commission started to show substantive interest in European security and defence beyond its industrial dimension: since 2016, the year in which then Commission President Jean-Claude Juncker announced the creation of a European Defence Fund,[64] and the Commission published the European Defence

[58] See on this point Menon and Weatherill (n 53) 117.

[59] See section 2.2 of this chapter.

[60] This temporal categorization is based on the insights provided by Hylke Dijstra and the thorough analysis developed by Panos Koutrakos. See Dijkstra (n 44) 46–77; Koutrakos (n 27) 5–21, 37–54.

[61] Dijkstra (n 44) 71–74.

[62] Council Decision (EU) 2017/971 of 8 June 2017 determining the planning and conduct arrangements for EU non-executive military CSDP missions and amending Decisions 2010/96/CFSP on a European Union military mission to contribute to the training of Somali security forces, 2013/34/CFSP on a European Union military mission to contribute to the training of the Malian armed forces (EUTM Mali) and (CFSP) 2016/610 on a European Union CSDP military training mission in the Central African Republic (EUTM RCA) [2017] OJ L146/133.

[63] Council Decision (CFSP) 2017/2315 of 11 December 2017 establishing permanent structured cooperation (PESCO) and determining the list of participating Member States [2017] OJ L331/57.

[64] State of the Union 2016—Towards a better Europe: a Europe that protects, empowers and defends, speech delivered by Jean-Claude Juncker on 14 September 2016.

Action Plan,[65] the Commission has pursued its own integration agenda in the field of security and defence.[66] The following analysis concentrates on the first three phases of this process.

## 2.2 An arduous integration and institutionalization process

Given the described delegation and institutionalization dynamics, characterized by hesitation and a preference for intergovernmental institutional design and agent selection, the initial integration delay in EU security and defence was overcome only after the fall of the Iron Curtain, despite the first attempts to tame the pugnacious demons menacing European peace dating back to the 1950s. As the long road to integrated European security and defence—which is closely tied to the development of the EU's foreign and security policy dimension—has been told well and extensively elsewhere,[67] the analytical focus of this section is on key events and elements only.

With a view to allowing for a broader and deeper community, France suggested in late 1950 a merger of European armies to form the European Defence Community (EDC). But the EDC, based on an ambitious institutional proposal of a supranational character (the Pleven Plan), failed: it was voted down by the French Assemblée Nationale for national political considerations in 1954[68] (the very year in which Karl Deutsch published his progressive security community study). This traumatic inception would leave its mark on the policy field for several decades. After the rejection in 1962 of the Fouchet Plans—another French initiative but of an intergovernmental nature[69]—the security and defence dimension of European integration, as well as foreign policy matters, remained for more than twenty years outside the Treaties. As a result, European security became a matter of the Western European Union (WEU)[70] and

[65] COM(2016) 950 final, 'European Defence Action Plan' (30 November 2016).

[66] A thought-provoking account of aspects of the Commission's recent involvement in EU security and defence can be found in Pierre Haroche, 'Supranationalism Strikes Back: A Neofunctionalist Account of the European Defence Fund' (2019) 26 Journal of European Public Policy.

[67] For a concise overview of this development until the entry into force of the Treaty of Lisbon, see in particular Koutrakos (n 27) 5–25.

[68] For a detailed study of the EDC and its failure, see David Scannell, 'Third Time Luck: The Pre-History of the Common Security and Defence Policy' in Anthony Arnull and others (eds), *A Constitutional Order of States? Essays in EU Law in Honour of Alan Dashwood* (Hart Publishing 2011) 566–82.

[69] For further information, see Simon Duke, *The EU and Crisis Management: Development and Prospects* (European Institute of Public Administration 2002) 4–5; Jaap W de Zwaan, 'Foreign Policy and Defence Cooperation in the European Union: Legal Foundations' in Steven Blockmans (ed), *The European Union and Crisis Management: Policy and Legal Aspects* (TMC Asser Press 2008) 19.

[70] The WEU was a defensive alliance created in 1954 as an alternative to the failed EDC. It comprised ten Member States (Belgium, France, Germany, Greece, Italy, Luxembourg, the Netherlands, Portugal, Spain, and the United Kingdom). The WEU was based on the modified Brussels Treaty (signed in October 1954), which amended the Brussels Treaty initially concluded in 1948 between

NATO.[71] This marginalization, however, falls short of a paradox; after all, security concerns had been at the very origin of the 'ever closer Union among the peoples of Europe'.[72]

After the failure in 1954 of the EDC project, matters with foreign policy implications had been relegated to informal consultation agreements, which took the form of the European Political Cooperation (EPC). The EPC was gradually put in place between the Member States in the 1970s,[73] and was later codified through Title III of the Single European Act (SEA) of 1896, which was the first primary law instrument to lay down existing foreign affairs practices at the European level.

### 2.2.1 Reluctant integration and distinctive codification of high politics

The SEA undeniably set the tone of codification and institutionalization patterns for the decades to come. As for the legal framework, foreign affairs were consciously kept apart from other strands of EU law. Indicative hereof is the *two-treaty pattern* regarding foreign affairs, security, and defence matters at the EU level, which eventually lead to a special constitutional status. The underlying logic of this pattern is that *high* politics are formalized along intergovernmental lines, whereas *low* politics follow the supranational codification regime. The SEA was exemplary of this pattern. Those provisions dealing with foreign policy, security, and defence (Article 30 SEA) were contained in a separate title (Title III 'Provisions on European Cooperation in the Sphere of European Foreign Policy'). What is more, until an advanced stage of the negotiations this title was intended to constitute a treaty on its own. An indication hereof is the diverging denomination of the signatory parties: whereas Title III SEA refers to 'the High Contracting Parties', the rest of the Treaty uses the denomination 'Member States'.[74] This illustrates that Member States wanted—in whatever form—to keep this policy field apart from other European politics and to maintain the intergovernmental legal framework of traditional international relations. For many years then, the law that could be found in the context of EU foreign and security matters resembled traditional international

France, the United Kingdom, and the Benelux countries as a military assistance pact against Germany. The amended version of the 1954 Treaty, however, allowed for the accession of Italy and Germany, and importantly, for the latter's rearmament and integration into NATO. According to Article IV of the modified Brussels Treaty, the responsibility for military matters was de facto passed on to NATO (to avoid the duplication of structures). With the entry into force of the Treaty of Lisbon in 2009, the WEU structures were integrated into the EU (CFSP/CSDP) and the organization was closed down in 2011. For further information, see Scannell (n 68) 581–83; Stephan Keukeleire and Jennifer MacNaughtan, *The Foreign Policy of the European Union* (Palgrave Macmillan 2008) 41–43.

[71] Daniel Thym, 'GASP und äußere Sicherheit' in Andreas von Arnauld (ed), *Europäische Außenbeziehungen* (Nomos 2014) 949.

[72] TEU, Preamble, Article 1, para 2. Formulation first used in 1957 in the Treaty of Rome.

[73] A detailed description of the coming into being and functioning of the EPC can be found in Philippe de Schoutheete, *La coopération politique européenne* (Editions LABOR 1980) 17–85; Simon J Nuttall, *European Political Co-Operation* (Clarendon Press 1992).

[74] This intriguing point was made by Koutrakos (n 27) 14.

law rather than EU law.[75] As a result, foreign and security policy (high politics) was legally treated as a matter apart from economic issues (low politics)—and this dichotomy has been maintained ever since.

In addition, institutional design and agent selection followed intergovernmental patterns as Member States remained reluctant to delegate functions. While Member States created a secretariat for the EPC in Brussels, they refrained from providing the secretariat with permanent staff; they did, however, agree to second six diplomats from each Member State. The EPC secretariat was, hence, at best a rudimentary bureaucracy as it not only had limited human resources, but was without a budget, had vague functions, and no specific mandate.[76] With a view to ensuring consistency, Member States decided to put in place a six-month rotating presidency, which later became the Troika secretariat (composed of diplomats from the preceding, current, and succeeding presidencies of the Council of the EU (the Council)).[77] The codification of the EPC through the SEA, though, did not alter the intergovernmental institutional setting of the (in)formal consultation agreements in the field of foreign policy: cooperation was intentionally kept on an intergovernmental footing, and was conducted separately from the activities related to economic integration.[78]

Only after the end of the Cold War was EU security and defence revived. The Treaty of Maastricht (1992) introduced the CFSP as the second, distinctively intergovernmental pillar of the EU.[79] Security featured in two out of the five CFSP objectives (Article J.1(2) Treaty on European Union, Maastricht). This represented a crucial step forward in terms of integration of security and defence. But even though foreign and security policy matters were considerably upgraded by the creation of the second pillar, foreign affairs, security, and defence were again kept legally apart. The relevant provisions were contained in a separate Title that, even though it spelled out the prospect of a common European defence policy 'which might in time lead to a common defence' (Article J.4), left the intergovernmental setting unaltered. Rather, the creation of the CFSP as the second, distinctively intergovernmental pillar of the new EU consolidated the idiosyncratic nature of the policy at stake. The reason for the preservation of the purely intergovernmental nature of the CFSP was that several Member States, concerned about the increasing influence of the Commission headed by Jacques Delors in the aftermath

[75] Koskenniemi (n 57) 28–29; Peter van Elsuwege, 'EU External Action After the Collapse of the Pillar Structure: In Search of a New Balance Between Delimitation and Consistency' (2010) 47 Common Market Law Review 987, 994.

[76] Dijkstra (n 44) 51.

[77] Ana E Juncos and Karolina Pomorska, 'Secretariat, Facilitator or Policy Entrepreneur? Role Perceptions of Officials of the Council Secretariat' (2010) 14 European Integration Online Papers 1, 8–9.

[78] Eric Stein, 'European Political Cooperation (EPC) as a Component of the European Foreign Affairs System' (1983) 43 Zeitschrift für ausländisches öffentliches Recht und Völkerrecht (ZaöRV) 49, n 14. See also Koutrakos (n 27) 10.

[79] Title V, TEU (Maastricht).

of the fall of Berlin Wall, aimed at limiting the Commission's influence over foreign policy matters and at maintaining their decision-making power.[80] Member States therefore consciously created a bureaucracy within the Council and not within the Commission, where capacities and expertise in this field were already (partly) acquired and operational.[81] They did so to avoid boosting the external dimension of existing supranational structures and thereby preferred the potential duplication through the establishment of intergovernmental bureaucratic structures within the Council.[82] In the same vein, this intergovernmental penchant regarding institutional design and staffing remained characteristic of the bureaucracy. As a result, the little delegation of functions that took place in the context of the Treaty of Maastricht was exclusively directed at intergovernmental structures. Through the merger of the EPC secretariat with structures within the Council, a CFSP unit was created within the Council General Secretariat; the unit was given twenty-six members of staff—one seconded civil servant from each Member State plus personnel from the Council and the Commission.

The Treaty of Amsterdam (1997) further scaled up matters with foreign policy, security, and defence implications. While the intergovernmental design of the CFSP remained unaltered, the Treaty of Amsterdam represented a first 'major instance of delegation in foreign policy',[83] which would constitute the basis for further security and defence structures. There were three notable changes. First, the position of the Secretary-General of the Council/High Representative for the CSFP (SG/HR) was created for the purpose of external representation.[84] Secondly, the SG/HR was to be assisted by a Policy Planning and Early Warning Unit (Policy Unit), established for the purpose of information analysis within the Council General Secretariat.[85] Thirdly, the Treaty incorporated the Petersberg tasks into EU primary rules.[86] Activities in this field would henceforth encompass humanitarian and rescue tasks, peacekeeping activities, and tasks of combat forces in crisis management, including peace-making.[87]

80 Dijkstra (n 44) 53–54; Keukeleire and MacNaughtan (n 70) 49–50.

81 Special report of the Court of Auditors No 2/1996 concerning the accounts of the Administrator and the European Union Administration, Mostar (EUAM) accompanied by the replies of the Commission and the Administrator of Mostar paras 61–64.

82 Dijkstra (n 44) 67–68.

83 ibid 55.

84 Art 26 TEU (Amsterdam).

85 Art 26 TEU (Amsterdam); Treaty of Amsterdam amending the Treaty on European Union, the Treaties establishing the European Communities and certain related acts signed at Amsterdam 2 October 1997 [1997] OJ C340/1, 6. Declaration on the establishment of a policy planning and early warning unit.

86 The Petersberg tasks were set out in 1992 in a ministerial declaration released after WEU Council of Ministers in Petersberg (near Bonn). Art II.4 of the said declaration spelled out three purposes for which military units of WEU member states could be employed, namely (i) humanitarian and rescue tasks; (ii) peacekeeping tasks; and (iii) tasks of combat forces in crisis management, including peacemaking. Petersberg Declaration, issued by the Council of Ministers of the Western European Union, Bonn, 19 June 1992 Art II.4.

87 Art 17(2) TEU (Amsterdam).

While this incorporation did not immediately lead to the conferral of functions to specific institutions, it constituted the legal foundation upon which later institutional and operational developments in the field of EU peacekeeping and peacebuilding would be based.

### 2.2.2 External events driving security and defence integration and institutionalization

In the wake of the Kosovo crisis (1998/99), when European nations were again unable to respond to the atrocities committed in their geopolitical backyard,[88] and after a joint Franco-British initiative pushing for more integration in security and defence matters in December 1998,[89] the CSDP was added to the CSFP at the European Council in Cologne (June 1999) to provide the EU with the necessary operational capacity.[90] At the same occasion, Javier Solana was appointed as the SG/HR, which constituted a step towards personification of the CFSP. These two novelties were only (partly) codified through the Treaty of Nice (2001).[91]

Henceforth, the CSDP underwent an unexpected and astonishingly quick development to meet a range of institutional, functional, and operational demands. At subsequent Council meetings (1999–2000), Heads of State and Government created the first Brussels-based CSDP bureaucracies and set out strategic targets in terms of capacities and activities. Interestingly, the agents to whom Member States handed over functions again remained exclusively of an intergovernmental nature: all agents were seconded personnel of Member States. Most importantly, the Political and Security Committee (PSC) was established to keep track of the international situation and to help define policies within the CFSP, including the CSDP, under the auspices of the Council.[92] As the primary motivation and priority of Member States was placed on military capacity building,[93] two additional bodies of a military nature were called into being: the European Union Military Committee (EUMC)[94]

[88] Ministerial Declaration 'ESDP Ten Years—Challenges and Opportunities', 2974th External Relations Council meeting, Brussels, 17 November 2009 para 1.

[89] Joint Declaration on European Defence issued at the Franco-British Summit, Saint-Malo, 2–4 December 1998.

[90] Presidency Conclusions of the Cologne European Council (2–4 June 1999), Annex III: Presidency Report on Strengthening of the common European policy on security and defence.

[91] Most importantly, the Political and Security Committee (PSC) was codified in primary law through Art 25 TEU (Nice).

[92] Formalized in its present form through Council Decision 2001/78/CFSP of 22 January 2001 setting up the Political and Security Committee [2001] OJ L27/1, and Annex thereto.

[93] Jolyon Howorth, 'The CESDP and the Forging of a European Security Culture' (2002) 4 Politique européenne 88, 94; Radek Khol, 'Civil-Military Co-Ordination in EU Crisis Management' in Agnieszka Nowak (ed), *Civilian Crisis Management—The EU Way* (Institute for Security Studies 2006) 18.

[94] The European Union Military Committee (EUMC) is composed of national Chiefs of Defence. It provides the PSC with advice and makes recommendations on military matters. It was formalized through Council Decision 2001/79/CFSP of 22 January 2001 setting up the Military Committee

and the European Union Military Staff (EUMS).[95] In addition, Heads of State and Government laid down strategic targets for military capacities and activities.[96]

At the European Council in Feira (2000), the first civilian structure was set up, namely the Committee for Civilian Aspects of Crisis Management (CIVCOM).[97] Like the EUMC for military aspects, the CIVCOM was to provide advice to the PSC on civilian matters within the CFSP/CSDP framework. From this institutional nucleus, civilian crisis management would develop within a few years into a core operational element of EU security and defence, as section 4 of this chapter shows.

Prior to outlining the current state of codification, it is judicious to recapitulate the intricate integration and institutionalization trajectory of EU foreign affairs, including the inception of the EU's security and defence dimension, whose key events are summarized in Table 2.1. Three elements deserve particular attention. First, Member States have been hesitant, not to say reluctant, to integrate security and defence at the EU level after the failure of the first integration attempt in the 1950s. Therefore, Member State governments have proceeded with integration in small steps, with little risk, and according to an intergovernmental blueprint—in normative, procedural, and institutional terms. Secondly, external drivers, such as the fall of the Berlin wall, the war in Kosovo, or lately the Brexit vote, play a crucial role in EU security and defence cooperation and integration. And thirdly, integration and institutionalization take place outside formal Treaty revision procedures: cooperation starts with informal arrangements and operational activities, both of which are codified—at least in part—only later. The incremental development of European foreign affairs, security, and defence has indeed largely been driven by irreversible policy choices (leading to day-to-day practice) taken outside of intergovernmental conferences, when primary law provisions are negotiated and eventually determined. Practice therefore complements and often foreshadows law.

of the European Union [2001] OJ L27/4. Amended in 2005 through Council Decision 2005/395/CFSP of 10 May 2005 amending the Decision on the establishment of the Military Staff of the EU [2005] OJ L132/17.

[95] The European Union Military Staff (EUMS), which reports to the EUMC, is in charge of early warning, situation assessment, and strategic planning concerning CSDP activities and missions. It was formalized through the Council Decision 2001/80/CFSP of 22 January 2001 on the establishment of the Military Staff of the European Union [2001] OJ L27/7.

[96] Presidency Conclusions of the Helsinki European Council (10–11 December 1999), Annex 1 to Annex IV: Presidency progress report to the Helsinki European Council on strengthening the common European policy on security and defence.

[97] Formalized through Council Decision 2000/354/CFSP of 22 May 2000 setting up a Committee for civilian aspects of crisis management [2000] OJ L127/1.

**Table 2.1** Landmarks of the CFSP/CSDP (chronology until 2019)

| Year | Major event | Short description |
|---|---|---|
| 1950 | *Pleven Plan* | France proposes to establish a supranational European Defence Community (EDC) |
| | | Establishment of NATO |
| 1952 | *European Defence Community Treaty* | Treaty signed by Belgium, France, Germany, Italy, Luxembourg, and the Netherlands |
| 1954 | | EDC Treaty not ratified by the French Parliament |
| | *Modified Brussels Treaty* | Creation of the Western European Union (WEU) |
| 1961/62 | *Fouchet Plan (I + II)* | (Failed) proposal(s) made by France to put in place an intergovernmental union of States with a common foreign and security policy |
| Late 1960s | | Informal arrangements between Member States to coordinate foreign and security policy |
| 1970 | *Luxembourg report* | European Political Cooperation (EPC) put in place |
| 1986 | *Single European Act (SEA)* | Cooperation in foreign policy and in the field of security given a legal basis in primary EU law through the provisions contained in Title III of the SEA. |
| 1989/90 | | Collapse of the USSR, dissolution of Yugoslavia and German reunification |
| 1991 | | Beginning of hostilities in the Balkan region |
| 1992 | *Treaty of Maastricht* | Introduction of the Common Foreign and Security Policy (CFSP) as the second pillar of the European Union (EU). |
| 1997 | *Treaty of Amsterdam* | Creation of the position of the High Representative (HR) for CFSP; |
| | | Petersberg tasks incorporated into EU primary law, envisaging the use of civilian means |
| 1998/99 | | Hostilities in Albania; Kosovo crisis |
| 1998 | *Declaration of Saint-Malo* | Franco-British Joint Declaration on European Defence, calling for the development of European military and defence structures |
| 1999 | *Cologne European Council* | European Security and Defence Policy (ESDP) established against the backdrop of the Kosovo crisis |
| | *Helsinki European Council* | First 'Action Plan' for civilian crisis management set out by the Presidency Conclusions |
| | | Political and Security Committee (PSC) established |

**Table 2.1** *Continued*

| Year | Major event | Short description |
|---|---|---|
| 2000 | | Committee for Civilian Aspects of Crisis Management (CIVCOM) set up within Council of the EU (Council) |
| | *Feira European Council* | Definition of four priority areas of civilian CSDP (police, rule of law, civil administration, and civil protection) |
| 2001 | *Treaty of Nice* | Institutionalization of existing CSDP structures |
| 2003 | | First CSDP mission launched (EUPM Bosnia & Herzegovina) |
| | *European Security Strategy* | The use of civilian tools is underlined |
| 2004 | *Brussels European Council* | Adoption of the Action Plan for the Civilian Aspects of the CSDP, adding two more priority areas (monitoring and SSR) |
| | | Endorsement of Civilian Headline Goal 2008 |
| 2007 | | Adoption of Civilian Headline Goal 2010 |
| | | Creation of the Civilian Planning and Conduct Capability (CPCC) within the Council structures |
| | *Treaty of Lisbon* | Pillar structure abolished (entered into force 2009); |
| | | Mutual assistance clause introduced (Article 42(7) Treaty on European Union (TEU)); |
| | | European External Action Service (EEAS) programmed |
| 2009 | | Creation of the Crisis Management and Planning Directorate (CMPD) |
| | | EEAS put in place |
| | | Civilian CSDP structures integrated into the EEAS |
| 2013 | | CSDP Warehouse becomes operational |
| 2016 | *EU Global Strategy* | Civilian missions are labelled as 'trademark of CSDP' |
| | | Creation of a European Defence Fund (EDF) announced by Commission President Juncker |
| | | Commission proposal on a European Defence Action Plan released |
| 2017 | | Military Planning and Conduct Capability (MPCC) established within the EEAS |
| | *Tallinn European Council* | Launch of Permanent Structured Cooperation (PESCO) |
| 2018 | *Brussels European Council* | Council Conclusions on strengthening civilian CSDP are adopted, followed by the approval of the Civilian CSDP Compact |

## 3. Primary Law as it Stands

With a view to completing the unpacking of the 'policy area' box, this section looks at the current state of EU foreign affairs, security, and defence, which constitutes an integral, though distinctive, part of the EU legal order. The current legal framework of EU security and defence has been set out by the Treaty of Lisbon (2007). While the latest Treaty revision brought about one legal order by abolishing the former pillar structure, the CFSP/CSDP has remained distinctive in terms of procedures, competences, and institutional arrangements.[98] This is why some authors have argued that the CFSP/CSDP continues to be a second pillar all but in name.[99] Indicative hereof are (at least) three features, namely (i) the maintenance of the two-treaty pattern, (ii) the unaltered executive preponderance, and (iii) the continuation of institutional particularities. The ensuing analysis therefore first covers the revisited legal positioning of the CFSP/CSDP in the EU's legal order. Secondly, it sheds light on CFSP/CSDP governance. And thirdly, the section addresses the institutional changes—and continuities—brought about by the latest Treaty revision, notably the creation of the EEAS.

### 3.1 Recasting legal distinctiveness

As previously mentioned in section 2.2.1, EU foreign affairs, security, and defence have always been kept legally apart from other EU policies. This two-treaty pattern has survived the latest Treaty revision. Provisions on the CFSP, and consequently on the CSDP, are contained in the Treaty on European Union (TEU), whereas all other substantive policy competences, including other forms of external action, are laid down in the Treaty on the Functioning of the European Union (TFEU). Bearing in mind that according to Article 1(3) TEU both Treaties—the TEU and the TFEU—have the same legal value, one could comprehend this legal anomaly as the result of the previously existing Treaty structure, which kept foreign policy matters separate from other parts of EU law. But it has been reasoned that, in light of the Treaty of Lisbon expressively aiming at unity in EU law, the preservation of this legal anomaly is a clear and conscious signal that the CFSP is separate—and will in the near future remain separate—from other policy fields.[100] This strong signal was said to result from the UK pressuring for the CSFP to be contained in the TEU instead of keeping it in the TFEU with the remaining provisions on external action, where the Constitutional Treaty had located the policy at stake.[101] As a result, the CFSP/CSDP

[98] Marise Cremona, 'The Two (or Three) Treaty Solution: The New Treaty Structure of the EU' in Andrea Biondi, Piet Eeckhout, and Stefanie Ripley (eds), *EU Law After Lisbon* (Oxford University Press 2012) 70.

[99] Koutrakos (n 27) 29; Piris (n 38) 260.

[100] Cremona (n 98) 49–50.

[101] Piris (n 38) 260; Cremona (n 98) 50.

retains its sui generis character, which clearly demarcates this policy area from other EU policies,[102] and moreover leads to a distinctive constitutional status.[103]

## 3.2 Intact executive prerogatives

Indicative of the distinctiveness of the CFSP/CSDP is the dominance of national governments in EU high politics. Following the trajectory of past Treaties, the Treaty of Lisbon confirms that decision-making is exclusively conferred to intergovernmental fora, namely the European Council and the Council (Article 24(1) TEU), and in principle follows the unanimity rule (Article 31(1) TEU). The European Council determines the grand strategic orientations, which the Council then translates into action (Article 26(1)–(2) TEU), inter alia by agreeing on mandates and adopting decisions to launch or prologue civilian crisis management missions. Decision-making on the political control and strategic direction of a specific crisis management operation or mission can be delegated to the PSC (Article 38 TEU), which has become a pivotal body in CSDP matters.

In line with the Member States' preference for an intergovernmental framework, Treaty law ascribes a 'specific role' to the European Parliament (EP) and the Commission (Article 24(1) TEU), which is modest and primarily passive. The function of the EP is limited to regular consultations and expressions of views (Article 36 TEU).[104] In the same vein, the participation of the Commission is restricted to backing up certain actions of the High Representative of the EU for Foreign Affairs and Security Policy (HR), such as questions and initiatives addressed to the Council (Article 30 TEU), as well as its involvement once EU instruments are used under the CSDP (Article 42(4) TEU). Even though this is not mentioned in the TEU but in the relevant provisions of the TFEU, the Commission is also in charge of implementing the budget allocated to civilian missions (Article 41(1)–(2) TEU, read in conjunction with Article 317 TFEU). Yet, the Commission is deprived of the right of initiative. Hence, while the Commission is in charge of administering the CFSP expenditure charged to the EU budget, the Council continues to be the sole decision-maker. Already in the early days of the CFSP and prior to the CSDP going operational, this construction was judged incompatible with 'all traditions of democratic governance'[105] as it renders the Commission a

[102] Piet Eeckhout, 'The EU's Common Foreign and Security Policy After Lisbon: From Pillar Talk to Constitutionalism' in Andrea Biondi, Piet Eeckhout, and Stefanie Ripley (eds), *EU Law After Lisbon* (Oxford University Press 2012) 265; Koutrakos (n 27) 27.

[103] Koutrakos (n 27) 34.

[104] For an overview of the development of parliamentary scrutiny of European foreign affairs issues, see Esther Barbé and Anna Herranz Surralés, 'The Power and Practice of the European Parliament in Security Policies' in Dirk Peters, Wolfgang Wagner and Nicole Deitelhoff (eds), *The Parliamentary Control of European Security Policy* (ARENA 2008) 77–107.

[105] Jörg Monar, 'The Finances of the Union's Intergovernmental Pillars: Tortuous Experiments with the Community Budget' (1997) 35 Journal of Common Market Studies 57, 78.

'mere "cashier" of intergovernmental co-operation deprived of political responsibility'.[106] The double-hatted High Representative, in turn, has in theory the right to make proposals (Article 27(1) TEU), but in reality has little say at both the strategic and operational level of civilian crisis management despite some executive responsibilities in the context of the CFSP/CSDP.[107]

Furthermore, judicial review by the EU judicature is limited under the current Treaty provisions. The second sub-paragraph of Article 24(1) TEU and the first paragraph of Article 275 TFEU stipulate that the Court of Justice of EU (CJEU) has no jurisdiction with respect to the CFSP/CSDP, except for policy delimitation (Article 40 TEU) and sanctions, that is, restrictive measures directed against legal and natural persons (second paragraph of Article 275 TFEU).

Executive prerogatives are not limited to law, but do also surface in practice. Coinciding with the entry into force of the Treaty of Lisbon, the departure of the respected and experienced Javier Solana as 'Mister CFSP' did not go unnoticed, and the nomination of the relatively unknown and inexperienced Catherine Ashton to the position of the HR was, moreover, not an innocent choice by the Member States.[108] In cases of actual crisis, Member States have for some years after the entry into force of the Treaty of Lisbon preferred to play the leading role themselves while leaving EU actors—in particular the HR—with a supporting role at best.[109] Thereby, national governments have underscored that there is an underlying principal drift in CSFP/CSDP matters—the Member States being the principal, the Brussels-based CSDP structures being the agent.[110] The way in which Member States dealt with the Arab Spring, the situation in Libya in 2011, or the Syrian crisis in 2012 was telling in this regard: matters of high politics were handled at the national level.[111] The migratory pressures of 2015 have exacerbated this executive-friendly trend, as the EU–Turkey statement of March 2016 (and its confirmed judicial unreviewability) illustrated.[112]

[106] ibid.

[107] As regards the responsibilities and tasks of the High Representative/Vice-President, see section 3.3 of this chapter.

[108] A similar point was made by Smith (n 18) 252; Daniel Thym, 'The Intergovernmental Constitution of the EU's Foreign, Security & Defence Executive' (2011) 7 European Constitutional Law Review 453, 457.

[109] On the role played by the HR and the Member States in cases of crisis and the underlying dynamics at work, see the case studies provided by Dijkstra on the Israeli–Lebanese war (2006) and the South Ossetia war (2008) in Hylke Dijkstra, 'EU External Representation in Conflict Resolution: When Does the Presidency or the High Representative Speak for Europe?' (2011) 15 European Integration Online Papers 1.

[110] On the issue of *agency* drift v *principal* drift in the EU, see Menon and Weatherill (n 53) 119.

[111] On this matter, see Panos Koutrakos, 'The European Union in the Global Security Architecture' in Bart van Vooren, Steven Blockmans, and Jan Wouters (eds), *The EU's Role in Global Governance—The Legal Dimension* (Oxford University Press 2013) 85–86; Youri Devuyst, 'The European Council and the CFSDP after the Lisbon Treaty' (2012) 17 European Foreign Affairs Review 327, 331–40.

[112] Joined Cases C-208/17 P to C-210/17 P *NF, NG and NM v European Council* [2018] EU:C:2018:705.

## 3.3 (Novel) institutional particularities

Let us now turn to the institutional context under the current primary law regime. The Treaty of Lisbon introduced two major institutional reforms in the CFSP which, however, did not alter the distinctive intergovernmental nature of the policy. These changes have to be seen against the wider backdrop of the particular delegation pattern (reluctance prevailing) and the distinctive integration trajectory (intergovernmental solutions being privileged) of EU foreign affairs, security, and defence.

The first important institutional reform was the merger of the formerly separate position of the HR/SG with the position of the Commissioner for External Relations. The drafters of the Treaty have undertaken this amalgamation of posts with a view to increasing the consistency of EU external action. Yet, it leaves the High Representative[113] with a long list of functions and missions, all of which are to be carried out simultaneously: the HR holds the office of the Vice-President of the European Commission (VP);[114] takes part in the meetings of the European Council;[115] presides over the meetings of the Foreign Affairs Council;[116] is in charge of representing the EU at the international level;[117] is tasked to coordinate the action of Member States in International Organizations and at international conferences;[118] heads the EEAS, liaises with the EP on CFSP/CSPD matters;[119] is responsible for the EU Special Representatives;[120] heads the European Defence Agency;[121] and chairs the board of the European Union Institute for Security Studies located in Paris.[122] To this already impressive list can be added a set of executive responsibilities incumbent upon the HR in the context of the CFSP/CSDP: the HR shall conduct the EU's foreign and security policy, the shall contribute to the development of the CFSP by their proposals,[123] and they shall also put into effect the CSDP together with Member States.[124] It has been underlined that this job description is too long for one person and that the HR/VP position is not the result of a merger, but rather resembles a personal union in which one person has two jobs.[125] Concretely, this means that the HR is fairly absent from

[113] The HR is appointed by the European Council by qualified majority according to Art 18(1) TEU.
[114] Art 18(4) TEU.
[115] According to Art 15(2) TEU, the HR shall take part in the work of the European Council.
[116] Art 18(3) TEU and Art 34(2).
[117] Art 27(2) TEU.
[118] Art 34(1) TEU.
[119] Art 36 TEU.
[120] Art 33 TEU.
[121] Art 7(1) Council Decision 2011/411/CFSP of 12 July 2011 defining the statute, seat and operational rules of the European Defence Agency and repealing Joint Action 2004/551/CFSP [2011] OJ L183/16.
[122] Art 5(2) Council Decision 2014/75/CFSP of 10 February 2014 on the European Union Institute for Security Studies [2014] OJ L41/13.
[123] Art 18(2) TEU and Art 27(1).
[124] Art 24(1) TEU, Art 27(1) TEU, and Art 26(3) TEU.
[125] Norheim-Martinsen (n 27) 59.

the strategic and operational stage of CSDP activities given their otherwise heavy workload.

The second major institutional change introduced by the Treaty of Lisbon was the creation of the EEAS, which is to assist the HR.[126] While Article 27(3) TEU stipulates that the staff of the EEAS is to 'comprise officials from relevant departments of the General Secretariat of the Council and of the Commission as well as staff seconded from national diplomatic services of the Member States', many other crucial points were left undefined by primary law. These points included the institutional nature of the service and the distribution of posts across the Council and the Commission. As a result, the core issue of the negotiations on the future EEAS circled—as many times before in the history of the CFSP/CSDP—around (decision-making) power in a given institutional setting.[127] Not surprisingly, then, fears of sovereignty loss were associated with the EEAS.[128] Indeed, the creation of a true European external affairs service—in other words, a European ministry of foreign affairs—was a fundamental change that led Member States to overhaul their national foreign policy machineries in the wider European context; this rearrangement, in turn, meant a lot of power politics at the European level.[129] An expression of this anxiety can be found in Declaration 13 concerning the common foreign and security policy annexed to the Treaty of Lisbon, which emphasizes that the current responsibilities of Member States—foreign policy formulations as well as conduct, and representation in third countries as well as international organizations—remain unaltered by the changes in primary law.[130] Finally, the outcome of the negotiations led to a complex institutional design compromise, endorsed by Council Decision 2010/427/EU:[131] as it stands today, the EEAS is neither supranational nor intergovernmental, but a sui generis body, officially labelled as a 'functionally autonomous body of the European Union'.[132] Supranational and intergovernmental

[126] Art 27(3) TEU.

[127] Detailed descriptions of the creation and the legal as well as institutional framework of the EEAS can, for instance, be found in Leendert Erkelens and Steven Blockmans, 'Setting Up the European External Action Service: An Institutional Act of Balance', *CLEER Working Papers 2012/1* (Centre for the Law of the EU External Relations (CLEER) 2012); Bart van Vooren, 'A Legal-Institutional Perspective on the European External Action Service' (2011) 48 Common Market Law Review 475.

[128] An analysis of the establishment of the EEAS and the underlying national interest can be found in Michael Kluth and Jess Pilegaard, 'The Making of the EU's External Action Service: A Neorealist Interpretation' (2012) 17 European Foreign Affairs Review 303; Koutrakos (n 27) 48–49.

[129] Dijkstra (n 44) 73.

[130] Consolidated Version of the Treaty on European Union (TEU) [2016] OJ C202/343, Declarations 13 and 14 concerning the common foreign and security policy.

[131] A thorough analysis of Council Decision 2010/427/EU can be found in Steven Blockmans and Christophe Hillion (eds), *EEAS 2.0—A Legal Commentary on Council Decision 2010/427/EU Establishing the Organisation and Functioning of the European External Action Service* (Centre for European Policy Studies 2013).

[132] Art 1(2) Council Decision 2010/427/EU of 26 July 2010 establishing the organisation and functioning of the European External Action Service [2010] OJ L201/30, and Annex thereto. For more information on the sui generis nature of the EEAS, see Van Vooren (n 127) 481–84.

branches of the EU's external action nonetheless continue to co-exist within the EEAS.[133]

These modifications—the new mandate of the HR/VP and the creation of the EEAS—have transformed the institutional scenery of EU foreign affairs. Yet, a closer look at the CFSP/CSDP lays open that these changes have not impacted EU security and defence: while the institutional stage setting has been refurbished, both the actors and the plot (ie processes) of CSDP matters have remained unchanged.

An examination of the different areas of activity of the EEAS is indeed revealing in terms of institutional design patterns and agent selection. All CSDP structures, including those dedicated to civilian missions, were initially established within the General Secretariat of the Council; some of these structures were then transferred *en bloc* to the EEAS in the post-Lisbon institutional architecture.[134] This relocation has only taken place on paper (in the organization chart) as the units concerned have not physically moved into another building: they continue to work in the Avenue de Cortenbergh, while the EEAS has its address at the Schuman roundabout.[135] The said structures have indeed been granted a special treatment: they continue to report and operate along intergovernmental lines, and retain a specific intergovernmental recruitment scheme and status.[136] Hence, one will find that the personnel in charge of CSDP matters remain primarily seconded national civil servants or experts. CSDP structures are therefore internally cocooned sub-units,[137] functioning according to their own *modus operandi*. This confirms that there was and still is a preference for intergovernmental institutional design and agents within EU security and defence structures.

Empirical studies have shown that the 'intergovernmental' staff members of the EEAS—that is, those seconded national civil servants and experts working in crisis management structures—still identify the European Council and the Foreign Affairs Council as the most important source of political signals for decision-making.[138] It remains to be seen whether the institutional anchorage of the civilian crisis management bureaucracy with the EEAS will in the medium- or long-term change the behaviour or loyalty of implicated agents. Until now, their operational distinctiveness has not gone without criticism,[139] in reaction to which the architectural structure of the EEAS and specifically its intergovernmental components have been altered in late 2015: existing reporting lines were

[133] Thym (n 71) 971.

[134] See Art 4(3)(a) Council Decision 2010/427/EU [2010] OJ L201/30.

[135] A move of CSDP crisis management structures to a compound situated between Rue d'Arlon and Rue de la Science is imminent. See EEAS Annual Human Resources Report 2018 (July 2019) 35.

[136] See Art 4(3)(a) Council Decision 2010/427/EU [2010] OJ L201/30.

[137] Hans Merket, *The EU and the Security-Development Nexus* (Brill/Nijhoff 2016) 188.

[138] Thomas Henökl, 'Conflict and Continuity in European Diplomatic Cultures: Accountability, Scrutiny and Control in EU External Affairs' (2016) 4 International Relations and Diplomacy 324, 335.

[139] EEAS Review, European External Action Service 2013 1, 5, 16, 18.

modified by interposing Deputy Secretary-Generals between the different crisis management actors and the HR.[140] The primary goal of this reporting innovation was to bring crisis management structures closer to other EEAS departments.[141] In a similar vein, the division for CSDP Coordination and Support and the division for Conflict Prevention, Peacebuilding and Mediation were merged in 2017 into the new division with the catchy acronym PRISM (Prevention of Conflicts, Rule of Law/Security Sector Reform, Integrated Approach, Stabilisation and Mediation). The latest refurbishment of the Service's crisis management structures, undertaken in 2019 reportedly with a view to aligning EEAS structures to the new integrated approach to crisis management,[142] further decreases the institutional distinctiveness of CSDP actors within the EEAS. Crisis management will henceforth be writ large, including CSDP measures *and* integrated security and defences dossiers, namely external security measures beyond the CSDP (ie overlapping or parallel AFSJ activities). Accordingly, a new Managing Directorate dedicated to CSDP and Crisis Response was created. Two divisions operate under the umbrella of this new Managing Directorate, namely Integrated Approach for Security and Peace (ISP), which by and large takes over the functions previously carried out by the Crisis Management and Planning Directorate (CMPD), and the slightly readjusted division Security and Defence Policy (SECDEFPOL).[143] But as with previous—often cosmetic—changes to the organigram, it is unclear whether the latest reshuffling will (profoundly) alter the sui generis institutional and procedural intergovernmental regime of the civilian crisis management apparatus. In light of the integrated approach, however, civilian CSDP will certainly get closer to other strands of external action, in particular activities carried out under the former third pillar (AFSJ).

That said, the Commission has through the EEAS reshuffle lost a great deal of its resources to the new service, which was said to have considerably weakened the former's stand in EU external affairs.[144] The same is not true for the Council as, in the end, '[t]he Council and its preparatory bodies retain their decision-making powers, while the administrative infrastructure steps into the open and becomes visible within in EEAS'.[145] With the Treaty of Lisbon, Member States have thus not renounced their decision-making prerogatives, which they traditionally enjoy in

[140] Namely the Deputy Secretary-General Political Affairs/Political Director for the politico-strategic level, and the Deputy Secretary-General CSDP and Crisis response for the strategic planning and operational implementation units.
[141] Merket (n 137) 190.
[142] EEAS, Annual Activity Report 2018 (1 July 2019) 13.
[143] EEAS, 'Organisation Chart of the EEAS' (July 2019) <https://eeas.europa.eu/headquarters/headquarters-homepage/3602/organisation-chart-of-the-eeas_en> accessed 18 February 2020.
[144] Dijkstra (n 44) 73–74.
[145] Daniel Thym, *Holding Europe's CFSP/CSDP Executive to Account in the Age of the Lisbon Treaty* (CEU Ediciones 2011) 9.

foreign, security, and defence policy. This confirms the general trend in EU security and defence, namely that throughout the incremental development of the Brussels-based crisis management bureaucracy, intergovernmental institutional design and agent selection has remained predominant. This also holds for the reforms brought about by the Treaty of Lisbon, where intergovernmental tendencies were strong but somewhat camouflaged. Despite their 'novelty', the institutional reforms introduced by the Treaty of Lisbon, therefore, perpetuate existing institutional—that is intergovernmental—particularities. In sum, high politics have been and still are treated differently at the EU level than low politics. This holds for institutional, procedural, and normative aspects. As for normative distinctiveness, EU foreign affairs, security, and defence share a single but differentiated legal order with other EU policies. The prevalence of unanimity—instead of qualified majority voting—constitutes an important procedural difference. Regarding institutional distinctiveness, national executive actors (formally) call the shots at high-level meetings and intergovernmental agents take care of crisis management within Council and EEAS structures, without the Commission or EP playing a meaningful role.

## 4. Civilian Crisis Management, the 'Trademark of CSDP'

After having explored step by step the international security environment (largest box), as well as the distinctive policy field of the CFSP/CSDP (middle-sized box), the current section delves into the realities of EU civilian crisis management (smallest box). The section first outlines the unexpected institutional and operational ascent of civilian crisis management, an initially underestimated policy tool. The discussion then moves to the gradual recalibration of civilian and military CSDP and, finally, focuses on the often conflict-ridden overlap of civilian missions with other (similar) external activities of the EU.

### 4.1 The unexpected ascent of civilian crisis management

When the CSDP was crafted in the late 1990s and its institutions gradually put in place in the early 2000s, security-related external action was believed to fit into two distinct categories: *military* and *civilian*. In line with this presumed civil–military dichotomy, soldiers were assigned to fight and win battles, whereas civilian personnel were expected to make peace last by taking care of an array of ancillary, non-military activities, such as rule of law reforms or police training. In other words, civilian peacebuilding activities were seen as a by-product of military operations; they aimed at stabilization and conflict prevention once the military guys had done their job. This perception explains why policy-makers initially accorded only a secondary importance to the civilian element of the CSDP.[146] Scandinavian advocacy, however, helped to overcome Member States' hesitation regarding non-military activities, and paved the way for the development of civilian crisis management capacities at the EU level.[147] And so, in late 1999, Heads of State and Government adopted an action plan for *non*-military (ie civilian) crisis management.[148] Two decades later, civilian crisis management constitutes an innovation hub for peacebuilding activities—both within the EU's crisis management structures and processes, as well as for action on the ground.[149]

Regarding the operational track record, civilian missions account for two-thirds of the EU's thirty-four peace operations. Thus, there is an apparent operational tilt to civilian action types under the CSDP. To date, the EU has deployed a total of twenty-two civilian missions, comprising seven police missions, three rule-of-law missions, two monitoring missions, two border assistance missions, four security sector reform missions, and four missions with both civilian and military components under the framework of civilian CSDP.[150] Table 2.2 provides an overview of all civilian CSDP missions deployed from 2003 to 2019, including the type and duration of missions and their maximum staff level.[151]

[146] Anand Menon and Ulrich Sedelmeier, 'Instruments and Intentionality: Civilian Crisis Management and Enlargement Conditionality in EU Security Policy' (2010) 33 West European Politics 75, 81–84; Khol (n 93) 18.

[147] The Finnish and Swedish presidencies (respectively in place from July to December 1999 and from January to June 2001) were strongly advocating for *non*-military crisis management capacities. See Peter Viggo Jakobsen, 'Small States, Big Influence: The Overlooked Nordic Influence on the Civilian ESDP' (2009) 47 Journal of Common Market Studies 81; Howorth (n 93) 94.

[148] Presidency Conclusions of the Helsinki European Council (10–11 December 1999), Annex 2 to Annex IV: Presidency Report on Non-Military Crisis Management of the European Union (Action Plan).

[149] Smith (n 18) 2, 155, 208.

[150] Prefixes vary according to mission types. *Police* missions carry the prefix EUPOL/EUPM (EU Police Mission) or EUPAT (EU Police Advisory team). *Rule of law* missions have the prefix EULEX or EUJUST. EU *monitoring* missions are referred to as AMM or EUMM. *Border* missions bear the prefix EUBAM (EU Border Assistance Mission). Missions related to *security sector reform* are designated by SSR (Security Sector Reform), SEC (Security), or EUAM (EU Advisory Mission). Finally, *hybrid* missions have, next to EUAVSEC (EU Aviation Security Mission) the prefix EUCAP (EU Capacity Building Missions).

[151] Some specifications are judicious here. The mission EUBAM Moldova and Ukraine is not deployed by the Council under the framework of the CSDP, but by the Commission in the context of the European Neighbourhood and Partnership Instrument. Moreover, the support to AMIS (Sudan) was labelled as civil–military supporting action, not as a crisis management mission. See Council Joint Action 2005/557/CFSP of 18 July 2005 on the European Union civilian–military supporting action to the African Union mission in the Darfur region of Sudan [2005] OJ L188/46. Finally, as regards EUCAP NESTOR, the mission was renamed into EUCAP Somalia by Council Decision (CFSP) 2016/2240 of 12 December 2016 amending Decision 2012/389/CFSP on the European Union Mission on Regional Maritime Capacity Building in the Horn of Africa (EUCAP NESTOR) [2016] OJ L337/18. This said, the numbers displayed in Table 2.2 indicate (i) the *maximum recorded* personnel for *completed missions* and (ii) the *current (authorized) staff level* for *ongoing missions* (as of October 2019) with the maximum recoded personnel in brackets if the maximum differs considerably from the current deployment strength. The numbers, comprising both international and local personnel, are retrieved from the information provided by the Council/the EEAS for ongoing and completed missions. Another source of information constituted the 'EU Engagement Database' elaborated by Danilo Di Mauri, Ulrich Krotz, and Katerina Wright. See Danilo Di Mauro, Ulrich Krotz and Katerina Wright, 'EU's Global Engagement: A Database of CSDP Military Operations and Civilian Missions Worldwide', *Version 2.0* (European University Institute 2017) <doi:10.2870/14148>. Concerning EUCAP Sahel Mali, a Regional Advisory

**Table 2.2** Civilian CSDP missions deployed from 2003 to 2019

| Name | Location | Duration | Staff |
|---|---|---|---|
| *Police Missions* | | | |
| EUPM BiH | Bosnia and Herzegovina | 2003–12 | 500 |
| EUPOL PROXIMA | FYROM | 2003–5 | 200 |
| EUPAT | FYROM | 2005–6 | 30 |
| EUPOL KINSHASA | DRC | 2005–7 | 27 |
| EUPOL COPPS | Palestinian territories | 2006–present | 110 |
| EUPOL RD Congo | DRC | 2007–14 | 60 |
| EUPOL AFGHANISTAN | Afghanistan | 2007–16 | 390 |
| *Rule of Law Missions* | | | |
| EUJUST THEMIS | Georgia | 2004–5 | 20 |
| EUJUST LEX | Iraq | 2005–13 | 70 |
| EULEX KOSOVO | Kosovo | 2008–present | 503 (3,000) |
| *Monitoring Missions* | | | |
| AMM | Aceh, Indonesia | 2005–6 | 220 |
| EUMM GEORGIA | Georgia | 2008–present | 411 |
| *Border Missions* | | | |
| (EUBAM Moldova and Ukraine | Moldova/Ukraine border | 2005–present | ~120) |
| EUBAM Rafah | Rafah Crossing Point | 2005–present | 16 (70) |
| EUBAM Libya | Libya | 2013–present | 65 |
| *Security Sector Reform Missions (with a military component)* | | | |
| EUSEC RD Congo | DRC | 2005–16 | 50 |
| EU SSR GUINEA-BISSAU | Guinea-Bissau | 2008–10 | 20 |
| EUAM Ukraine | Ukraine | 2014–present | 323 |
| EUAM Iraq | Iraq | 2017–present | 98 |
| *Other Hybrid Missions (civilian and military components)* | | | |
| (AMIS EU Supporting Action | Sudan | 2005–7 | 50) |
| EUAVSEC-South Sudan | South Sudan | 2012–14 | ~50 |
| EUCAP Sahel Niger | Niger | 2012–present | 210 |
| EUCAP NESTOR [Somalia] | Horn of Africa | 2012–present | 170 |
| EUCAP Sahel Mali | Mali | 2014–present | 209 |

This operational dynamism rests on institutional foundations. The progressive institutionalization of Brussels-based structures, which were specifically set up for the purpose of steering, planning, and implementing civilian missions, began shortly after the adoption of the first action plan for non-military CSDP activities in 1999.[152] In 2000 government representatives established the first structure solely dedicated to civilian CSDP matters within the Council General Secretariat, namely the CIVCOM.[153] At the European Council meeting in Santa Maria da Feira, which took place later the same year, policy-makers circumscribed the operational scope of future civilian crisis management activities: policing, the rule of law, civilian administration, and civil protection were laid down as 'priority areas' with concrete targets.[154] These priority areas were quickly extended to include the support of Special EU Representatives, monitoring, and security sector reform.[155]

In 2003, the EU was proud to launch its first ever CSDP mission in Bosnia and Herzegovina: a civilian police mission.[156] Given the military preponderance, it was rather unexpected that the operational baptism of fire of the CSDP would be in the field of civilian crisis management. Only two years later, in 2005, there were already 12 civilian missions. This pace of deployment clearly went beyond the capacities of the existing civilian CSDP structures. As a reaction, the Civilian Planning and Conduct Capability (CPCC) saw the light in 2007 within the Council General Secretariat.[157] Its structure and staffing level resulted from a German compromise proposal, reconciling a rather low-level profile (preferred by the UK) with a quasi-military set-up (favoured by France).[158] It is worth recalling at this juncture that the bureaucratic structures dedicated to crisis management, including CIVCOM and the CPCC, were initially all pooled under the roof of the General Secretariat of the Council. Nowadays, however, crisis management actors are affiliated with two

and Coordination Cell (RACC) with 15 staff was launched in 2017 to liaise with the G5 Sahel. While the RACC is embedded into EUCAP Mali—expenditures are covered by the budget of the EUCAP Sahel Mali mission—the thematic and geographical scope of the RACC mandate is broader. The displayed staff numbers include EUCAP Sahel Mali personnel (194) and RACC staff members (15).

152 For a detailed description of this process, see Faleg (n 13) 90–95.

153 Formalized through Council Dec. 2000/354/CFSP [2000] OJ L127/1.

154 Presidency Conclusions of the Santa Maria da Feira European Council (19–20 June 2000), Annex I: Presidency Report on Strengthening the Common European Security and Defence Policy, Appendix 3: Study on concrete targets on civilian aspects of crisis management.

155 Council Doc 15863/04 of 7 December 2004, 'Civilian Headline Goal 2008', endorsed by the European Council on 7 December 2004.

156 Council Joint Action 2002/210/CFSP of 11 March 2002 on the European Union Police Mission [2002] OJ L 70/1.

157 Hylke Dijkstra, 'The Council Secretariat's Role in the Common Foreign and Security Policy' (2008) 13 European Foreign Affairs Review 149, 162. The CPCC was set up in 2007 following the Council's approval of the Guidelines for Command and Control Structure for EU Civilian Operations in Crisis Management. See Council Doc 9919/07 EXT2 of 1 February 2008, 'Draft Guidelines for Command and Control Structures for EU Civilian Operations in Crisis Management', Annex (partial declassification of document 9919/07 RESTREINT UE of 23 May 2007).

158 Raphael Bossong, 'EU Civilian Crisis Management and Organizational Learning' (2013) 22 European Security 94, 104.

EU structures, namely the Council—when it comes to strategic matters—and the EEAS—primarily when operational issues are at stake, including budget coordination and cooperation with the Service for Foreign Policy Instruments (FPI) of the Commission.[159]

After considering the operational and institutional development of civilian CSDP, let us now turn to capabilities. Based on the defined priority areas in 2000, Member States took successive steps to equip the civilian dimension of the CSDP with operational means. In the early days of civilian CSDP, the Heads of State and Government adopted several action plans, and set and revised strategic as well as capacity targets, notably the Civilian Headline Goals (2008 and 2010).[160] In addition, several commitment and improvement conferences were held between 2004 and 2007 at the ministerial level to gauge the progress made, enhance the development of civilian capabilities, and assess future challenges.[161] The permanent CSDP Warehouse, which was set up in 2012 and became operational in 2013, was another milestone in providing civilian crisis management with the necessary operational means to rapidly react in times of crisis.[162] In the post-Lisbon context, a multi-annual capability development approach was favoured, leading in 2012 to the Council adopting the Civilian Capability Development Plan (CCDP). The implementation of the CCDP was, however, much delayed: it was only kicked off in 2015.[163] In November 2016, that is after the release of the EUGS advocating for an integrated approach, the Council endorsed the Implementation Plan for Security and Defence, which echoed the need for combining different crisis management tools and moreover backed the establishment of a list of generic civilian CSDP tasks across missions; the Council furthermore welcomed the deployment of specialized expert teams (to speed up otherwise slow deployment), and called for an improvement of pre-deployment training.[164]

[159] For more details on the budgetary arrangements regarding civilian CSDP, see section 5 of this Chapter and Chapter 5.

[160] In reverse chronological order: Council Doc 14823/07 of 19 November 2007, 'Civilian Headline Goal 2010', approved by the ministerial Civilian Capabilities Improvement Conference and noted by the General Affairs and External Relations Council on 19 November 2007; Civilian Headline Goal 2008; Action Plan for Civilian Aspects of ESDP [European Security and Defence Policy], adopted by the European Council, Brussels, 17–18 June 2004; Presidency Report to the Göteborg European Council (15–16 June 2001) on European Security and Defence policy, Annex III to the ANNEX: New Concrete Targets for Civilian Aspects of Crisis Management, Council Doc 9526/1/01 REV 1 (11 June 2001); Presidency Report to the Göteborg European Council (15–16 June 2001) on European Security and Defence policy, Annex I to the ANNEX: Police Action Plan, Council Doc 9526/1/01 REV 1 (11 June 2001).

[161] Nicoletta Pirozzi, 'The European Union and Civilian Crisis Management after Lisbon' (2015) 20 European Foreign Affairs Review 287, 291.

[162] Initially set up in 2012, the warehouse's legal foundations were revisited in 2018. See Council Decision 2012/698/CFSP of 13 November 2012 on the establishment of a warehouse for civilian crisis management missions [2012] OJ L 314/25. Repealed in 2018 by Council Decision (CFSP) 2018/653 of 26 April 2018 on the establishment of a warehouse capability for civilian crisis-management missions [2018] OJ L108/22.

[163] Nina Antolovic Tovornik, 'CSDP Civilian Capability Development' in Thierry Tardy (ed), *Recasting EU civilian crisis management* (European Union Institute for Security Studies 2017) 33.

[164] Implementation Plan on Security and Defence 19.

Building on these recommendations and following a reflection phase on the future of civilian CSDP, the Civilian CSDP Compact (Civilian Compact) was adopted in 2018. This Compact, which is to be implemented at the latest by the summer of 2023, is a major step forward for civilian crisis management, not least because it entails a range of novel capability developments. It has to be stressed that, although significant progress has been made on the capabilities front, past attempts at improving civilian means has not led to the desired outcome. Intricate planning processes continue to slow down deployment, as do difficult recruitment arrangements. Next to the difficulty of finding (enough) skilled personnel, there is the persistent lack of uniform training.[165] What is more, institutional and operational sustainability through stable commitments and institutional memory building remains weak. The latest capabilities development plan therefore tries to overcome some of these long-standing capability issues, in particular staffing, readiness, and deployability. The 2018 Civilian Compact first stipulates that the share of seconded personnel among the internationals shall increase to 70% (instead of 50–60% at present).[166] Secondly, the Core Responsiveness Capacity, an expert group which can be sent to a crisis zone on very short notice, shall comprise 50 (instead of 30) members.[167] Thirdly, the EU shall be able to deploy 200 civilian experts in 30 days.[168] To reach these goals and to allow for a proper review of commitments and achievements, the High Representative and the Commission have been asked to specify the necessary steps at the EU level, and the Member States agreed to draw up National Implementation Plans until late 2019.[169] But while the EEAS and the Commission delivered their joint Action Plan to implement the compact in April 2019, progress at the national level has been slow. This delay at the national level is indicative of enduring (civilian) CSDP pathologies: in the absence of concrete targets or a defined review process, and with many Member States caring far more about military capability building, the development of civilian CSDP capabilities remains structurally weak. It therefore remains to be seen whether Member States will use the momentum created by the 2018 Civilian Compact to eventually boost civilian crisis management, or whether national governments will continue to treat civilian CSDP as an unwelcome stepchild of military CSDP.

[165] The problem of lacking pre-deployment training and, in particular, of insufficient staffing has been regularly pinpointed by the Court of Auditors in its Special reports dealing with (aspects of) civilian missions, most recently in relation to EUCAP Nahel Niger and EUCAP Sahel Mali. See Special report of the Court of Auditors No 15/2018, 'Strengthening the capacity of the internal security forces in Niger and Mali: only limited and slow progress' paras 25–27, 31–33; Special report of the Court of Auditors No 7/2015, 'The EU police mission in Afghanistan: mixed results' para 81; Special report of the Court of Auditors No 18/2012, 'European Union assistance to Kosovo related to the rule of law' para 109.

[166] Civilian CSDP Compact 5.

[167] ibid 8.

[168] ibid.

[169] ibid 10–11.

## 4.2 Recalibrated civil–military interaction

The unexpectedly fast institutional build-up and operational dynamism of civilian CSDP has obviously impacted on the civil–military balance of EU security and defence. In the early days of the CSDP, the connectedness of civilian and military components played a minor role, not least because civilian aspects were thought to merely complement the peace-making work of armed personnel. The underlying ideas were that there was a sequencing of 'military first and civilian later'.[170] Over the years, however, the relation between the civilian and the military dimension of the policy has considerably changed—both on the institutional and conceptual plane.[171]

With regards to the institutional dimension, liaison entities at both the politico-strategic and the operational crisis management levels have been put in place to attenuate the initially dichotomous civil–military bureaucratic organization. The creation of the Civil–Military Cell (CivMilCell) in 2005 marked the beginning of this hesitant but steady rapprochement. The Cell, which was set up to enhance strategic planning capacities, including in the context of joint civil–military activities, was affiliated to an existing military body: the European Union Military Staff.[172] The CivMilCell, however, did not deliver on the expectation of improving civil–military interaction at a politico-strategic level,[173] the military anchorage possibly having played a role in this disappointing performance. Therefore, an important institutional refurbishment occurred in 2009 with the aim of eventually overcoming the persistent civil–military division regarding *strategic* planning.[174] In the wake of the Lisbon Treaty and the scheduled creation of EEAS, a merger of existing military and civilian planning structures of the Council General Secretariat took place, resulting in the establishment of the CMPD.[175]

Quickly after its establishment, the CMPD took over agenda-setting in EU crisis management, even after its integration into the EEAS.[176] Within the CMPD, civilian and military staff jointly drew up the first planning document of any CSDP

[170] Adapted quote from an interview with the former HR Javier Solana (2005). General Secretariat of the Council of the European Union, 'Interview with Javier Solana, Secretary General of the Council, High Representative for the CFSP' [2005] ESDP newsletter 10, 12.

[171] For a concise overview of this development, see Carolyn Moser, 'Two Become One? On the Civil–Military Amalgamation of the CSDP' (*Verfassungsblog.com*, 30 March 2019) <https://verfassungsblog.de/two-become-one-on-the-civil-military-amalgamation-of-the-csdp/> accessed 18 February 2020.

[172] A detailed account of the CivMilCell can be found in Khol (n 93).

[173] Smith (n 18) 256.

[174] Council Conclusions on ESDP, adopted by the Council on 17 November 2009, Council Doc 16500/09, Annex (23 November 2009) para 56. The establishment of the CMPD had been programmed by the Presidency Conclusions of the Brussels European Council (11–12 December 2008), Annex 2: Declaration by the European Council on the enhancement of the European Security and Defence Policy (ESDP) para 6.

[175] The CMPD resulted from the merger of DG VIII for Defence Issues and of DG IX for Civilian Crisis Management of the Council General Secretariat.

[176] Dijkstra (n 44) 80.

activity, namely the Crisis Management Concept (CMC), upon which additional planning and implementation details were based.[177] But as the CMPD employed more military than civilian personnel,[178] planning looked slightly more military than civilian. In 2017 however, an interesting change in the EU crisis management bureaucracy occurred: the coordination unit, thus far affiliated to the CMPD, was moved to operate within the EUMS (under the heading 'horizontal coordination'), where its predecessor (the CivMilCell) had been located. Moreover, as mentioned in section 3.3, a new division for conflict and crises was established within the EEAS, called PRISM, merging the previously distinct division dealing with CSDP Coordination and Support with the division for Conflict Prevention, Peacebuilding and Mediation.

The latest bureaucratic reshuffle took place in 2019, when CSDP structures affiliated with the EEAS—in particular those in charge of planning—underwent a significant restructuring in the name of the EU's integrated approach to crisis response.[179] As a result, most tasks previously carried out by the CMPD are now in the hands of the newly created division named Integrated Approach for Security and Peace (in particular its sub-division ISP.3). This recomposed division, in turn, belongs to the novel CSDP and Crisis Response Managing Directorate within the EEAS, which also comprises SECDEFPOL. The CPCC, on the contrary, was spared any reorganization measure; it maintains its *à part*-character as a quasi-department. It is too early to tell how the new organizational set-up will impact the division of labour between different crisis management actors operating at the strategic and the implementation level. But we can assume that the reconfiguration of crisis management structures is likely to reinforce crisis management writ large, which in turn shifts the balance in favour of non-military tools, including mediation, civilian CSDP, and AFSJ activities. Instead of seeing a civil–military nexus, operational CSDP realities might in the future be characterized by a civil–civil–military nexus stretching beyond the CSDP—an arrangement which we already observe in the Mediterranean (see section 4.3).

Efforts to improve civil–military coherence at the *operational* level are also recent. They occurred in 2017 as a result of the overdue creation of a permanent operations headquarters for non-executive military operations, the Military Planning and Conduct Capability (MPCC),[180] which was modelled

[177] Apart from its strategic planning functions, the CMPD also performed strategic reviews of current on the ground CSDP activities and distilled lessons learned.

[178] Per M Norheim-Martinsen, 'Managing the Civil-Military Interface in the EU: Creating an Organisation Fit for Purpose' in Sophie Vanhoonacker, Hylke Dijkstra and Heidi Maurer (eds), *Understanding the Role of Bureaucracy in the European Security and Defence Policy* (European Integration online Papers 2010) 16.

[179] EEAS 2018 Activity Report 13.

[180] Council Decision (EU) 2017/971 [2017] OJ L146/133.

after its civilian counterpart, the CPCC. The establishment of a Joint Support Coordination Cell (JSCC) between the MPCC and the CPCC was signalled, marking the latest development in civil–military institutional rapprochement. So far, however, this liaison unit does not appear on the organization chart of the EEAS.[181]

Despite this institutional rapprochement, the initial military predominance has led to a long-lasting civil–military divide. Civilian CSDP has therefore been described as 'suffer[ing] from a form of second child syndrome, affected by a lack of professionalization and visibility, and limited investments compared to its military counterpart'.[182] Until today, civilian and military CSDP structures differ in their institutional settings, their procedures regarding mission planning, their control and command mechanisms, and their recruitment and operational doctrines.[183] Furthermore, the reluctance of Member States to invest in civilian CSDP can still be seen, as military CSDP structures are far better staffed than their civilian equivalents: the CPCC counts approximately seventy civil servants, while the comparable military structures have in total five times more personnel—the MPCC is planned to have sixty permanent staff (and an additional ninety-four personnel for the conduct of executive operations), the EUMS counts some 200 personnel, and the Operations Headquarter is run by 150 staff.

But there have also been significant improvements, in particular regarding the *conceptual and operational connectedness* of civilian and military CSDP elements. The first deployment to Bosnia and Herzegovina, where a civilian police mission (EUPM) operated in parallel to a military operation (EUFOR Althea), already revealed that the mere simultaneous presence of civilian and military units on the ground without institutional coordination or operational cooperation was insufficient to tackle multi-factorial crises and new security threats. Hence, the idea of improved civil–military coordination at the EU level gained traction, leading to the adoption in 2003 of the first CSDP concept for civil–military coordination (CMCO),[184] which aimed at joint planning and implementation of civilian and military crisis management activities.[185] Under the heading 'comprehensive approach to crisis management', the CMCO called for a '*culture* of co-ordination',

[181] The latest consultable version dated July 2019. EEAS (n 143).

[182] Pirozzi (n 37) 1.

[183] Dijkstra (n 44) 15.

[184] Council Doc 14457/03 of 7 November 2003, 'Paper on EU Civil Military Co-ordination (CMCO)'.

[185] The CMCO complemented the previously endorsed concept for civil–military cooperation (CIMIC), which had addressed the *external* interface of civilian and military actors on the ground with a view to ensuring force protection. Council Doc 7106/02 of 18 March 2002, 'Civil-Military Co-operation (CIMIC) Concept for EU-Led Crisis Management Operations', endorsed by the EU Military Committee on 8 March 2002. Updated by Council Doc 11716/1/08 REV1 of 3 February 2009, 'EU Concept for Civil-Military Co-operation (CIMIC) for EU-led Military Operations', declassified version of Council Doc 11716/08 of 11 July 2008.

which was to inform the entire crisis management cycle so as to enable an efficient use of the EU's large civil–military toolbox. This approach was and still is put in practice in the Horn of Africa, where the EU engages in joint civil–military CSDP efforts. In line with the 2012 Strategic Framework for the Horn of Africa,[186] the naval anti-piracy operation EU NAVFOR Atalanta is complemented both by a land-based military EU Training Mission (EUTM) and a civilian EU Capacity Building Mission (EUCAP). The rationale behind this civil–military deployment strategy is that long-term success against piracy at sea will crucially depend on complementary capacity building on land. In other words, there will be no sustained (economic) development without security and, conversely, no stability and thus no security without economic development.

This *security–development nexus* has left its mark on the CSDP far beyond the Horn of Africa. Conceiving of security and development as two intrinsically linked components of successful peacebuilding has indeed stirred the progressive convergence of the civilian and military branches of the CSDP, not to say their hybridization. An important factor for this development is that the interconnectedness of security and development leads to what scholars described as the 'securitization of development' and, vice versa, the 'developmentalization of security'.[187] The integrated approach to security threats adopted by the EU in the 2003 ESS was indicative of this amalgamation of security and development issues;[188] the same is true for the 2016 Global Security Strategy,[189] as well as the joint EEAS–Commission paper on the implementation of the EU integrated approach to external conflicts and crisis of 2017.[190]

Deployment patterns also trace this securitization–developmentalization trend. First, the growing number of civilian missions focussing on security sector reform, law enforcement training, and military capacity building, along with the significant number of 'civilian' tasks increasingly inserted into the mandates of military operations (eg training, consulting, or capacity building) illustrate a gradual conceptual convergence coupled with an operational hybridization of the civilian and military dimension of the CSDP. Indeed, many of the more recently launched civilian crisis management missions are of a hybrid nature, entailing both development

[186] Council Doc 16858/11 of 14 November 2011, 'A strategic framework for the Horn of Africa, Annex to the Annex of Council Conclusions on the Horn of Africa', as adopted by the Council on 14 November 2011.

[187] Panos Koutrakos, 'The Nexus Between the European Union's Common Security and Defence Policy and Development', *A Constitutional Order of States? Essays in EU Law in Honour of Alan Dashwood* (Hart Publishing 2011) 590–600; Koutrakos (n 27) 210–25; Panos Koutrakos, 'The External Dimension of the AFSJ and Other EU External Policies. An Osmotic Relationship', *The External Dimension of the European Union's Area of Freedom, Security and Justice* (PI E Peter Lang 2011) 152–60.

[188] For an analysis of the integrated approach, see Norheim-Martinsen (n 27) 40–51.

[189] EUGS 50–51.

[190] 'The EU Integrated Approach to external conflicts and crises', EEAS/Commission services Issues Paper for PSC, dated 2 June 2017, Ref Ares(2017)2821812 paras 2–3.

and security elements. As a result, the clear lines between 'civilian' and 'military' have come to be blurred, which leaves us with a conceptually and operationally 'integrated' CSDP—except for combat activities. Secondly, sub-Saharan Africa has become the central zone of security-related activities, the majority of which tackles border control and, in particular, migration management.[191] The threats that the (civilian) CSDP is to contain have thus developed a clear security–development flavour. In view of these developments, it is very likely that civil–military coherence will remain highly relevant concerning not least border control and cyber or maritime security. Indicative hereof is that recent CSDP policy documents—namely the Civilian CSDP Compact and the Council conclusions on strengthening the CSDP—underline the importance of civil–military synergies in the CSDP.[192]

But much of the future development of the civil–military nexus in the CSDP will depend on political will: the will to overcome institutional divisions, to bridge financial differences, and to develop a long-term vision. Socialization will also play a role. Even though the stereotypical civil–military images of the courageous warrior figure on the one side and the technocratic civilian expert on the other have faded, the interaction of civilian and military CSDP actors (in Brussels) is still cautious, to say the least. Past attempts to overcome the civil–military bureaucratic trenches have led to mixed results; the future success of civil–military interaction is hence uncertain. What we know for sure, though, is that the security-centred approach obviously favours securitization tendencies, which in turn is a means of de-politicization.[193] Another certainty is that the increasing operational hybridity of missions somehow blurs institutional affiliations, which renders it more difficult to clearly ascribe responsibilities and competences—and ultimately to hold actors to account.

The operational hybridization of CSDP endeavours has been accompanied by an intriguing conceptual shift: the *comprehensive* approach to crisis management of the early days of crisis management (2003) was, replaced in 2018 by the *integrated* approach in line with the logic underpinning the EUGS.[194] This integrated approach is not limited to CSDP activities but extends to cross-policy cooperation and coordination.[195] The objective is to better align instruments from different external policies, particularly security and defence, development, and the AFSJ. In the past, however, this civil–military nexus writ large has been a major source of discontentment for various EU players, as the next section (4.3) shows.

[191] Pirozzi (n 37) 4.

[192] Civilian CSDP Compact 4; Council Conclusions on strengthening civilian CSDP para 5.a.

[193] Thierry Balzacq, 'The Policy Tools of Securitization: Information Exchange, EU Foreign and Interior Policies' (2008) 46 Journal of Common Market Studies 75, 93.

[194] Council Conclusions on the Integrated Approach to External Conflicts and Crises, adopted by the Council on 22 January 2018, Council Doc 5413/18.

[195] EEAS/Commission paper on the integrated approach para 3.

### 4.3 Conflict-ridden intersection with other strands of external action

Indeed, a discussion of EU peacebuilding would not be complete without addressing issues of policy delimitations or, in other words, without mentioning the usual turf wars at the EU level. These turf wars bring us back to the fact that civilian crisis management is conceptually and operationally situated at the crossroads of different strands of external action (development, neighbourhood policy, enlargement, and security and defence). What is more, as a relatively recent post-Cold War phenomenon, civilian missions encroached upon existing policies and initiatives. The gradual institutional development of the CSDP, accompanied by a growth in operational activity, has not proceeded without interinstitutional friction at the EU level. Tensions have been linked to questions of competence and procedure regarding different policy strands, both of which have to do with interinstitutional balance. Therefore, the delimitation of peacebuilding from development policies, as well as from measures taken under the umbrella of the external dimension of the AFSJ, is examined in the following analysis, with the focus being on operational aspects.[196]

A major part of interinstitutional contention is linked to the overlap (or intrusion) of peacebuilding activities and development measures (in a broad sense).[197] It has been repeatedly stressed that a range of activities carried out by civilian CSDP missions could equally be carried out under policies conducted by the Commission and vice versa.[198] The most prominent example of interinstitutional tensions related to development is the *ECOWAS* case, which opposed the Commission and the Council (discussed in detail in Chapter 6).[199] But there are many more examples from practice that demonstrate the frequent operational overlap of CSDP activities and development work. In 2003, when the first civilian mission was launched, both the Council and the Commission simultaneously deployed personnel to carry out work in the field of policing in the Former Yugoslav Republic of Macedonia.[200] Operational intersection was equally present in the Kosovar context, where the largest civilian CSDP mission so far, EULEX Kosovo, co-existed with a considerable financial assistance programme managed by the Commission, though with limited coordination (and cooperation).[201] Operational overlap without sufficient coordination, however, is not a matter of the past, but also occurs in current activities.

[196] The legal aspects to policy delimitation are dealt with in detail in the Chapter 6 on legal accountability.

[197] For a detailed study of the interface and overlap of development and CFSP instruments, see Merket (n 137) 104–40.

[198] On the overlap of activities, competences, and expertise, see also COM(2001) 647 final, 'Financing of civilian crisis management operations' (29 November 2001) pt 3.

[199] Case C-91/05 *Commission v Council* [2008] EU:C:2008:288.

[200] On this point, see for instance Dijkstra (n 44) 69–70.

[201] Special report of the Court of Auditors No 18/2012 (EULEX Kosovo) 27–28.

In its 2016 report on EU assistance to Ukraine from 2014 onwards, the European Court of Auditors highlighted that the initiatives simultaneously put in place by the Commission under the Neighbourhood Policy (namely the Support Group for Ukraine, SGUA) and by the Council (ie the EU Advisory Mission for Civilian Security Sector Reform, EUAM) overlapped, especially as regards anti-corruption work—which was, in addition, already tackled by the EU Delegation in place.[202] Therefore, the operational ambit of the two initiatives was redesigned to accommodate the concurrent provision of anti-corruption input.[203] This operational parallelism makes apparent that the line between security and development is thin, and thus highlights the security–development nexus mentioned in section 4.2. It is at times difficult or even impossible to determine precisely where security concerns end and development issues begin.

Another source of contention has been (and still is) the operational overlap of the external dimension of the AFSJ and civilian missions. While the AFSJ activities are subject to the 'Community method',[204] civilian missions are deployed under the CSDP and therefore along intergovernmental lines.[205] As regards the relationship between the AFSJ and the CFSP/CSDP, a remarkable development has taken place since the inception of both policy strands through the Treaty of Maastricht (1992). Initially, the AFSJ was to constitute an umbrella and not a policy per se (unlike the CFSP), and this also holds for its external dimension, which has developed incrementally from 1999 onwards. However, the external dimension of the AFSJ has become more than a mere complement to the AFSJ's internal dimension. Indicative hereof is that many Council decisions on the AFSJ bear external relations elements.[206]

The expansive nature of the external dimension of the AFSJ contributes to a progressive erosion of the separation of the two policy fields, namely the CFSP and the AFSJ, and poses questions as to their policy contents and framework. This inevitably leads to the question of whether the external dimension of the AFSJ is complementary to or replacing certain other types of external policies, especially regarding the CSDP.[207] Put differently, is the gradual build-up of the external dimension of the AFSJ and the (civilian dimension of the) CSDP indicative of a *rapprochement*, an encroachment, or an infiltration?

[202] Special report of the Court of Auditors No 32/2016, 'EU assistance to Ukraine' 17.

[203] ibid.

[204] The term Community method describes the prevailing mode of cooperation and decision-making at the EU level, which is the ordinary legislative procedure. According to the Community method, the Commission holds the sole right of legislative initiative, the Council and the EP co-decide legislation, and qualified majority voting applies in the Council.

[205] Intergovernmental cooperation is, as described in Chapter 1, characterized by executive decision-making by Member State representatives (European Council, Council) on the basis of unanimity. The Commission has no right of initiative and the role of the EP is purely consultative.

[206] Monar (n 23) 249.

[207] Mounier (n 22) 44.

It is true that, even though these two policy fields have evolved separately since their coming into being, they both deal with transboundary public order and security phenomena. Also, they both follow the logic of the internal–external security nexus.[208] However, while civilian missions are first and foremost preventive in nature, AFSJ activities can bear a repressive facet. Nonetheless, CSDP as well as AFSJ activities pursue shared objectives, namely the protection and promotion of constitutional principles and norms *within* the EU, and to this end employ overlapping (at times even similar) instruments *outside* the EU's borders.[209] In the eyes of the late Advocate General (AG) Yves Bot, the use of civilian instruments outside of the EU's territory implies that the external dimension of the AFSJ is absorbed by the EU's foreign policy competences under the CFSP.[210] In other words, according to AG Bot, the external dimension of the EU's internal security is ensured through CFSP/CSDP activities only. AG Juliane Kokott concurred with this interpretation and equally argued in favour of a division of labour based on both geographic and teleological aspects. She underlined that CFSP/CSDP measures are meant to ensure *international* security *outside* the EU, whereas AFSJ activities are intended to foster *security within the EU* by undertaking coordination *within* the territory of the EU.[211] This take, however, is not shared by all European actors, in particular the EP and the Commission, whose powers are stronger in the AFSJ than in the CFSP realm. Moreover, the politico-strategic as well as operational projection contained in the latest EU policy documents clearly diverges from AG Bot's and AG Kokott's views when addressing the CSDP/AFSJ intersection: increased strategic coordination and better operational coordination between CSDP actors on the one hand, and AFSJ agencies (eg Frontex, Europol, Eurojust) on the other, is high on the agenda.[212] There is, therefore, a political impulse for institutional and operational CSDP/AFSJ interweaving.

This said, in an assessment of whether the shared objectives are met with conflicting realities, different elements must be considered, namely the imposition of sanctions in the context of counter-terrorist activities, the conclusion of international agreements, and the conduct of capacity-building activities in third countries, notably regarding policing and security sector reforms. The first two items—sanctions and international agreements—have already been subject to

[208] Wolff, Wichmann, and Mounier (n 12) 11.

[209] Carolyn Moser, '¿Union de Droit, Union de Sécurité? Sobre La Interacción Entre Actuación Interior y Exterior Respecto a Los Valores y Normas de La UE' in J I Ugartemendia, A Saiz Arnaiz and M Morales Antoniazzi (eds), *La jurisdicción constitucional en la tutela de los Derechos Funda-mentales de la Unión Europea* (Instituto Vasco de Administración Pública; MPIL 2017).

[210] Case C–658/11 *European Parliament v Council* [2014] EU:C:2014:41, Opinion of AG Bot of 30 January 2014 para 118.

[211] Case C–263/14 *European Parliament v Council* [2015] EU:C:2015:729, Opinion of AG Kokott of 28 October 2015 paras 62–68.

[212] Civilian CSDP Compact 4, 9–10; Council conclusions on strengthening civilian CSDP paras 3, 5.b.

judicial proceedings before the CJEU.[213] These cases (discussed in Chapter 6), opposing the EP and the Council, epitomize the progressive slide from a two-track approach of dealing with transboundary security and public order phenomena to a situation of overlap or even absorption of policy contents and operational activity as well. And it is probably only a matter of time until the parallel conduct of capacity-building activities end up in court. This, in turn, raises several questions as to the policy framework, notably with regard to competences and procedural arrangements set out by primary rules.

These questions are heightened by the increasing hybridity of missions. This is particularly true for peacebuilding activities carried out under the framework of the CSDP. As mentioned in section 4.2, the more recent missions mainly focus on security-related matters, such as security sector reform, law enforcement training, and military capacity building. In particular, since the significant migratory increase of 2015, their (implicit) objective is to help curb migratory pressures—emanating in particular from sub-Saharan Africa—through better border control and law enforcement work.[214] This less preventive but more (law) enforcement operational scope, in turn, comes very close to many institutional capacity-building activities undertaken under the AFSJ umbrella and on the basis of bilateral agreements.[215] Frontex, the most prominent AFSJ agency in charge of external border control, has only recently concluded bilateral agreements—strongly resembling the Status of Mission Agreements (SOMAs) concluded for civilian CSDP missions—with a range of governments from the Western Balkans to strengthen transboundary police cooperation on border control issues.[216] The improvement of intelligence sharing with African countries on migratory issues through capacity building is also an important field of activity; the core project in this domain is 'Strengthening the Africa-Frontex Intelligence Community', which is planned to run from 2017 to 2020).[217] It is under this project's umbrella that, in the summer of 2019, Frontex launched capacity-building and cooperation activities on transboundary crime (ie data sharing) in Niger; the agency further announced that it intended to set up similar arrangements with other countries of the Sahel region

[213] Case C–658/11 *European Parliament v Council* [2014] EU:C:2014:2025; Case C–263/14 *European Parliament v Council* [2016] EU:C:2016:2436.

[214] Pirozzi (n 37) 4; Böttcher (n 37) 2.

[215] For an analytical overview of objectives pursued and activities conducted, see Koutrakos (n 187) 152–60; Jörg Monar, *The External Dimension of the EU's Area of Freedom, Security and Justice. Progress, Potential and Limitations after the Treaty of Lisbon* (Swedish Institute for European Policy Studies 2012) 60–66.

[216] Agreements have been signed (in alphabetical order) with Albania, Bosnia and Herzegovina, Montenegro, North Macedonia, and Serbia. See, by way of example, the agreement concluded with the Republic of Albania. Status agreement between the European Union and the Republic of Albania on actions carried out by the European Border and Coast Guard Agency in the Republic of Albania [2019] OJ L46/3.

[217] Frontex, 'Strengthening of AFIC as an Instrument to Fight Serious Cross-Border Crimes Affecting Africa and the EU' (EU 2018).

in 2019–20.[218] However, while Africa (from a geographical perspective) has so far been CSDP turf, border control and management have to date constituted genuine AFSJ expertise. Potential delimitation conflicts regarding the geographic and thematic scope of activities are therefore not unlikely.[219]

There lingers another increasingly salient issue for CSDP activities, namely to contribute to the fight against terrorism. The Treaty of Lisbon has brought about important modifications in this regard, as it added a new operational field to CSDP missions and operations. Primary rules were amended to stipulate that the conduct of all CSDP tasks 'may contribute to the fights against terrorism' (Article 43(1) TEU). This amendment, in turn, brings us back to the difficult relationship between and delimitation of the CSDP and the external dimension of the AFSJ, not least because both are intended to contribute to the fight against terrorism. As mentioned above, it remains to be seen whether this operational overlap will at some point lead to judicial contestations, especially as the external action in the AFSJ field lacks formal legal competences.[220]

The intersection of EU peacebuilding activities with other strands of EU external action, on the one hand, emphasized the conceptual and operational interconnectivity of policy dossiers. But, on the other hand, the existing overlap also underlines that Member States preferred a *dédoublement fonctionnel* and even *institutionnel* over boosting the competences of supranational actors (ie the Commission) in the aftermath of the fall of the Berlin Wall.[221] The consequences of this choice remain noticeable today—both in practice and in law. Despite recurrent pleas for enhanced CSDP–AFSJ interaction, there is still plenty of room for improvement, as the recent high-level policy calls for closer cooperation and coordination illustrate.[222] But there is at least one positive example from the field regarding CSDP–AFSJ coordination and cooperation, coming from concerted activities in the Mediterranean Sea. The naval operation EU NAVFOR Sophia and the civilian mission EUBAM Libya on the one hand, and Frontex and Europol on the other hand jointly combat illegal border crossing by smugglers—and migrants—regardless of their CSDP or AFSJ affiliation.[223] This shows that pressing needs

[218] The other countries are Ghana, Gambia, Senegal, Kenya, Nigeria, Guinea, and Mali. See Frontex, 'News Release: Frontex Opens First Risk Analysis Cell in Niger' (Frontex 2018) <https://frontex.europa.eu/media-centre/news-release/frontex-opens-first-risk-analysis-cell-in-niger-HQIoKi> accessed 18 February 2020.

[219] Similar concerns are voiced in Paula García Andrade, 'EU External Competences in the Field of Migration: How to Act Externally When Thinking Internally' (2018) 55 Common Market Law Review 157, 182–85.

[220] Monar (n 215) 7; Mounier (n 22) 23.

[221] On this point, see sections 1 and 2 of this chapter.

[222] Civilian CSDP Compact 4, 9–10; Council Conclusions on strengthening civilian CSDP paras 3, 5.b.

[223] Panos Koutrakos, 'The Nexus between the CFSP/CSDP and the Area of Freedom, Security and Justice' in Steven Blockmans and Panos Koutrakos (eds), *Research Handbook on the EU's Foreign and Security Policy* (Edward Elgar 2018) 302–7.

coupled with sufficient political will is essential to ease long-standing coordination bottlenecks at the operational level and to overcome entrenched turf wars at the institutional level. Civil–civil–military cooperation is thus possible. Although we should not forget that enhanced CSDP–AFSJ coordination and cooperation is certainly desirable from an operational perspective, it also raises the often contentious question of institutional balance (the classical 'legal basis' debate).[224] The increasing osmosis of preventive and rather repressive external action tools sparks further accountability concerns, not least because repression (ie law enforcement) activities require a higher level of individual legal protection.

## 5. Understanding the Sui Generis Bureaucratic Edifice of Civilian CSDP

With a view to further unpacking the smallest box (the policy tool of EU civilian missions), we now move to the administrative and operational realities of EU civilian crisis management.

### 5.1 The 'who's who' of EU peacebuilding

The progressive development of Brussels-based bureaucracies, which started at the turn of the century, leaves us throughout the civilian crisis management cycle (schematically depicted in Figure 2.2) with a handful of institutionalized and, in composition, predominantly intergovernmental key players (outlined in Figure 2.3). The ensuing discussion concentrates on crisis management—ie the period *after* a crisis has been identified—and therefore does not cover monitoring, early warming, or advance planning.[225] Likewise, crisis response planning and decision-making prior to deployment is discussed on the margins only. This narrowing down is in line with the overall analytical focus of the book, which tries to disentangle accountability arrangements covering the operational phase of crisis management.

At the politico-strategic heart of this bureaucracy is the PSC, as Figure 2.3 shows.[226] Composed of one ambassadorial-level representative per Member State and chaired by a representative of the EEAS, the PSC sits bi-weekly and keeps the High Representative informed about the CSDP. The PSC is de jure merely a preparatory body of the Council. In reality, though, the PSC constitutes *the* decisional

[224] ibid 307–11.

[225] The analysis therefore does not cover the work delivered by the EU Intelligence Analysis Centre (IntCen) or the EU Situation Room.

[226] Formalized in its present form through Council Decision 2001/78/CFSP [2001] OJ L27/1, and Annex thereto.

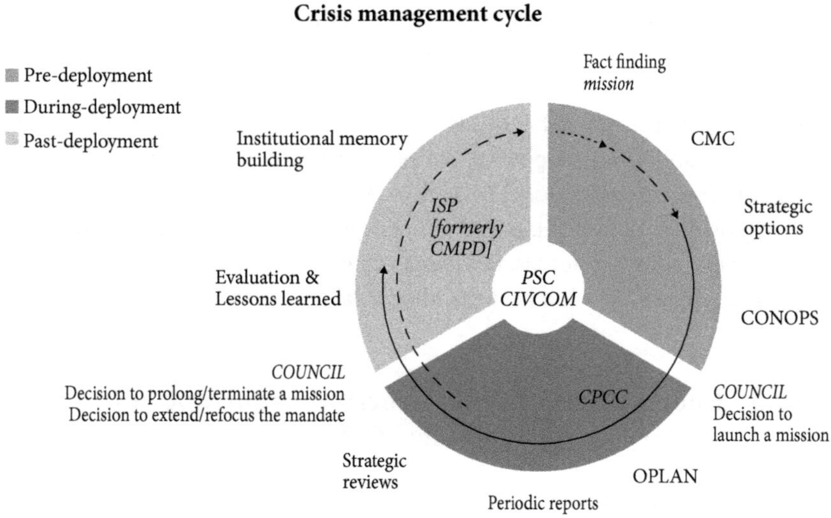


**Figure 2.2** Simplified scheme of the crisis management cycle

CFSP body,[227] or as its founding document indicates, it is the 'linchpin' of the policy.[228] Indeed, the PSC is in charge of monitoring international developments and helps to define EU foreign affairs, security, and defence policies. Importantly, the body exercises both political control and strategic direction of crisis management activities under the authority of the Council (Article 38 TEU), by whom it is entrusted with decision-making and to whom the body regularly reports. This function entails the final approval of a range of planning documents leading to the launch and implementation of a mission. Moreover, the function of exercising political control and strategic direction comprises the discussion of the bi-annual reports provided by the missions, detailing the progress made on mission tasks and objectives, as well as the strategic review prepared by the EEAS.

The PSC receives advice in civilian matters from the CIVCOM.[229] The CIVCOM, a working group at expert level composed of early to mid-career national diplomats as well as a Commission and a Council representative,[230] is key to ensuring the EU's institutionalized expertise in peacebuilding. The CIVCOM, inter alia, provides input to the Crisis Management Concept (CMC) before the document

[227] ibid.

[228] On the crucial importance of the PSC for CFSP/CSDP policy-making, see Ana E Juncos and Christopher Reynolds, 'The Political and Security Committee: Governing in the Shadow' (2007) 12 European Foreign Affairs Review 127.

[229] Formalized through Council Decision 2000/354/CFSP [2000] OJ L127/1.

[230] Dijkstra (n 44) 84; Catriona Gourlay, 'Parliamentary Accountability and ESDP: The National and the European Level' in Hans Born and Hans Hänggi (eds), *The 'Double Democratic Deficit'. Parliamentary Accountability and the Use of Force Under International Auspices* (Ashgate 2004) 408.

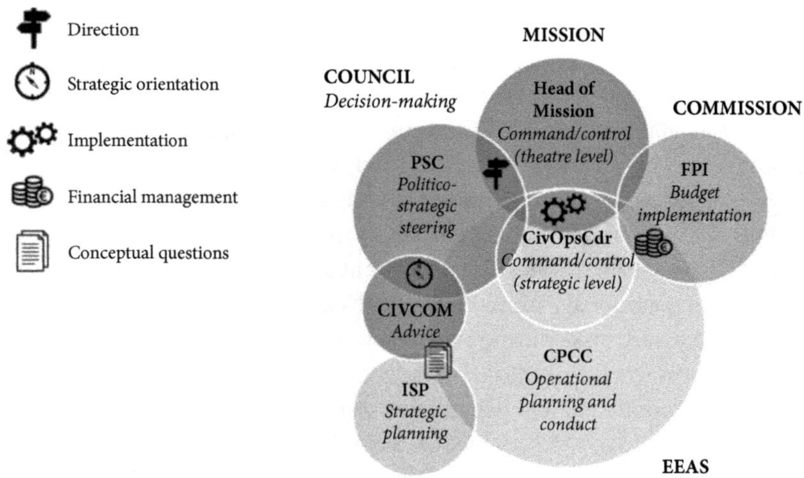


**Figure 2.3** The 'who's who' of EU peacebuilding

is presented to the PSC for approval, and comments further on periodic mission reports.

Within the EEAS, there is the Managing Directorate CSDP and Crisis Response, whose structure resulted from the latest bureaucratic refurbishment in 2019. The new Managing Directorate, which is in charge of crisis management writ large, regroups the two divisions of SECDEFPOL and ISP.[231] In particular, the latter unit is important for civilian missions as it, by and large, inherits the tasks formerly carried out by the CMPD.[232] Henceforth, one sub-division of the ISP (ISP.3) will be in charge of planning, including the drafting of the CMC, and another sub-division will take care of institutional memory building (ISP.1). However, there is an important novelty: to increase information-sharing and to allow for better coordination and cooperation, AFSJ-actors are from now on planned to be associated, where appropriate, with concept development and planning processes.[233]

At the operational level, the CPCC is the cornerstone of the civilian crisis management bureaucracy: under the political control and strategic direction of the

[231] EEAS Organisation Chart (n 143).

[232] The CMPD was set up in 2009 to foster civil–military cooperation regarding strategic planning and implementation (Council Conclusions on ESDP, adopted by the Council on 17 November 2009, Council Doc 16500/09, Annex (23 November 2009) para 56; Presidency Conclusions of the Brussels European Council (11–12 December 2008), Annex 2: Declaration by the European Council on the enhancement of the European Security and Defence Policy (ESDP) para 6). The civil–military CMPD structure used to draw up the CMC which, upon approval by the Council, constitutes the basis for further planning and implementation of a civilian mission. The CMPD also undertook strategic reviews (including mission mandates, size, objectives, etc) and distilled lessons learned from past activities.

[233] Civilian CSDP Compact para 20; Council Doc 8962/19 of 30 April 2019, 'Joint Action Plan Implementing the Civilian CSDP Compact', elaborated by the EEAS and the European Commission 14–16.

PSC, some seventy staff members ensure the autonomous operational conduct—from planning to implementation—of *all* civilian missions.[234] Indeed, the CPCC is involved in the drafting of all planning and implementation documents once the CMC has been approved: the CPCC formulates the Strategic Options for potential civilian missions on the basis of the CMC and, as soon as the CSDP hierarchy has given the green light, drafts the Concept of Operations (CONOPS), which sets out the details of the mission. After the CONOPS and the budgetary details have been approved by the Member States, the implementation phase begins with the CPCC preparing the Operational Plan (OPLAN).[235] Next to these planning functions, the CPCC fulfils all core tasks during the operational peacebuilding phase as it constitutes the permanent Operational Headquarters of civilian missions where the unified chain of command for civilian crisis management missions ends. In its role as Operational Headquarters, the CPCC is in daily contact with field personnel, frequently interacts with the relevant Council structures on operational issues (in particular CIVCOM), coordinates budget matters with the Commission (ie its FPI), and discusses recruitment matters with Member States. Recruitment for civilian CSDP missions is indeed managed by the CPCC, which each year advertises about 700 jobs in different civilian missions and processes some 6,000 applications. In the context of the annual budgetary exercise, the CPCC is also in regular contact with the Council's Working Party of Foreign Relations Counsellors (RELEX). Likewise, the CPCC interacts with the European Court of Auditors (ECA) when the latter conducts performance audits; it facilitates, inter alia, access to information and helps to get the ECA in contact with personnel (also in the field). Last but not least, the CPCC interacts with its military counterpart, the MPCC, including through the JSCC.

The Director of the CPCC, nominated by the Council (in coordination with the chair of the PSC),[236] is simultaneously the Civilian Operations Commander (CivOpsCdr). The CivOpsCdr issues instructions at the strategic level to the different Heads of Mission and provides the latter with advice and technical support. The CivOpsCdr reports directly to the PSC and to the Council through the HR. While the CPCC is institutionally embedded in the EEAS, the Director of the CPCC reports to the Council, and much coordination is done with CIVCOM; therefore, this entity has an ambiguous standing.

The Head of Mission (HoM) is responsible for and exercises command and control of the respective mission at theatre level. With a view to ensuring the effective conduct of the respective mission, the HoM is responsible for personnel questions,

[234] The CPCC was set up in 2007 following the Council's approval of the Guidelines for Command and Control Structures for EU Civilian Operations in Crisis Management.

[235] A detailed account of the decision-making process related to planning and implementation can be found in Dijkstra (n 44) 82–92.

[236] Draft Guidelines for Command and Control Structures for EU Civilian Operations in Crisis Management para 16.

budget implementation, disciplinary control, and thus assumes both coordination and day-to-day management tasks. The HoM is appointed by the Council (but employed by the Commission), and follows the strategic instructions of the CivOpsCdr in Brussels to whom s/he also report.[237] The budget allocations are implemented by the HoM and other senior mission staff in close coordination with the FPI of the Commission and the CPCC.

This budgetary arrangement, linking the Commission to civilian crisis management, goes back to a 'constitutional oddity'[238] introduced by the Treaty of Maastricht. According to this constitutional oddity, supranational funds can be disbursed for intergovernmental activities conducted under the CSDP. Indeed, Article 41(1)–(2) TEU stipulates that both administrative and operating expenditure without military and defence implications arising from CFSP/CSDP activities are charged to the EU budget. This, in turn, signifies that the Council and the EP must find an agreement on the budget appropriations allocated to the CFSP, including peacebuilding activities, and that this budget is eventually implemented by the Commission (first paragraph of Article 317 TFEU, together with the pertinent financial rules, most importantly the Financial Regulation applicable to the general EU budget).[239] By a delegated act, the Commission confers the budget implementation to the theatre level of civilian crisis management (prior to 2014, to the HoM; since 2014, directly to the respective mission), but retains the final budgetary responsibility and control (both ex ante and ex post) for the disbursed funds. As in practice, the line between financial decisions with operational implication (for which the FPI is responsible) and operational decisions with financial implications (for which the CPPC/mission is responsible) is very thin, and the Commission is frequently associated with decision-making at the strategic and operational level. The mission, the FPI, and the CPCC are, hence, coordinating financial decisions with operational implications, as well as operational decisions with financial implications several times per week—mostly by phone. In addition to these rather informal ex ante consultation and coordination mechanisms, there is an annual ex post budget evaluation by the Commission in the context of which crisis management actors cooperate in a more formal way, that is mainly by written communication according to codified procedures. Although not explicitly mentioned in the chapter on foreign policy, the Commission thus fulfils important administrative functions in civilian crisis management and is involved in financial micro-management decisions and procedures through its supervision, evaluation, and control tasks. What is more, the FPI is in charge of supervising the proper

237 ibid 11, 17, 18.

238 Monar (n 105) 59.

239 Regulation (EU, EURATOM) 2015/1929 of the European Parliament and of the Council of 28 October 2015 amending Regulation (EU, Euratom) No 966/2012 on the financial rules applicable to the general budget of the Union [2015] OJ L286/1.

management of the funds allocated to the warehouse capacity of civilian CSDP, which is roughly EUR 52 million (2018–21).[240]

## 5.2 Europeanized intergovernmentalism resulting from concealed agencification

As the preceding description of crisis management actors and their respective assignments shows, Member States have progressively entrusted Brussels-based bodies with functions throughout the entire policy cycle of civilian crisis management. All relevant tasks—from agenda-setting, strategic planning, decision-making, and steering to implementation, and evaluation of civilian missions—are run through the hands of a dedicated peacebuilding bureaucracy in Brussels.[241] Supportive functions and (operational) command, as well as control functions, have progressively been conferred from the national plane to Brussels. Hence, even though the incremental transfer of functions to this bureaucracy has happened according to an intergovernmental trajectory, in terms of institutional design and agent selection,[242] practice has turned the initial *supportive* bureaucratic services into '*autonomous* administrative structures'[243] in charge of EU (civilian) crisis management. Civilian CSDP has thus outgrown intergovernmentalism.

### 5.2.1 Outgrowing the intergovernmental framework

To demonstrate that practice has gone beyond intergovernmentalism, the degree of intergovernmentalism of civilian crisis management is ascertained in the following analysis, based on four interdependent criteria developed by Helene Sjursen in the broader context of EU foreign policy. These criteria include (i) the nature of actors involved in decision-making, (ii) the procedures governing decision-making, (iii) the scope and potential reversibility of delegation, and (iv) the nature of interest(s) underpinning cooperation.[244] In a truly intergovernmental environment, actors would be national representatives, decision-making unanimous (thus including a veto option), delegation potentially revocable, and the rationale behind cooperation would be the defence of national interests and preference.

As for the first two criteria—the nature of decision-makers and the decision-making procedures—it is argued here that the 'visible' part of CSDP decision-making has an intergovernmental character, whereas the 'invisible' part follows Europeanized rules. Regarding actors, formal decisions—that is, CFSP decisions

240 Art 4(1) Council Decision (CFSP) 2018/653 of 26 April 2018 on the establishment of a warehouse capability for civilian crisis-management missions [2018] OJ L108/22.

241 Dijkstra (n 44) 79–99.

242 ibid 46–77, 191–93.

243 Emphasis added. Koutrakos (n 27) 67.

244 Sjursen (n 56).

in the primary law sense—are adopted by Member State representatives. Yet, there are two elements attenuating this formal intergovernmental setting. First, although 'formal' decisions are taken by the Council (or the PSC), they are prepared by Brussels-based bureaucrats.[245] These Brussels-based bureaucrats are mainly seconded national experts who, after some time, 'go native' in Brussels.[246] The frame of reference of this specific type of 'national Eurocrats'[247] is no longer national (eg ministerial structures or processes) but European (eg practices and habits of their Brussels work environment). Indeed, a behavioural and cognitive process of internalization and socialization among crisis management actors takes place, generating a genuine *esprit de corps* among CSDP actors.[248] This also impacts procedures. The unanimity rule applicable at the strategic level (set out in Article 31(1) TEU) is valid but not followed at the sub-Council working level, where a distinct culture of negotiation and consensus has been forged over the years by the seconded personnel.[249] This, in turn, implies that the Brussels-based bureaucrats in CSDP structures tend to eschew governmental control.

Secondly, the adoption of decisions in the primary law sense (legal acts) is not the rule but the exception in CFSP/CSDP matters. On the one hand, this rule–exception relationship exists because informal procedures and communication methods are preferred over formal legal instruments for a range of day-to-day diplomatic business and delicate policy questions.[250] On the other hand, primary law codifies only CFSP decisions adopted by the Council and certain decisions adopted by the PSC (Article 38 TEU), acting as a Council-substitute. But Treaty provisions remain silent as to the sub-Council level soft administrative rule-making; that is, numerous derivative decisions of an administrative nature adopted by the members of the Brussels-based bureaucracy.[251]

The de facto change in the nature of decision-makers and decision-making procedures corresponds to the development that Carol Harlow described already in the early 2000s with regard to other (preparatory) Brussels-based bodies involved in intergovernmental decision-making, namely the Committee

[245] Simon Duke and Sophie Vanhoonacker, 'Administrative Governance in the CFSP' (2006) 11 European Foreign Affairs Review 163, 169–70.

[246] Ana E Juncos and Karolina Pomorska, 'Invisible and Unaccountable? National Representatives and Council Officials in EU Foreign Policy' (2011) 18 Journal of European Public Policy 1096, 1103–9.

[247] Karin Geuijen and others, *The New Eurocrats: National Civil Servants in EU Policy-Making* (Amsterdam University Press 2008) 13–15.

[248] Juncos and Pomorska (n 246) 1098–110; Per M Norheim-Martinsen, 'Beyond Intergovernmentalism: European Security and Defence Policy and the Governance Approach' (2010) 48 Journal of Common Market Studies 1351, 1356–58.

[249] Juncos and Reynolds (n 228) 141–44.

[250] Thym (n 108) 463.

[251] Thym (n 71) 967–70. These derivative CFSP decisions resemble, in many instances, soft administrative rule-making, which has been criticized for its gaps in procedural checks and balances, leading to legal uncertainty and to difficult (not to say lacking) judicial reviewability. See, for instance, Linda Senden and Ton van den Brink, 'Checks and Balances of Soft EU Rule-Making', *Study PE 462.433* (European Parliament 2012).

of Permanent Representatives, which is better known under its French acronym COREPER: there is a discrepancy between law and practice in that 'decisions have in effect—though not, of course, legally—been passed to a corps of invisible and unaccountable public servants'.[252] Almost a decade later, a similar observation of invisible and unaccountable public servants was made in relation to EU foreign policy by Ana Juncos and Karolina Pomorska.[253]

When it comes to the third criterion—the quality and quantity of powers delegated—it is questionable whether the delegation process in the context of EU peacebuilding activities is reversible. Due to their unique process and content expertise, their institutional position giving them an informational advantage, and their administrative resources, Brussels-based civilian experts have outgrown their intermediary or support role for Member State governments: they have become actors in their own right.[254] In reality, expertise and administrative resources are considerably higher in Brussels than in many national settings and, in addition, there is very little control over civilian CSDP by Member States in the absence of a coordinated approach to civilian crisis management at the national level.[255] In many Member States, there is no national administrative entity mirroring the work delivered by the Brussels-based bureaucratic machinery—which is a meaningful difference to other intergovernmental policy settings (including COREPER). It would be very hard indeed to imagine deploying civilian experts under the CSDP without the Brussels-based bureaucracy taking over planning, steering, and implementation tasks. Moreover, an important share of the costs of EU peacebuilding activities is covered by the EU budget according to Article 41(1)–(2) TEU. Financial decisions are taken by (senior) mission staff in close coordination with the Brussels-based CPCC and the Commission (ie FPI, collocated in the EEAS building). Considering these elements together, it would be counterintuitive to revoke delegation from a practical point of view, even if the delegated powers could be de jure readjusted or limited.

Finally, the *raison d'être* of cooperation, namely the defence of particular interests, is not purely (inter)governmental either but Europeanized. At the highest political level, national interests certainly play a crucial role, but at the working level the abovementioned *esprit de corps* prevails, which is the expression of a shared European vision rather than of particular national interests.[256] This has been

[252] Carol Harlow, *Accountability in the European Union* (Oxford University Press 2002) 34.

[253] Juncos and Pomorska (n 246).

[254] Thym (n 108) 464.

[255] Hylke Dijkstra, 'The Influence of EU Officials in European Security and Defence' (2012) 21 European Security 31, 314, 323; Pirozzi (n 161) 298.

[256] Juncos and Pomorska identified five factors contributing to *esprit the corps* within the EEAS, namely (i) leadership, (ii) communication, (iii) mutual trust, (iv) public image, and (v) training. Ana E Juncos and Karolina Pomorska, 'Manufacturing Esprit de Corps: The Case of the European External Action Service' (2014) 52 Journal of Common Market Studies 302, 306.

highlighted by a range of empirical studies on the civilian crisis management bureaucracy covering both the pre- and post-Lisbon institutional architecture.[257]

In sum, the law and practice of EU peacebuilding activities diverge: a range of administrative and operational arrangements going beyond intergovernmentalism complement the fundamentally intergovernmental legal foundations.[258] This is a combined effect of, on the one hand, delegation and institutional design dynamics—hesitant integration and codification coupled with an intergovernmental preference in terms of institutions and actors—and, on the other hand, adjustment to existing needs through practice.

### 5.2.2 Innovative conceptualizing offering new insights

This schizophrenic structure of civilian crisis management, where law and practice point in different directions, does not fit the traditional categories of intergovernmentalism or supranationalism. Scholars have so far used a range of terms to conceptualize EU security and defence in its entirety, which is to say both its civilian and military dimension, including notions such as transgovernmental(ism),[259] supranational intergovernmentalism, intergovernmental supranationalism,[260] legal intergovernmentalism,[261] new intergovernmentalism,[262] or a compound 'intergovernmental' legal system.[263]

Yet, bearing in mind the distinctive institutional and procedural features codified in primary law, and the administrative as well as operational specificities of civilian crisis management, this book puts forward that civilian crisis management is a truly sui generis edifice, which can be best described by the novel concept of *Europeanized intergovernmentalism*. This means that the formal institutional and procedural framework remains intergovernmental, while the administrative and operational realities have been subject to Europeanization: 'a process in which

[257] Thomas Henökl, 'How Do EU Foreign Policy-Makers Decide? Institutional Orientations within the European External Action Service' (2015) 38 West European Politics 679; Dijkstra (n 44) 196; Juncos and Reynolds (n 228) 141–44.

[258] Norheim-Martinsen, 'Beyond Intergovernmentalism: European Security and Defence Policy and the Governance Approach' (n 248); Sjursen (n 56).

[259] Frédéric Mérand, *European Defence Policy beyond the Nation State* (Oxford University Press 2008) 13, 84. Stephanie C Hofmann, 'CSDP: Approaching Transgovernmentalism?' in Xymena Kurowska and Fabian Breuer (eds), *Explaining the EU's Common Security and Defence Policy* (Palgrave Macmillan 2010).

[260] Jolyon Howorth, 'Decision-Making in Security and Defense Policy: Towards Supranational Intergovernmentalism?' (2012) 47 Cooperation and Conflict 433.

[261] Thym (n 108) 454.

[262] Michael E Smith, 'The New Intergovernmentalism and Experiential Learning in the Common Security and Defence Policy' in Chris J Bickerton, Dermot Hodson, and Uwe Puetter (eds), *The New Intergovernmentalism: States and Supranational Actors in the Post-Maastricht Era* (Oxford University Press 2015).

[263] Christina Eckes, 'Common Foreign and Security Policy: The Consequences of the Court's Extended Jurisdiction' (2016) 22 European Law Journal 492, 496.

powers are transferred vertically (from the national to the EU level) rather than horizontally (from Community [EU] institutions to specialized agencies)'.[264]

What does this vertical transfer of power imply, and how did it take place? Given the reluctance of Member States to delegate and codify, primary law suggests that no transfer of power has occurred: Member States remain the masters of the policy, with some high-level decision-making taking place in intergovernmental fora (Council and European Council, and, if appropriate, the PSC). This is generally referred to as the phenomenon of Brusselization,[265] implying the steady enhancement of decision-making in EU foreign affairs in Brussels. Yet, the Brusselization concept falls short of the fact that the enhancement of civilian CSDP went much further than the geographic relocation of decision-making to Brussels: the working level of civilian crisis management has equally been (re) positioned at Brussels. This development in turn resembles what Jarle Trondal qualified as agencification, which 'signifies a *transfer* of government activities to bodies vertically specialized outside ministerial departments' and, in the EU context, is 'basically about transferring action capacity from the constituent states to the EU level'.[266]

A closer look at the incremental institutionalization of civilian crisis management reveals that a vertical transfer of both governmental decision-making and action capacity from national ministerial departments to a specialized Brussels-based bureaucracy has indeed taken place. The autonomous bureaucratic crisis management structures, however, have not explicitly been established under EU law as a body, office, or agency of the EU. On the contrary, the agencification of civilian crisis management has happened from its own momentum. To describe this unusual agencification path, this book introduces another novel notion—*concealed agencification*—which describes an informal vertical transfer of both governmental decision-making and action capacity from national ministerial departments to a specialized Brussels-based bureaucracy. As a result of this concealed agencification, the civilian crisis management bureaucracy possesses a range of the attributes generally ascribed to EU agencies: it is a specialized, though institutionally heterogeneous, administrative entity, created by (several pieces of) secondary EU law, with its own budgetary resources and staff, which exercises on a permanent basis public power autonomously from EU institutions.[267]

[264] Renaud Dehousse, 'Misfits: EU Law and the Transformation of European Governance' in Christian Joerges and Renaud Dehousse (eds), *Good Governance in Europe's Integrated Market* (Oxford University Press 2002).

[265] David Allen, '"Who Speaks for Europe?" The Search for an Effective and Coherent External Policy' in John Peterson and Helene Sjursen (eds), *A Common Foreign Policy for Europe? Competing visions of the CFSP* (Routledge 1998) 42.

[266] Jarle Tondral, 'Agencification' (2014) 74 Public Administration Review 545, 546.

[267] As for the attributes of national agencies, see ibid 545. The specific characteristics of EU agencies are described in E Madalina Busuioc, *European Agencies: Law and Practices of Accountability* (Oxford University Press 2013) 21.

There is a further (informational) consequence of concealed agencification. The 'formal' CFSP decisions taken by the Council (or by the PSC) surface in Treaty law and are subject to mandatory publication in the Official Journal (in the L-series under 'non-legislative acts') according to Article 297(2) TFEU, whereas derivative CFSP decisions taken by the Brussels-based bureaucracy are not—as they are not mentioned in primary law, they are not subject to publication requirements set out in the Treaties. Concretely, Council decisions launching or prolonging missions, as well as decisions modifying mission mandates, are formal legal acts whose publication in the Official Journal is mandatory. The same holds for substitute decisions by the PSC (eg related to appointments of HoMs or third State contributions). All other decisions relating to civilian missions emanating from soft administrative rule-making are *not* (mandatorily) published in the Official Journal, and only a small share of these numerous derivative CFSP decisions—primarily of an administrative nature—are displayed in the (online) registers of the EEAS or the Council. But, as in EU peacebuilding, the adoption of formal legal acts by the Council (or the PSC) is far less frequent than the adoption of derivative CFSP decisions related to administrative or operational matters by the bureaucratic structures, the work of the civilian crisis management bureaucracy remains largely below the threshold of formality and visibility. This lack of visibility is heightened by the strict disclosure rules in place, rendering access to (administrative) CFSP documents listed in the register an intricate endeavour.[268]

It is therefore argued here that EU civilian crisis management operates in a framework of *Europeanized intergovernmentalism*—meaning that the framework is intergovernmental, whereas the realities are Europeanized—because of concealed agencification. Hence, the strategic and operational centre of gravity of civilian crisis management is undoubtedly located in Brussels, and not in national capitals as primary law suggests. But as the exercise of power by the Brussels-based bureaucracy is not codified in primary law—neither in institutional nor procedural terms—accountability formally continues to be channelled through national institutions. These national institutions, however, have a hard time holding the Brussels-based structures to account, given that much of their work is 'informal' and 'invisible'.

The innovative conceptualization of the civilian dimension of the CSDP offers three advantages. First, studying civilian crisis management through the lens of Europeanized intergovernmentalism adds a dynamic element to the equation. What might seem like a minor linguistic detail—the shift from nouns (eg transgovernmentalism) accompanied by qualifying adjectives (eg supranational and legal) to a noun-participle combination, namely Europeaniz*ed* intergovernmentalism—gives the study a novel conceptual twist: it acknowledges that the policy is in motion. Europeanized intergovernmentalism

[268] On the access-to-document regime, see Chapter 3.

combines static elements (the intergovernmental institutional and procedural framework) with dynamic factors (the process leading to Europeanized operational and administrative realities). This process might have come to an end (or a temporary halt), but it might also continue and further transform civilian crisis management. This dynamic conceptualization can include elements in the analysis that would otherwise not fit the traditional intergovernmental (or supranational) model.

Secondly, drawing on insights from EU agency/agencification literature to disentangle the mechanisms behind the Europeanization process offers a new theoretical framework for understanding past developments and the current state of civilian crisis management. Instead of thinking within the narrow categories of intergovernmental or supranational integration, it opens a salutary additional integration and institutionalization path, namely agencification, which takes place irrespective of the codified framework. The *context*, the nature of the framework, thus becomes secondary to the *content*, the actual transfer and allocation of power, which is at the heart of accountability.

Thirdly, law and practice are neither portrayed as antagonists nor as separate phenomena but as complementary elements. In other words, EU civilian crisis management is not what it is *despite* law being like this (profoundly intergovernmental) and practice being like that (not so intergovernmental after all), but precisely *because of* law and practice following diverging but intersecting paths (Europeanization of the intergovernmental setting). This turning away from traditional binary law–practice considerations engenders a more nuanced and comprehensive analysis of the civilian dimension of EU security and defence. Consequently, this differentiated scrutiny is essential for identifying (i) who holds decision-making and action capacity and (ii) who can be held to account for their action or omission.

## 6. Indispensable Accountability

This brings us to the issue of accountability regarding EU security and defence activities. While some readers might think that accountability does not square with (the civilian dimension of) EU security and defence, this section presents two arguments to explain why accountability is an indispensable feature of EU peacebuilding: one touches upon normative requirements laid down in primary law, and the other has to do with pragmatic considerations. Prior to outlining these two argumentative strands, it is judicious to reiterate that (i) this accountability study concentrates on process accountability rather than on output accountability,[269] and that (ii) the analysis covers the operational phase of EU

[269] A comprehensive description regarding *process* accountability compared to *outcome* accountability can be found in Shefali V Patil, Ferdinand Vieider, and Philip E Tetlock, 'Process versus

peacebuilding only (that is everything that happens after the deployment decision has been adopted). In other words, the underlying concern is not effectiveness or efficiency, according to which one would ask whether EU peacebuilding missions actually achieve their ambitious goal, namely, to pacify and stabilized a conflict zone. On the contrary, this analysis is informed by governance considerations on whether and how different actors exercise de jure and de facto decisional and operational powers.

## 6.1 Bound by law: the 'practice what you preach' formula

The first argument is tied to the *constitutional principles* underpinning EU peacebuilding activities. Article 21(1) TEU defines a set of principles guiding all strands of the EU's external action. According to the said Treaty provision, the EU's external action,

> shall be guided by the principles which have inspired its own creation, development and enlargement, and which it seeks to advance in the wider world: democracy, the rule of law, the universality and indivisibility of human rights and fundamental freedoms, respect for human dignity, the principles of equality and solidarity, and respect for the principles of the United Nations Charter and international law.[270]

The guiding principles are complemented by a series of objectives according to which the EU's external action shall be defined and pursued, as set out in Article 21(2) TEU. These objectives entail, inter alia, the consolidation and support of democracy, the rule of law, human rights, and principles of international law (paragraph b). In line with the internal–external identity nexus discussed in section 1.2, these provisions create a link between the EU's internal and external aspect: they envisage the EU's international role as a continuation of its internal norms and achievements and thereby create a connection between the EU's self-*perception* and self-*projection*.[271]

Interestingly, the drafters have not stopped at this identity-driven alignment of internal and external EU norms and values: they inserted a progressive stipulation to ensure that policy *goals* and policy *processes* match up regarding the EU's external action. According to Article 21(3) TEU:

Outcome Accountability' in Mark Bovens, Robert E Goodin and Thomas Schillemans (eds), *The Oxford Handbook of Public Accountability* (Oxford University Press 2014) 69–89.

[270] Art 21(1) TEU.
[271] See Chapter 2.

> [t]he Union shall respect the principles and pursue the objectives set out . . . in the *development and implementation* of the different areas of the Union's external action covered by this Title.[272]

It can be inferred from the above primary law provisions that, in the conduct of its external action, the EU is bound by the very principles it seeks to promote abroad.[273]

It is remarkable to observe the logic inherent to Article 21 TEU: the references made to the EU's core norms and values are rendered increasingly concrete as they evolve from an ideational statement on principles (paragraph 1) and programmatic policy objectives (paragraph 2) to an operational requirement incumbent upon the EU (paragraph 3). The codified discourse on the EU as a force for good in this way establishes boundaries to policy choices, both in terms of substance and legitimacy.[274] As a result, the EU is bound to practice what it preaches. This obligation was also highlighted by AG Niilo Jääskinen in his Opinion of May 2015 in the *Elitaliana* case (C–439/19 P), in which an Italian company engaged an action for annulment against a measure adopted by EULEX Kosovo in the context of a public procurement procedure. Jääskinen recalled that the constitutional principles underpinning EU external action must be adhered to by EU institutions, and their observance monitored by the CJEU. He further stated that 'in accordance with Article 21(3) TEU, the European Union *is* to respect the principles which inspired its own creation . . . in the development and implementation of external action'.[275] His interpretation of the Treaty provisions thus leads to a tighter obligation—*is* instead of *shall*—incumbent upon the EU to respect certain principles in EU external action.

One core principle underpinning EU external action—and thus peacebuilding activities—is the rule of law. Within the EU polity, the rule of law plays a primordial role of identification and consolidation. The EU's attachment to the rule of law is stated twice in the preamble of the TEU (paragraphs 2 and 4) and, more importantly, forms part of the values upon which the EU is built (Article 2 TEU). The rule of law concept is also pivotal for the EU's posture on the world stage, both in law

[272] Emphasis added.

[273] This argument reflects what Piet Eeckhout calls the normativity of the Normative Power Europe concept. According to him, a legal reading of Normative Power Europe means that 'the EU is required to act externally in accordance with its own constitutionally determined normative basis, ie its values and objectives'. Piet Eeckhout, 'A Normative Basis for EU External Relations? Protection Internal Values Beyond the Single Market' in Markus Krajewski (ed), *Services of General Interest Beyond the Single Market. External and International Law Dimensions* (Springer 2015) 226.

[274] More generally, on the role of discourse in foreign policy, see Thomas Diez, 'Speaking Europe, Drawing Boundaries: Reflections on the Role of Discourse in EU Foreign Policy and Identity' in Caterina Carta and Jean-Frédéric Morin (eds), *EU Foreign Policy through the Lens of Discourse Analysis. Making Sense of Diversity* (Ashgate 2014) 28.

[275] Emphasis added. Case C–439/13 *P Elitaliana SpA v EULEX Kosovo* [2015] EU:C:2015:341, Opinion of AG Jääskinen of 21 May 2015 para 28.

and practice. According to the abovementioned Article 21(1) TEU, the rule of law is a principle that the EU seeks to advance in the world and whose consolidation and support form part of the objectives to be pursued through common external policies and actions (Article 21 (2)(b) TEU), as well as in the context of civilian crisis management. It is worth mentioning that the rule of law is listed as a principle of EU external relations and not as a value. This differing categorization is not without impact: while values are more indeterminate, principles 'possess a more defined structure which makes them more suitable for the creation of legal rules',[276] and—it can be added here—obligations, too.

The rule of law has been described as 'the backbone of any modern constitutional democracy',[277] as it ensures that public powers are exercised within the constraints defined by law through the interplay of institutional arrangements, procedural requirements, and substantive components. The enumeration of these elements presupposes a 'thick' understanding of the rule of law, according to which both formal and substantive requirements are to be met—in contrast to the 'thin' understanding limited to formal requirements.[278] As Marise Cremona concisely puts it: 'At its most basic the rule of law refers to a State where power is exercised according to, and accountable to, the law.'[279] The rule of law and accountability are thus intrinsically connected.[280] This connectivity does not, however, insinuate that the rule of law can be equated with accountability or vice versa. Rather, this connectivity leads to the conclusion that accountability is a constitutive element of the rule of law.

While the precise meaning and scope of the rule of law principle in the EU context is not defined by Treaty law, neither as regards its internal nor its external dimension, it can be inferred from (institutional) practice that the rule of law contains several core elements, such as the separation of powers, including an executive subject to the law, the prevention of the abuse of powers (and thus the

[276] Illaria Vianello, 'Guiding the Exercise of Union's Administrative Power in the EU Wider Neighbourhood. The Rule of Law from Paper to Operationalisation', *EUI Working Paper LAW 2015/08* (EUI 2015) 3. In a similar vein, see Marise Cremona, 'Structural Principles and Their Role in EU External Relations Law' (2016) 69 Current Legal Problems 35, 47.

[277] COM(2014) 158 final, 'A new EU Framework to strengthen the Rule of Law' (11 March 2014) 2.

[278] See, on this point, Simon Chesterman, 'Rule of Law', *The Max Planck Encyclopedia of Public International Law*, vol VIII (Oxford University Press 2012) 1014–16; Frank Schimmelfennig, 'Rule of Law Promotion Policies in Comparison of Major Western Powers' in Michael Zürn, André Nollkaemper, and Randy Peerenboom (eds), *Rule of Law Dynamics: In an Era of International and Transnational Governance* (Cambridge University Press 2014) 113–14.

[279] Marise Cremona, 'The European Neighbourhood Policy: Partnership, Security and the Rule of Law' in Nathaniel Copsey and Alan Mayhew (eds), *European Neighbourhood Policy and Ukraine* (University of Sussex European Institute 2005).

[280] According to Carol Harlow, the rule of law is, together with the separation of powers and constitutionalism, at the very heart of accountability. She writes that, 'the rule of law, which is the foundational principle for every western legal order; the constitutional doctrine of separation of powers; and the notion of "constitutionalism", which embodies the idea of limited government [provide] a framework within which accountability can flourish'. Carol Harlow, 'Accountability and Constitutional Law', *The Oxford Handbook of Public Accountability* (Oxford University Press 2014) 198–99.

prohibition of arbitrary executive behaviour), legality and legal certainty, effective judicial remedies, judicial review by an independent and impartial judiciary, non-discrimination, and the protection of fundamental rights.[281] These core elements are also part of the rule of law principle that the EU seeks to promote abroad.[282]

EU peacebuilding activities perfectly fit this conceptual framework as they seek to precisely enhance the capacity of police units, the judiciary, and the armed forces. It is therefore unsurprising that the rule of law, which generally underpins EU peacebuilding efforts, constitutes one of the priority areas of EU civilian crisis management.[283] Consequently, several civilian CSDP missions have specifically been designed as 'rule of law' missions.[284] These missions can fall under two types of categories. First, the EU can decide to set up a mission with a view to strengthening the rule of law through training, advice, and mentoring activities. Secondly, an EU rule of law mission can act as a substitution for the judiciary/legal system of the respective host state, in which case executive functions are carried out (eg EULEX Kosovo). Regardless of the type of mission, their general objective is 'to provide for complete and sustainable judiciary and penitentiary systems under local ownership and meeting rule of law and human rights standards in the mission area and to improve these systems' capacities in accordance with the demands of a democratic society'.[285]

This motivation to engage in capacity building so as to support democratic societies is not limited to rule of law missions. It constitutes the impetus for *all* types of peacebuilding activities (eg security sector reform, police training). This ambitious policy *goal* to foster the rule of law comes with an obligation of *conduct*:[286] the Treaty provisions examined above call for the policy *process*, that is the launch

[281] See, for instance, COM(2019) 163 final, 'Further strengthening the Rule of Law within the Union—State of play and possible next steps' 1; Council of Europe (Venice Commission), 'Rule of Law Checklist', CDL-AD(2016)007-e, Venice, 11–12 March 2016); COM(2014) 158 final, 'A new EU Framework to strengthen the Rule of Law'(11 March 2014) 4; Council of Europe (Venice Commission), 'Report on the Rule of Law', Study No 512/2009, CDL-AD(2011)003rev, Strasbourg, 4 April 2011 para 41.

[282] Ricardo Gosalbo-Bono, 'The Significance of the Rule of Law and Its Implications for the European Union and the United States' (2010) 72 University of Pittsburgh Law Review 229, 311.

[283] Presidency Conclusions of the Santa Maria de Feira European Council (19–20 June 2000), Annex I, Appendix 3.

[284] See the decisions establishing the three (to date) EU missions solely dedicated to the rule of law under the CSDP in chronological order of deployment. (i) EUJUST Themis in Georgia (2004): Council Joint Action 2004/523/CFSP of 28 June 2004 on the European Union Rule of Law Mission in Georgia, EUJUST THEMIS [2004] OJ L291/17. (ii) EUJUST Lex Iraq (2005): Council Joint Action 2005/190/ CFSP of 7 March 2005 on the European Union Integrated Rule of Law Mission for Iraq, EUJUST LEX [2005]OJ L62/37. (iii) EULEX Kosovo (2008): Council Joint Action 2008/124/CFSP of 4 February 2008 on the European Union Rule of Law Mission in Kosovo, EULEX KOSOVO [2008] OJ L42/92.

[285] Council Doc 14513/02 of 19 November 2002,'Comprehensive EU concept for missions in the field of Rule of Law in crisis management, including annexes' 10.

[286] This qualification of an obligation of conduct has been inspired by Stefan Oeter, who writes that 'the principles and objectives codified in the article do not provide for specific outcomes of external action decision making, but shall serve as a point of reference for decision makers'. Stefan Oeter, 'Article 21 [The Principles and Objectives of the Union's External Action]' in Hermann-Josef Blanke and Stelio Mangiameli (eds), *The Treaty on European Union (TEU). A Commentary* (Springer 2013) 840.

and conduct of a civilian mission, to equally rest on the rule of law. Accountability being a constitutive element of the rule of law, both the development and the implementation of civilian crisis management missions need to feature accountability to meet the 'practice what you preach' formula enshrined in primary law.

## 6.2 Mind the gap: reputational aspects

The second argument that stipulates accountability to be indispensable in the context of EU peacebuilding originates from *impact considerations*. Civilian missions primarily try to export principles, standards, and mechanisms to non-EU countries with a view to restoring or strengthening stability and security. In this study, peacebuilding activities are therefore regarded as a soft power instrument at the disposal of the EU, which is based on persuasion (in contrast to coercion).[287] The extent to which the propelled principles, standards, and mechanisms are espoused abroad largely depends upon the EU's persuasiveness or on its 'normative power', a concept coined by Ian Manners.[288] Europe's normative power resides in its (international) image, which in turn relies on the correspondence or at least interaction between policy goals (what) and policy means (how).[289] As reputation is a key ingredient of soft power,[290] the success of the crisis management endeavour thus heavily depends on the EU's reputation, which is linked to its legitimacy and credibility.[291]

The question, then, is the following: how credible and legitimate, both nationally and internationally, is a polity calling itself '*Union de droit*'[292] to promote the rule of law abroad if fundamental standards in this area—the rule of law, and accountability being one of them—are not met at home? Conversely, imposing at home the same governance standards, principles, and mechanisms that it tries to foster and improve with third parties is a signal that the institution is practising what is

[287] Joseph S Nye, *Soft Power: The Means to Success in World Politics* (PublicAffairs 2004) X.

[288] Ian Manners, 'Normative Power Europe: A Contradiction in Terms?' (2002) 40 Journal of Common Market Studies 235.

[289] Ian Manners, 'The Normative Ethics of the European Union' (2008) 84 International Affairs 45, 46; Richard G Whitman, 'Norms, Power and Europe: A New Agenda for Study of the EU and International Relations' in Richard G Whitman (ed), *Normative Power Europe: Empirical and Theoretical Perspectives* (Palgrave Macmillan 2011) 16.

[290] Ruth W Grant and Robert O Keohane, 'Accountability and Abuses of Power in World Politics' (2005) 99 American Political Science Review 29, 37.

[291] For a general analysis of the impact of governance/rule-of-law-related activities (anti-corruption measures) and stakeholder reception, see Alina Mungiu-Pippidi, 'Contextual Choices in Fighting Corruption: Lessons Learned' (Norwegian Agency for Development Cooperation (NORAD) 2011) Study Report 4/2011 80. The point has also specifically been made with regard to CSDP activities in Whitman (n 289) 15–16.

[292] The term *Union de droit* (Union based on the rule of law) was first used in Case C–550/09 *Criminal proceedings against E and F* [2010] EU:C:2010:382 para 44. The analogous notion *communauté de droit* (community based on the rule of law) was first employed in the judgment of Case 294/83 *Parti écologiste 'Les Verts' v European Parliament* [1986] EU:C:1986:166 para 23.

preaches. Through procedural and institutional safeguards, accountability mechanisms ensure that power is not held and exercised in an unconstrained manner; it indicates that the exercise of power takes place within a clearly demarcated set-up, which aims at preventing the abuse of power. Put differently, providing for accountability mechanisms is a way to lead by example and to thereby sustain one's reputation.[293] Jolyon Howorth expressed these concerns about reputation and impact already in the early days of the CSFP and CSDP when he stated that 'issues of transparency, legitimacy and even democratic accountability are likely to be central to the success of EU defence and security policy'.[294] In a similar vein, Ruth W Grant and Robert O Keohane find that '[i]f governance above the level of the nation-state is to be legitimate in a democratic era, mechanisms for appropriate accountability need to be institutionalized'.[295]

Following this line of thought, it is argued here that the EU needs to live up to its own standards in peacebuilding activities in order to maintain the credibility and legitimacy necessary for gaining support at the EU level, and to have an impact on the ground. Therefore, actors entrusted with power need to be held to account for their action in this policy field. Accountability and civilian crisis management are, hence, not mutually exclusive but mutually reinforcing.

With this in mind, we move on to explore the concept of accountability in Chapter 3 after having recapitulated the content of this chapter, which successively explored different dimensions of EU peacebuilding activities, namely the policy context (international security architecture), the policy area (EU foreign affairs, security, and defence), and the policy tool (civilian crisis management realities). As for the policy context, civilian missions emerged in the early 1990s to cope with a new international security environment, which was (and still is) characterized by a diversification of security threats and actors after the end of the Cold War. The rationale behind increased exterritorial civilian activities is both ideational (norm-focused) and instrumental (security-driven). In the last decade, security concerns have been on the rise, leading to an increase in security-oriented peacebuilding activities. When it comes to the policy area, it is important to remember the complex integration and institutionalization trajectory of this policy field, marked by hesitant and small-scale integration through practice (later codified by law) stirred by external factors. This particular integration trajectory has given rise to a distinctive framework. Indicative of this distinctiveness is the maintenance of the two-treaty pattern (legal distinctiveness), the unaltered executive preponderance in decision-making and agenda-setting (procedural distinctiveness), and the continuation of institutional particularities (institutional distinctiveness). Another important

[293] E Madalina Busuioc and Martin Lodge, 'The Reputational Basis of Public Accountability' (2015) 29 Governance 247, 248.

[294] Jolyon Howorth, *European Integration and Defence: The Ultimate Challenge?* (WEU Institute on Security Studies 2000) 90.

[295] Grant and Keohane (n 290) 29.

aspect is the conceptual and operational proximity of civilian missions with other strands of external action, in particular development and, increasingly, the external dimension of the AFSJ. Under the heading 'policy tool', the analysis brings to the fore the idiosyncratic governance features of EU civilian crisis management, which is intergovernmental in conception but Europeanized through practice. At the core of this Europeanization is a web of specialized administrative structures located in Brussels, which Member States have progressively put in place since the early 2000s. Almost two decades later, these Brussels-based structures have undeniably outgrown their support job, as the entire policy cycle of civilian crisis management is in the hands of some seventy dedicated Eurocrats. As a result of concealed agencification, EU peacebuilding activities take place in a setting of Europeanized intergovernmentalism: a framework that fundamentally is institutionally and procedurally intergovernmental, while administrative and operational realities have been Europeanized. This setting in turn prompts accountability questions that are salient both for normative and effectiveness considerations.

# 3
# Accountability: A Complex Concept for a Compound Policy Tool

'A body of men holding themselves accountable to nobody, ought not to be trusted by anybody.' This observation on accountability and trust, and therefore also (implicitly) on legitimacy, sounds like a contemporary catchphrase, drawn from today's newspaper, current academic publications, or policy documents. And yet, these words—in appearance simple, but complex in essence—have weathered several centuries: they were written in the late eighteenth century by the political thinker Thomas Paine. In his now famous *Rights of Man* (1791),[1] a response to Edmund Burke's *Reflections on the Revolution in France* (1790),[2] Paine defends popular, constitutional sovereignty and opposes hereditary rule and monarchy. To bolster his argument, Paine enumerates several reasons why the aristocracy should not be entrusted with the function of law-making. The quotation cited above is one of the reasons he provides in this context, insinuating that the absence of accountability leads to a lack of trustworthiness, which in his eyes is a crucial prerequisite to hold the powerful position of legislator.[3]

More than two centuries later, Thomas Paine's observation still offers a suitable point of departure for reflecting upon public accountability, notwithstanding that this study deals with a different era—namely the twenty-first century—and a different context—peacebuilding conducted under the Common Security and Defence Policy (CSDP) of the European Union (EU)—and not the French Revolution. This persistent suitability is because the question of accountable decision-makers is at the very heart of popular sovereignty and, consequently, of exercising public power in a constitutional democracy, be it in the eighteenth or the twenty-first century.

Inspired by Paine's accountability reflections, one can ask a series of questions in relation to EU peacebuilding. (i) How can accountability be conceptualized, including in the realm of international relations, which is the habitat of the EU's security and defence policy? (ii) What does the accountability landscape look like

[1] Thomas Paine, *Rights of Man* (edited with introduction and notes by Gregory Claeys, Hackett Publishing Company 1992).

[2] Edmund Burke, *Reflections on the Revolution in France: And on the Proceedings in Certain Societies in London Relative to That Event. In a Letter Intended to Have Been Sent to a Gentleman in Paris* (J Dodsley 1790).

[3] In the original text, the sentence reads as follows: 'Fourthly, Because a body of men holding themselves accountable to nobody, ought not to be trusted by any body.' Paine (n 1) 53.

*Accountability in EU Security and Defence.* Carolyn Moser, Oxford University Press (2020). © Carolyn Moser.
DOI: 10.1093/oso/9780198844815.001.0001

in civilian CSDP? (iii) And how can accountability be operationalized in the intricate setting of Europeanized intergovernmentalism, which characterizes EU civilian crisis management? Attempting to answer these three questions, the present chapter sets out the conceptual and analytical framework of the book. It first discusses the nexus between public power and accountability. It then goes on in section 2 to unpack the concept of accountability: after outlining the three stages of the accountability process, it sketches out relevant accountability types. Instead of restricting accountability to legal matters, accountability is seen as a crucial vector for the rule of law and eventually governance. Building on these conceptual underpinnings, the third section contextualizes accountability in the governance setting of international relations, where executive agenda-setting and decision-making prevails. In addition to the preponderance of executive actors at the international level, there is the risk of a 'multiple accountabilities deficit': a situation where actors are neither called to account at the national nor at the international level. Against this broader governance backdrop, accountability catalysts and inhibitors are discussed, namely institutional design and accountability architecture, and information-sharing modes. In a fourth section, a taxonomy of civilian crisis management accountability is developed, familiarizing the reader with accountability actors and fora in civilian CSDP, both at the strategic and operational level. In section 5, the chapter also discusses challenges for (studying) accountability in the context of civilian crisis management, both being of an analytical and practical nature. Special attention is paid to the very restrictive information-disclosure policy regarding EU security and defence matters. The final section of the chapter sketches out the research agenda of this accountability study.

## 1. Construing Accountability as a Corollary to Power

Accountability is an elusive concept that means 'very different things to different people and to different audiences [and reflects] a range of understandings rather than a single core paradigm'.[4] For this very reason, it is often regarded as a 'conceptual umbrella',[5] subsuming an array of aspects and situations that might be loosely related, but that might also be disconnected. As a 'buzzword of modern governance',[6] which lacks a general statutory definition,[7] accountability is frequently

[4] Deidre Curtin, Yannis Papadopoulos, and Peter Mair, 'Positioning Accountability in European Governance: An Introduction' (2010) 33 West European Politics 929, 930.

[5] Mark Bovens, Deidre Curtin, and Paul 't Hart, 'Studying the Real World of EU Accountability: Framework and Design' in Mark Bovens, Deidre Curtin, and Paul 't Hart (eds), *The Real World of EU Accountability* (Oxford University Press 2010) 32.

[6] Mark Bovens, Thomas Schillemans, and Robert E Goodin, 'Public Accountability' in Mark Bovens, Robert E Goodin, and Thomas Schillemans (eds), *The Oxford Handbook of Public Accountability* (Oxford University Press 2014) 1.

[7] Mario Costas, *The Accountability Gap in EU Law* (Routledge 2017) 6.

mentioned together with, or as a synonym for, other governance terms such as transparency, responsibility, participation, control, or integrity. The European Commission (the Commission), for instance, used the term interchangeably with most of the aforementioned governance terms and even equated accountability with deliberation in its 2001 White Paper on Governance and subsequent documents related to the topic.[8] Ultimately, the multiplicity of meanings poses the risk of rendering the concept vague, ambiguous, and even incoherent.[9]

In large part, this multiplicity of meanings (and understandings) can be attributed to the etymological anchorage of the concept: accountability made its appearance as a medieval Anglo-Norman notion that lacks, until today, an obvious corresponding semantic expression in other European and many non-European languages.[10] In French, for example, no semantic differentiation is made between responsibility and accountability as both notions are translated with *responsabilité*, whereas the obligation to render account for one's action is translated with *obligation de rendre compte*.[11] As a result, the French version of Paine's 'men holding themselves accountable to nobody' reads '*un corps d'hommes qui n'est responsable à personne*'.[12] In German, on the contrary, one will encounter many terms circumscribing aspects of accountability—such as *Rechenschaftspflicht* (duty to render account and, to some extent, liability), *Haftung* (liability), and *Verantwortlichkeit* (responsibility)—but there is no exact translation of the overarching concept of accountability, as *Verantwortung* translates both as responsibility and accountability. Given the existing semantic differences, individuals have diverging views on the precise content of accountability, as their understanding is often shaped by the expressions, including connotations, offered by their respective language(s).[13]

The disparate use of the term accountability also holds for scholarly works. In many disciplines, including legal studies, political science, public administration,

[8] Mark Bovens, 'Two Concepts of Accountability: Accountability as a Virtue and as a Mechanism' (2010) 33 West European Politics 946, 949. For a detailed analysis of the said White Paper, see Daniel Wincott, 'The Governance White Paper, the Commission and the Search for Legitimacy' in Anthony Arnull and Daniel Wincott (eds), *Accountability and Legitimacy in the European Union* (Oxford University Press 2002).

[9] On this matter see Melvin J Dubnick, 'Seeking Salvation for Accountability' (2002) <http://mjdubnick.dubnick.net/papersrw/2002/salv2002.pdf> accessed 18 February 2020.

[10] Carol Harlow, *Accountability in the European Union* (Oxford University Press 2002) 13–18; Bovens, Curtin, and 't Hart (n 5) 32; Bovens, Schillemans, and Goodin (n 6) 2–3.

[11] A similar point on the translation of accountability in French has been made in Carol Harlow, 'Accountability and Constitutional Law', *The Oxford Handbook of Public Accountability* (Oxford University Press 2014) 197–98.

[12] Thomas Paine, *Droits de l'homme: en réponse à une attaque de M. Burke sur la Révolution française* (François Soulès tr, F Buisson 1791) 63.

[13] The same observation can be made with regard to other grand concepts, such as the rule of law. In continental Europe, no semantic (and conceptual) translation of the term rule of law exists. *Rechtsstaat, Etat de droit, Stato di diritto*, or *Estado de derecho* differ from *rule of law*: semantically, there is a State (authority) in the former but not in the latter. This difference obviously also has an impact on the conceptual meaning attributed to the notion. For a definition of the term see, for instance, Simon Chesterman, 'Rule of Law', *The Max Planck Encyclopedia of Public International Law*, vol VIII (Oxford University Press 2012) 1014–16.

and international relations, accountability is indeed used in a quasi-inflationary manner with differing and not necessarily compatible definitions and, therefore, varying meanings and scopes.[14] Legal scholars tend to use accountability as a substitute for responsibility or liability in the event of an actor's justiciable wrongdoing, while political scientists generally understand accountability as an important control vehicle in the principal–agent relationship.[15] But despite—or precisely because of—its conceptual blurriness,[16] authors continue to use accountability for its evocativeness and its generally positive connotation.

This phenomenon is not restricted to academia, but extends to the practice of international relations. An examination of the linguistic meaning attributed to accountability by international institutions shows that these institutions put forward differing, not to say opposing, and often amorphous conceptualizations of accountability. While the European Commission counts accountability among the necessary ingredients of European institutional governance and highlights its procedural nature, the United Nations (UN) Secretariat adheres to an output-oriented definition that circles around the virtuous behaviour of individual UN staff members.[17] The accountability of the UN as an organization is not subject to discussion, as the Haiti cholera incident sadly illustrated. Even though an internal UN report revealed that the 2010 cholera outbreak on Haiti was caused by the arrival of a UN peacekeeping unit,[18] the UN refused to acknowledge any legal obligation to compensate the numerous victims and invoked its immunity. The UN Security Council (UNSC), for its part, makes increasing reference to accountability in its resolutions, but as the latter touch upon a panoply of issues stretching from general socio-political issues (eg the fight against corruption and the promotion of good governance) to questions of individual responsibility (eg criminal liability for serious crimes), the content of the notion remains vague.[19] In addition, many international institutions adopt an active stance on accountability;[20] accordingly,

[14] Richard Mulgan, '"Accountability": An Ever-Expanding Concept?' (2000) 78 Public Administration 555, 555–73; Andreas Schedler, 'Conceptualizing Accountability' in Andreas Schedler, Larry Diamond, and Marc F Plattner (eds), *The Self-Restraining State: Power and Accountability in New Democracies* (Lynne Rienner Publishers 1999) 13–28.

[15] On the different approaches to accountability, see Gijs Jan Brandsma and Carolyn Moser, 'Accountability in a Multi-Jurisdictional Order' in Miroslava Scholten and Alex Brenninkmeijer (eds), *Controlling EU Agencies. The Rule of Law in a Multi-jurisdictional Legal Order* (Edward Elgar 2020) 60–79.

[16] Mark Bovens, 'Analysing and Assessing Accountability: A Conceptual Framework' (2007) 13 European Law Journal 447, 449.

[17] Exemplary is this regard is the document Towards an accountability system in the United Nations Secretariat, report of the Secretary-General of 29 January 2010, A/64/640 paras 10–11.

[18] This information was released by international media having seen the report in question. See, for instance, Clarke/Pilkington, 'Leaked UN reports faults sanitation at Haiti bases at time of cholera outbreak', 5 April 2016, available at: <https://theguardian.com/world/2016/apr/05/leaked-un-report-sanitation-haiti-bases-cholera-outbreak> accessed 18 February 2020.

[19] Jeremy M Farrall, 'Rule of Accountability or Rule of Law? Regulating the UN Security Council's Accountability Deficits' (2014) 19 Journal of Conflict and Security Law 389.

[20] On *active* and *passive* accountability, see Bovens (n 8) 949, 951.

it is the international institution holding another entity or individual to account. A prime example in this respect is again the UNSC. In its resolutions mentioning accountability, the UNSC calls other entities (eg a State) to account, for instance, on human rights violations or poor governance. Its own severely limited legal and political accountability is, however, not subject to discussion.[21] The same finding applies to the Organization for Security and Co-operation in Europe (OSCE), whose institutions and bodies tend to conceive accountability as a mission statement rather than an organizing governance principle of the institution.[22]

Bearing the concept's elusiveness in mind, the present study construes accountability as the *corollary to the exercise of public power*—and the introductory quote by Thomas Paine points in the same direction. This vision of accountability as a conceptual counterpart to power, however, is relatively recent. When the English concept of accountability emerged in the late eleventh and early twelfth century in a territory marked by the Norman Conquest (1066), it was still very much tied to its etymological origins: accounting in the sense of bookkeeping, translating the French expression *comptes à rendre*. The possessions of royal agents were recorded in the Domesday Books for tax purposes, but also to ensure their alliance to the crown.[23] It was the powerful sovereign who held his subjects to account. This initial logic has been reversed over the centuries. Nowadays, accountability in public discourse implies that citizens ask those entrusted with power, namely the public authorities, to render an account of their (in)action.[24] 'Accountability concerns agents, not subjects. It concerns those who exercise power, not those who are subordinate to it', as Andreas Schedler states.[25] The transition from monarchic rule to constitutional democracy has been accompanied by a shift in perception: the active, top-down attitude towards accountability allowing power-wielders to *hold to* account their subjects has been replaced by a passive bottom-up approach, according to which the power-holder *is held to* account by the citizens.

Since the Enlightenment, the dyad of power and accountability has become an intrinsic element of modern democratic thinking on popular sovereignty and on public institutions: the conferral of (decision-making or executive) power to an agent via delegation, elections, or other means necessarily implies questions regarding the accountability of that agent.[26] Thus, there is a *power–accountability nexus*.[27] 'Power entails accountability, that is the duty to account for its exercise',

21 Christian Henderson, 'Authority without Accountability? The UN Security Council's Authorization Method and Institutional Mechanisms of Accountability' (2014) 19 Journal of Conflict and Security Law 489.

22 Carolyn Moser, 'Conceptualising Accountability in the Legal and Institutional Framework of the OSCE' in Mateja Steinbrück Platise, Carolyn Moser, and Anne Peters (eds), *The Legal Framework of the OSCE* (Cambridge University Press 2019) 286.

23 Dubnick (n 9); Bovens (n 16) 448–49; Bovens, Schillemans, and Goodin (n 6) 3.

24 Bovens (n 16) 449; Mulgan (n 14) 563; Bovens (n 8) 955.

25 Schedler (n 14) 20.

26 Harlow (n 10) 8.

27 As Schedler puts it, accountability is 'antithetical to monologic power'. Schedler (n 14) 15.

the International Law Association concisely puts it.[28] Consequently, those holding power have 'the obligation to explain and justify conduct'.[29] This brings us back to Thomas Paine, who argues that those entrusted with power (in the given case, law-making power) need to be accountable in order to be trustworthy and, hence, to have the legitimacy to exercise power.[30] It follows that, according to our contemporary conception of public accountability, the chain of power delegation has to be accompanied in some way by a reversed chain of accountability.[31] This explanation and justification obligation incumbent upon the power-holder illustrates that accountability is a 'power relationship [in which] one's autonomy and one's power over others [is] constrained'.[32] But it is also true that people are generally not well disposed to being held to account. As previously stated, many international institutions cherish an exclusively active stance on accountability. However, accountability can be part of the mandate ascribed to an international institution—meaning that the international institution in question can find itself playing the role of the forum entitled to an account (active)—without thereby precluding this very same institution from being an actor subject to accountability mechanisms itself (passive).

The comprehension of accountability as a vehicle to constrain and tame power in a political and constitutional system corresponds to a *constitutional* perspective on accountability.[33] As the exercise of public power ought not to go unchecked according to the constitutional accountability paradigm, countervailing powers need to be established. Pivotal in forging the required web of accountability relations and arrangements are the central concepts of constitutional law, and, in particular, the rule of law doctrine(s).[34] Accountability, therefore, has a restrictive function: it

[28] International Law Association, Final Report on the Accountability of International Organisations, 2004 5.

[29] Bovens (n 16) 450.

[30] Oliver W Lembcke writes that 'the legacy of the enlightenment era [is] that political power can only be justified when its claim to power is democratically legitimized and legally limited. This is one element that contributed to the process of *juridification of politics*' (emphasis added). Further information on the (historical) interrelation of law and politics, leading to a politicization of law and a juridification of politics can be found in Oliver W Lembcke, 'Balancing Law and Politics—The Contribution of Political Theory' in Stephan Kirste and others (eds), *Interdisciplinary Research in Jurisprudence and Constitutionalism* (Franz Steiner Verlag 2012) 59–76.

[31] This point was also made by Kaare Strøm when discussing accountability in parliamentary democracies. See Kaare Strøm, 'Delegation and Accountability in Parliamentary Democracies' (2000) 37 European Journal of Political Research 261, 267.

[32] Robert O Keohane, 'Accountability in World Politics' (2006) 29 Scandinavian Political Studies 75, 79.

[33] Bovens, Curtin, and 't Hart (n 5) 51–52.

[34] On this issue, see Harlow (n 11) 198–205. According to a 'thick' understanding of the term, the rule of law contains several core elements, such as the separation of powers (including an executive subject to the law), the prevention of the abuse of powers (and thus the prohibition of arbitrariness of the executive), legality and legal certainty, effective judicial remedies, judicial review by an independent and impartial judiciary, non-discrimination, and the protection of fundamental rights. See, for instance, COM(2019) 163 final, 'Further strengthening the Rule of Law within the Union—State of play and possible next steps' 1; Council of Europe (Venice Commission), 'Rule of Law Checklist', CDL-AD(2016)007-e, Venice (11–12 March 2016); COM(2014) 158 final, 'A new EU Framework to

allows for the exercise of public power to be subject to a set of constitutionally enshrined rule of law standards.[35] Typically, the two most important and constitutionally embedded players in this power-balancing exercise are parliaments and courts, respectively in charge of political and legal accountability. Accountability is thus regarded as a constitutive element of the rule of law,[36] which helps to operationalize the rule of law: while the rule of law is a constitutionally embedded organizational model for constraining public powers,[37] accountability is an institutional mechanism for holding those entrusted with public powers to account for the use of these powers. This is why accountability is apprehended here as an institutional mechanism and not a virtue:[38] it has to do with countervailing powers in contrast to behavioural or moral standards. Hence, this book ascertains whether public agents can be held accountable for their (in)action or not and whether their action has been conducted in a virtuous way. The crucial question to be addressed is *who* is accountable *to whom*, *for what*, and *on which basis*.

## 2. Conceptualizing Accountability as a Three-stage Mechanism

To conceive of accountability as a mechanism that contributes to good governance by ensuring a dynamic equilibrium between core state powers is not a novel approach. The underlying conceptual framework, developed by Mark Bovens, has commonly underpinned legal analyses and political science studies of the EU and the accountability of different manifestations of EU governance.[39] Bovens describes accountability as 'a relationship between an actor and a forum, in which the actor has an obligation to explain and to justify his or her conduct, the forum can pose questions and pass judgement, and the actor may face consequences'.[40] This widely used definition of accountability, schematically depicted in Figure 3.1, is also employed in this book.

strengthen the Rule of Law' 4 (11 March 2014); Council of Europe (Venice Commission), 'Report on the Rule of Law', Study No 512/2009, CDL-AD(2011)003rev, Strasbourg, 4 April 2011 para 41.

[35] Harlow (n 11).

[36] According to Carol Harlow, the rule of law is, together with the separation of powers and constitutionalism, at the very heart of accountability. She writes that, 'the rule of law, which is the foundational principle for every western legal order; the constitutional doctrine of separation of powers; and the notion of "constitutionalism", which embodies the idea of limited government [provide] a framework within which accountability can flourish'. See ibid 198–99.

[37] A new EU Framework to strengthen the Rule of Law 3–4.

[38] Bovens (n 8) 946–67.

[39] See, inter alia, the writings of (in alphabetical order) Mark Bovens, Gijs Jan Brandsma, Madalina Busuioc, Deidre Curtin, Carol Harlow, Paul 't Hart, Yannis Papadopoulos, Thomas Schillemans, and Miroslava Scholten. Three publications have particularly contributed to building the theoretical framework of this book, namely Bovens, Curtin, and 't Hart (n 5); Bovens (nn 8 and 16).

[40] Bovens (n 16) 450.

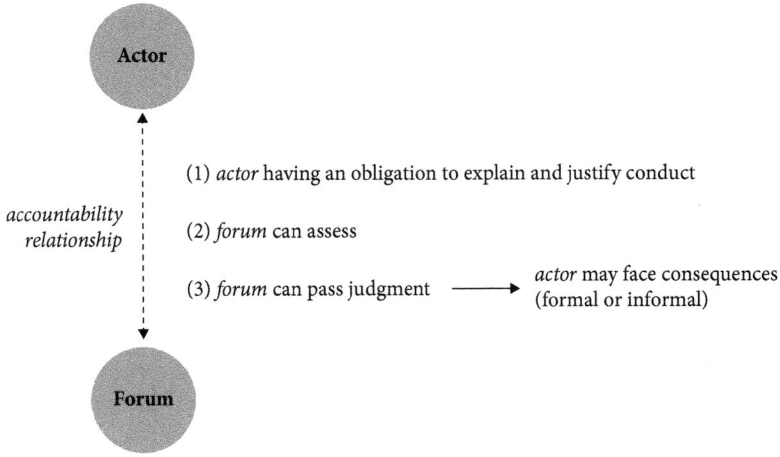


**Figure 3.1** Actor–forum accountability relationship (adapted from M Bovens)

## 2.1 A mechanism with three interconnected stages

In line with the definition by Bovens, the accountability relationship unfolds in three interconnected stages. In the *first stage*, the actor shares *information* with the forum. The information to be disclosed by the actor to the forum can vary in nature (ranging from confidential to publicly available) and type (eg policy briefs, reports, and statistics). The topics on which information has to be provided can relate to procedures or outcomes on both strategic and operational aspects. Furthermore, timelines and intervals of information-sharing differ: an actor might have the obligation to provide information on a weekly, monthly, yearly, or on an ad hoc basis (eg in the event of a special report or internal investigation). The key role of information is reflected in the three-stage model employed: as information-sharing is the very first step, the mechanism stands and falls with the provision of information between the actor and the forum. Providing information is indeed the *sine qua non* condition for accountability, as it enables the (in)action of the power-holder to be scrutinized.[41]

But even though information is pivotal for accountability, it is insufficient to achieve effective accountability. This is why, in the *second stage*, *scrutiny* by the forum takes place so as to closely assess the information provided by the actor. Characterized by a dialectic interaction, this stage of accountability is about being

[41] Deirdre Curtin, 'Holding (Quasi-)Autonomous EU Administrative Actors to Public Account' (2007) 13 European Law Journal 523, 532; Peter Dyrberg, 'Accountability and Legitimacy: What Is the Contribution of Transparency' in Anthony Arnull and Daniel Wincott (eds), *Accountability and Legitimacy in the European Union* (Oxford University Press 2002) 83.

responsible or answerable *to* another person or institution for one's actions.[42] This dialectic interaction is essential for ensuring and maintaining trust and legitimacy, especially when comprehending accountability as a means to discipline power. In the absence of such interaction, agents entrusted with power tend to lose the trust that citizens initially placed in them. The quotation from Thomas Paine on unaccountable lawmakers who ought not to be trusted precisely because they are not responsible *to* another body illustrates this point.[43]

In the third and *last stage*, the forum then goes on to pass a *judgment* on the conduct or performance of the actor in terms of procedures or outcomes, with the possibility of sanctions in the event of a negative judgment.[44] As the consequences prevail over the explanatory interplay between the actor and the forum, this aspect of accountability is about an actor being responsible *for* one's conduct or performance to another person or institution. The possibility of sanctions is a constitutive element of accountability if accountability is to amount to more than a mere discursive exercise or, differently put, answerability.[45]

It is judicious at this point to make three clarifying remarks on (i) actor–forum constellations, (ii) the nature of the accountability relationship, and (iii) timing. First, accountability obviously needs two entities to work: only if there is an actor *and* a forum can we speak of an accountability relationship. Indeed, accountability essentially consists of an interaction between the power-wielder and the accountability-demander. Therefore, there must be a certain distance and distinction between the *who* (actor) and the *whom* (forum). This is also why self-control, for instance in the form of (self-imposed) compliance procedures monitored by the actor, cannot qualify as accountability, not least because it lacks the interaction between the power-holder and the accountability-demander.[46] Secondly, the accountability relationship between the actor and the forum can be formal or informal in nature, or both. It need not be codified by law or regulated by some other procedure but can be based on informal arrangements. The (in)formality relates to all elements—the obligation incumbent upon the actor to be held to account, the

[42] Robert O Keohane writes about this dimension of accountability: 'We also need the capacity to interpret information intelligently, which entails the ability to ask pointed questions of power-holders and to demand answers.' Keohane (n 32) 84.

[43] See the French translation of the English text, where 'accountable to' reads '*responsable à*'. Paine (n 12) 63.

[44] 'Judgment' is used here in the broader sense of 'evaluation' or 'assessment' and not in the narrow legal sense of a court judgment.

[45] Bovens (n 16) 451. Andreas Schedler writes that '[u]nless there is some punishment for demonstrated abuses of authority, there is no rule of law and no accountability'. Schedler (n 14) 17.

[46] Philipp Dann, 'Accountability in Development Aid Law: The World Bank, UNDP and Emerging Structures of Transnational Oversight' (2006) 44 Archiv des Völkerrechts 381, 384, 398. A critical account of internal oversight policies and mechanisms with regard to international financial institutions can be found in Celine Tan, 'Mandating Rights and Limiting Mission Creep: Holding the World Bank and the International Monetary Fund Accountable for Human Rights Violations' (2008) 2 Human Rights and International Legal Discourse 79. The salience of the actor–forum distinction with regard to European security actors, namely the OSCE, was reiterated in Moser (n 22) 277.

scrutiny and judgment of the forum, and the potential consequences. Therefore, reputational damage caused by the forum's scrutiny can also be a consequence. Thirdly, accountability takes place *ex post facto*. This retrospective character, however, does not preclude the accountability mechanism from having potential ex ante effects, as 'the line between retrospective accounting and proactive policy making can be thin in practice'.[47] The threat or shadow of sanctions can indeed influence actors aware of the fact that their conduct or performance will be scrutinized and eventually evaluated by an accountability forum.

## 2.2 Accountability types and constellations

There are different types of accountability relationships based on different criteria, such as the nature of the forum, the actor, the conduct, or the obligation.[48] As the present book adopts a constitutional perspective on accountability, accountability-demanders play a vital role. Therefore, the *nature* of the forum is the core categorizing parameter that will be discussed in more detail in the following paragraphs.

If the forum is political in nature, one can speak of *political accountability*. This type of accountability is the most prominent in liberal democratic systems. Parliamentarians, political parties, the electorate, media, and increasingly civil society organizations play the role of the forum.[49] They exercise their function in a framework of formal and informal accountability arrangements and at times operate separately or concomitantly. Parliamentary debates or 'question time' formats during which government representatives—often ministers—have to explain their policy choices in Parliament represent a classic example of political accountability. Another typical case of political accountability in liberal democratic systems are elections: the voter (the forum) can sanction the elected representative (the actor) for their performance. In political accountability, sanctions are often informal: the sanction for the actor can be the detrimental reputational effects caused by the forum's scrutiny or by bad press, engendering a loss of credibility or legitimacy. The French *affaire du sang contaminé* of the 1990s is exemplary in this regard: although acquitted by a special court, the political career of then Prime Minister Laurent Fabius would remain tainted by the scandal.[50] In some cases, scrutiny as such is (part of) the informal sanction. A further example of political accountability, taken in a wider sense, is the implication of non-governmental organizations (NGOs) and other civil society actors. By 'accessing, interpreting, and distributing information

[47] Bovens (n 16) 453.
[48] Approach developed by Bovens. See ibid 454–62.
[49] Accountably channelled through civil society fora can also be labelled as *social* accountability.
[50] Cour de justice de la République, judgment of 9 March 1999, affaire n°99-001, *Laurent Fabius, Georgina Dufoix et Edmond Hervé*.

to multiple stakeholders in usable and accessible formats', they increase demands for accountability addressed to power-holders.[51]

Where the forum is a judicial body (ie courts), the accountability arrangement can be qualified as *legal accountability*. However, it is not always clear which court is competent to adjudicate. Therefore, the (determination of the) competence of a jurisdictional body is a precondition to legal accountability. The scrutiny undertaken by courts takes place in a clear framework once the procedures and applicable laws or precedents are known. Consequently, it is essential to determine the applicable law, as the respective civil, penal, or administrative legislation formally sets out the obligation incumbent upon the actor. The codified framework, furthermore, lays down the procedures to be followed by the court and provides reference to previous judgments. Next to identifying the competent court and the applicable law, it is important to understand to whom the disputed measure can be attributed, as this defines against whom an action can be brought. Finally, access to court conditions (in particular standing requirements) are an important aspect of (and often hurdle to) judicial accountability. Once a procedure is opened in court, the competent judicial body can opt for a procedural review (to check whether the procedures for adopting or implementing the disputed measure have been respected) or for a substantive review (to check whether the disputed measure is legally sound). A court's judgment is, per se, formal, as are most of the consequences. Hence, while political accountability can leave actors with formal and informal consequences of their conduct, legal accountability generally implies formal consequences—be they positive or negative for the actors.

Another important type is *administrative accountability*. Here, the forum exercises administrative—including quasi-judicial or financial—oversight. With the rise of New Public Management techniques, the importance of these accountability relationships has considerably increased. While administrative fora—including courts of auditors, inspectors, ombudspersons, and controllers—exercise their administrative or financial oversight on the basis of statues, specific standards, and norms—as do their legal counterparts—their scrutiny can go beyond legality and cover improper though not necessarily illegal behaviour, as is often the case for ombudsman offices. The forum's judgment can be both formal and informal, depending on the institutional anchorage of the body at stake. While the decision of an ombudsperson is in many systems not binding, the report of an auditing body can comprise compulsory recommendations.

Most forms of political accountability can be qualified as principal–agent relations, the forum being the principal and the actor the agent.[52] The chain of

[51] Albert Meijer, 'Transparency' in Mark Bovens, Robert E Goodin, and Thomas Schillemans (eds), *The Oxford Handbook of Public Accountability* (Oxford University Press 2014) 517; Albert van Zyl, 'How Civil Society Organizations Close the Gap between Transparency and Accountability' (2014) 27 Governance 347.

[52] Bovens (n 16) 455.

accountability then follows precisely the inverted pattern of the chain of power delegation, starting from the other end of the chain. But chains of delegation tend to be very long, as policy documents and bills run through many hands prior to approval. Responsibilities can therefore be somewhat blurred: there is the 'problem of many hands'[53] on the actor side and the 'problem of many eyes'[54] on the forum side. This combined hands–eyes *problématique* is particularly present in a multilevel setting, as is EU peacebuilding. However, the principal–agent framework mostly does not fit legal, quasi-legal, or administrative accountability mechanisms. In a constitutional democracy, where the rule of law is applied, branches of government are separated, and the judiciary is independent. Therefore, the legal forum is in general not the principal of the actor (being the agent) even though higher judicial institutions, such as supreme or constitutional courts, can be principals of lower judicial institutions, which then act as agents. Put differently, judges are not principals of ministers or public officials acting as agents. On a broader plane, though, (quasi-)judicial authorities are in a principal–agent relation: they are agents of the popular sovereign acting as principal.[55] That said, in the presence of (quasi-)legal accountability, the forum is likely to be situated *outside* the delegation pattern, so that the chain of accountability tends not to mirror one-to-one the course of the chain of delegation.

Moreover, accountability mechanisms can cover different dimensions of the exercise of public power, namely at the strategic and operational level. Whereas agendas and policy choices are determined at the strategic level, steering and implementation are central tasks at the operational level. Actors tend to vary across these levels. Executive actors (mostly high-ranking national representatives) are in the majority when it comes to strategic choices, while single rather than collective actors (often, albeit not always, lesser senior civil servants) are more prominent for operational issues. This difference obviously matters for accountability, as does the fact that accountability arrangements related to strategic issues tend to be political in nature, whereas those arrangements related to operational aspects are more diverse, covering political, administrative, and legal issues.

## 3. Contextualizing Accountability in the International Arena

What happens when the conceptual framework described in section 2 is applied to the international level? In the international arena, policy problems and their

[53] Dennis F Thompson, 'Moral Responsibility of Public Officials: The Problem of Many Hands' (1980) 74 American Political Science Review 905.

[54] Bovens (n 16) 455–57.

[55] Indicative of this principal–agent relation existing between the judiciary and the people is the fact that certain judicial decisions are delivered 'in the name of the people' (eg by the French Conseil d'État or the German Bundesverfassungsgericht).

solutions are transnational in nature, as is the exercise of public power. Yet, the institutional and procedural blueprint of national constitutional systems, including their accountability schemes, is not easily transposable to the international arena—the habitat of civilian missions deployed under the EU's security and defence dimension. The fundamental question thus remains: *sed quis custodiet ipsos custodes*?[56] Bearing this question in mind, the following section tries to identify key governance characteristics and accountability patterns of the international sphere, which are also typical of EU peacebuilding activities.

## 3.1 Governance above the nation-state: some conceptual specificities

In the international arena, the exercise of public power takes place in a particular governance context where *executive agenda-setting and decision-making* prevails—a finding that also holds true for EU security and defence. This asymmetrical allocation of public power on the international plane derives, to a great extent, from the prerogatives granted to the executive in foreign policy issues at the national level. The strengthening of executive governance, however, is not limited to the international level. In the domestic sphere, too, the internationalization of policy issues relocates political resources from legislative actors to executive actors.[57] Shifting policy issues from the domestic to the international realm therefore bears the risk of putting these very issues out of sight and reach of domestic institutions traditionally in charge of oversight, such as national parliaments and courts.[58]

In the past decades, international cooperation has considerably increased, as has the number of formal and informal international actors/institutions, including their powers and significance.[59] This internationalization has changed governance patterns.[60] It has shaped a new order 'dominated by executive powers who jump

[56] On this aspect, see August Reinisch, 'Securing the Accountability of International Organizations' (2001) 7 Global Governance 131, 132.

[57] Andrew Moravcsik, 'Why the European Union Strengthens the State: Domestic Politics and International Cooperation', *CES Working Paper no. 52* (Harvard University, Centre for European Studies 1994).

[58] The motive behind the internationalization of domestic politics is often the circumvention of domestic constraints. On this point, see Sebastiaan Princen, *Agenda-Setting in the European Union* (Palgrave Macmillan 2009) 28–29.

[59] Niels Blokker, 'Proliferation of International Organizations: An Exploratory Introduction' in Niels Blokker and Henry Schermers (eds), *Proliferation of International Organizations. Legal Issues*, vol 37 (Kluwer Law International 2001) 2–11; Benedict Kingsbury, Nico Krisch, and Richard B Steward, 'The Emergence of Global Administrative Law' (2005) 68 Law and Contemporary Problems 15; Armin von Bogdandy, Philipp Dann, and Matthias Goldmann, 'Developing the Publicness of Public International Law: Towards a Legal Framework for Global Governance Activities' in Armin von Bogdandy and others (eds), *The Exercise of Public Authority by International Institutions: Advancing International Institutional Law* (Springer 2010).

[60] James N Rosenau, 'Governance in the Twenty-First Century' (1995) 1 Global Governance 13.

the fence of their national constitutional and democratic systems and who exercise public power over an increasing range of politically and socially salient issues'.[61] The enhanced international or, more precisely, inter*state* and trans*governmental* cooperation of the last decades has led to the creation of various overlapping or superposed 'executive orders'.[62] These executive orders are often characterized by informal procedures, leading to a lack of visibility.[63]

This *informality–opacity nexus*, in the absence of appropriate control mechanisms, bears the risks of unlashing executive power above the nation-state. Despite some eclectic pockets of accountability in international politics,[64] there are by design no legal or institutional safeguards built into the international system ensuring that the exercise of power above territorial units is subject to monitoring or scrutiny. As a result, 'most collectivities in globalized space are not accountable for their actions in the sense required even by a minimalist theory of democratic governance'.[65] This finding is not limited to State actors but also applies to international institutions. In other words, the shift in governance to the international level has rarely been followed by a shift in accountability mechanisms.[66] Indeed, in the international realm, both the problem of many hands on the actor side and the problem of many eyes on the forum side (mentioned in section 2.2) is aggravated by the intricacy and multidimensionality of the system. Instead of suffering from a 'multiple accountabilities disorder',[67] international politics and especially international institutions tend to display a *multiple accountabilities deficit*. In this situation, national actors remain the principal decision-makers in a collective international level without, however, being held to account by their domestic institutions (for international decisions) or at the international plane (as the central actors are national).

This observation rests on a conceptualization of accountability that is broader than the traditional legal–institutional perspective. Instead of restricting accountability to legal matters, accountability is seen in this book as a crucial vector for the rule of law and, eventually, governance: it is a mechanism whose objective is to constrain and, by using this means, to prevent the abuse of power. Yet, the

[61] Curtin, Papadopoulos, and Mair (n 4) 932.

[62] ibid 933.

[63] See, in this context, the analysis of Yannis Papadopoulos on network governance. Yannis Papadopoulos, 'Problems of Democratic Accountability in Network and Multilevel Governance' (2007) 13 European Law Journal 469, 472–83.

[64] Expression inspired by Robert O Keohane (2002), 'Global Governance and Democratic Accountability, Miliband Lecture at the London School of Economics' (17 May 2002) London School of Economics 25 <doi:10.1.1.610.6432>.

[65] James N Rosenau, 'Change, Complexity, and Governance in Globalizing Space' in Jon Pierre (ed), *Debating Governance: Authority, Steering, and Democracy* (Oxford University Press 2000) 192.

[66] Deirdre Curtin and André Nollkaemper, 'Conceptualizing Accountability in International and European Law' (2005) 36 Netherlands Yearbook of International Law 3, 6.

[67] Jonathan G S Koppell, 'Pathologies of Accountability: ICANN and the Challenge of "Multiple Accountabilities Disorder"' (2005) 65 Public Administration Review 94.

accountability of international institutions and actors is, from a legal point of view, often approached under the narrow headings of responsibility or liability, both of which presuppose a violation by the international institution of its obligations (under international law).[68] Indeed, accountability designates in traditional legal scholarship a response to a justiciable wrongdoing and is thus employed by most lawyers as a surrogate for responsibility or liability.[69] This narrow legal perspective imposes four significant limitations on accountability, both in terms of substance and procedure: (i) the limitation to justiciable issues, (ii) the precondition of the actor having international legal personality, (iii) the unclear competence of international judicial fora, and (iv) the exceptional and ad hoc character of court proceedings.[70]

The traditional international legal perspective, incrementally developed for an interstate international system, is unsuited for studying EU peacebuilding under the CSDP. Applying only the traditional and narrow concepts of (international) law to EU civilian crisis management would make it impossible to grasp the multidimensional and multilevel power constellations at play.[71] Therefore, the claim underpinning this study is that accountability needs to be considered within new categories that go beyond the liability and responsibility category and extend to governance parameters with a view to preventing the avoidance of accountability by international actors.[72] Accountability needs to also cover political and administrative (including financial) aspects to ensure that there is no power–accountability gap above the nation-state.[73] The often idealized State paradigm offers, however, no suitable point of departure for a meaningful comparison.[74] The idea is not to replicate national constitutional solutions, as this would obviously lead to misplaced analogies, but to imagine 'functional equivalences of domestic procedures'[75] providing for accountability mechanisms. The rule of law standard serves as *fil conducteur* in this endeavour.

[68] Ige F Dekker, 'Making Sense of Accountability in International Institutional Law' (2005) 36 Netherlands Yearbook of International Law 83, 85–86.

[69] ibid; Harlow (n 11) 6–7.

[70] Moser (n 22) 281–82.

[71] By analogy, see also Curtin and Nollkaemper (n 66) 6–7.

[72] The successful avoidance of external accountability by an international actor can also be a sign of power. Keohane (n 64) 16.

[73] In substance, this understanding of accountability comes close to what the International Law Association called the *first level of accountability* (internal and external scrutiny in general), and more precisely to the *subcomponents of the principle of good governance*, namely,

> transparency in both the decision-making process and the implementation of the ensuing institutional and operational decisions; a large degree of democracy in the decision-making process; access to information open to all potentially concerned and/or affected by the decisions at stake; the well-functioning of the international civil service; sound financial management; and appropriate reporting and evaluation mechanisms.

International Law Association, Final Report on the Accountability of International Organisations, 2004, 8.

[74] Christina Eckes, *EU Powers under External Pressure* (Oxford University Press 2019) 13.

[75] Rosenau (n 65) 192.

## 3.2 Accountability catalysts and inhibitors

Several elements are particularly salient with regard to the identification of functional equivalences as they impact the effectiveness of the accountability process. As they feed into the accountability equation, these elements can either be accountability catalysts or, on the contrary, constitute accountability inhibitors.

### 3.2.1 Institutional design and accountability architecture

The first element is related to institutional design. The exercise of power does not take place in a vacuum but unfolds within a given framework, be that framework formal or informal in nature. Institutional design choices determine the allocation of strategic and operational power, which in turn impacts on the methods of interaction within this framework. But institutional design choices do not only relate to determining which body or entity is in charge of what; they substantially impact on procedural issues (eg decision-making and voting procedures) and staffing questions (eg seconded personnel or international public officials). As a matter of fact, policy choices will be prepared and taken differently depending on the respective institutional environment—in the EU there is the choice between either an intergovernmental setting dominated by national representatives deciding on a consensual basis or, alternatively, a supranational administration or transnational regulatory body composed of experts where majority-voting might apply. In addition, long and intricate chains of accountability make it more difficult to determine who is accountable to whom in international institutions. Identifying the power-wielder is a truly challenging task as the problem of many hands is acute. In the international arena, decision-makers and agenda-setters are often high-ranking national representatives acting on the basis of consensus or unanimity; in many cases, their decisions are prepared by semi-bureaucratic structures also composed of national envoys. It is difficult, therefore, to disentangle the decision-*maker* from the decision-*preparer*. EU peacebuilding activities are no exception in this regard.

Intrinsically linked to the element of institutional design is the question how accountability arrangements are structured in a multilevel setting. Shall accountability be exercised through traditional national channels (eg national parliaments and courts), or shall accountability mechanisms be lifted up to the international arena to match the transnational exercise of power, or both? The first solution appears prima facie attractive as it rests on existing accountability structures, at least in some nation-states. But there are several reasons to advocate the 'up-lifting' solution. First, traditional, national accountability mechanisms might not fit the new governance patterns, and therefore be inadequate. Whereas decisions are taken collectively at the international level, only the representative of a given State can be held to account by the institutions of that State. Secondly, using nationally anchored accountability mechanisms for the exercise of public power on the international plane leads to fragmented accountability, which reposes on the constitutional provisions and institutional structures as well as the resources of the respective territorial States. This would eventually result in patchwork accountability, unequal in breadth and depth across the different national systems. Thirdly, channelling accountability for international cooperation through national institutions misses a crucial point: the shift in governance. In international cooperation, the exercise of strategic and often operational functions is de facto or de jure relocated to the international level, even if international cooperation remains formally intergovernmental. Therefore, it is necessary to establish accountability mechanisms adapted to this post-national situation in which power is leaking away and dispersed.[76] Differently put, the increased internationalization of policy issues also enhances the salience of novel transnational accountability mechanisms, operating in parallel or cumulatively to the existing national mechanisms. This aspect also plays an essential role for EU peacebuilding activities.

### 3.2.2 Information-sharing

There is another important aspect to bear in mind: information-sharing arrangements. Information asymmetries constitute a persistent companion of accountability in international relations. These information asymmetries derive from the very scheme of international cooperation and stretch across governance levels. As executive actors dominate the international arena, they are not only *power*-holders but, by extension, also *information*-holders. Therefore, at both the international and the national level, (potential) fora—such as parliamentary bodies, judicial actors, or the media—that could hold the power-holders to account, are structurally in a shortage of information. Indeed, '[h]iding information is endemic to organizations, even when their leaders do not engage in systematic deceit'.[77] It goes without saying that this finding extends to public (international) institutions.[78] In world politics, procedural and institutional arrangements ensuring that information is shared on a regular basis by power-wielders—simultaneously being information-holders—are key but are often (by design) lacking. This is why it is particularly important to include information circuits in the institutional design shaping the governance framework, including in the context of civilian crisis management, where information flows are crucial for both strategic and operational accountability.

It is important to underline at this juncture the fundamental role of information for a well-functioning accountability mechanism. On this point, Andreas Schedler argues that it is the opacity of power from which the demand for accountability originates, and that 'in a world of perfect information, it would be pointless to

[76] Curtin and Nollkaemper (n 66) 7.

[77] Keohane (n 32) 84.

[78] Albert Meijer, 'Understanding the Complex Dynamics of Transparency' (2013) 73 Public Administration Review 429, 432.

ask … actors what they have been doing, or intend to do, and why'.[79] It is an interesting paradox that the opposite situation also leads to an absence of demand or diminished demand, but for entirely different reasons: the lack of information or transparency undermines the quest for accountability.[80] How would one want to know about or even question the exercise of power if there was no information on the matter, that is to say, if it was not made public that power was held or exercised?[81] This illustrates that information is necessary to create a certain level of public awareness, which in turn constitutes the basis for (public) accountability demands. Transparency and accountability are hence interdependent: while lacking transparency engenders a loss of accountability,[82] increased transparency reinforces accountability.[83]

Information has been described as a *power resource* in the public sphere: access to information actually implies access to power.[84] Information-sharing arrangements are therefore key to the distribution of power. This point is particularly relevant when conceiving accountability as a means to constrain power: in this scenario, providing information changes the allocation of power as information allows for the questioning of the decisions and actions or omissions of power-wielders. Information constitutes thus an instrument of empowerment: it is a means by which power is transferred from the actor (information-*holder*) to the forum (information-*recipient*). If the power-wielder is at the same time the information-holder without the obligation to share this information monopoly, accountability cannot take place. Interestingly, the need for information is expressed by the word 'accountability' itself: what would the 'ability' be without the 'account'? A mere ability. The provision of information is therefore considered to be the linchpin of accountability.[85]

Many academics working in the humanities and social sciences have stressed the crucial role that information plays for accountability.[86] There is little doubt that information can be regarded the prerequisite to and backbone of any form of accountability.[87] As underlined in section 2.1, this is also reflected by the three-stage accountability mechanism: as sharing information is the first stage of the accountability relationship between the actor and the forum, the latter would not be operational without the provision of information. This is particularly true in the field of foreign and security policy where decisions are often taken behind closed doors

[79] Schedler (n 14) 20.
[80] On the reverse relation of transparency and accountability, see Meijer (n 51) 513–14.
[81] A similar point has been made by Peter Dyrberg. Dyrberg (n 41) 83.
[82] Andreas Nothelle, 'The Parliamentary Assembly: Driving Reform' *OSCE Yearbook 2006* 348.
[83] Meijer (n 51) 518.
[84] Meijer (n 78) 431. In a similar vein, see Anne Peters, 'Towards Transparency as a Global Norm' in Andrea Bianchi and Anne Peters (eds), *Transparency in International Law* (Cambridge University Press 2013) 554–55.
[85] On this point, Mulgan (n 14) 560, 564.
[86] ibid 567; Keohane (n 32) 84.
[87] Curtin (n 41) 532; Dyrberg (n 41) 83.

and activities conducted far away from home and thus also from public opinion and public scrutiny. How would one raise questions about accountability matters with regard to a specific (element of) external action or security activity without even knowing that this external action or security activity has taken place?

Yet, the security realm has been qualified as an 'enclave of secrecy', or, in other words, an enclave of limited access to information: it is characterized by specifically developed systems of document classification preventing easy access to or broad disclosure of information.[88] This 'enclave' qualification also applies to EU security and defence, where a high level of secrecy and confidentiality has been consciously upheld to retain strategic and operational autonomy.[89] As a matter of fact, the rules on classification and access to documents currently in place per default render the bulk of CSDP documents inaccessible; they are (often in their entirety) shielded from the public eye in order to protect public security, defence and military matters, and international relations, as will be discussed in more detail in section 5.2.[90] Hence, in this policy domain traditionally associated with secrecy,[91] the provision of information can be regarded as an (accountability) end in itself.

However, it is not only the mere provision of information that matters for accountability purposes; equally vital are its *quality* and *appropriateness*. The actor has to provide information to the forum, which is deemed useful and appropriate to allow the latter to fulfil its mandate, namely assessing and judging the conduct or performance of the former. Producing lengthy reports without meaningful content or handing over large quantities of complicated statistics does not help the forum in doing its job.[92] In other words, the shared information has to make sense.

Providing information in the context of accountability is not a matter of public relations or propaganda, it is about explaining and justifying conduct, to paraphrase Mark Bovens.[93] In this context, Robert O Keohane has made an attractive remark about the provision of information when the actor is an institution: 'institutions should be judged not merely by their transparency [that is to say the provision of information], but by the epistemic quality of our understanding of them' and that 'too much information without coherent interpretation, is merely confusing noise'.[94] This statement is particularly interesting with regard to the EU and

[88] Meijer (n 51) 517; Vigjilenca Abazi, *Official Secrets and Oversight in the European Union* (Oxford University Press 2019) 57–68.

[89] This statement refers to the analysis put forward in Meijer (n 78) 435.

[90] Art 4(l)(a) and Art 4(3) Regulation (EC)1049/2001 of the European Parliament and of the Council of 30 May 2001 regarding public access to European Parliament, Council, and Commission documents [2001] OJ L145/43. A detailed assessment of these provisions can be found in section 5 of this chapter.

[91] Adrian Hyde-Price, 'Decision-Making under the Second Pillar' in Anthony Arnull and Daniel Wincott (eds), *Accountability and Legitimacy in the European Union* (Oxford University Press 2002) 55–56.

[92] In a similar vein, Richard Mulgan writes that '[u]nless those calling subordinates to account have full access to the relevant people and the relevant information their investigations and assessments will be frustrated'. Mulgan (n 14) 567.

[93] Bovens (n 16) 451.

[94] Keohane (n 32) 84.

its institutions, whose legal, procedural, and institutional set-up is complex, if not to say complicated. Bearing this in mind, the analysis presented in this book will also be concerned with the question of whether the information disclosed in the context of CSDP enables different fora—composed of public officials, elected representatives at both the national and European level, judges, or citizens—to understand the relevant institutions and their conduct.[95]

To recapitulate this section, the accountability context of international relations is a particular one: in an environment characterized by informality and a lack of transparency, executive agenda-setting and decision-making prevails. Generally, the accountability architecture is not adapted to the shift of power from the national to the international level, leading to a multiple accountabilities deficit: decision-makers are neither held to account in their territorial units nor at the international plane. To counter this deficit, it is judicious to imagine functional equivalences of domestic procedures—instead of transplanting national solutions to the international level—to ensure that the shift in governance is mirrored by a shift in accountability. Two elements are key in this regard, as they can either help or impede accountability: institutional design (linked to accountability architecture) and information-sharing.

## 4. Charting Accountability: A Taxonomy of EU Peacebuilding

For an accountability relationship to exist, there obviously needs to be an actor and a forum. Yet, which are the actors, and which are the fora in EU civilian crisis management? While (primary) law sets out a fundamentally intergovernmental institutional and procedural framework, the administrative and operational realities of civilian crisis management have been subject to Europeanization, that is, 'a process in which powers are transferred vertically (from the national to the EU level) rather than horizontally (from [EU] institutions to specialized agencies)'.[96] Civilian crisis management thus operates in a context of *Europeanized intergovernmentalism*. A closer look reveals that *concealed agencification*—an informal vertical transfer of both governmental decision-making and action capacity from national ministerial departments to a specialized Brussels-based bureaucracy—has led to the strategic and operational centre of gravity of EU peacebuilding activities being undoubtedly situated in Brussels and not in national capitals.[97]

[95] This question will be addressed in particular in Chapter 6 on legal accountability and Chapter 7 on administrative accountability.

[96] Renaud Dehousse, 'Misfits: EU Law and the Transformation of European Governance' in Christian Joerges and Renaud Dehousse (eds), *Good Governance in Europe's Integrated Market* (Oxford University Press 2002).

[97] For more details on concealed agencification and Europeanized intergovernmentalism, see Chapter 2.

The accountability effects of concealed agencification, leading to Europeanized intergovernmentalism, are significant. Who actually takes decisions and defines strategies in this intricate institutional, procedural, and administrative set-up? Who prepares these decisions and strategies? And who implements policies and oversees operational activity in this multilevel policy? Basing the responses to these questions solely on primary law would lead to an incomplete and consequently misleading picture: the answer would be that EU peacebuilding is an inter*governmental* business, with actors (and potential fora) remaining in the realm of Member States. This explanation, though, does not correspond to the Europeanized realities. The Brussels-based civilian crisis management bureaucracy, composed of several units, fulfils both strategic and operational tasks. Therefore, section 4.1 sets out to disentangle reporting schemes within civilian crisis management structures to unravel existing accountability arrangements, while section 4.2 outlines both formal and informal fora. The analytical focus is on administrative and operational business taking place after the deployment decision has been adopted.

## 4.1 Distilling strategic and operational actors from intricate reporting lines

A crucial element of accountability is to identify who needs to account to whom, about what, and on what basis. Lines of reporting indicate chains of command and control, and are paramount for accountability queries as they specify who is in charge and, consequently, to whom/which entity decisions can be attributed.[98] In civilian crisis management, lines of reporting differ according to the specific exercise of activities.

It is important to stress at this juncture that one would search in vain for primary law provisions that set out institutional relationships or reporting requirements. Only one entity of the CSDP bureaucratic apparatus, namely the Political and Security Committee (PSC), surfaces in Treaty law. Consequently, one has to explore sources of secondary and supplementary EU law (eg decisions of the Council of the EU (Council), internal (administrative) documents and directives, or jurisprudence), read policy documents (eg annual reports, organization charts), and analyse practice to disentangle institutional affiliation, cooperation modes, and reporting schemes. Taken together, the intricacy and opacity of existing reporting constellations is not conducive to accountability (queries). It is unsurprising, then, that accountability-demanders had and still have difficulties identifying the

[98] Gerard C Rowe, 'Administrative Supervision of Administrative Action in the European Union' in Herwig C H Hofmann and Alexander H Türk (eds), *Legal Challenges in EU Administrative Law: Towards an Integrated Administration* (Edward Elgar 2009) 191.

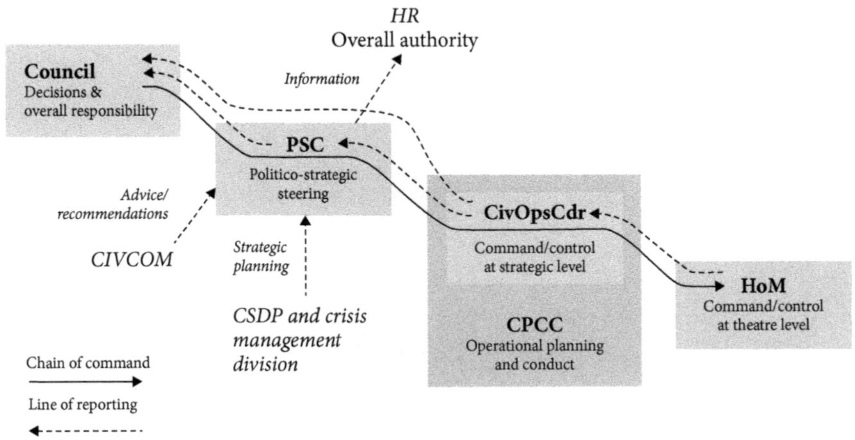


**Figure 3.2** Reporting configuration regarding day-to-day management

appropriate accountability actor.[99] The following description therefore constitutes a valuable addition to the literature as it charts, for the first time, existing formal and informal reporting requirements in civilian crisis management that are crucial for accountability (demands).

When it comes to *general crisis management business*, Council documents outline command responsibilities and formal reporting requirements.[100] In short, the line of reporting runs inversely to the chain of command, as Figure 3.2 on reporting constellations for day-to-day management highlights. The Head of Mission (HoM) reports to the Civilian Operations Commander (CivOpsCdr), who reports to the PSC and to the Council through the High Representative of the EU for Foreign Affairs and Security Policy (HR), having 'overall authority'. Furthermore, the PSC reports to the Council. Inversely, the Council takes decisions or delegates certain types of decisions to the PSC, under whose political and strategic direction the CivOpsCdr exercises strategic command and control over the HoM, who is in charge of command and control at theatre level. Therefore, the highest authority of decision-making and reporting is the Council, in particular in its Foreign Affairs Council (FAC) configuration—that is foreign ministers from all Member States and, on defence issues, defence ministers. In addition to these formal reporting requirements, civilian crisis management actors communicate frequently to coordinate daily business.

[99] Exemplary of such lack of clarity is Case T-213/12 *Elitaliana SpA v EULEX Kosovo* [2013] EU:T:2013:292 para 39. The case is discussed in detail in Chapter 6.

[100] Eg Council Doc 9919/07 of 1 February 2007, 'Draft Guidelines for Command and Control Structure for EU Civilian Operations in Crisis Management' RESTREINT EU; Council Doc 11277/07 of 28 June 2007, 'Standard language for planning documents and legal acts for civilian ESDP operations' LIMITE.

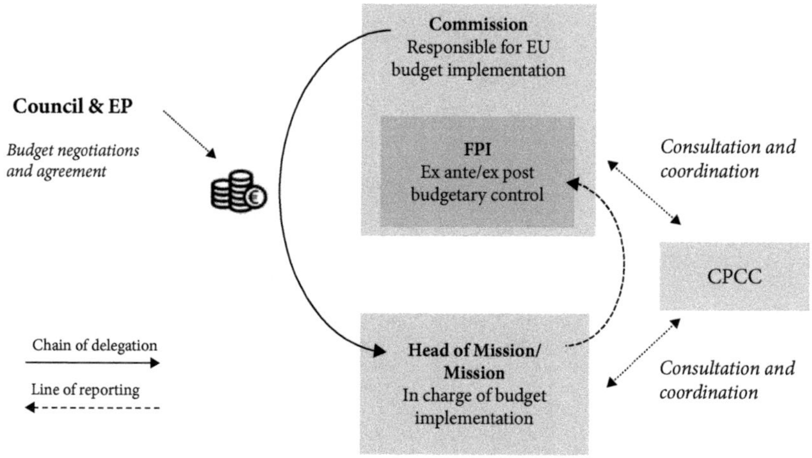


**Figure 3.3** Reporting configuration regarding financial matters

The situation differs for *financial issues*, as illustrated by Figure 3.3. Given the budgetary responsibilities of the Commission in the context of civilian crisis management, due to the primary law provisions in place,[101] the line of reporting obviously runs through the Commission. The Commission, and more precisely its Service for Foreign Policy Instruments (FPI), exercises both ex ante and ex post control, including internal audits to verify that appropriations for the respective missions have been spent in line with the applicable financial rules. This supervision requirement arises from the fact that the Commission entrusts the mission by a delegated act with the implementation of the appropriations of the Common Foreign and Security Policy (CFSP) contained in Chapter 19.03 of the EU budget (agreed upon by the Council and the European Parliament).[102] On a side note, it is worth mentioning that, prior to the conferral of legal capacity to civilian missions, the Commission delegated the implementation of the budget directly to the HoM (*ad personam* delegation), who then bore the responsibility and personal liability for correct implementation.[103] The mission administers the funds in compliance with principles of sound financial management,[104]

[101] For a thorough discussion of these provisions see Chapters 2 and 5.

[102] Art 58(1)(c) Regulation (EU, EURATOM) 2015/1929 of the European Parliament and of the Council of 28 October 2015 amending Regulation (EU, Euratom) No 966/2012 on the financial rules applicable to the general budget of the Union [2015] OJ L286/1.

[103] Art 58(1)(c)(viii) ibid. See furthermore the arrangements regarding financial liability insurance at 3c.(d) C(2009)9502/1 (30 November 2009) (Administrative Decision), 'Specific Rules for Special Advisers of the Commission entrusted with the implementation of operational CFSP actions and contracted international staff'; C(2012)4052 final (26 June 2012) (Administrative Decision), 'Rules for the Financial Management of the Common Foreign and Security Policy Missions.'

[104] This includes the duty to prevent, detect, correct, and notify irregularities and fraud to the Commission, and to carry out ex ante and ex post controls. See art 60(3) Financial Regulation.

and concludes the necessary contracts (eg procurement of personnel and services) in consultation with Brussels-based structures. Financial management is thus in the hands of (senior) mission staff under the supervision of the Commission's FPI and takes place in close consultation with the Civilian Planning and Conduct Capacity (CPCC).

The above taxonomy of responsibilities and reporting configurations in civilian crisis management leaves us with a handful of actors, all of which are situated in Brussels (except for the HoM). These actors can be assembled in two broad categories, namely actors at the strategic level and actors at the operational level as the schematic overview of Figure 3.4 outlines. On the one hand, the Political and Security Committee (PSC), the Committee for Civilian Aspects of Crisis Management (CIVCOM), and the European External Action Service (EEAS) division in charge of strategic planning, namely the ISP (Integrated Approach for Security and Peace, formerly the Crisis Management Planning Directorate (CMPD)) are grouped as actors belonging to the *strategic* level of EU peacebuilding activities. On the other hand, the Civilian Planning and Conduct Capability (CPCC), the HoM, and the FPI of the Commission count as actors at the *operational* level. Somewhere in between is situated the Civilian Operation Commander who holds a position at the intersection of strategic and operational matters. The contours of the two levels are in practice not sharp, but blend into each other—both in terms of actors and activities. Yet, the approximate categorization of actors into broader categories helps to tailor and operationalize accountability arrangements. Based on this classification, the next step is to elucidate *to whom* these strategic and operational actors must account.

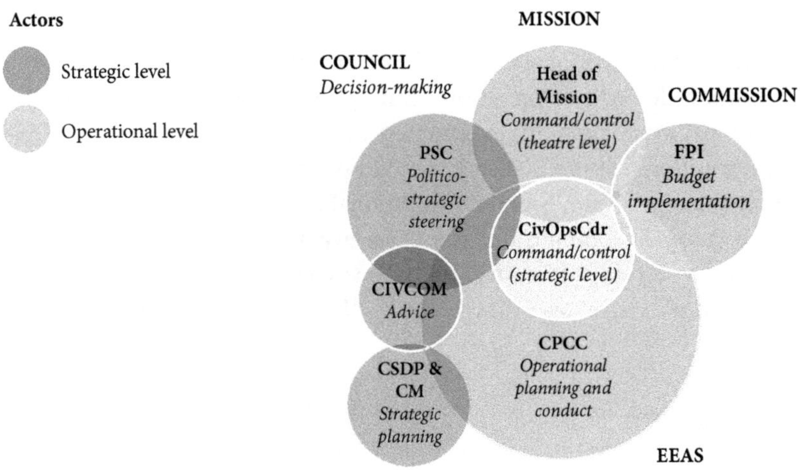


**Figure 3.4** Civilian CSDP actors: strategic and operational levels

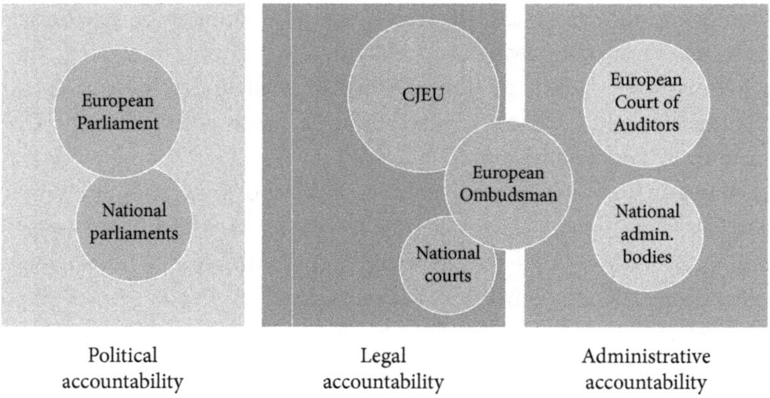


**Figure 3.5** Political, legal, and administrative fora in civilian crisis management

## 4.2 Multilevel forum-mapping

Because of Europeanized intergovernmentalism, fora are both in the national realm—following the de jure intergovernmental logic—and at the EU level—mirroring the Europeanized realities of crisis management. As the nature of the forum is the core categorizing parameter of this study,[105] there is an array of potential accountability fora of a political, legal, and administrative nature across governance levels, all of which are shown in Figure 3.5.

Parliaments at the Member State and EU level are the natural candidates for political accountability. While national parliamentarians, in some countries, have to consent to the deployment (decision) of civilian missions, the Members of the European Parliament hold an important trump card: they co-decide on and control the budget allocated to EU civilian crisis management. Regarding legal accountability, national and EU courts act as legal fora (even though they are at times called to rule on administrative and disciplinary matters). Finally, administrative accountability is exercised by national and European administrative institutions. At the EU level, the European Court of Auditors qualifies as an administrative forum, gauging institutional performance tied to financial issues. The European Ombudsman has a somewhat particular positioning: an administrative forum in nature, the Ombudsman acts as a hybrid between a court and an administrative oversight body.[106] The Ombudsman sits between the

[105] See Chapter 3.

[106] Paul Magnette, 'Between Parliamentary Control and the Rule of Law: The Political Role of the Ombudsman in the European Union' (2003) 10 Journal of European Public Policy 677, 678; Katja Heede, 'Enhancing the Accountability of Community Institutions and Bodies: The Role of the European Ombudsman' (1997) 3 European Public Law 587, 603.

administrative and legal chairs and is therefore placed between legal and administrative accountability in Figure 3.5.

## 5. Challenging Accountability: Outlining Constraints

Now that actors and fora have been mapped, it is time to identify the analytical and practical difficulties or challenges for (assessing) accountability in the context of EU peacebuilding activities.

### 5.1 Analytical and practical difficulties

First, the very *nature of the subject* matter renders (studying) accountability challenging. Peacebuilding is a security and defence policy tool and, therefore, subject to the distinctive rules pertaining to external affairs and matters with defence implications: in the *domaine réservé*, executives enjoy a wide strategic and operational margin, while usual accountability mechanisms, which, inter alia, would imply the participation of the legislative branch and judiciary, are traditionally discarded. This strong executive governance impacts on the conceptualization and implementation of accountability mechanisms in civilian CSDP, which need to be adapted to the allocation of power to be effective.

It is here that the second difficulty originates: there is a *difference between law and practice*. For EU security and defence, the relevant Treaty provisions set out a fundamentally intergovernmental institutional and procedural framework. Secondary legislation attenuating this executive penchant is, with some minor exceptions, absent. In contrast to the de jure intergovernmental framework, administrative and operational realities of civilian crisis management are Europeanized. Civilian crisis management has been subject to a process of Europeanization that has taken the form of concealed agencification; indeed, an informal vertical transfer of both governmental decision-making and action capacity from national ministerial departments to a specialized Brussels-based bureaucracy has taken place.[107] In other words, a transfer of power from national capitals to Brussels-based actors in charge of peacebuilding activities has occurred even though primary rules do not mirror this development. As a result, EU civilian crisis management is de jure intergovernmental but de facto Europeanized. Consequently, accountability mechanisms related to EU peacebuilding activities, which mirror a purely intergovernmental environment as programmed by law, would not be effective as practice tells a different (Europeanized) story. Analytically, then, intergovernmentalism

[107] A detailed analysis of the Europeanization process in form of concealed agencification can be found in Chapter 2.

and supranationalism are not suitable points of reference but constitute the two ends of the broad spectrum on which accountability arrangements are situated, fitting an informally agencified setting. Apprehending the current Europeanized state of civilian crisis management as the result of concealed agencification indeed impacts the accountability yardstick. If a policy is no longer purely intergovernmental but Europeanized, why would the accountability architecture remain intergovernmental?

This brings us to the third challenge, namely the *complexity of activities* undertaken in a multilevel and multi-actor environment. There is, firstly, a politico-strategic dimension to the launch or prolongation of a mission and to the scope and objective of its mandate. Secondly, there is an operational dimension that includes the implementation of the mandate on the ground and the supervision by Brussels-based structures, which constitutes the focus of this study. Although these dimensions are inseparably interlaced, they follow different logics, involve different types of actors, and stretch across several policy and legal levels. This intricacy makes it difficult to disentangle the accountability regime(s) in place, especially as there is no 'one size fits all' accountability regime that would be applicable to both dimensions.

Fourthly, *(in)formality* poses a challenge to (studying) accountability in the context of civilian CSDP. On the one hand, formality or the absence thereof pertains to accountability relationships. Some accountability arrangements in place might be so informal that it will be difficult to qualify them as an arrangement. Vice versa, formal accountability arrangements might not work out in practice. The right balance between formal and informal accountability elements has to be struck. Moreover, there are also practical hurdles to accountability. Formal arrangements being rather weak, an overload of informal accountability arrangements—as an overreaction to the lack of formal accountability—has to be avoided as it could paralyse the operational dimension of civilian crisis management. On the other hand, informality is tied to the *modus operandi* of civilian crisis management. The bulk of (administrative) work in civilian CSDP remains below the threshold of formality (in the primary law sense) and visibility: the numerous derivative decisions are not explicitly codified in primary law or, additionally, subject to a strict disclosure regime.[108] How can an actor be held to account for an action that is 'informal' and 'invisible'?

Finally, and this aspect is linked to the previous point, a major difficulty for analysing and operationalizing accountability in civilian CSDP is the *shortage of information*. Information-gathering and processing is a difficult endeavour in the area of the CFSP/CSDP, including civilian crisis management, given the rules in place on confidential and classified documents. As the scarcity of information is a major

[108] On these issues, see Chapters 2 and 3.

accountability challenge in the context of EU peacebuilding activities, section 5.2 offers a more detailed discussion of the matter.

## 5.2 Access me if you can: on a very restrictive information policy

The rules on handling (classified) information pertaining to EU foreign affairs, security, and defence were introduced at the turn of the century as a response to the gradual build-up of bureaucratic structures for civilian and military CSDP activities, in the context of which the circulation and exchange of sensitive information considerably increased.[109] At this time, the CFSP/CSDP still constituted a separate pillar under EU law, so that rules internal to the Council were adopted to protect classified information in the absence of a Community legal basis (ie a legal basis under the first pillar) allowing for an overarching legislative act.[110] But the first attempt to regulate the classification and processing of sensitive information in the CFSP/CSDP realm did not square with the pro-transparency thrust underpinning the then ongoing negotiations on a regulation pertaining to public access to EU documents:[111] the so-called Solana coup of 2000 excluded per default from the access-to-documents regime all Council documents classified *très secret UE/ EU top secret, secret EU*, and *confidentiel UE* related to EU security and defence matters with and without military implications.[112] What is more, according to the rule of originator control, documents supplied by Member States or third parties required the disclosure consent of the originator (orcon).[113] After a severe inter- and intra-institutional confrontation on disclosure matters,[114] the otherwise progressive regulation on public access to EU documents, which was agreed upon in 2001, left unaltered the blanket exclusion of documents classified *très secret UE/ EU top secret, secret EU*, or *confidentiel UE*.[115] In addition, documents drawn up

[109] An insightful study of (the introduction) of access-to-document rules in the foreign affairs realm of the EU can be found in Maarten Hillebrandt, *Living Transparency. The Development of Access to Documents in the Council of the EU and Its Democratic Implications (Doctoral Thesis)* (University of Amsterdam 2017) 179–207.

[110] David Galloway, 'Classifying Secrets in the EU' (2014) 52 Journal of Common Market Studies 668, 675.

[111] On the pro-transparency and contra-transparency dynamics underpinning the (re)cast of Regulation 1049/2011 see Maarten Z Hillebrandt, Deirdre Curtin, and Albert Meijer, 'Transparency in the EU Council of Ministers: An Institutional Analysis' (2014) 20 European Law Journal 1, 12–13.

[112] Art 2(1) Council Decision 2000/527/EC of 14 August 2000 amending Decision 93/731/EC on public access to Council documents and Council Decision 2000/23/EC on the improvement of information on the Council's legislative activities and the public register of Council documents [2000] OJ L 212/9.

[113] Arts 1 and 2(3) ibid. A detailed analysis of how the 'orcon' requirement made its way into the legal framework can be found in Hillebrandt (n 109) 187–91; Abazi (n 88) 63–66.

[114] On this protracted struggle, see, inter alia, Hillebrandt, Curtin, and Meijer (n 111); Guri Rosén, 'EU Confidential: The European Parliament's Involvement in EU Security and Defence Policy' (2015) 53 Journal of Common Market Studies 383.

[115] Art 9(1) read in conjunction with Art 4(1)(a) Regulation (EC) 1049/2001 regarding access to documents.

for internal use relating to a yet undecided matter or documents containing opinions for internal use as part of deliberations and preliminary consultations could, even for decided matters, equally be excepted from public access if disclosure would or could undermine the institution's decision-making process.[116] In other words, documents linked to (prospective) derivative CFSP decisions can, until today, be withheld from public access. Administrative proceedings and decisions of Europeanized crisis management structures therefore rarely make it into the public realm.

These already restrictive provisions on mandatory and optional exceptions to disclosure are tightened up by internal security regulations on EU classified information (EUCI):[117] the respective rules of the Council and the EEAS introduce an additional fourth category of classified documents, namely *restreint UE*.[118] Statistics show that most of the approximately 7,500 EU classified documents handled annually by the Council relate to the CFSP, with documents labelled *restreint UE* constituting on average more than 90% of all classified information.[119] In addition to these classified documents, there exists another category of secret (that is controlled) documents: *limité*-documents. Falling under professional secrecy rules, the disclosure of documents labelled *limité* could, according to the Council, negatively affect the institution's decision-making processes.[120] Almost a third of all documents registered in the Council register fall under the '*limité*' category.[121] This 30% benchmark is stable, as the Council's Annual Reports of Access to Documents from previous years confirm.

As the numbers underscore, the legal patchwork of secondary legislation and internal rules boils down to a considerably restricted public access to documents—and thus to information—regarding civilian CSDP. Most CSFP/CSDP documents fall under the classification scheme and are thus, per default, covered by the exceptions regime. Even if a document is not classified, it can be withheld from public access under the 'internal use' provision of the 2001 Regulation. This substantially reduces access to information on administrative

[116] Art 4(3) ibid.

[117] *EU classified information* (EUCI) 'means any information or material designated by an EU security classification, the unauthorised disclosure of which could cause varying degrees of prejudice to the interests of the European Union or of one or more of the Member States'. Art 2 Council Decision 2013/488/EU of 23 September 2013 on the security rules for protecting EU classified information [2013] OJ L274/1.

[118] In their current version, see ibid; Decision of the High Representative of the Union for Foreign Affairs and Security Policy of 19 September 2017 on the security rules for the European External Action Service ADMIN(2017) 10 OJ C 126/1.

[119] Council Doc 10684/12 of 4 June 2012, 'Breakdown of documents by security classification levels' LIMITE.

[120] First mentioned in 2000 (by the 'Solana Decision' discussed in this chapter and in Chapter 5), the handling of such *limité* documents is currently regulated by Council Doc 11336/11 of 9 June 2011, 'Handling of documents internal to the Council'.

[121] Galloway (n 110) 672; Deirdre Curtin, 'Overseeing Secrets in the EU: A Democratic Perspective' (2014) 52 Journal of Common Market Studies 684, 685–86.

matters, including the numerous derivative decisions taken by the Brussels-based bureaucracy.

This access restriction was practically experienced in the context of this study. First, a request to access a non-classified document on guidelines applying to reporting arrangements (CivOpsCdr instruction No 03-2013 of 26 April 2013) was denied by the EEAS, which based its refusal on two exception provisions of the 2001 Regulation: (i) the risk that disclosure could undermine public security, defence, and military matters, as well as international relations according to Article 4(1)(a); and (ii) the risk that disclosure could seriously undermined the decision-making process outlined in Article 4(3).[122] While in its response the EEAS contended that the instructions contained in the requested document addressed 'internal deliberations, command matters and the cooperation with the host country of civilian CSDP missions in the practical implementation of their mandates, as agreed by the Council', it had described the very same document in a compilation listing best practices in civilian CSDP as comprising above all reporting modes. In particular, reporting requirements, the proposed structure and contents of mission reports, watch points for report writing, formatting questions, and templates were reportedly included in the requested document.[123] In light of the EEAS description of the requested document in the best practice compilation, it is not clear why access to the document was denied (for the entire document). How could it be detrimental to a civilian mission or the EU if an academic knew who had to report to whom, how, on what, and at which intervals? Secondly, a request to access a non-classified EEAS working document comprising an analysis of recent jurisprudence on ongoing legal proceedings before EU and national courts related to civilian CSDP activities (EEAS(2019)809 of 17 July 2019) was denied. Again, the EEAS refused access to the said document on the grounds of the 2001 Regulation, arguing that the disclosure of the internal assessment would (i) seriously undermine the EEAS's internal decision-making process in relation to the conduct and management of EU civilian crisis management (Article 4(3) of the Regulation) and (ii) undermine the protection of court proceedings (Article 4(2) of the Regulation).[124] This time, however, the reply stated that the EEAS had considered partial disclosure (but decided not to grant it) and, moreover, indicated that the judgments of closed cases before the Court of Justice of the EU (CJEU) and national courts were available.

[122] An access-to-document request was made on 23 February 2017 through the EEAS online portal for requesting documents (request reference 2017/031). The reply, refusing access to the quested document, was received via electronic mail on 22 March 2017 (Ref Ares(2017)1540817—22/03/2017).

[123] Council Doc 5705/15 of 28 January 2015, 'Civilian CSDP Best Practice Compilation' [EEAS document Ares(2014)4217483] 26.

[124] An access-to-documents request was lodged on 6 August 2019 through the EEAS online portal for requesting documents (request reference 2019/145), and additional information on the applicant provided to the competent EEAS entity by email (on 8 August 2019). The reply, refusing access to the quested document, was received via electronic mail on 28 August 2019 (eeas.sg.affg en.2 (2019)6028746).

Denied access notwithstanding, the quality of the refusal was therefore higher than in 2017, where partial disclosure had not been considered. It is interesting to note, though, that the requested document seems to have been removed from the public register of the EEAS after the access-to-document request had been made. The requested legal analysis is thus left to its fate as one of numerous 'invisible' administrative documents produced by the Europeanized Brussels-based bureaucracy.

What these two interludes illustrate is that, next to the, at times criticized, over-classification of documents related to CFSP issues (including civilian CSDP),[125] a rather generous interpretation of the applicable exceptions renders public access to documents particularly difficult in (civilian) CSDP. This in turn cements the structural information asymmetry characteristic of external action and, in this way, potentially precludes claims of accountability: if one does not know, one cannot question.[126]

The generally weak proactive disclosure of information by involved institutions does not help this already difficult access situation. Exemplary hereof was the disclosure regime applied to the supposedly public review report produced in 2015 by the external expert (Jean-Paul Jacqué) in the EULEX Kosovo corruption case referred to in Chapter 1. The said report certainly contained sensitive information (eg case material, and names of victims and alleged criminals) which needed to be redacted prior to release to meet confidentiality requirements. This, however, did not justify to systematically erase *all* names—including those of publicly known (high-ranking) EULEX and Brussels-based officials (eg the Head of Mission or the Civilian Operations Commander)—together with sensitive information. The general deletion of names seriously impeded the understanding of crucial passages of the report and led to confusion. It is, moreover, questionable in how far this particular disclosure approach was in line with the Draft Terms of Reference asking for a *public* report and *adequate* arrangements for classified information.[127] One can hence say that the review report not only shed light on crucial questions related to the allegations in the EULEX Kosovo case, but also threw shadows on civilian crisis management in terms of information management and transparency.[128]

Yet, it is only fair to add at this juncture that although the EU is not a model pupil when it comes to transparency and access to documents in the security and

[125] Guri Rosén, 'Secrecy versus Accountability. Parliamentary Scrutiny of EU Security and Defence Policy', *ARENA Working Paper 1/2014* (ARENA Centre for European Studies 2014) 15.

[126] David Pozen, 'Deep Secrecy' (2010) 62 Stanford Law Review 257, 270.

[127] Draft Terms of Reference, Ref.Ares(2014)3899224 (24 November 2014).

[128] See Jean-Paul Jacqué, 'Review of the EULEX Kosovo Mission's Implementation of the Mandate with a Particular Focus on the Handling of the Recent Allegations' Report commissioned by the High Representatives and released (with annexes) on 31 March 2015 <https://eulex-kosovo.eu/eul/repository/docs/150331_jacque-report_en.pdf> and <https://eulex-kosovo.eu/eul/repository/docs/150331_jacque-report-annexes_en.pdf> both accessed 18 February 2020.

defence realm, Member States generally fare no better. At the national level, access to sensitive information on security and defence is far from easy. Due to specific national access-to-information legislation restricting the type of document that can be requested and imposing extensive exception rules, access for citizens can be even harder at the domestic than the EU level—and the same holds true for members of national parliaments as numerous Member State governments are rather ungenerous when it comes to sharing classified information with national parliamentarians.[129]

Bearing both the public access-to-information regime and the restrictive disclosure policy in mind, different expressions of the informational challenges arising in civilian crisis management are addressed in the three in-depth chapters (5–8) looking at the political, legal, and administrative accountability of EU peacebuilding under the CSDP.

## 6. Customizing Accountability to Civilian CSDP

The scarcity of publicly available information and the difficulty of accessing information in the realm of EU peacebuilding activities is indeed a core element in and of this book, in which information is seen as both a *means* to and an *end* of accountability. This brings us to a differentiation of accountability finalities.

### 6.1 Accountability finalities

According to the accountability definition of Mark Bovens cited in section 2, the provision of information is the first stage of the accountability process upon which all further stages rest—no accountability without information. In the second stage, the information provided is scrutinized, leading in the third stage to a 'judgment', which might entail formal or informal consequences. The crucial question is: *for what* can an actor be sanctioned by the respective forum? Is it for the appropriateness of the conduct, the quality and quantity of information provided, or is it for both? Mark Philp argued in this regard that the power of a forum to sanction the actor for the failure to provide information is a *necessary* condition of accountability, while the power to sanction for the content of the account is a *contingent* condition of accountability.[130] Inspired by this argument, the study

[129] Giovanna Bono, 'Challenges of Democratic Oversight of EU Security Policies' (2006) 15 European Security 431, 443–44; Rosén (n 114) 383, 389.

[130] Mark Philp, 'Delimiting Democratic Accountability' (2009) 57 Political Studies 28, 28–36.

at hand differentiates between accountability for the provision of information—accountability for *information*, $A_i$—and accountability for the actor's action or omission—accountability for *conduct*, $A_c$.

The analytical differentiation between $A_i$ and $A_c$ is particularly salient in relation to accountability for matters with foreign affairs, security, and defence implications. First, governments traditionally enjoy a high level of discretion and secrecy in this field and are not willing to put in place formal or informal arrangements reducing their strategic and operational leeway. This means that there is a considerable informational asymmetry between actors and potential fora. And yet, information-sharing is a precondition for accountability. That is because information and accountability are closely intertwined variables: lesser provisions of information (ie a low level of transparency) leads to reduced accountability, while greater provision of information fosters accountability.[131] Therefore, information-sharing is understood to constitute an accountability *end*-in-itself in the particular context of foreign and security policy activities. What is more, from the constitutional perspective on accountability—according to which accountability is conceived as a means to constrain power—receiving appropriate information (in time) is *the* core element for ensuring countervailing powers. The provision of information indeed changes the allocation of power as information allows the decisions and (in)action of the power-holders to be questioned.

Secondly, the differentiation between $A_i$ and $A_c$ tailors the study to the context of EU peacebuilding activities. The idea behind this contextualization is that particular governance characteristics—in our case executive prevalence coupled with chronic information-shortage—necessitate particular accountability features if accountability is to be effective. As a tool of EU security and defence, civilian missions belong to the *domaine réservé*, which is characterized by executive governance. Accountability is not a traditional feature of the *domaine réservé*. Changing this pattern, however, is essential given the steady increase in executive action above the nation-state. Realistically, then, strengthening accountability in foreign and security matters implies a reduction in the scope of executive prerogatives but not an abolition of the *domaine réservé* as such. Applying the distinction between accountability for information and accountability for conduct allows for a context-adequate approach: strategic decision-making, for instance, remains executive business (little $A_c$) but is subject to more stringent transparency rules, including timely information-sharing with non-executive players (higher $A_i$). In this way, accountability is increased without necessarily reducing the action capacity of crisis management actors.

[131] Meijer (n 51) 518.

## 6.2 Research agenda

This leads us to the research agenda for the present study, which seeks to answer the question: *to what extent has the transfer of powers by Member States to Brussels-based EU civilian crisis management structures been matched with the establishment of appropriate accountability mechanisms at the European level?*

Accountability is construed as a corollary to holding and exercising public power. This power-centred perspective on accountability is a constitutional one, linking accountability to key constitutional elements, such as the rule of law or the separation of powers. Accountability is thus conceptualized as a mechanism the purpose of which is to hold those entrusted with power to account for the use of that power. This mechanism, involving an actor and a forum or several fora, unfolds in three interconnected stages: (i) information, (ii) scrutiny, and (iii) judgment (potentially implying sanctions).[132] The objective of this book is to identify and explore accountability arrangements constraining and taming the power(s) exercised in EU peacebuilding activities. Hence, accountability is not restricted to legal matters but is understood as a crucial vector for the rule of law and eventually governance.

This, in turn, brings us to an essential challenge, which is the informality of the transfer of power regarding EU civilian crisis management. Primary law provisions set out a fundamentally intergovernmental institutional and procedural framework in which national executive actors remain the masters of decision-making. In other words, no power has de jure been conferred to a body or entity above the nation-state. Therefore, accountability continues to be formally channelled through national institutions. However, de facto decision-making and action capacity has been transferred from Member States to Brussels-based structures that now autonomously run the entire civilian crisis management business. Hence, civilian crisis management operates in a setting of Europeanized intergovernmentalism: the institutional and procedural framework is formally intergovernmental, whereas the administrative and operational realities have informally been subject to Europeanization, that is, an informal vertical transfer of power to the EU level following the path of concealed agencification. In short, law and practice diverge.

This finding is crucial for (studying) accountability in two respects. First, both law *and* practice need to be investigated to understand the allocation of power and to disentangle accountability arrangements in the context of peacebuilding activities. Secondly, for accountability arrangements and mechanisms to be effective, they need to be designed primarily to keep in check those actors who *actually* hold and exercise power. Regarding civilian crisis management, this shifts the analytical

[132] Bovens (n 16) 450–51.

focus to the said Brussels-based structures that autonomously plan, steer, and implement activities on the ground.

The analysis therefore extends to both the strategic and the operational level of the exercise of public power in civilian CSDP. Important policy choices are made and agendas are set at the strategic level, whereas steering and implementation is taken charge of at the operational level. In real life, the two levels are not so neatly separated, but overlap as strategic choices impact operational issues, whereas operational realities influence strategic decisions. Thus, actors on both the strategic and the operational level are inquired. On the forum side, the study covers political, legal, and administrative fora both on the EU and the national plane.

For each of the accountability types explored—political, legal, and administrative arrangements—the analysis, which covers both accountability for *information* ($A_i$) and accountability for *conduct* ($A_c$), unfolds in four steps. First, the context is briefly outlined. Secondly, national accountability arrangements are studied, where power remains de jure rooted. Thirdly, the EU level, where power is de facto exercised, is closely examined. Finally, cross-level or transversal aspects are addressed in order to paint the broader accountability picture.

Prior to engaging in this transversal analysis of de jure and de facto accountability arrangements in EU peacebuilding activities providing for $A_i$ or $A_c$, Chapter 4, on the research design, outlines the methodological details of this accountability study.

# 4
# Research Design

The chapter at hand provides insights into the methodology used in this book, which intends to answer the question: *to what extent has the transfer of powers by Member States to Brussels-based European Union (EU) civilian crisis management structures been matched with the establishment of appropriate accountability mechanisms at the European level?*

The point of departure of the study is the finding that EU law sets out a fundamentally intergovernmental institutional and procedural framework to which the administrative and operational realities of civilian crisis management no longer correspond. Indeed, a Europeanization process has occurred: the informal vertical transfer of both governmental decision-making and action capacity from national ministerial departments to a specialized Brussels-based bureaucracy—defined as *concealed agencification*—has led to the strategic and operational centre of gravity of civilian crisis management being undoubtedly situated in Brussels and not in national capitals. The entire policy cycle of civilian crisis management—from planning to implementation and evaluation—is run by this Brussels-based machinery. EU civilian crisis management thus operates in an environment of *Europeanized intergovernmentalism*, meaning that the formal setting is intergovernmental, whereas the realities are Europeanized. The question is then whether accountability arrangements correspond to this sui generis edifice. In other words, is there a sufficient accountability capacity counterbalancing the considerable decision-making and action capacity in EU peacebuilding activities?

Accountability is in this book defined as 'a relationship between an actor and a forum, in which the actor has an obligation to explain and to justify his or her conduct, the forum can pose questions and pass judgement, and the actor may face consequences'.[1] It is a mechanism with three interconnected stages in which (i) an actor provides information on decisions and actions or omissions to a qualified forum, which (ii) then scrutinizes and (iii) passes a judgment on the actor's conduct or performance. While in theory the different stages are ordered, and the actor as well as the forum are graspable, accountability in the real world looks a lot messier.[2]

[1] Mark Bovens, 'Analysing and Assessing Accountability: A Conceptual Framework' (2007) 13 European Law Journal 447, 450. See also Mark Bovens, 'Two Concepts of Accountability: Accountability as a Virtue and as a Mechanism' (2010) 33 West European Politics 946, 946–67.

[2] Gijs Jan Brandsma and Thomas Schillemans, 'The Accountability Cube: Measuring Accountability' (2013) 23 Journal of Public Administration Research and Theory 953, 956.

*Accountability in EU Security and Defence.* Carolyn Moser, Oxford University Press (2020). © Carolyn Moser.
DOI: 10.1093/oso/9780198844815.001.0001

It is important, therefore, to develop an analytical framework capable of capturing accountability arrangements existing both in theory and in practice. In the following pages, the methodological choices made with regard to the *what* and *how* of this accountability inquiry are explained. After a brief exploration of the analytical focus (section 1), the method (section 2) and specific yardsticks are discussed (section 3) and, lastly, the sources outlined (section 4).

## 1. Brussels at the Centre of Attention

The study has intentionally been designed as an inquiry into the EU civilian crisis management apparatus. There are two reasons for this methodological choice. The first and main motivation to primarily scrutinize the Brussels-based structures (instead of national institutions) is tied to the actual allocation of power in EU peacebuilding. As a matter of fact, the strategic and operational centre of gravity of all (types of) EU peacebuilding activities deployed under the EU's Common Security and Defence Policy (CSDP) is de facto situated in Brussels. This is the result of concealed agencification, having engendered the Europeanization of the formally intergovernmental setting. Logically, then, the analytical focus of the present research is on the Europeanized structures at the EU level, where power is actually held and exercised. But as national institutions and actors are still de jure in the driving seat (both on the actor and on the forum side), the analysis also extends to accountability arrangements at the national level and equally covers cross-level aspects.

The second set of reasons for concentrating on the civilian CSDP apparatus—in contrast to a specific (type of) civilian mission—is related to the operational realities of civilian crisis management. Missions vary considerably in size, scope, and context. There are no uniform parameters that would allow for a meaningful comparison. Hence, selecting one single mission to study accountability mechanisms would not lead to generalizable conclusions and, in the worst case, could result in distorted findings. A comparative inquiry into missions of the same type (eg police training, rule of law strengthening) would also be difficult to realize because of the greatly varying variables (number of personnel, mandate, duration, context, etc). Likewise, missions sent to the same country or area (eg the Western Balkan, sub-Saharan Africa) show considerable differences in terms of size and mandates so that country-specific assessments conflating mission types equally bear the risk of an inadequate analysis. A temporal approach is equally problematic, given that both the institutional framework and operational scope of EU peacebuilding activities have evolved over time and have become more complex. The increased number of hybrid missions—that is, missions combining civilian and military activities (eg in the field of security sector reform)—is indicative of this enhanced operational complexity. It would thus be misleading to compare an early-stage police training mission to a recently deployed, multi-faceted capacity-building mission with a police training component.

Now that the analytical *locus* of this book has been outlined—the Brussels-based bureaucratic apparatus—its *focus* needs to be addressed. In the context of external action, policy results are in most cases intangible and therefore difficult to evaluate given the complexity and long-term effects of measures or activities. In our case, the 'output' would be the stabilization of a conflict zone and bringing about peace, which is a very ambitious objective that is hardly measurable. Policy processes, on the other hand, can be assessed as compliance with procedural requirements, legal provisions, and (in)formal arrangements can be subject to scrutiny. This book therefore concentrates on *processes*—rather than on results—involving the civilian crisis management apparatus located in Brussels.[3] These processes are common to all types of peacebuilding activities. Factual as well as analytical elements drawn from specific case studies related to field activities feed into this overall investigation. By choosing this broader analytical angle, findings are applicable to the edifice of EU civilian crisis management as a whole. Another clarification pertains to the phases of peacebuilding activities, which the book's in-depth investigation covers. The analytical focus is on the processes taking place *after* the adoption of the deployment decision; consequently, only events during and after deployment are scrutinized. In contrast, pre-deployment, politico-strategic decisions are not part of this accountability study. The reason for this choice is that pre-deployment considerations—whether a crisis is virulent enough to launch a mission, what geographical and operational zone the mission should cover, what the appropriate mandate and staffing might be—are inherently discretionary and, moreover, subjective, not least because they depend on the weighing of different geopolitical and geostrategic elements. These discretionary choices are difficult to assess from a governance perspective, as they are fundamentally political in nature.

## 2. Exploring Law and Practice

The peculiar edifice of Europeanized intergovernmentalism resulting from concealed agencification calls for a particular method that can connect the dots in the

[3] A comprehensive description of *process* accountability compared to *outcome* accountability can be found in Shefali V Patil, Ferdinand Vieider, and Philip E Tetlock, 'Process versus Outcome Accountability' in Mark Bovens, Robert E Goodin, and Thomas Schillemans (eds), *The Oxford Handbook of Public Accountability* (Oxford University Press 2014) 69–89.

(in)formal patchwork that shrouds civilian crisis management. This is why this book explores both law *and* practice. This choice reposes on two observations.

First, in EU civilian crisis management, law and practice diverge: while law translates an intergovernmental scheme in terms of actors and procedures, practice is characterized by Europeanized administrative arrangements and operational realities. Secondly, there is a high degree of informality, both regarding the institutional setting and day-to-day routines. In many instances, codification in (civilian) CSDP has been preceded by informal institutional and operational arrangements (eg the codification of the European Political Cooperation (EPC) or the formalization of the CSDP). One aspect of this informality, related to the overall framework, is that practice foreshadows future law or might modify existing law. Another aspect—this time linked to day-to-day issues—is that many institutional arrangements or operational undertakings remain below the threshold of formality, in the primary law sense, as practice is not comprehensively codified. Only decisions adopted by the European Council, the Council of the EU (Council), and the Political and Security Committee are explicitly codified by Treaty law, whereas no mention is made of day-to-day derivative decisions, mostly of an administrative nature, taken by the Brussels-based bureaucracy. Thus, most working level activities of civilian crisis management fall under the 'informality' category.

Given the divergence of law and practice as well as the prominence of informality, both law *and* practice must be taken into consideration in order to comprehensively examine accountability processes in EU peacebuilding activities. Limiting an accountability study to de jure considerations would paint an incomplete and inaccurate picture of the actual situation. In contrast, combining an examination of the law in the books with the assessment of the law as it is exercised in or complemented through practice offers a more nuanced and realistic approach to accountability.[4] Real-world accountability arrangements can be 'thinner' or 'thicker' depending on a combination of different de jure and de facto factors.[5] This holds particularly true for civilian crisis management, where accountability arrangements are not solely determined by black letter law, but depend to a considerable degree on what happens in practice, which departs from or adds elements to the codified accountability scheme: there can be more de jure than de facto accountability (or vice versa). Therefore, this inquiry is based on a desk study of pertinent legal rules (de jure dimension), which is combined with and refined by an analysis of policy documents, reports, internal regulations, and institutional practice.

[4] See, inter alia, Gijs Jan Brandsma, *Controlling Comitology: Accountability in a Multi-Level System* (Palgrave Macmillan 2013); Brandsma and Schillemans (n 2).

[5] On this point, see also Chapter 3.

## 3. Differentiated Accountability

Having outlined the locus and focus of this inquiry (processes involving the Brussels-based crisis management structures during the operational phase of EU peacebuilding) and the approach (a study of law and practice) it is now time to discuss in more detail the concept of accountability. As previously mentioned, accountability is defined as an institutional mechanism. Its core function is to hold those entrusted with power to account for the use of that power. Construing accountability as a corollary to (the exercise of) power reflects a *constitutional perspective on accountability*, which in turn is stirred by constitutional law considerations.[6]

To fulfil its function as a power-constrainer and power-tamer, and to prevent a power–accountability gap, accountability arrangements need to be adapted to the allocation of power. The edifice of Europeanized intergovernmentalism renders this endeavour challenging as the informal transfer of decision-making and action capacity blurs the distinction between those who hold power and those who do not, as well as those who consequently must account (to whom) on the use of this power and on what (in)formal basis. To ascertain whether accountability mechanisms exist de jure or de facto, it is crucial to examine in detail who has to account to whom, for what, and on what basis.

### 3.1 Who to whom?

Accountability is essentially a relationship between an actor (who) and a forum (to whom). Therefore, a fundamental element of any accountability study is to identify the power-wielder(s) and appropriate accountability-demander(s). The who and the whom cannot be the same individual or entity—a relationship necessarily requires a meaningful other—implying that (self-imposed) compliance procedures monitored by the actor do not amount to accountability.[7]

As for the *actor* side in civilian crisis management, some actors operate at the strategic level (ie definition of grand directions, formal decision-making, strategic planning, and oversight) while others primarily work at the operational level (ie operational planning, steering and implementation, operational command and oversight). These two levels are not neatly separated in practice, neither in terms

[6] Mark Bovens, Deidre Curtin, and Paul 't Hart, 'Studying the Real World of EU Accountability: Framework and Design' in Mark Bovens, Deidre Curtin, and Paul 't Hart (eds), *The Real World of EU Accountability* (Oxford University Press 2010) 51–52.

[7] Philipp Dann, 'Accountability in Development Aid Law: The World Bank, UNDP and Emerging Structures of Transnational Oversight' (2006) 44 Archiv des Völkerrechts 381, 384, 398. The salience of this distinction with regard to European security actors, namely the OSCE, was reiterated in Carolyn Moser, 'Conceptualising Accountability in the Legal and Institutional Framework of the OSCE' in Mateja Steinbrück Platise, Carolyn Moser, and Anne Peters (eds), *The Legal Framework of the OSCE* (Cambridge University Press 2019) 277.

of functions nor actors. Nonetheless, the distinction between the strategic and the operational level offers a valuable analytical framework for studying accountability. This is because the different levels are staffed with different types of actors with varying responsibilities. At the strategic level, power-wielders are primarily high-ranking members of national governments who act collectively (eg decision-making bodies operating on the basis of unanimity). At the operational level, power-wielders are in general (albeit not always) lesser senior civil servants, and there are more individual actors (eg Heads of Mission, mission or country desk officers, legal advisers) who also closely interact. These different actor–task constellations, in turn, impact on the accountability architecture. To offer a comprehensive picture of civilian CSDP, this study covers both strategic and operational aspects of the exercise of power.

Regarding the *forum* side, fora both at the EU level and at the national level are studied, given the de jure–de facto discrepancy of Europeanized intergovernmentalism. However, the focus lies on fora at the EU level as power is effectively exercised in a Europeanized context. That said, this book examines in detail (i) political, (ii) judicial, and (iii) administrative accountability mechanisms regarding the civilian dimension of the CSDP. Financial accountability does not constitute a category on its own, as financial/budgetary aspects are addressed transversally throughout the analysis and ascertained in detail in section 4 of Chapter 7 on the European Court of Auditors (ECA).

The analysis of the three accountability types—political, legal, and administrative—develops in four steps along the lines of the research questions stated in Table 4.1. After sketching out the context (i), the analysis unpacks national accountability arrangements (ii) prior to assessing in detail EU level arrangements (iii). In a final step (iv), multilevel or transversal elements are outlined.

## 3.2 For what and on which basis?

The assessment of de jure and de facto accountability arrangements with a political, legal, and administrative nature at the strategic and operational level can be finetuned and further enhanced by adding analytical layers. This is why this book introduces a differentiation regarding the object or finality of the accountability process: between accountability for the provision of information (accountability for *information*, $A_i$) and accountability for the actor's action or omission (accountability for *conduct*, $A_c$).

Regarding accountability for *information*, the focal point of the accountability arrangement is on the provision of information by the actor to the forum, and on the power of the forum to sanction non-compliance regarding the provision of information. In the policy area of security and defence, where executive predominance is the rule and not the exception, and additionally where chronic

**Table 4.1** Research questions: overview

| **To what extent has the transfer of powers by Member States to Brussels-based EU civilian crisis management structures been matched with the establishment of appropriate accountability mechanisms at the European level?** | |
|---|---|
| *Political accountability* | – What parliamentary function is desirable and practicable in the *domaine réservé?*<br>– How does parliamentary scrutiny of the CFSP/CSDP unfold across different governance levels?<br>– How has the division of labour between national parliaments and the EP in this field evolved over time?<br>– To what extent has the current division of parliamentary labour adapted to the edifice of Europeanized intergovernmentalism? |
| *Legal accountability* | – Which judicial body—national, European, or both—is competent to adjudicate on matters related to extraterritorial EU civilian missions?<br>– How can legal accountability be reconciled with Europeanized intergovernmentalism?<br>– How is legal accountability exercised, and in respect of which aspects and actors? |
| *Administrative accountability* | – To what extent has the legal and procedural framework of civilian crisis management enabled administrative accountability?<br>– What is the role of administrative fora? Do they tackle cross-cutting administrative questions or solve individual cases? And how has their role evolved over time?<br>– In how far are the existing de jure and de facto administrative accountability arrangements aligned with Europeanized intergovernmentalism? |

information-shortage seriously hampers accountability demands, it is paramount to oblige (executive) actors to provide timely and encompassing information about their decisions and measures. Information is thus more than an accountability prerequisite, but constitutes the purpose of accountability in itself. The requirement to share information can derive either from rights held by the forum, such as access-to-information rights, or from obligations incumbent on the actor, including the delivery of annual reports or the required appearance in public hearings. The information requirement is not necessarily due to the forum, but can also be enforced by the forum on behalf of another individual or entity, for instance when a court is called to decide on whether a public institution's refusal to grant a citizen access to documents was lawful. The benchmarks to evaluate the quantity and quality of the information provided vary for different accountability types and fora. Parliamentarians, on the one hand, will scrutinize the provision of information according to the informal and subjective yardstick of political salience (Does the information provided enable them to exert political influence through debate or decision-making?). A judge, on the other hand, will have recourse to codified rules as well as procedures and jurisprudence, for instance when ascertaining whether an access-to-document request should have been granted in full or in part to an individual or entity. The $A_i$-benchmark against which the forum scrutinizes and eventually sanctions the actor is thus context dependent.

Much of the above is equally true regarding accountability for *conduct*, where the crucial aspect is the (in)action of the actor. (The scope is thus broader than in the $A_i$-scenario.) Conduct can be scrutinized in relation to the forum itself (eg a parliament sanctioning an executive actor for not having respected parliament's participation rights in a procedure) or to a third entity (eg an ombudsperson endorsing a complaint by a citizen who argues that their rights were infringed upon). The yardstick according to which conduct is evaluated is also context dependent, albeit mostly formal in nature. Parliament will, for instance, assert its legally enshrined budgetary powers and sanction an actor for not respecting its decision-making rights in this matter. The (compliance) criteria applied by an auditing body regarding administrative procedures and financial rules will equally be formalized. A (quasi-)judicial forum will assess the conduct of the actor against the backdrop of codified rules and procedures, and established case law, for instance when it has to deal with a case on the right to effective remedy. Faced with a disputed disciplinary measure, a (quasi-)judicial forum will ask on what basis and according to what criteria the contested measure was adopted, and whether the procedure followed allows the concerned individual to appeal against the measure.

To recapitulate, the forum can require the actor to provide information and, depending on the finality of the accountability arrangement (information or conduct), can sanction for an incomplete (or a total lack of) provision of information ($A_i$), or for (mis)conduct ($A_c$). The scrutiny benchmarks vary according to the type of forum (political, legal, or administrative), and tend to be more formal for $A_c$. It is worth adding that, in light of the low level of codification and the high degree of informality of (civilian) CSDP, many yardsticks are not explicitly laid down or referred to in law, but are identified by the respective fora by means of implied rules and principles or by way of analogy.

## 3.3 The appropriateness question

This brings us to the crucial point of the appropriateness of accountability arrangements in EU civilian crisis management. Indeed, this book is not limited to charting existing de jure and de facto accountability arrangements, but also aims at assessing whether these arrangements are appropriate. Accountability has thus both a descriptive and a normative facet.

Recurring to national (constitutional) frameworks for determining what constitutes appropriate accountability in civilian crisis management would be of little help: accountability arrangements regarding security and defence matters are generally scarce at the domestic level, offering the executive wide decisional and operational leeway with few (to no) countervailing powers. However, the low level of accountability is not a model to be replicated at the EU level if civilian CSDP is not to resemble a 'multi-level process of self-reinforcing executive dominance [triggering] questions regarding the democratic anchoring of the polity as a whole'.[8] Indeed, the exercise of power (ie decision-making and action capacity) needs to go hand in hand with accountability mechanisms at the level where power is actually exercised; for Europeanized intergovernmentalism, this would be at the European level. To be appropriate, these mechanisms need to be adapted, on the one hand, to the particular context of security and defence—traditionally a realm of executive power and secrecy—and, on the other hand, need to safeguard fundamental constitutional features.

What are these features? According to the 'practice what you preach' formula enshrined in Treaty law (Article 21(3) of the Treaty on European Union (TEU)), the EU has an obligation of conduct when engaging in external action, including peacebuilding activities.[9] This obligation of conduct imposes on the EU's action abroad to be in accordance with—and with the aim of promoting—inter alia, democracy, the rule of law, and the respect of human and fundamental rights. These are, obviously, great ambitions and grand concepts, but they provide a valuable *fil conducteur* for sketching out appropriateness standards in the context of civilian CSDP. The rule of law is particularly salient as it determines both the *content* of peacebuilding activities (ie strengthening public institutions that are crucial to the rule of law) and their *context* (a constitutionally enshrined principle). According to the 'thick' understanding of the rule of law (entailing both formal and substantive requirements) employed in this book,[10] one can count among the core elements of the rule of law the separation of powers (including an executive subject to the law), the prevention of the abuse of powers (and thus the prohibition of arbitrariness of the executive), legality and legal certainty, effective judicial remedies, judicial review by an independent and impartial judiciary, non-discrimination, and the protection of fundamental rights.[11] In addition, the good governance principles developed

[8] Helene Sjursen, 'The EU's Common Foreign and Security Policy: The Quest for Democracy' (2011) 18 Journal of European Public Policy 1069, 1071.

[9] On the obligation of conduct imposed on the EU in external action, see Chapter 2.

[10] See, on this point, Simon Chesterman, 'Rule of Law', *The Max Planck Encyclopedia of Public International Law*, vol VIII (Oxford University Press 2012) 1014–16; Frank Schimmelfennig, 'Rule of Law Promotion Policies in Comparison of Major Western Powers' in Michael Zürn, André Nollkaemper, and Randy Peerenboom (eds), *Rule of Law Dynamics: In an Era of International and Transnational Governance* (Cambridge University Press 2014) 113–14.

[11] See, for instance, COM(2019) 163 final, 'Further strengthening the Rule of Law within the Union—State of play and possible next steps' 1; Council of Europe (Venice Commission), 'Rule of Law Checklist', CDL-AD(2016)007-e, Venice, 11–12 March 2016); COM(2014) 158 final (11 March 2014), 'A new EU Framework to strengthen the Rule of Law' 4; Council of Europe (Venice Commission), 'Report on the Rule of Law', Study No 512/2009, CDL-AD(2011)003rev, Strasbourg, 4 April 2011 para 41.

by the International Law Association provide guidance. Among these principles figure transparency (in decision-making and implementation), access to information, a well-functioning administration, sound financial management, and reporting mechanisms.[12]

Bearing these elements in mind, we now return to circumscribing appropriateness in civilian crisis management. Appropriateness bears three dimensions, namely (i) quantity, (ii) quality, and (iii) capacity. The *quantity* criterion obviously implies how many accountability arrangements are in place. The *quality* standard is tied to the scope and intensity of the accountability process. The *capacity* benchmark in turn has to do with the power of the forum to fulfil its role to ensure a countervailing power. While the first two criteria are rather formal in nature, the third evaluative yardstick entails a substantive element. What is more, there is a progression from descriptive criteria (quantity and quality) to a more normative criterion (capacity).

As for the first dimension—quantity—the contours for EU peacebuilding activities are clear: appropriate means that enough accountability mechanisms exist when and where power is effectively exercised to keep in check the power-wielder. In civilian CSDP, where the strategic and operational centre of gravity is with the Brussels-based bureaucratic structures, this quantity requirement implies that there be accountability arrangements at the EU level on both the strategic and the operational plane of decision-making and action capacity, covering political, legal, and administrative matters.

The contours of appropriateness are blurrier when it comes to the second dimension—quality. What is an appropriate scope or intensity of scrutiny? And what powers of the forum/fora are adequate? The accountability mechanism consists of three interconnected stages—information provision, scrutiny, and potential sanctions—and its quality depends on all three stages being effective. In other words, inquisitive and sanctioning powers of the forum/fora need to be strong enough to keep in check the actor(s) throughout the process. When applied to EU civilian crisis management this means that the quality of accountability arrangements is appropriate if the respective forum has the ability to (i) require information from the actor allowing for substantive scrutiny and (ii) sanction actors either for an incomplete (or a non-existent) provision of information ($A_i$) or for (mis)conduct ($A_c$).

Finally, the contours of the third dimension of appropriateness—capacity—are the most difficult to circumscribe. It is worth recalling at this point that this research is driven by a core element of modern democratic thinking, according to which power and accountability are a conceptual unity. The exercise of public power needs to be accompanied by accountability mechanisms on the use of that

[12] International Law Association, Final Report on the Accountability of International Organisations, 2004 8.

**Table 4.2** Accountability appropriateness evaluation criteria

| Dimension | Evaluation criteria | |
|---|---|---|
| *Quantity* | Existence at the EU level of political, legal, and administrative accountability arrangements on both the strategic and the operational plane of civilian crisis management | |
| *Quality* | Ability of the respective forum (i) to require information from the actor allowing for substantive scrutiny, and (ii) to sanction either for the lacking or incomplete provision of information ($A_i$) or for (mis) conduct ($A_c$) | |
| *Capacity* | Political accountability | Scrutiny of decisional and operational activity, including budgetary aspects |
| | Legal accountability | 1. Safeguard of constitutionally enshrined institutional and procedural arrangements |
| | | 2. Individual legal protection |
| | Administrative accountability | 1. Redress routes and complaint options |
| | | 2. Financial oversight (both compliance and performance) |

power, regardless of this power being exercised on formal grounds or informally as a result of practice. In line with the constitutional perspective on accountability, appropriateness is closely tied to '[t]he extent to which an accountability arrangement curtails the abuse of executive power and privilege'.[13]

In light of the above, the following capacity criteria in the context of EU peacebuilding activities are identified, which are summarized in Table 4.2. First, let us turn to political accountability. As civilian crisis management is executive and not legislative in nature, the envisioned accountability capacity signifies that parliaments are able to control the measures taken by the executive—in contrast to making and adopting laws. Therefore, in an ideal scenario, the legislative branch would have the capacity to scrutinize both decisional and operational civilian crisis management activities, including budgetary matters (eg passing the financial bill and discharge procedures). This control function, however, presupposes that executive actors swiftly provide the legislative branch with sufficient and sound information on decisions adopted and measures implemented. Parliamentarians could gauge the progress made by a mission, discuss day-to-day issues with high-ranking members of the Brussels-based bureaucracy or mission personnel, ask pointed budget questions, or propose possible operational adjustments. Yet,

[13] Bovens (n 1) 466.

parliamentarians could not co-decide on the launch or mandate of a mission, or require the Council to deploy a mission, and they could not nominate high-ranking personnel either, as this comes within executive competences.

With regards to legal accountability, rule-of-law considerations play a crucial rule in the determination of the appropriate accountability capacity. On the one hand, the rule-of-law benchmark would imply that judicial bodies could safeguard constitutionally enshrined institutional and procedural arrangements. On the other hand, judges should be in a position to ensure individual legal protection, which can be a difficult task given *locus standi* requirements in security and defence issues. There is also the question of the scope and intensity of judicial reviews. While procedural reviews might be sufficient in relation to strategic CFSP decisions to address competence questions and ensure compliance with primary law, substantive reviews might be required once the case circles around the potentially infringed rights of individuals by an operational or (derivative) administrative measure.

Finally, the capacity regarding administrative accountability is twofold. First, and this is again tied to rule-of-law considerations, there should be effective redress options as well as complaint mechanisms for individuals concerned by an administrative decision. Secondly, financial oversight—both for compliance and performance aspects—would ideally exist.

## 4. Sources

To allow for an accurate assessment of all facets of accountability in civilian CSDP—that is (i) de jure *and* de facto mechanisms of a (ii) political, legal, and administrative nature at (iii) the domestic level, the EU plane, and across levels, and (iv) their strengths and weaknesses—the book draws on a multitude of sources. Next to a broad thematic range of academic literature (including legal analyses, political science readings, public administration studies, and international relations scholarship), this analysis relies on both legal sources and empirical data. This diversity of sources, in turn, allows for a triangulation of findings. While the legal sources helped to disentangle the intricate de jure framework of civilian crisis management, the secondary sources—and in particular the empirical material—revealed the Europeanized facet of EU peacebuilding. Indeed, legal and para-legal sources contributed to elucidating the distinctive legal, institutional, and procedural setting of EU peacebuilding activities and provided the initial hints about the strengths and weaknesses of this formally intergovernmental framework. The empirical data, on the other hand, put into perspective the insights drawn from the desk study of legal and para-legal sources and, importantly, allowed the gaps in the literature to be closed, in particular for the informal (or only partly codified) administrative and operational practice of EU peacebuilding missions.

The first category of sources—legal sources—entails three components. First, EU law is the major reference for the analysis, comprising primary law provisions, pertinent secondary EU law (decisions, regulations, interinstitutional agreements, etc), and supplementary legal sources, namely case law of the Court of Justice of the European Union (CJEU). Para-legal documents, primarily including policy documents from European institutions (eg presidency conclusions or white books) and third-party reports (eg by the European Parliament (EP), the ECA, or the European Ombudsman), provide further analytical nuances. National laws as well as regulations, policy documents, and national jurisprudence are referred to as subsidiary legal sources. The same holds for international norms and procedural standards.

The second category of sources—empirical data—is made up of interviews and case studies, both of which follow a qualitative approach. The purpose of the empirical data is indeed to contextualize and put into perspective insights drawn from the desk study of legal and para-legal sources. In addition, the empirical material fills certain gaps in the literature. For example, administrative procedures related to civilian missions, including disciplinary matters, remain both underregulated and understudied. Therefore, academic literature, as well as legal and para-legal sources are not sufficient to shed light on these questions. Moreover, much day-to-day business in EU peacebuilding is informal (ie not codified by primary law or based on informal cooperation methods). Disentangling these informal arrangements or practices of civilian crisis management was a vital thread when conducting interviews. In these situations, where insights from practice are the only available sources, special caution was applied to the extrapolation of empirical data.

Regarding the interviews, respondents both from the actor and the forum side were selected. With a view to allowing for a nuanced picture, respondents from different policy levels (EU and national sphere), belonging to different types of institutions (executive, legislative, administrative, or judicial), and with different tasks (decision-making, oversight, implementation, etc) and ranks (from senior leadership to more junior-level personnel) were interviewed. Between September 2016 and May 2017, thirteen semi-structured interviews were conducted at different places with interlocutors affiliated with the Council of the European Union, the CJEU, the European Commission (the Commission), the ECA, the European External Action Service, the European Ombudsman, the EP, Member State parliaments, and civilian missions. Due to the highly politicized field, the names of the respondents are not disclosed. For the same reason, information obtained in the interviews is used as background information, but is not referred to explicitly in this book (in a footnote, for instance). Concerning the interview set-up, all respondents were contacted via email, detailing the nature of the research project and issues to be discussed during the interview. Interview questions revolved around three to four identified thematic fields, which were shared with the respective respondent, either at the beginning of the interview or prior to the interview via email. These identified thematic fields varied according to the type of accountability studied (legal, political, and administrative) and the institutional affiliation of the respondent. During the interviews, which lasted on average between one and one-and-a-half hours, handwritten notes were taken and later typed. The answers were closely examined both in comparison to the findings of the desk study and with regard to answers of other respondents.

Concerning case studies, two requests to access case files concerning civilian CSDP were made with the European Ombudsman in December 2016 and in July 2017 respectively. Case files of nineteen files (both complaint-based and triggered by own-initiative inquiries of the European Ombudsman) were requested. One file constituted a joint complaint, and one own-initiative inquiry had thirteen underpinning complaints. Access was granted in full to thirteen redacted case files (and seven underpinning complaints of the said own-initiative inquiry). Almost full access was granted for one case file (only two documents were withheld). Access was denied for five case files: in four of these cases, the proceedings had already been closed and the decisions of the Ombudsman—stating the complaint, putting forward the arguments of the involved actors, outlining the assessment of the Ombudsman, and indicating the outcome—were accessible via the online database of the Ombudsman; for the fifth refusal, access was denied so as not to impair the then still ongoing inquiry. The alleged irregularity could, however, be inferred from the information displayed in the Ombudsman's database, and the same holds for the decision later rendered by the Ombudsman. From the same online database, seven further case files were identified as relevant and included in the study, without access to documents being requested. In total, twenty-six case files were scrutinized in depth. The analysis, which focused on (informal) administrative procedures, allowed for accountability patterns to be identified, including *lacunae*, regarding administrative accountability in civilian CSDP.

To conclude, this book investigates in depth three types of accountability mechanisms—namely political, legal, and administrative accountability—existing at both the strategic and operational level of civilian crisis management. The assessment concentrates on procedures, and covers both national and European arrangements, while the focus is on the latter. To grasp the entire picture of accountability in civilian crisis management, de jure and de facto arrangements are covered in the analysis. This law and practice approach is also reflected in the sources that include empirical data next to legal sources.

# 5
# Political Accountability: Unsteady Parliamentary Involvement

In modern democratic systems, parliaments constitute the cornerstone of political accountability: in addition to their crucial role as lawmakers, parliaments have an important oversight function as they ensure that executive actors account for their decisions and actions. Yet, there are policy fields where this oversight function is tricky. Security and defence are among these delicate policy fields: governments traditionally enjoy *domaine réservé* prerogatives that shield them from (overly tight) parliamentary supervision. Foreign affairs, security, and defence at the European Union (EU) level is no exception in this regard. On the contrary, the multilevel and multi-actor setting of the EU's Common Foreign and Security Policy (CFSP) and its Common Security and Defence Policy (CSDP) renders parliamentary scrutiny a truly intricate affair.

This holds particularly true for the civilian dimension of EU security and defence, which unfolds in an environment of *Europeanized intergovernmentalism*: whereas the institutional and procedural features of civilian CSDP remain formally intergovernmental, the daily routine of civilian crisis management has become Europeanized. This means that both decision-making and action capacity has been transferred vertically from the ministerial departments and institutions of Member States to specialized Brussels-based bureaucratic structures—a phenomenon known from EU agencies.[1] As this transfer has, however, taken place informally—meaning outside of Treaty law and as a momentum of its own—agencification is concealed.[2] Thus, much of what happens in civilian crisis management is (i) not codified in primary law, including derivative decision-making and implementation, and consequently (ii) remains below the threshold of formality and visibility.

This leaves us with a complex de jure–de facto accountability structure. On the one hand, national parliaments, whose powers in the field of foreign and security policy vary considerably across Member States, are de jure in charge of holding national actors to account as the setting is formally intergovernmental.

[1] Jarle Tondral, 'Agencification' (2014) 74 Public Administration Review 545, 545, 546. See also Renaud Dehousse, 'Misfits: EU Law and the Transformation of European Governance' in Christian Joerges and Renaud Dehousse (eds), *Good Governance in Europe's Integrated Market* (Oxford University Press 2002).

[2] For a more detailed analysis of Europeanized intergovernmentalism and concealed agencification, see Chapter 2.

*Accountability in EU Security and Defence.* Carolyn Moser, Oxford University Press (2020). © Carolyn Moser.
DOI: 10.1093/oso/9780198844815.001.0001

But parliamentarians are confronted with a situation in which they have to keep track of numerous dossiers and scrutinize an array of decisions taken by *their own* executive in the context of the CFSP/CSDP—and potentially that of *twenty-six other* governments, as representatives act unanimously in this policy field.[3] What is more, many decision-making and implementation tasks have been transferred to a Brussels-based bureaucracy, including the Political and Security Committee (PSC) or the bodies belonging to the civilian crisis management structures of the European External Action Service (EEAS). Most of these bureaucratic structures operate, as previously touched upon, below the threshold of formality in the primary law sense—both in institutional and decisional terms—and thus beyond the range of national parliamentary vision.[4] The European Parliament (EP), on the other hand, is well placed to interact closely with the Europeanized Brussels-based actors, but lacks formal powers to hold national governments to account because of the *informal* transfer of functions. In addition, in a multilevel parliamentary field,[5] parliamentary scrutiny can hardly be confined to either the national or the European level. Cooperation across levels is needed, inter alia, to foster the exchange of information necessary for effectively holding executive actors to account. Faced with this intricate situation, the present Chapter investigates political accountability and, more precisely, the role of parliaments as accountability fora in the context of EU civilian missions.

*To what extent has the transfer of powers by Member States to Brussels-based EU civilian crisis management structures been matched with the establishment of appropriate accountability mechanisms at the European level?* Against the backdrop of this overarching research question guiding this study, the chapter at hand tries to answer a set of questions regarding political accountability; accountability being defined as a three-stage mechanism involving an actor and a forum.[6] (i) What parliamentary function is desirable and practicable in the domaine réservé? (ii) How does parliamentary scrutiny of the CFSP/CSDP unfold across different governance levels? (iii) How has the division of labour between national parliaments and the EP in this field evolved over time? (iv) And to what extent has the current division of parliamentary labour adapted to the edifice of Europeanized intergovernmentalism? In searching for answers, the study looks at both de facto and de jure arrangements providing for accountability for *information* ($A_i$) and

[3] On the great disparity of parliamentary control of CFSP activities at the national level, see Suzana Anghel and others, 'National Parliamentary Oversight of ESDP Missions' in Dirk Peters, Wolfgang Wagner, and Nicole Deitelhoff (eds), *The Parliamentary Control of European Security Policy* (ARENA 2008).

[4] Ariella Huff, 'Problems and Patterns in Parliamentary Scrutiny of the CFSP and CSDP', *OPAL Online Paper Series 14/2013* (Observatory of Parliaments after the Lisbon Treaty) 6–7.

[5] Ben Crum and John E Fossum, 'The Multilevel Parliamentary Field: A Framework for Theorizing Representative Democracy in the EU' (2009) 1 European Political Sciences Review 249.

[6] Mark Bovens, 'Analysing and Assessing Accountability: A Conceptual Framework' (2007) 13 European Law Journal 447, 450.

for accountability for *conduct* ($A_c$). While in the former constellation (accountability for information) the focus is on the inquisitive and sanctioning powers of the forum in relation to the (timely and encompassing) provision of information, the central element in the latter constellation (accountability for conduct) is on the forum's ability to scrutinize and sanction the actor for its (in)action.

The analysis develops against the backdrop of the three dimensions of appropriate accountability, namely (i) quantity, (ii) quality, and (iii) capacity. We will thus keep an eye on the existence of sufficient political accountability arrangements at the level where strategic and operational power is actually exercised: at the EU level (quantity). Further, the inquisitive and sanctioning powers of the forum/fora play a role when assessing the scope and intensity of the accountability arrangement (quality). Finally, the power-restraining facet of accountability is assessed (capacity): scrutiny of decisional and operational activity, including budget matters.

The chapter starts in section 1 with some reflections on parliamentary scrutiny in the *domaine réservé*, a policy field where parliamentary activity has traditionally been low, but becomes increasingly salient given the growing scope and impact of international policy-making. Section 2 then develops a discussion of the fairly limited oversight role of national parliaments regarding EU security and defence. General patterns of parliamentary involvement and particular features of scrutiny related to EU peacebuilding activities are assessed. In the third section, the analysis highlights the enhanced significance of the EP as political forum in the CFSP/CSDP context through a range of formal and informal vehicles, which, however, only marginally contribute to parliamentary scrutiny of civilian missions. Building on section 4 that ascertains the hurdles to interparliamentary cooperation, the final section of the chapter underscores the significance of effective supranational parliamentary scrutiny of peacebuilding activities in the edifice of Europeanized intergovernmentalism.

## 1. Parliaments and the *domaine réservé*

Prior to examining different expressions of political accountability by means of parliamentary oversight mechanisms, it is judicious to make a preliminary remark on the role of parliaments in the sensitive area of foreign affairs, security, and defence *tout court*. The traditional—though increasingly disputed—stance on this matter refutes the usefulness and appropriateness of parliamentary scrutiny, which is considered to be problematic for, if not detrimental to, policies falling under this category given the distinctive nature of *domaine réservé* issues.[7]

[7] Arguments supporting executive preponderance in foreign affairs, security, and defence can be found in, inter alia, Daniel Thym, 'Beyond Parliament's Reach? The Role of the European Parliament in the CFSP' (2006) 11 European Foreign Affairs Review 109, 123–26; Adrian Hyde-Price, 'Decision-Making under the Second Pillar' in Anthony Arnull and Daniel Wincott (eds), *Accountability and*

The argument circles around effectiveness and efficiency considerations and can be divided into procedural concerns on the one hand, and substantive concerns on the other. As to the procedural dimension, the underlying assumption is that putting these issues on the parliamentary agenda would slow down the decision-making process and would thus bear the risk of unnecessarily delaying the executive's response in the speedy international relations business. Concerning the substantive element, it is repeatedly argued that bringing parliaments on board would inevitably endanger the secret or confidential character of external affairs and diplomacy, and thereby alter their very course. The concern underpinning or related to the latter claim is that publicly debating foreign policy and defence issues narrows down the array of options at the executive's disposal as not all options would find public or parliamentary support. Parliamentary scrutiny regarding foreign and defence issues interlaces internal and external policy matters; this interlacement, in turn, may lead to reduced flexibility as it obliges decision-makers to find a way to square internal with external imperatives.[8] Wary of this two-level situation, many executives are reluctant to put international matters on the national parliamentary agenda. This reluctance is highlighted for the CFSP/CSDP, where two hot topics converge: (i) security policy and (ii) European integration.[9]

However valid the abovementioned concerns may be, they are expressed in relation to ex ante parliamentary oversight. The situation looks different, though, when parliamentary involvement happens after the event, which is the case with accountability mechanisms. In this context, scrutiny takes place *ex post facto*, although with potential effects on future policy choices. Therefore, the arguments traditionally voiced against parliamentary overview in the *domaine réservé* are not justified when it comes to political accountability mechanisms fulfilled through parliamentary activity. The timeframe concern according to which parliamentary involvement would delay proceedings is not applicable, as the inquiry into a foreign policy or defence decision or action takes place retrospectively. Accountability

*Legitimacy in the European Union* (Oxford University Press 2002) 55–56. A critical stance on the exclusion or restriction of parliamentary involvement is, for instance, adopted in Dirk Peters, Wolfgang Wagner and Nicole Deitelhoff, 'Parliaments and European Security Policy. Mapping the Parliamentary Field' in Dirk Peters, Wolfgang Wagner, and Nicole Deitelhoff (eds), *The Parliamentary Control of European Security Policy* (ARENA 2008) 3, 5–8; Piet Eeckhout, *EU External Relations Law* (2nd edn, Oxford University Press 2011) 500; Geert de Baere, *Constitutional Principles of EU External Relations* (Oxford University Press 2008) 166–67; Jolyon Howorth, *European Integration and Defence: The Ultimate Challenge?* (WEU Institute on Security Studies 2000) 90; Christopher Lord, 'The Political Theory and Practice of Parliamentary Participation in the Common Security and Defence Policy' (2011) 18 Journal of European Public Policy 1133; Berthold Rittberger, '"No Integration without Representation!" European Integration, Parliamentary Democracy, and Two Forgotten Communities' (2006) 13 Journal of European Public Policy 1211; Isabelle Ley, *Opposition im Völkerrecht—Ein Beitrag zur Legitimation internationaler Rechtserzeugung* (Springer 2014).

[8] On the issue of interlaced policy levels, see Robert D Putnam, 'Diplomacy and Domestic Politics: The Logic of Two-Level Games' (1988) 42 International Organization 427, 460.

[9] Peters, Wagner and Deitelhoff (n 7) 7.

has, of course, also an anticipatory facet and could restrain policy or operational options in the future. In a move of precautionary responsiveness,[10] the executive could choose to take into consideration possible parliamentary objections. Yet, it is far from evident why the indirect limitation of the executive's choice to those options that would stand up to parliamentary scrutiny would be negative per se. On the contrary, given (i) the increasing internationalization of politically and socially salient topics (including security),[11] and (ii) the wide-ranging (in)direct effects of foreign affairs and security decisions on citizens, 'the democratization of security might even be viewed as the culmination of democracy'.[12] This democratization would primarily consist of increasing oversight—in contrast to enhancing parliamentary participation in decision-making. That is because *domaine réservé* issues are mostly executive—non-legislative—in nature.[13] The primary function of parliaments, hence, is to act as a democratic controller of government through discursive (inter-)action and not as a (co-)legislator. Therefore, the provision of information (stage 1 of the accountability process) allowing for scrutiny (stage 2) is particularly salient when studying political accountability. This said, the *ex post facto* involvement of parliamentary bodies does *not* constitute an impediment to policy-making and implementation in external, security, and defence affairs, but is a crucial means of holding executive actors to account for the use of their external action powers.[14] In fact, providing for parliamentary scrutiny of external action can be regarded as an 'inherent value' in a democratic society.[15]

## 2. National Parliamentary Scrutiny at a Safe Distance

Bearing in mind that both procedural and substantive concerns voiced against political accountability in foreign affairs, security, and defence matters exercised through parliamentary participation can be rebutted, this section assesses the significance of national parliaments in the context of EU security and defence. At this juncture, it is important to recall that EU security and defence is de jure a predominantly intergovernmental policy field even though a de facto Europeanization of (civilian) CSDP has occurred. This implies that representatives taking decisions

[10] Formulation inspired by Jelena von Achenbach, 'Informationsrechte von Bundestagsabgeordneten über Rüstungsexporte' (2015) 70 Juristenzeitung 96, 98.

[11] On this point, see Chapter 3.

[12] Peters, Wagner, and Deitelhoff (n 7) 5–6.

[13] Imposing restrictive measures (sanctions) is an exception in this regard.

[14] A similar conclusion on ex post political accountability through parliamentary inquiry is reached by Hänggi with regard to the use of force in peace operations. Hans Hänggi, 'The Use of Force Under International Auspices: Parliamentary Accountability and "Democratic Deficits"' in Hans Born and Hans Hänggi (eds), *The 'Double Democratic Deficit'. Parliamentary Accountability and the Use of Force Under International Auspices* (Ashgate 2004) 14.

[15] Case C-263/14 *European Parliament v Council* [2015] EU:C:2015:729, Opinion of Advocate General (AG) Kokott of 28 October 2015 para 78.

in the Council of the EU (hereafter the Council) formally remain under the scrutiny of their respective national parliaments,[16] even if policy-making has in reality moved beyond intergovernmentalism.[17] This is why it is crucial to understand the national institutional and constitutional frameworks within which parliamentary scrutiny of European foreign and security affairs unfolds. It is important to ascertain to what extent the transfer of powers to Brussels has been matched with the establishment of appropriate political accountability mechanisms in the given multilevel parliamentary field.

## 2.1 The role of national parliaments according to EU law

Two primary law elements shape the participation of national parliaments in EU affairs. First, the Treaty on European Union (TEU) assigns national parliaments a prominent position in the EU architecture as they 'contribute actively to the good functioning of the Union' (Article 12 TEU). The participation of national parliaments is programmed by primary law in six instances, namely (i) through information-sharing including draft legislative acts; (ii) by ensuring that the principle of subsidiarity is respected; (iii) by playing an active role in the evaluation mechanisms regarding the Area of Freedom, Security and Justice, as well as the political monitoring of Europol and Eurojust; (iv) by involvement in Treaty revision procedures; (v) through the provision of information on accession applications; and (vi) by fostering interparliamentary cooperation with the EP.[18] This enumeration illustrates that the list of policy issues for which national parliaments have information rights or a say is long. Yet, it also brings to the fore that national parliamentary scrutiny, despite the policy being fundamentally intergovernmental, does *not* extend to EU foreign affairs, security, and defence—at least not explicitly. National parliaments might play a role here, but then indirectly under the headings of subsidiarity (and proportionality) or interparliamentary cooperation.[19]

This, in turn, signifies that parliamentary supervision of the CFSP/CSDP takes place according to the constitutional provisions of each Member State. This is underlined by the Declarations 13 and 14 concerning the common foreign and security policy annexed to the Treaty of Lisbon. Both declarations stress that Treaty

[16] de Baere (n 7) 167; Anna Herranz Surrallés, 'The EU's Multilevel Parliamentary (Battle)Field: Inter-Parliamentary Cooperation and Conflict in Foreign and Security Policy' (2014) 37 West European Politics 957, 966.

[17] Helene Sjursen, 'Not so Intergovernmental after All? On Democracy and Integration in European Foreign and Security Policy' (2011) 18 Journal of European Public Policy 1078.

[18] Art 12(a)–(f) TEU.

[19] Michael Hilger, 'An Insider's View. Perspectives for Interparliamentary Cooperation of European Security Policy' in Dirk Peters, Wolfgang Wagner, and Nicole Deitelhoff (eds), *The Parliamentary Control of European Security Policy* (ARENA 2008) 134, 136. As for subsidiarity, see Consolidated Version of the Treaty on European Union (TEU) [2016] OJ C202/206, Protocol no 2 on the application of the principles of subsidiarity and proportionality.

law neither modifies existing legal arrangements and responsibilities in the formulation and conduct of national foreign policies nor prejudices the specific character of the security and defence policy of the Member States.[20]

The picture is more nuanced when extending the evaluation to the second primary law element, namely the provisions of Protocol no 1 on the role of national parliaments in the EU annexed to the Treaty of Lisbon.[21] The said protocol reiterates the crucial importance of national parliaments in the EU's architecture, and grants significant information rights concerning legislative matters, which are primarily (draft) legislative acts.[22] Yet, policy issues with foreign affairs, security, and defence implications, in the great majority of cases, do not involve legislative activities as they are executive in nature. Protocol no 1, therefore, does not prima facie contribute to strengthening the direct access to information of national parliaments regarding EU security and defence matters. However, Articles 9 and 10 of the said protocol entail provisions on regular parliamentary cooperation. The exchange of information and best practices between parliamentary levels, as well as 'on specific topics, in particular to debate matters of common foreign and security policy, including the common security and defence policy', is to be achieved through an interparliamentary conference. Access-to-information matters are thus indirectly tackled. Such an interparliamentary conference was indeed established in 2012 to cover both the CFSP and the CSDP.[23] While these arrangements provide for some information-sharing and enhanced debate across policy levels, including in the field of EU security and defence, they relate to parliamentary actors only and do not extend to executive decision-makers.[24]

## 2.2 Accountability patchwork across Member States

Given the comparatively little direct involvement EU primary law ascribes to national parliaments in EU security and defence matters, it is important to understand the national legal frameworks regulating the role of national parliaments in the oversight of EU security and defence in general. These national frameworks are almost as numerous as they are diverse. Therefore, 'there is no standard way in which member state parliaments are engaged in European security affairs and no guarantee that national parliaments are involved at all'.[25] As undertaking an

[20] Consolidated Version of the Treaty on European Union (TEU) [2016] OJ C202/343, Declarations 13 and 14 concerning the common foreign and security policy.

[21] Consolidated Version of the Treaty on European Union (TEU) [2016] OJ C202/203, Protocol no 1 on the role of national parliaments in the European Union.

[22] Title I (Information for national parliaments) ibid.

[23] Known as the Inter-Parliamentary Conference for the Common Foreign and Security Policy (CFSP) and the Common Security and Defence Policy (CSDP).

[24] The effects of these arrangements for political accountability are discussed in more detail in section 3 of this chapter.

[25] Peters, Wagner, and Deitelhoff (n 7) 11.

exhaustive comparative study on the diversity—not to say disparity—in law and practice across Member States would go beyond the scope of the present chapter, the following analysis draws on empirical insights offered by several comparative studies dealing with parliamentary oversight of EU security and defence at both the EU and national level.[26] Each of these studies is based on a detailed set of responses to wide-ranging questionnaires and in-depth country case studies. In addition, a range of semi-structured interviews conducted in the context of this study offer supporting empirical material.

What the aforementioned comparative studies illustrate is that the broad spectrum of diverging national legal frameworks and practices regarding the involvement of national parliaments in EU security and defence matters can be subdivided into four categories.[27] These categories, which also deal with ex ante parliamentary consultation and approval, offer valuable insights as to the broader framework within which parliamentary participation in EU security and defence matters unfolds. An overview of the four categories is provided in Table 5.1. The first category entails Member States (eg Finland, Luxembourg, and Sweden) whose national parliaments have to authorize their government to take a Council decision in favour of launching an EU civilian or military crisis management mission. The second category relates to those countries in which the national parliament has to authorize the deployment of troops. This constellation, for instance, can be found in Austria, Ireland, and the Netherlands for all sorts of EU security and defence activities, and in Cyprus, Estonia, Germany, and Spain for military deployments only.[28] The third category encompasses Member States in which legal provisions or practices assign national members of Parliament (MPs) a consultative and debating role regarding EU security and defence. Lacking parliamentary approval, the respective governments can still proceed with deciding on the launch of a civilian mission or military operation and deploy personnel as they are not bound by the consultative parliamentary decision; this is the case, inter alia, in Belgium, France, Poland, Portugal, and the UK. Lastly, in a handful of Member States, policy-making and decision-making matters pertaining to European security and defences issues are excluded from parliamentary scrutiny. Bulgaria, Greece, and Romania fall under this category,

[26] Hans Born and others, 'Parliamentary Oversight of Civilian and Military ESDP Missions: The European and National Levels', *Study PE 348.610* (European Parliament 2007); Dirk Peters, Wolfgang Wagner, and Nicole Deitelhoff (eds), 'The Parliamentary Control of European Security Policy', *RECON report No. 6* (ARENA 2008); Ariella Huff, 'Executive Privilege Reaffirmed? Parliamentary Scrutiny of the CFSP and CSDP' (2015) 38 West European Politics 396.

[27] For more details, see Born and others (n 26) 51–52; Anghel and others (n 3) 72–75; Peters, Wagner, and Deitelhoff (n 7) 11–12; Hans Born and Hans Hänggi, 'The Use of Force under International Auspices: Strengthening Parliamentary Accountability', *DCAF Policy Paper No 7* (Geneva Centre for the Democratic Control of Armed Forces (DCAF) 2005) 8.

[28] The German framework for parliamentary involvement (including required parliamentary consent for deployment) will be discussed in more detail in the ensuing comparative analysis (with France) in section 2.3.

**Table 5.1** Involvement of national parliaments in EU security and defence

| | Role in EU security and defence | Examples of Member States | Level of involvement |
|---|---|---|---|
| *Category 1* | Ex ante approval of a Council decision to launch both civilian and military CSDP activities | Finland, Luxembourg, Sweden | High—allows for ex ante decisional control of the executive |
| *Category 2* | Ex ante approval of deployment | Both military and civilian deployments: Austria, Ireland, Italy, Latvia, The Netherlands<br>Military deployments only: Cyprus, Estonia, Germany, Spain | Relatively high—programmes involvement once operational action has been decided by the executive |
| *Category 3* | Consultative and debating role | Belgium, France, Poland, Portugal, UK | Low—executive not bound to act in accordance with parliamentary vote |
| *Category 4* | Exclusion of parliamentary scrutiny | Bulgaria, Greece, Romania | Non-existent—MPs are not in the loop |

where neither military operations nor civilian missions are subject to parliamentary scrutiny.

## 2.3 EU peacebuilding missions: a parliamentary blind spot

It can be inferred from the above typology that limited parliamentary scrutiny of EU security and defence is a common feature across many Member States (indicative hereof are categories 3 through 4, and to a lesser degree category 2).[29] This is particularly true for EU civilian missions. It is argued here that this low level of parliamentary oversight is connected to four factors,[30] all of which impact both accountability for *information* ($A_I$) and accountability for *conduct* ($A_c$).

First, many national parliaments have only *reduced formal powers* when it comes to supervising civilian CSDP activities.[31] Generally, national parliaments are not too closely associated with EU security and defence, and, if they are, their oversight

[29] Born and Hänggi (n 27) 18.

[30] Other authors unfold their analysis along three criteria, namely (i) authority, (ii) ability, and (iii) attitude. A definition of the triad can be found in Hänggi (n 14) 11–15.

[31] Hänggi deals with this issue under the heading of 'authority'. See ibid 12–14.

mainly covers military matters. More precisely, while the deployment of troops is subject to an array of ex ante and ex post overview regimes, parliamentary consent is generally not required for the dispatch of (seconded) civilian experts or for mandate prolongations. Concretely, ex ante parliamentary decisions on EU civilian crisis management activities are required and binding only in Austria, Finland, Ireland, Italy, Latvia, Luxembourg, the Netherlands, and Sweden.[32] Hence, only eight out of twenty-seven Member States have a framework currently in place that allows their respective national parliament to formally have a say on the launch of a civilian mission. These reduced formal powers lessen parliaments' capacity to effectively influence or sanction the conduct of executive actors, and therefore constitute an important weakness with regard to $A_c$.

The second aspect pertains to *information circuits* across policy levels and policy fields, leaving national parliamentarians often out of the loop. The intensity of parliamentary scrutiny depends to a large extent on the access to timely and accurate information, an issue which is challenging in the two-level environment of EU peacebuilding activities.[33] As touched upon earlier, national parliaments have not only to follow a range of dossiers and oversee numerous decisions taken by their own executive in the context of the CFSP/CSDP but they potentially also have to scrutinize the conduct of twenty-six more governments as decisions rest upon unanimity. This is a truly Herculean task, especially as national parliaments rarely have direct access to information on salient EU security and defence issues and therefore rely on their governments to receive pertinent information.[34] Yet, many Member State governments are not well disposed to share classified information with national parliamentarians.[35] As a result, there are significant informational bottlenecks on both strategic and operational aspects between executive decision-makers and information-holders (actors) on the one hand, and legislative accountability-demanders and information-recipients (fora) on the other.[36]

Generally, information on draft legislative acts has to be forwarded to national parliaments, which then have eight weeks for scrutiny.[37] But legislative acts are precluded under the CFSP/CSDP (Article 31(1) TEU).[38] Hence, under EU law

[32] The launch of EU civilian missions used to be subject to parliamentary scrutiny in the Czech Republic and Romania, too, but the legal framework in these countries was reportedly amended to exclude national MPs from oversight. Anghel and others (n 3) 56.

[33] de Baere (n 7) 167–68; Hänggi (n 14) 14.

[34] Catriona Gourlay, 'Parliamentary Accountability and ESDP: The National and the European Level' in Hans Born and Hans Hänggi (eds), *The 'Double Democratic Deficit'. Parliamentary Accountability and the Use of Force Under International Auspices* (Ashgate 2004) 185.

[35] Giovanna Bono, 'Challenges of Democratic Oversight of EU Security Policies' (2006) 15 European Security 431, 443–44; Guri Rosén, 'EU Confidential: The European Parliament's Involvement in EU Security and Defence Policy' (2015) 53 Journal of Common Market Studies 383, 383, 389.

[36] Peters, Wagner, and Deitelhoff (n 7) 13.

[37] Art 2 and 4 Protocol no 1 on the role of national parliaments in the European Union.

[38] In addition, in the event that an international agreement exclusively relating to the CSFP/CSDP is concluded by the Council, this agreement is not subject to parliamentary consent at the EU level (Art 218(6) TFEU). Even if the EP has to be immediately and fully informed about the ongoing procedure

national parliaments do not need to be informed of decisions relating to the CFSP/ CSDP in due time or within prescribed consultation periods. They only receive such information if the constitutional provisions of their Member State provide otherwise. In most European jurisdictions, however, such provisions do not exist so that the rule is that little (or no) information is shared by executive actors with the respective MPs. In addition, the web of specialized administrative structures located in Brussels generally does not see (national) parliamentarians as natural interlocutors. This lack of information, in turn, is a major stumbling block for $A_i$ at the national level in the context of EU civilian missions as it seriously endangers the accountability-process being kicked off (stage 1 being the provision of information).

This structural shortage of information is further aggravated by the decision-making modes and procedures at the EU level. On the one hand, formal CFSP decisions—that is decisions in the primary law sense—are adopted on the basis of unanimity (Article 31(1) TEU). How can national parliaments identify the position of their own government in such a setting and pin down national decision-makers, especially if decision-makers, acting as information gate-keepers, are reluctant to share information on negotiations and voting behaviour?[39] Because of the specific rules and procedures at work, decision-making in EU security and defence remains opaque.[40] In addition, when information is transmitted from the executive to the legislative, this often happens at a very late stage, so that MPs face an irreversible fait accompli.[41] On the other hand, most policy issues are prepared, and their implementation administered by the Brussels-based crisis management bureaucracy. This bureaucracy, however, operates below the threshold of formality and visibility. That is largely because derivative CFSP decisions emanating from crisis management structures, many of whom belong to the EEAS, are informal and thus not published, and can therefore hardly be scrutinized by national parliaments.[42] Indeed, the shortage of information is intensified by the fact that many decisions tied to deployment and implementation regarding EU civilian crisis management are mostly taken (within the Brussels-based bureaucracy) at a comparatively low executive level—lower than for military questions—and 'with no obligation to report the decision to parliament'.[43] While national MPs have in some countries the possibility to visit deployed personnel, this information channel cannot make up for otherwise weak information-sharing. The aforementioned

in such a case (Art 218(10) TFEU), there is an information bottleneck for national parliaments. On this issue, see section 3 of this chapter.

39 de Baere (n 7) 168; Peters, Wagner, and Deitelhoff (n 7) 13.
40 On the combined effect of unanimity and flexibility, see Bono (n 35) 442.
41 ibid 441; Anghel and others (n 3) 58; Huff (n 4) 15.
42 Huff (n 4) 5–8.
43 Born and others (n 26) 28.

information asymmetry between executive and legislative actors is therefore particularly significant in the context of civilian missions.[44] These framework conditions are not conducive to endowing national parliaments with strong inquisitive powers. Deirdre Curtin therefore writes that 'unilateral control over information and decision-making at the expense of parliaments'[45] is a core feature of the CFSP. The prospect of accountability both for $A_i$ and for $A_c$ through parliamentary scrutiny at Member State level is therefore considerably attenuated.

The third crucial factor for political accountability is related to the *division of labour within national parliaments*, an element which ties in with the available (administrative) resources.[46] In numerous Member States, several parliamentary committees are in charge of overseeing EU missions and operations. The list of committees potentially involved in scrutinizing EU security and defence is long: the committee list entails foreign affairs, EU affairs and defence, interior policies, development aid, budget, and human rights.[47] This panoply of potential accountability-demanders with overlapping mandates, coupled with the generally low working pace of committee structures, is said to dissipate awareness on CSDP matters.[48] Rather unsurprising then, scrutiny processes regarding EU security and defence matters are most effective when oversight is jointly undertaken by or coordinated between the involved committees.[49] In the absence of mainstreamed oversight and bundled administrative resources, however, the *dédoublement fonctionnel* at best results in eclectic demands for accountability and, in the worst case, paralyses political accountability regarding EU security and defence in general. Moreover, civilian missions are often part of the 'interior policies' portfolio because of their mandate (eg rule of law programmes, policing, civil–military capacity-building) and staffing (eg police experts, judges, customs officers). Information-sharing between actors in charge of external policies and those dedicated to internal policies is often difficult. This is an impediment to both $A_i$ and $A_{c,}$ as many resources are needed for information processing and coordination. In other words, the political accountability mechanism at Member State level mostly begins to falter between phase 1 (the provision of information) and phase 2 (scrutiny), leaving the actor without sanctions (phase 3) and thus the forum without teeth.

This in turn is related to yet another factor impacting on political accountability exercised through parliamentary overview, namely *political will*.[50] It is true that civilian crisis management activities generally carry less political weight and receive

[44] ibid 25, 28; Huff (n 4) 5–6, 15; Anghel and others (n 3) 52.

[45] Deirdre Curtin, 'Challenging the Executive Dominance in European Democracy' (2014) 77 The Modern Law Review 1, 2.

[46] On the importance of a parliament's ability to scrutinize, see Hänggi (n 14) 14–15.

[47] Anghel and others (n 3) 60; Born and others (n 26) 28, 67–68.

[48] Born and others (n 26) 28; Huff (n 26) 404.

[49] Huff (n 26) 402–5.

[50] On the importance of political will, or 'attitude', see Hänggi (n 14) 15.

significantly less media coverage than military operations even though EU civilian missions are far more numerous. The political salience of troop deployments is, indeed, higher in most countries than the dispatch of a group of policemen, lawyers, or customs officers.[51] Parliamentary control in this field demands much 'input' in terms of time and resources, but offers little 'output' as it attracts little political attention. Accordingly, the political will to scrutinize EU peacebuilding activities is low. This leads to a situation in which civilian activities undertaken by the EU remain largely unknown to national politicians and to the average voter.[52] The low level of political interest generates negligible demands on the national plane regarding $A_i$ and, as a consequence of information shortage, even fewer demands concerning $A_c$ (ie decision-making). A noteworthy deliberative exception in this regard is the European Scrutiny Committee of the UK House of Commons. The said committee is persistent in asking the UK government to account for EU civilian missions. Indicative of this parliamentary tenacity is the corruption case concerning EU rule of law mission (EULEX) to Kosovo, which became public in 2014.[53] The European Scrutiny Committee has repeatedly requested government bodies to provide information and explanations about the past and current situation, and has made critical remarks as to the internal investigation and review process instigated by the EEAS.[54] This has helped to increase the $A_i$ of UK government bodies.

The combination of the four aforementioned factors—(i) reduced formal powers, (ii) the shortage of information, (iii) the at times problematic division of labour, and (iv) the lack of political will—leads to a situation in which EU civilian

[51] Huff (n 26) 406, 408–9.

[52] Interestingly, academic studies reverberate this situation: they mostly deal with parliamentary involvement regarding military operations (and neglect civilian missions). See, inter alia, Christian Mölling and Alicia von Voss, 'The Role of EU National Parliaments in Defence Affairs. A Comparison of Decision-Making Powers across Europe Concerning International Troop Deployments and Procurement Processes', *SWP Working Paper FG03-WP No 01* (Stiftung Wissenschaft und Politik 2015); Sandra Dieterich, Hartwig Hummel, and Stefan Marschall, 'Parliamentary War Powers: A Survey of 25 European Parliaments', *DCAF Occasional Paper No 21* (Geneva Centre for the DCAF 2007); Wolfgang Wagner, 'Parliamentary Control of Military Missions: Accounting for Pluralism', *DCAF Occasional Paper No 12* (Geneva Centre for the DCAF 2006); Hans Born and Hans Hänggi (eds), *The Use of Force Under International Auspices: Parliamentary Accountability and 'Democratic Deficits'* (Ashgate 2004); Assembly of Western European Union, 'National parliamentary scrutiny of intervention abroad by armed forces engaged in international missions: the current position in law', Document A/1762 (2001) 2001 22.

[53] The incident is outlined in detail in Chapter 1.

[54] Exemplary of the perseverance of the European Scrutiny Committee in the allegations of corruption concerning EULEX Kosovo is a series of reports issues on the matter. See, for instance, some of the reports from 2014 to 2015: House of Commons, European Scrutiny Committee, 'Common Security and Defence Policy: EULEX Kosovo: allegations of corruption', Twentieth report HC 219-xix (2014–15), chapter 16 (19 November 2015); House of Commons, European Scrutiny Committee, 'Common Security and Defence Policy: EULEX Kosovo: allegations of corruption', First report HC 342-i (2015–16), chapter 29 (21 July 2015); House of Commons, European Scrutiny Committee, 'Common Security and Defence Policy: EULEX Kosovo: allegations of corruption', Thirty-seventh report HC 219-xxxvi (2014–15), chapter 28 (18 March 2015); House of Commons, European Scrutiny Committee, 'Common Security and Defence Policy: EULEX Kosovo: allegations of corruption', Twenty-fifth report HC 219-xxiv (2014–15), chapter 14 (10 December 2014).

missions fly under the radar of most national parliaments. Across Member States there is, with some exceptions, little $A_i$ and even less $A_c$. For both dimensions of accountability, the three-stage process resembles an inversed pyramid: there is little information (stage 1), even less dialectic interaction (stage 2), and almost no sanctioning mechanism for a lack of information or for misconduct (stage 3). As a result, political accountability is thinned out at every stage of the process.

The ensuing comparative analysis of parliamentary scrutiny of EU peacebuilding missions in France and Germany highlights the generally weak stance of national parliaments regarding civilian CSDP. The analysis will cover three aspects, namely (i) formal powers, (ii) information-sharing, and (iii) the political context of parliamentary oversight. Let us first turn to formal powers. In France, the constitutional amendments of 2008 have provided Parliament with slightly more de jure prerogatives. According to the amended constitutional provisions, the French government has to inform parliament about its decision to deploy armed forces (*forces armées*) abroad, at the latest three days after the beginning of the intervention.[55] If the intervention lasts longer than four months, the new stipulations envisage that government has to seek for parliamentary authorization to prolong the intervention.[56] While, in theory, the French Sénat (upper chamber of the French parliament) counts civilian dispatches, such as police missions or support missions, among those deployments constitutionally subject to ex post parliamentary control,[57] its interest in EU civilian missions seems marginal in practice—and the same holds for the Assemblée Nationale (lower chamber of the French parliament).[58] In Germany, formal parliamentary prerogatives with regard to civilian missions are equally limited. Compared to the considerable powers the Bundestag (the lower chamber of the German parliament) enjoys regarding military deployments,[59] both its ex ante and ex post involvement in EU civilian missions is weak. Parliamentary approval is *stricto sensu* only necessary when 'armed personnel' is deployed.[60] The powers of the German parliaments are further reduced by federal structures. Parliamentarians must be informed by the executive of its intention to dispatch

[55] Art 35, second paragraph, Constitution du 4 octobre 1958.

[56] Art 35, third paragraph, ibid. So far, the government has diligently followed these rules on troop deployments. See Amandine Blandin, 'Article 35 de la Constitution: état de l'information du Parlement sur les interventions militaires à l'étranger' [2016] Revue française de droit constitutionnel 3, 5–6.

[57] Jacques Gautier and others, 'Interventions extérieures de la France: renforcer l'efficacité militaire par une approche globale coordonnée', *Rapport d'information n°794* (Sénat 2016) 240.

[58] In contrast to civilian activities, the French parliament is very (pro-)active when it comes to military deployments. For a detailed analysis, see Carolyn Moser, 'Frieden durch Recht aus französischer Perspektive' in Sarah Jäger and Wolfgang S Heinz (eds), *Frieden durch Recht. Rechtstraditionen und Verortungen* (Springer 2020), 108–11.

[59] See, in particular, Art 3(2) Gesetz über die parlamentarische Beteiligung bei der Entscheidung über den Einsatz bewaffneter Streitkräfte im Ausland (ParlBG).

[60] Art 2(1) ibid. So far, German MPs have, however, given their approval to all EU missions involving military personnel, even for EU training missions. Currently, the German armed forces (*Bundeswehr*) participate in two EU-led training missions in Mali and Somalia. The initial mandates, including deployments, have been approved by the Bundestag respectively in 2013 and 2014.

federal police officers, and can request the termination of the deployment.[61] Yet, many civilians deployed in the context of EU civilian missions are not members of the federal police but belong to police services of the federal States (*Länder*), which are under the legislative control of the respective regional parliaments. Oversight powers are thus split—to the detriment of the federal parliament—and the two parliamentary levels do not engage in cooperative scrutiny.

The lack of formal powers of German parliamentarians is not compensated by information-sharing arrangements, which is the second aspect of this comparative analysis. Law prescribes that the federal executive informs the Bundestag comprehensively, continuously, and at the earliest possible moment on the CFSP/CSDP by transmitting, in principle in written form, an overview of tabled acts, including an evaluation of future steps.[62] In addition, the government has to orally inform MPs on all relevant developments and meetings pertaining to the CFSP/CSDP.[63] In practice, however, the German government applies a restrictive interpretation of this information obligation. As a result, the federal parliamentary committee primarily in charge of overseeing EU civilian missions—the Interior Committee—is not systematically informed by the Ministry of the Interior on the state of affairs; hence, the flow of information relies on the initiative taken by individual MPs.[64] The situation is similar with regard to the Committee for Foreign Affairs. Members of the Bundestag can visit deployed personnel, but this information channel cannot make up for otherwise weak information-sharing. In France, in contrast, information-sharing arrangements are more parliamentary-friendly. The French executive is under the obligation to submit to the committees in charge of European affairs of both parliamentary chambers—Sénat and Assemblée Nationale—all EU acts (including non-legislative acts under the CFSP/CSDP) transferred to the Council to receive ex ante clearing of political documents.[65] Even if, reportedly, this procedural obligation of ex ante clearing in practice is not applied to (all) CSDP activities,[66] it provides the two aforementioned committees in principle with timely information on planned and ongoing activities. In spite of these arrangements, parliamentary scrutiny of civilian missions is primarily confined to budget questions,[67] even though French MPs are entitled to visit deployed personnel.

[61] Art 8(1) Gesetz über die Bundespolizei (BPolG).

[62] Art 7(1) Gesetz über die Zusammenarbeit von Bundesregierung und Deutschem Bundestag in Angelegenheiten der Europäischen Union (EUZBBG); Unterrichtung durch die Kommission zur Überprüfung und Sicherung der Parlamentsrechte bei der Mandatierung von Auslandseinsätzen der Bundeswehr. Abschlussbericht der Kommission, Deutscher Bundestag, Drucksache 18/5000 (16.6.2015) 2015 54, 45–46.

[63] Art 7(3)–(4) EUZBBG.

[64] Anghel and others (n 3) 65.

[65] Art 88-4 Constitution du 4 octobre 1958.

[66] Born and others (n 26) 30.

[67] Gautier and others (n 57) 238; Anghel and others (n 3) 62.

This restraint of French parliamentarians can be (partly) explained by the political context. Considering the traditionally long list of military operations deployed simultaneously by the French Republic, including under the CSDP framework, the parliamentary deference or negligence towards civilian aspects might be understandable in practice, even though not desirable in theory. In Germany, the dire parliamentary oversight situation is also not helped by the political context: the fact that the German government judges superfluous parliamentary participation in this field, which it considers to be executive business.

The above comparison regarding parliamentary scrutiny of EU civilian missions on both sides of the Rhine confirms the existence of a considerable parliamentary weakness at the national level regarding EU security and defence, especially civilian crisis management.[68] The respective settings in place are not prone to foster accountability for conduct ($A_c$) as parliaments are left with little sanctioning powers. In addition, the French and German examples illustrate that there is generally little accountability for information ($A_i$) at the national level, because of the lack or circumvention of rules providing for the implication of national parliamentarians, diminishing the inquisitive powers of the fora.

Yet, peacebuilding missions are mostly mandated with wide-ranging tasks and responsibilities in the field of public governance and, moreover, increasingly contain a military component (hybrid missions). As a result of the relatively weak, formal national parliamentary powers, the structural shortage of information (provision) regarding CFSP/CSDP matters, problematic resource allocation within parliaments, and little political will stemming from MPs, we are left with both weak de jure and de facto accountability for information and accountability for conduct at the national level. This underwhelming parliamentary performance is alarming. It leads to EU peacebuilding—both its intergovernmental and its Europeanized facet—to a large extent going politically unchecked at the national level. In other words, current national parliamentary practice is at odds with the intergovernmental blueprint of the policy, which privileges national accountability channels—including in the parliamentary realm. In this light, it is not surprising that Geert de Baere concluded that, 'parliamentary control by Member States parliaments is a necessary complement to scrutiny by the European Parliament, [but] it cannot be a replacement'.[69] Indeed, the quasi-absence of national parliaments from political accountability processes highlights the importance of scrutiny by the EP to counterbalance the low level of national parliamentary oversight over EU peacebuilding activities.

[68] Anghel and others (n 3) 75.
[69] de Baere (n 7) 169.

## 3. The European Parliament: An Upgraded Accountability Forum

In line with the Member States' preference for an intergovernmental institutional and procedural framework regarding the CFSP/CSDP, Treaty law lays down a low-profile involvement of the EP. The institution is referenced twice in the chapter on foreign and security policy (Title V, Chapter 1), while no explicit mention of it is made in the chapter on security and defence (Title V, Chapter 2). The 'specific role' of the EP in this policy field (Article 24(1) TEU) is defined in Article 36 TEU, which reads as follows:

> The High Representative of the Union for Foreign Affairs and Security Policy shall regularly consult the European Parliament on the main aspects and the basic choices of the common foreign and security policy and the common security and defence policy and inform it of how those policies evolve. He shall ensure that the views of the European Parliament are duly taken into consideration. Special representatives may be involved in briefing the European Parliament.
>
> The European Parliament may address questions or make recommendations to the Council or the High Representative. Twice a year it shall hold a debate on progress in implementing the common foreign and security policy, including the common security and defence policy.

The above Treaty provision assigns the EP relatively little consultation and information rights and thereby formally bestows the institution with a modest and primarily passive role in the area of the CFSP and CSDP. This is also echoed in Declaration 14, stressing that 'the provisions covering the Common Foreign and Security Policy do not . . . increase the role of the European Parliament'.[70]

### 3.1 Marginalization of parliamentary scrutiny

The marginalization of supranational parliamentary scrutiny follows the traditional allocation of powers in this area at the EU level.[71] When foreign policy was first codified at the EU level in 1986, Article 30(4) of the Single European Act stipulated that the EP was to be *closely associated* with European Political Cooperation and had to be *kept informed* about foreign policy discussions taking place. The Treaty of

[70] Consolidated Version of the Treaty on European Union (TEU) [2016] OJ C202/343, Declaration 14 concerning the common foreign and security policy.

[71] For an overview of the development of supranational parliamentary scrutiny regarding European foreign affairs issues, see Ramses A Wessel, 'Good Governance and EU Foreign, Security and Defence Policy' in Deirdre M Curtin and Ramses A Wessel (eds), *Good Governance and the European Union: Reflection on Concepts, Institutions and Substance* (Intersentia 2005) 217–19.

Maastricht (1992) modified the wording, which was to remain unaltered until the latest Treaty revision: the article at stake laid down that the EP had to be *consulted* and *kept regularly informed* about the development of the EU's foreign policy.[72] Yet, despite the modified wording, the obligations incumbent on other actors (eg the Council and the European Commission (the Commission), and later the High Representative (HR)) remained vague in terms of substance, procedure, and timing.[73] In practice, this resulted in many informational bottlenecks—a situation that could partly have been remedied with the creation of the post of the HR in 1999.[74] Only in the latest Treaty revision (which entered into force in 2009) was the frequency of annual parliamentary debates on CFSP/CSDP matters increased from one to two.

But even though the EP has been given slightly more information, debating, and consultation rights over time, it enjoys a much less comfortable position than in other EU polices bearing an external dimension.[75] Essential in this regard is that, according to past and current Treaty provisions, information flows from different institutions (above all the HR) to the EP: it is consulted on the main aspects and basic choices of the CFSP and CSDP, and is informed on how they evolve, notably through an annual report from the Council. The EP has, however, no meaningful instruments at its disposal to influence or alter this one-way communication channel. In addition to the Members of the European Parliament (MEPs) being information-recipients (not inquirers), primary law stipulates that MEPs have to be informed about general policy trends only—*main aspects* and *basic choices*—without, however, being able to scrutinize individual decisions or actions. It has been noticed that this situation grants the EP even less information and fewer consultation rights than under the consultation procedure,[76] which offers the institution the lowest level of involvement in supranational EU decision-making.[77] What is more, the main decision-makers, namely the European Council and the Council, and by extension the PSC, remain unaccountable to the EP even if MEPs can ask questions or make recommendations to the Council (or the HR). All of the above elements lead to the conclusion that the CFSP and, by extension, the CSDP look like a 'parliamentary vacuum'[78] compared to other external policies of the EU when limiting one's assessment to primary law.

[72] Art J.7 TEU (Maastricht); Art 21 TEU (Amsterdam); Art 21 TEU (Nice).

[73] Wessel (n 71) 219; de Baere (n 7) 161; Peters, Wagner and Deitelhoff (n 7) 79. This observation, which was made with regard to a prior Treaty version, is still valid.

[74] Wessel (n 71) 221.

[75] Huff (n 4) 12–13. See several insightful studies contained in the edited volume Kolja Raube, Meltem Müftüler-Baç, and Jan Wouters (eds), *Parliamentary Cooperation and Diplomacy in EU External Relations. An Essential Companion* (Edward Elgar 2019).

[76] Thym (n 7) 112–13.

[77] The consultation procedure falls under the category of the special legislative procedure set out in Art 289(2) TFEU. In the event of a consultation procedure, the Council—the sole legislator in practice—is not legally obliged to take into account (but must await) the opinion voiced by EP, which may approve, reject, or propose amendments to a legislative proposal.

[78] Thym (n 7) 110, 111.

This parliamentary vacuum is worsened by another distinctive normative feature, namely the preclusion of legislative acts in the CFSP. Both Article 24(1) TEU and Article 31(1) TEU stipulate that under the CFSP '[t]he adoption of legislative acts shall be excluded'. The CFSP decision-making procedure follows neither the ordinary legislative procedure (the former co-decision procedure), which 'consists in the joint adoption by the EP and the Council of a regulation, directive or decision on a proposal from the Commission' (Article 289(1) Treaty on the Functioning of the European Union (TFEU)), nor the special legislative procedure (Article 289(2) TFEU).[79] This particular status is corroborated by the fact that legal acts adopted by either legislative procedure (ordinary or special) constitute legislative acts,[80] which are precluded in the area of foreign policy, security, and defence.

These Treaty provisions on the preclusion of legislative acts in the area of the CFSP can be understood as a relic of the aborted Treaty Establishing a Constitution for Europe, which differentiated between legislative acts and *non*-legislative acts.[81] The determining factor for acts to fall into the former or latter category was primarily the *procedure* employed to adopt the act and not its *substance*.[82] In other words, acts adopted with the participation of the EP and the Council were qualified as legislative acts as they satisfied the democratic standards of representation, whereas non-legislative acts did not.[83] As a general rule, legislative acts were subject to the ordinary legislative procedure (formerly co-decision);[84] non-legislative acts, in contrast, would follow a procedure without parliamentary participation.[85] According to this typology, the acts that could be adopted under the CFSP/CSDP were European decisions,[86] that is to say non-legislative acts binding in their entirety.[87] Even though this differentiation between legislative and non-legislative acts has not made its way into the Treaty of Lisbon, the idea of a 'legislative'

[79] Art 289 (2) TFEU stipulates that '[i]n the specific cases provided for by the Treaties, the adoption of a regulation, directive or decision by the European Parliament with the participation of the Council, or by the latter with the participation of the European Parliament, shall constitute a special legislative procedure'.

[80] Art 289(3) TFEU.

[81] Art I-34; Art I-35.

[82] Alexander Türk, 'The Concept of the "Legislative" Act in the Constitutional Treaty' (2005) 6 German Law Journal 1554, 1557.

[83] The Final Report of Working Group IX on Simplification of 29 November 2002 outlines (on page 2) that '[t]he democratic legitimacy of the Union is founded on its States and peoples, and consequently an act of a legislative nature must always come from the bodies which represent those States and peoples, namely the Council and the Parliament. Procedures must therefore be reviewed to ensure that they respect this simple principle: acts which have the same nature and the same legal effect must be produced by the same democratic procedure.' Final Report of Working Group IX on Simplification of 29 November 2002, CONV 424/02.

[84] Art I-34 (1–3).

[85] Non-legislative acts entailed European regulations, European decisions, recommendations, and opinions.

[86] Art I-40 (3); Art I-40 (6–7); Art I-41 (4).

[87] Art I-33.

procedure requiring parliamentary involvement has been maintained. And as general normative action is excluded from the policy at stake,[88] no legislative acts can be adopted in the context of the CFSP, where the role of the EP is de jure reduced to that of an informed spectator.[89]

This legal construction is, however, somewhat paradoxical. At first sight, one might think that the approach favouring procedure over substance leads to a reduced margin of executive manoeuvre in the field of the CFSP, notably because policy-makers cannot take normative action. However, this conclusion is misleading. Foreign policy is, per definition, more executive than legislative in nature; the adoption of legislative acts is thus the exception and not the rule. Preventing this exception from happening on the grounds of procedural considerations is therefore tautological. In theory, the participation of the EP is to ensure that democratic standards of representation are upheld. Where the standard is not met, legislative activity is precluded. But as legislative activity is generally low in foreign and security policy, the emphasis on procedure—instead of substance—in practice excludes the EP from overseeing mostly *non*-legislative activities *tout court*.

What do these de jure arrangements imply for political accountability? First, the primary institutional interface for the EP in the field of foreign policy is the HR, and so political accountability is diverted: while decision-makers remain out of parliamentary reach, accountability is channelled through the HR, a person in charge of implementation or, for crisis management, of representation. Secondly, the framework for parliamentary involvement set out by the Treaty of Lisbon is at odds with the three-stage accountability model used in this book. The modest political accountability exercised by the EP provided for by Treaty law already fails at the very first stage, namely the provision of information. Even though primary rules prescribe that the EP ought to receive some information, the quality and quantity of the information to be provided does not allow MEPs to kick off the accountability mechanism; the informational threshold is not reached. In addition to there being little room for scrutiny (stage 2), there is also an absence of formal sanctioning mechanisms (stage 3) in Treaty law. Furthermore, the procedure-oriented approach to the (non-)involvement of the EP eventually undermines democratic representation. In the end, the framework set out by primary law, by and large excluding the EP from the CFSP/CSDP, considerably hampers $A_i$ and equally impedes $A_c$.

88 Piet Eeckhout, 'The EU's Common Foreign and Security Policy After Lisbon: From Pillar Talk to Constitutionalism' in Andrea Biondi, Piet Eeckhout, and Stefanie Ripley (eds), *EU Law After Lisbon* (Oxford University Press 2012) 279–84.

89 Art 36 TEU.

## 3.2 Four successful strategies for increasing accountability

Yet, the EP—with the Committee on Foreign Affairs (AFET) and its subcommittee on Security and Defence (SEDE)[90]—has managed to extend its restricted role as an accountability forum in CFSP/CSDP matters programmed by the Treaty drafters. As the following analysis illustrates, the EP did so by taking a number of 'backdoors': by means of (i) interinstitutional agreements (IIAs),[91] (ii) litigation at the Court of Justice of the European Union (CJEU), and (iii) through intra-institutional practice, as well as (iv) day-to-day interinstitutional routine, the EP has extended its severely limited information and consultation rights outside the formal procedures of Treaty revision. In this way, the EP got hold of many Europeanized aspects of civilian crisis management (ie the activities of the Brussels-based bureaucracy) and even positioned itself as a suitable political forum for the scrutiny of intergovernmental aspects (ie decision-making).

### 3.2.1 Using the power of the purse

The first vector to enhanced parliamentary involvement in CFSP/CSDP matters constituted budgetary procedures, in which the EP plays a role. This is somewhat paradoxical as parliamentary control by the EP over expenses arising from CFSP actions had initially not been considered an option by the Treaty drafters as it implied the incursion of supranational policy-making modes and actors into a vigorously shielded intergovernmental policy field.[92] But both de jure and de facto aspects eventually opened a small backdoor for increased parliamentary involvement—and the EP gladly seized the opportunity to engage in a protracted but successful struggle to gain and eventually expand its 'power of the purse' concerning the CFSP/CSDP.[93]

The bone of contention was a 'constitutional oddity'[94] introduced by the Treaty of Maastricht (1992), according to which, in parallel with individual contributions by Member States, funds of the European Community could be used to finance the implementation of measures falling outside Community policies, namely the CFSP

[90] The AFET Committee, named after the acronym of its French title '*Affaires étrangères*', has two sub-committees: Human Rights (DROI) and Security and Defence (SEDE).

[91] As set out by Article 295 TFEU, '[t]he European Parliament, the Council and the Commission shall consult each other and by common agreement make arrangements for their cooperation. To that end, they may, in compliance with the Treaties, conclude interinstitutional agreements which may be of a binding nature.'

[92] Jörg Monar, 'The Finances of the Union's Intergovernmental Pillars: Tortuous Experiments with the Community Budget' (1997) 35 Journal of Common Market Studies 57, 60–61; Esther Barbé and Anna Herranz Surralés, 'The Power and Practice of the European Parliament in Security Policies' in Dirk Peters, Wolfgang Wagner, and Nicole Deitelhoff (eds), *The Parliamentary Control of European Security Policy* (ARENA 2008) 77.

[93] On this lengthy battle, see the description in Monar (n 92); Andreas Maurer, Daniela Kietz, and Christian Völkel, 'Interinstitutional Agreements in the CFSP: Parliamentarization through the Back Door?' (2005) 10 European Foreign Affairs Review 175; Barbé and Herranz Surralés (n 92).

[94] Monar (n 92) 59.

and Justice and Home Affairs (JHA).[95] In addition, a distinction between *administrative* and *operating* expenses was inserted that proved problematic because it gave rise to different budgetary procedures. On the one hand, operating expenditure arising from the implementation of the CFSP was subject to the regular budget procedure, and therefore implied the involvement of the EP.[96] Administrative expenditure, on the other hand, was tied to the costs incurred by the involved institutions. The handling of these administrative expenses, however, varied considerably for the Commission and the Council. On the basis of a Gentlemen's Agreement reached in 1970 between the Council and the EP, the two institutions refrained from scrutinizing each other's administrative expenditure.[97] As a consequence, parliamentary oversight for administrative expenses of the Council for CFSP matters was out of sight. Hence, Member States tried to label as much CFSP expenditure as possible as 'administrative' Council expenditure to preclude parliamentary scrutiny.[98] In other words, intergovernmental activities could be financed through supranational funds without involvement or prior MEP consent.[99]

Parliamentarians were, of course, unsatisfied with the arrangement and made fervent attempts to change the situation. In 1996, for instance, the EP requested a report from the European Court of Auditors (ECA) on the conditions governing the implementation of expenditure under the CFSP. The ECA report fleshed out major problems with funding for CFSP activities.[100] The EP then tabled a resolution denouncing the structural flaws inherent to the CFSP financing based on the findings of the ECA.[101] In addition, persisting practical hurdles and bottlenecks in the financing of CFSP actions through Member State contributions occurred, sobering the Council's expectations of charging more expenses to national budgets and less to the EU budget.[102] Finally, the EP's perseverance as well as the Council's realistic stance paved the way for the conclusion of an IIA on budgetary matters in 1997 between the EP, the Council, and the Commission, which has been subsequently amended several times (most recently in 2013).[103]

[95] Art J.11.2 TEU (Maastricht); Art K.8 TEU (Maastricht); and Art 199(2) TEC (Maastricht).

[96] Art J.11 and K.8 TEU (Maastricht).

[97] Barbé and Herranz Surrallés (n 92) 84–87; Monar (n 92) 59–60.

[98] Barbé and Herranz Surrallés (n 92) 84.

[99] Monar (n 92) 59–61; Peters, Wagner, and Deitelhoff (n 7) 77.

[100] Avis n°1/1997 de la Cour des Comptes sur les conditions régissant l'exécution des dépenses dans le cadre de la politique étrangère et de sécurité commune (PESC).

[101] Minutes of the sitting of Friday 19 December 1997 [1998] OJ C14/409.

[102] Barbé and Herranz Surrallés (n 92) 85–86.

[103] Interinstitutional agreement of 2 December 2013 between the European Parliament, the Council and the Commission on budgetary discipline, on cooperation in budgetary matters and on sound financial management [2013] OJ C 373/01; Interinstitutional agreement between the European Parliament, the Council and the Commission on budgetary discipline and sound financial management (2006/C 139/01) [2006] OJ C 139/1; Interinstitutional agreement of 6 May 1999 between the European Parliament, the Council and the Commission on budgetary discipline and improvement of the budgetary procedure [1999] C 172/1; Resolution on the proposal for an Interinstitutional agreement between the European Parliament, the Council and the European Commission on provisions regarding financing of the Common Foreign and Security Policy (A4-0249/97), Annex: Interinstitutional

The abovementioned constitutional oddity—the use of supranational funds for intergovernmental activities—subsists until today in law and practice. According to Article 41(1)–(2) TEU, both administrative expenditure and operating expenditure without military and defence implications arising from CFSP/CSDP activities are charged to the EU budget. This oddity, however, is smoothed out by complementary provisions contained in section E of the aforementioned 2013 IIA on budgetary matters,[104] regulating the concrete conditions of parliamentary control over CFSP expenses (including costs incurred for peacebuilding missions). Point 24 of the said IIA stipulates that the amount of budgetary appropriations allocated to the CFSP (operating costs) have to be agreed upon by the Council and the EP annually,[105] and that the total amount of CFSP operating expenditure has to be entered into one budget chapter of the EU budget (Chapter 19.03), entailing a specific line for civilian crisis management missions.[106]

The number of exchanges between the EP and other institutional actors were considerably increased by the stipulations of the IIA: joint consultation meetings with the HR have to be held at least five times a year (first sub-paragraph of point 25),[107] and the Commission has to inform the MEPs on a quarterly basis about the implementation of CFSP activities and financial forecasts (last sub-paragraph of point 25). Moreover, the 2013 IIA (third sub-paragraph of point 25) entails the obligation for the HR to inform the EP 'immediately, and in any event no later than five working days' after a decision containing expenditure is taken by the Council, which means that parliamentarians have to be provided with a *fiche financière*. This also implies that the Council has to keep MEPs up to date on individual decisions (with financial implications); this, however, is not programmed by primary law, as outlined above. In addition, the HR has to consult the EP each year 'on a forward-looking document' regarding financial matters, main aspects, and basic choices of

agreement between the European Parliament, the Council and the European Commission on provisions regarding financing of the Common Foreign and Security Policy [1997] OJ C 286/80.

104 IIA on budgetary matters (2013).

105 According to point 24 of the 2013 IIA, in the absence of an agreement, 'the amount contained in the previous budget or the amount proposed in the draft budget, whichever is lower' shall be entered in the budget.

106 The budgetary envelop dedicated to the CFSP forms part of the resources allocated to different EU policies in the field of external relations. These policies are contained in Title 19 'Foreign Policy Instruments' of the EU budget allocated to the Commission (section III). The CFSP budget is outlined in Chapter 3 of said Title (19.03), and the expenditure for civilian crisis management missions is listed under the budgetary line 19.03.01, entitled 'Support to preservation of stability through Common Foreign and Security Policy (CFSP) missions and European Union Special Representatives'. On the different steps of the budgetary procedure and their development over time, see Günter Sautter, 'The Financing of Common Foreign and Security Policy—on Continuity and Change' in Hermann-Josef Blanke and Stelio Mangiameli (eds), *The European Union after Lisbon: Constitutional Basis, Economic Order and External Action* (Springer 2012) 572–74.

107 The formalization of the joint consultation meetings was, to a large extent, the result of a fierce confrontation between the EP and the Council in the run-up to the re-negotiations over the IIA in 2006. For more information on this issue, see Barbé and Herranz Surralés (n 92) 81.

the CFSP according to the first sub-paragraph of point 25 of the said IIA. The crucial element here is the adjective *forward-looking*, as it explicitly introduces an ex ante consultation mechanism. This fundamental change is the result of a lengthy battle fought by the EP with the Council over parliament's timely consultation regarding choices on future foreign policy developments.[108] The declaration by the HR on political accountability of 2009 contains, however, many adjectives that seem to reduce the leeway for ex ante consultation as they leave a wide margin of appreciation to the decision-makers. Paragraph 1 states that '[a]ny exchanges of views prior to the adoption of mandates and strategies in the area of CFSP will take place in the *appropriate* format, *corresponding to the sensitivity and confidentiality* of the topics discussed'.[109]

The above attenuating elements notwithstanding, complementary arrangements of the IIA regarding budgetary control have important implications for the role of the EP in the context of civilian crisis management. The EP's 'hard' power is increased by joint consultation meetings involving both AFET and the Committee on Budgets (BUDG). In these meetings, formally scheduled to discuss expenses, a small delegation of MEPs can *in camera* debate all sorts of issues related to CFSP matters with the Chair of the PSC and alongside experts from the Commission.[110] This gives MEPs (indirectly) some operational insight.

But it should not be forgotten that considerable amounts spent on civilian crisis management missions are supported by the Member States, which bear all expenditure related to seconded personnel, including salaries, medical coverage, and travel expenses;[111] here, the principle of 'costs lie where they fall' applies. This, in turn, implies that the EP is not overseeing total spending related to civilian missions because not all expenditure is charged to the EU budget. These intergovernmental funding streams have been qualified by the EP as 'shadow budgets', which are allegedly preventing a coherent and comprehensive budgetary control by the institution.[112]

All in all, the IIA on budgetary matters strengthened the position of the EP as an accountability forum in CFSP matters. As regards the provision of information (stage 1), both the quality and quantity of information shared with the MEPs has increased. This in principle enables the EP to better follow policy developments and keep track of implementation issues, and thereby increased the EP's inquisitive

[108] On the EP's struggle for ex ante consultation, see for instance de Baere (n 7) 161–62.

[109] Emphasis added. The stance adopted by the EP on the consultation and provision of information to the institution in the context of the CFSP reads less attenuated. See in particular Rule 112, Rules of Procedure of the European Parliament, 8th parliamentary term, July 2016.

[110] The Rules of Procedures of the European Parliament spell out that '[e]xceptionally, at the request of the Vice-President/High Representative, a committee may decide to hold its proceedings in camera'. Rule 112(2), ibid.

[111] Council Doc 7291/09 of 10 March 2009, 'Guidelines for allowances for seconded staff participating in EU civilian crisis management missions'. See further Sautter (n 106) 569; Barbé and Herranz Surrallés (n 92) 92.

[112] Barbé and Herranz Surrallés (n 92) 92.

power. As a result, the scrutiny by the EP has been intensified in terms of frequency and substance (stage 2). Via additional agreements, MEPs are able to ask pointed questions to representatives of the Council and the EEAS. This is, for instance, what happened when the corruption scandal surrounding the rule of law mission to Kosovo (EULEX) erupted in late 2014: MEPs asked for an ad hoc meeting with representatives of the PSC and the relevant EEAS crisis management structures. As for the last stage (sanctions), the EP has managed to augment its power of the purse: it can theoretically reject the amount proposed for CFSP activities, including civilian crisis management, and can moreover refuse to approve a discharge. But this is a last-resort measure, not least because it is very likely to prompt negative responses by the Council, which might in turn be tempted to increase the use of extra-budgetary expenditure through Member State contributions.[113] In other words, there are sanctioning powers in theory, to which the EP will not want to resort to in practice.

In sum, the institution strengthened $A_i$ and has also attained some $A_c$ through the enhanced control of budgetary spending. Importantly, these achievements regarding budgetary overview, and thus political accountability by the EP, have been recognized and refined by the 2009 declaration on political accountability made by the HR. In particular, the importance of joint consultation meetings with AFET and BUDG were underscored.[114]

### 3.2.2 Accessing sensitive information: a highly contentious issue

Another major improvement in terms of consultation and information rights was achieved in 2002 through the conclusion of another IIA, namely the one on sensitive information relating to the CSDP, which grants a small group of MEPs access to classified documents.[115] The conclusion of the agreement was, however, preceded by severe turbulences and laborious negotiations.[116] A crucial element in this regard was that Member States would initially not want to disclose to MEPs classified information that they either would not have to or would not want to share with national parliamentarians.[117] There were several important factors eventually leading to the conclusion of the 2002 IIA, despite initial (inter)governmental resistance. On the one hand, the Council had come to acknowledge that the EP had

[113] The financing mechanism for military operations, ALTHEA, was described to have in large parts resulted from such discontentment. See Thym (n 7) 116.

[114] European Parliament legislative resolution of 8 July 2010 on the proposal for a Council decision establishing the organisation and functioning of the European External Action Service (08029/2010 – C7-0090/2010 – 2010/0816(NLE)), P7_TA(2010)0280, Annex: Declaration by the High Representative on political accountability para 1.

[115] Interinstitutional agreement of 20 November 2002 between the European Parliament and the Council concerning access by the European Parliament to sensitive information of the Council in the field of security and defence policy [2002] OJ C298/01) pt 3.

[116] A detailed account of these negotiations can be found in Rosén (n 35).

[117] ibid 383, 389.

a legitimate role to play in the democratic scrutiny of the CSDP.[118] On the other hand, this realization had certainly been helped by the stick-and-carrot strategy pursued by the EP, of which recourse to the CJEU (or the threat thereof) was a central piece.

The Court's jurisprudence indeed opened a door for public access to certain types of documents, a subject matter that is intrinsically linked to the access of sensitive documents by parliamentarians. The cases under judicial scrutiny being discussed in the chapter on legal accountability,[119] it is important to briefly summarize the major dicta of the EU judicature at this point. In 1999 the Court of First Instance held that the Council could deny access to documents if their disclosure could have negative repercussions for the international relations of the EU according to an evaluation of their content and context.[120] Partial disclosure had to be granted to those parts of the documents not falling under the exceptions regime.[121] Also, the Court of First Instance found itself competent to scrutinize whether the procedural rules of (not) granting access had been respected by the Council, and this reasoning was upheld by the Court of Justice.[122]

Against this jurisdictional backdrop, the Council adopted a decision pertaining to public access to Council documents in August 2000.[123] The said decision, amended on the basis of provisions contained in a decision of the HR Solana of July 2000 on measures for the protection of classified information applicable to the General Secretariat of the Council,[124] led to the 'Solana coup', by which all Council documents classified *très secrèt*, *secrèt*, or *confidentiel* related to EU security and defence matters with or without military implications—thus both military operations and civilian missions—were per default excluded from public access.[125] Not amused by this drastic limitation of public access to Council documents, both the Dutch government and the EP launched an action before the CJEU to annul the decision.[126] In early 2001 the Council adopted new rules regulating public access to documents and again MEPs brought the matter to the Court in Luxembourg.

[118] ibid 390–91; Barbé and Herranz Surralés (n 92) 81.

[119] See Chapter 6.

[120] Case T–14/98 *Heidi Hautala v Council* [1999] EU:T:1999:157 para 72; Case T–188/98 *Aldo Kuijer v Council* [2000] EU:T:2000:101 paras 36–48. This reasoning was again unfolded and corroborated in a judgment delivered in 2002. See Case T–211/00 *Aldo Kuijer v Council* [2002] EU:T:2002:30 paras 60–64.

[121] Case T–14/98 [1999] para 87.

[122] ibid 72, 76. The Court of Justice upheld the 1999 first instance decision in a judgment delivered in 2001. Case C–353/99 *P Council v Heidi Hautala* [2001] EU:C:2001:661 paras 22–31.

[123] Council Decision 2000/527/EC of 14 August 2000 amending Decision 93/731/EC on public access to Council documents and Council Decision 2000/23/EC on the improvement of information on the Council's legislative activities and the public register of Council documents [2000] OJ L212/9.

[124] Decision of the Secretary-General of the Council/High Representative for the Common Foreign and Security Policy of 27 July 2000 on measures for the protection of classified information applicable to the General Secretariat of the Council [2000] OJ C239/1.

[125] Art 2(1) Council Decision 2000/527/EC [2000] OJ L212/9.

[126] Case C–369/00 *Netherlands v Council* (removed from the register by order of 6 March 2002 by the President of the Court); Case C–387/00 *European Parliament v Council* (removed from the register by order of 22 March 2002 by the President of the Court).

With the action for annulment pending, the negotiations on rules governing *public* access to documents and *parliamentary* access to sensitive documents continued. In October 2001 the contested Council decision was replaced by a regulation that echoed the Solana classification of documents excluded from public access presented above.[127] Yet, as the question of access by MEPs to sensitive CSDP documents remained unresolved, a deal was struck to pave the way for a separate IIA on access to sensitive (CSDP) matters. The EP, for its part, withdrew its pending action for annulment at the Court in Luxembourg,[128] and adopted internal rules on the handling of sensitive information.[129] The Council in turn knew that it could not, for reputational reasons, maintain its stance to keep MEPs away from any classified CSDP documents and so agreed to the compromise proposed by the EP to grant access to sensitive documents in accordance with best national practices.[130]

In the end, point 3.3 of the 2002 IIA on sensitive information provides for a 'special committee', composed by the Chairman of AFET and four specifically designated MEPs, which can gain access to sensitive information—documents classified *confidentiel UE* and above—on the premises determined by the Council.[131] Meetings with the HR, or with a substitute, take place every six weeks and can follow an ad hoc demand submitted by the EP. The information-sharing arrangement in place enables some 'elite-accountability'[132] in matters pertaining to the CSDP—especially for civilian crisis management—which is, however, limited in informational scope and substantive impact on (future) policy decision of the Council, as scrutiny is not public and the possibility of sanctions largely missing. Still, '[a]lthough security-cleared MEPs cannot share this confidential information with other MEPs, it can be useful for them for giving general advice for the EP's positioning'.[133] Access to sensitive documents results in more discursive interaction with external actors, in particular the HR and representatives from relevant crisis management units of the EEAS, and within the EP. This underscores that the 'availability of information frames and reframes debates',[134] even if this availability is restricted. In sum, the 2002 IIA allows the EP to keep a close eye on the dedicated

[127] Art 9(1) Regulation (EC) 1049/2001 of the European Parliament and of the Council of 30 May 2001 regarding public access to European Parliament, Council and Commission documents [2001] OJ L145/43. To be read in conjunction with Council Decision 2001/264/EC of 19 March 2001 adopting the Council's security regulations [2001] OJ L101/1.

[128] Rosén (n 35) 392.

[129] European Parliament Decision of 23 October 2002 on the implementation of the Interinstitutional agreement governing European Parliament access to sensitive Council information in the sphere of security and defence policy.

[130] Art 4 IIA on access to sensitive information.

[131] Parliamentarians involved need to have obtained a security clearance. Art 4(1) Rules of Procedure of the European Parliament, 8th parliamentary term, July 2016, ANNEX VII: Confidential and sensitive documents and information.

[132] Rosén (n 35) 385.

[133] Barbé and Herranz Surralés (n 92) 89.

[134] Albert Meijer, 'Understanding the Complex Dynamics of Transparency' (2013) 73 Public Administration Review 429, 431.

Europeanized administrative structures in Brussels in charge of preparing and implementing civilian missions.

But even if the access to documents was enhanced by the provisions of the pertinent IIA, there is still room for improvement. The 2002 IIA covers only documents labelled *confidentiel UE*, *secret UE*, and *très secret UE*. The vast majority of classified documents in the Council's register are, however, tagged *restreint UE*.[135] It has also to be mentioned at this point that MEPs have complained about the over-classification of CFSP documents.[136] Moreover, *limité* documents—that is internal Council documents used in the course of decision-making, which account for a third of documents registered with the Council[137]—are not included in the 2002 IIA.[138] That means that MEPs cannot consult a large amount of documents pertaining to the CSDP that are potentially relevant for parliamentary scrutiny, so that the provision of information rests in part on informal channels. Therefore, attempts were made by the HR (starting in 2012) to revise the existing arrangements,[139] but the negotiations on access to sensitive CSDP documents have ended in a stalemate, while in 2014 an Interinstitutional agreement was reached on the forwarding and handling of classified information held by the Council *except* for CFSP matters.[140]

In sum, the opening of some classified files to MEPs does not directly lead to the EP holding executive actors to account; but it leads to well-informed internal parliamentary debates (stage 2) and greater awareness, which in turn better positions MEPs to hold decision-makers to account within the limits of the powers formally and informally conferred to them (stage 3). The information rights accorded to the EP, including the increased interaction of MEPs with external actors, are underlined by the 2009 declaration on political accountability made by the HR.[141] As previously mentioned, the HR in 2012 followed up on her promise to 'review and where necessary propose to adjust the existing provisions on access for [MEPs] to classified documents and information in the field of security and defence policy' by

[135] On disclosure issues in the CFSP/CSDP realm, see Chapter 3.

[136] Guri Rosén, 'Secrecy versus Accountability. Parliamentary Scrutiny of EU Security and Defence Policy', *ARENA Working Paper 1/2014* (ARENA Centre for European Studies 2014) 15.

[137] See the numbers provided in Council Doc 10684/12 of 4 June 2012, 'Breakdown of documents by security classification levels' LIMITE.

[138] David Galloway, 'Classifying Secrets in the EU' (2014) 52 Journal of Common Market Studies 668, 672; Deirdre Curtin, 'Overseeing Secrets in the EU: A Democratic Perspective' (2014) 52 Journal of Common Market Studies 684, 685–686. This 30 per cent benchmark is stable, as Council Annual Report of Access to Documents of the last years confirm.

[139] Council Doc 15343/12 of 23 October 2012, 'Access by the European Parliament to classified information in the area of the Common Foreign and Security Policy' [proposal by the HR on a draft Arrangement].

[140] Interinstitutional agreement of 12 March 2014 between the European Parliament and the Council concerning the forwarding to and handling by the European Parliament of classified information held by the Council on matters other than those in the area of the common foreign and security policy [2014] OJ C95/1.

[141] Declaration by the High Representative on political accountability para 4.

proposing a draft agreement, which sought to allow parliamentarians to consult all types of classified EU documents, including those labelled *restreint UE*.[142] As the above evaluation underscores, the current regimes of access to sensitive information agreement does not imply more $A_c$ but heightens the chances to achieve $A_i$.

### 3.2.3 Jurisprudence backing democratic scrutiny of EU external action

The jurisprudence of the CJEU, to whom the EP had repeated recourse with a view to consolidating its involvement in CFSP matters, points in a similar direction. The contentious cases, which are discussed hereafter as they specifically regard the obligation incumbent upon the Council to keep the EP up to date on CFSP matters, concerned the conclusion of two international agreements in the context of the EU-led naval anti-piracy operation Atalanta in the Gulf of Aden—one with Mauritius in 2011,[143] and the other one with Tanzania in 2014.[144]

Essential in both court proceedings were the EP's information and consultation rights, that is, the Court's interpretation of Article 218(10) TFEU, which stipulates that '[t]he European Parliament shall be immediately and duly informed [by the Council] at all stages of the procedure'.[145] The Court of Justice held that this provision sets out an *information requirement*, which constitutes an *essential procedural requirement*, which extends to matters pertaining to the CFSP.[146] In both court cases, the judges found that an infringement of that information requirement had occurred, and therefore annulled the contested Council decisions while respectively maintaining their effect.[147] As the facts and reasoning of the two cases are discussed elsewhere in this book,[148] one can at this juncture underscore that the judgments rendered by the Court in 2014 and 2016 clearly emphasize the information rights of the EP on the grounds that the provision of information is a prerequisite of the modest democratic scrutiny of the EU's external action, which is made possible under the given primary law framework.[149] This reasoning must have provided the MEPs with great satisfaction: it resonates well with the

[142] Art 2 of the 2012 HR proposal on MEP access to sensitive CFSP documents.

[143] Council Decision 2011/640/CFSP of 12 July 2011 on the signing and conclusion of the Agreement between the European Union and the Republic of Mauritius on the conditions of transfer of suspected pirates and associated seized property from the European Union-led naval force to the Republic of Mauritius and on the conditions of suspected pirates after transfer [2011] OJ L254/1.

[144] Council Decision 2014/198/CFSP of 10 March 2014 on the signing and conclusion of the Agreement between the European Union and the United Republic of Tanzania on the conditions of transfer of suspected pirates and associated seized property from the European Union-led naval force to the United Republic of Tanzania [2014] OJ L108/1.

[145] This obligation had, in addition to primary law stipulations, been underlined by policy documents. See Declaration by the High Representative on political accountability para 2.

[146] Case C-658/11 *European Parliament v Council* [2014] EU:C:2014:2025 paras 79–80, 85; Case C-263/14 *European Parliament v Council* [2016] EU:C:2016:2436 para 70, 77, 84. AG Bot argued that Art 218(10) TFEU contained an information *obligation* for the Council. Case C-658/11 *European Parliament v Council* [2014] EU:C:2014:41, Opinion of AG Bot of 30 January 2014 para 143.

[147] Case C-658/11 [2014] para 94; Case C-263/14 [2016] para 92.

[148] See Chapter 6.

[149] Case C-658/11 [2014] para 79, 81; Case C-263/14 [2016] paras 70–71, 80, 84.

self-perception of the EP and, at the same time, corroborates its past achievements in the field of the CFSP.

The CJEU judgments indeed consolidate the EP as a forum for political accountability and strengthen its capacity to hold the Council to account for information ($A_i$). The decisions underline the obligation of the Council to provide the EP with information—ensuring that stage 1 and 2 of the accountability process work—and make clear that the EP has judicial means at its disposable to inflict sanctions to the Council in the event of non-compliance (stage 3). Yet, one should not overestimate the concrete impact of this jurisprudence on civilian CSDP. As regards peacebuilding activities, the international agreements concluded (eg Status of Mission Agreements or agreements with contributing third States) are based on standard documents and contain almost identical clauses. Increasing the information obligation incumbent upon the Council is thus symbolic in nature as, in reality, there is little surprise in these agreements. But even symbolic information-sharing can eventually improve substantive information-sharing and, hence, enhances the chances of accountability for information. The rather symbolic nature might also explain why the EP has so far not litigated on issues pertaining to EU peacebuilding activities, even though civilian CSDP is institutionally and operationally close to supranational external policies for which the EP already has a say.[150] So far, litigation has concentrated on other CFSP issues, with some potential positive implications for civilian crisis management. The increasing—and politically desired—rapprochement (or even interweaving) of activities carried out under civilian CSDP and the Area of Freedom Security and Justice (AFSJ) could, however, spark discontent and eventually end up in Luxembourg.[151]

### 3.2.4 Creating facts, expanding influence

Another vector for enhanced parliamentary oversight in the CFSP/CSDP field has been the capacity of the EP to make proactive use of the powers conferred to the institution and thereby consolidate and also extend their scope through practice. First, the EP has taken a proactive stance on the CFSP in general. Parliamentarians have produced numerous (own-initiative) reports, resolutions,[152] and recommendations on a range of foreign policy and defence matters, and have also commissioned research in this field.[153] Among the reports is the EP's annual assessment of the implementation of the CSDP, which the institution draws up in

[150] On the overlap of civilian CSDP with other, supranational EU policies, see Chapter 2.

[151] On this issue, see Chapter 6.

[152] Eg European Parliament resolution of 21 May 2015 on financing the Common Security and Defence Policy (2014/2258(INI)); European Parliament resolution of 21 May 2015 on the implementation of the Common Security and Defence Policy (based on the Annual Report from the Council to the European Parliament on the Common Foreign and Security Policy) (2014/2220(INI)).

[153] The SEDE Committee requested, for instance, an in-depth comparative study on parliamentary oversight of civilian and military CSDP missions (both at the European and national level), which paved the way for further research on this subject matter. Born and others (n 26).

response to the polished annual report delivered by the Council.[154] In addition, numerous hearings and exchanges of view on foreign affairs, security, and defence issues are held and parliamentary questions asked. Although these activities are not part of a formal procedure, they have generated considerable effects both in terms of agenda-setting[155] and policy substance,[156] even if some argue that they merely amount to no more than a '"virtual" parliamentary reality'.[157]

Secondly, the EP has also managed to exercise oversight over specific CSDP activities. MEPs have indeed been active in discussing ongoing and future operational activities carried out under the CSDP with representatives from the crisis management bureaucracy, and have, despite procedural hurdles, dispatched ad hoc delegations to crisis management missions and operations while or prior to deployment.[158] The EP has increased the scope of its oversight over CSDP practice programmed in primary law, and these achievements are also echoed in the 2009 declaration by the HR on political accountability.[159] Crucial in this regard has been the day-to-day parliamentary routine, incrementally consolidating developed practice regarding information-sharing and interinstitutional contacts, and long-term confidence building measures, especially with the Council.[160]

Both with regard to general CFSP/CSDP matters and particular crisis management activities, the EP wields its strongest political leverage as an accountability forum when it appears on the European political stage as a moral agitator.[161] In the case concerning corruption allegations surrounding EULEX Kosovo, for instance, the institution in late 2014 cleverly used several information channels to first trigger public awareness and attention (eg letter to the HR, press statements, interviews, hearings) and then to present itself as the EU's rule of law and democracy watchdog, stepping in to safeguard European normative standards. Even though this watchdog image does not per se confer to the EP any formal accountability role, it does indirectly increase its visibility, credibility, and, eventually, its importance as a political accountability forum. The parliamentary activism displayed by some MEPs with regard to CSDP matters has, at times, ameliorated the EP's stance during all stages of the accountability process (information-sharing, scrutiny, and sanction). Even if the sanctioning mechanisms at the disposal of the

[154] Eg the annual reports on the implementation of the CSDP. See, for instance, European Parliament report on the implementation of the Common Security and Defence Policy (based on the Annual Report from the Council to the European Parliament on the Common Foreign and Security Policy), 3 November 2016 (A8-0317/2016). See further European Parliament resolution of 12 December 2018 on the annual report on the implementation of the Common Foreign and Security Policy (2018/2097(INI)).

[155] de Baere (n 7) 166.

[156] Wessel (n 71) 223; Barbé and Herranz Surralés (n 92) 105.

[157] Thym (n 7) 120.

[158] Barbé and Herranz Surralés (n 92) 88–91; Born and others (n 26) 14.

[159] Declaration by the High Representative on political accountability para 4.

[160] Barbé and Herranz Surralés (n 92) 104.

[161] ibid.

EP remain weak in terms of codification or formality, they carry a considerable informal weight. An essential asset in this regard is that the EP knows how to go public with touchy issues. This blaming and shaming technique provides MEPs with a powerful tool of informal sanctioning for both the $A_i$ and $A_c$. Again, the EULEX corruption case epitomizes this point: after the EP had stepped in and made the misconduct both in Kosovo and Brussels public, the HR took mitigating measures—the commission of a report by an external expert—to reduce the risk of reputational damage. The EP has thus managed to kick off an accountability procedure within the crisis management machinery without any formal accountability arrangement providing for these proceedings.

## 3.3 Conditional interest: the difficult accountability sort of civilian crisis management

As the above analysis has shown, the EP managed to considerably improve its stance as an accountability forum in EU foreign affairs, security, and defence issues: while primary law leaves little parliamentary room for manoeuvre in CFSP/CSDP matters, the institution has de facto acquired more information and participation rights through IIAs, litigation, and day-to-day practice that allow for more debate and better scrutiny. In sum, $A_i$ in CFSP matters improved noticeably through the conclusions of two IIAs—one on information-sharing and one on budgetary matters—and by means of litigation. Likewise, $A_c$ for CFSP measures was (indirectly) enhanced through budgetary oversight and a proactive parliamentary stance on CFSP dossiers. This positive track record supposedly foreshadows an optimistic outlook on political accountability at the EU level regarding EU peacebuilding activities.

Yet, the EP's remarkable accountability achievements regarding CFSP have only marginal effects on the parliamentary scrutiny of EU civilian crisis management: whereas MEPs seem to display much interest in general CFSP questions and for military operations, parliamentary activity regarding civilian missions has remained low. What are the reasons for this parliamentary indifference to civilian CSDP? A look at the four factors impacting on political accountability—(i) formal and informal powers, (ii) information-sharing, (iii) resources, and (iv) political will—provides useful insights.

The formal powers of the EP are quite high for civilian missions and, in any case, higher than for the more closely followed military operations. That is because an important share of EU peacebuilding activities is financed through the EU budget. This gives MEPs in principle a say over money spent on civilian missions, both ex ante and ex post: parliamentarians have to strike a budget deal with the Council according to point 24 of the IIA on budgetary matters for the missions to come, and they have to give a discharge for past expenditure to the Commission (Article 319 of the TFEU), which is responsible for implementing the EU budget (Article 317 TFEU).[162] Yet, the responsibility to negotiate budget issues largely rests with the BUDG and not with AFET or SEDE, whose core function is CFSP/CSDP scrutiny. Both AFET and SEDE can provide sporadic directions, but BUDG is in the driving seat. This division of labour reduces the actual budgetary leverage of AFET/SEDE. This already moderate budgetary leverage was further lowered by the reduction of several budget items for civilian crisis management under the CFSP budget (Chapter 19.03) to one major item with three to four sub-items for major civilian missions (such as EULEX Kosovo or EUPOL Afghanistan). This means that it has become far more difficult for the EP to block money for specific activities (ie single missions) and MEPs have generally no interest in blocking CFSP or civilian crisis management funding *tout court*. It is the nuclear option that no one wants to put into practice. The comparatively strong formal budgetary powers are thus attenuated by institutional and political circumstances, de facto reducing the institution's sanctioning powers. This in turn diminishes the otherwise positive prospects of $A_c$.

These attenuating elements notwithstanding, the EP's budget rights have provided the institution with an information advantage. In addition to the IIA on information-sharing in CFSP/CSDP matters, which gives the EP privileged access to CSDP information in general, the supplementary arrangements on CFSP spending allow for direct interaction with the Brussels-based bureaucracy (ie joint consultation meetings). This is an additional and highly important information channel for MEPs. Yet, this channel is in practice rarely used to discuss EU peacebuilding activities. In principle, the conditions for enhanced $A_i$ are good, but they are not used to specifically scrutinize civilian CSDP.

Why is this? The assumption put forward in this book is that the lack of parliamentary scrutiny of civilian crisis management is primarily the combined effect of two (mutually reinforcing) factors, namely (i) resources and (ii) political will. The workload of MEPs sitting in the AFET/SEDE committees is indeed considerable, and the same holds true for the respective Secretariats given the many topics and manifold activities to be followed. Therefore, parliamentary activity in this area is directed at priority issues. As in day-to-day parliamentary routines, (smaller) civilian missions tend to attract less attention than more visible military operations,[163] and so the former keep on flying under the radar of the EP's scrutiny. In addition—or as a result thereof—the expertise of MEPs and staff members is limited in the field of civilian missions.

[162] For an analysis of the precise role of the Commission as regards the implementation of the CFSP budget, see Sautter (n 106) 579–82.

[163] Barbé and Herranz Surrallés (n 92) 91, 100.

This brings us to political will aspects. As in the national realm, parliamentary scrutiny of civilian CSDP demands much time, specific expertise, and sufficient resources, but offers little political visibility or media attention in return. It is therefore to be expected that the EP's interest in EU peacebuilding activities suffers from a negative input–output relation. As a result, civilian CSDP activities are not a priority on the EP's agenda, and are thus rarely subject to debate—except if they present an opportunity to increase the EP's say over other (CFSP) policy dossiers or if they attract significant media attention, as was the case in the EULEX Kosovo corruption case. Thus, the political will to scrutinize EU civilian crisis management depends on its political salience in relation to other topical issues. In other words, the EP's interest in EU peacebuilding activities is conditional. Indeed, most MEPs view civilian crisis management (at best) as ancillary to military operations or as an entry point to broader CFSP issues. Hence, civilian CSDP activities are addressed only occasionally as part of other issues. Parliamentary interventions on specific civilian CSDP questions are a rarity—the engagement in the EULEX Kosovo case constitutes a praiseworthy exception. And so, in the abovementioned EP's annual assessment of the implementation of the CSDP, civilian missions are mentioned as a side note. Likewise, civilian crisis management plays a minor role in the 'virtual parliamentary reality' discussed in section 3.2.4. Consequently, civilian CSDP benefits very little from the EP's proactive stance on general CFSP matters. This sobering finding holds for both the intergovernmental aspects (ie high-level decision-making) and the Europeanized realities (ie day-to-day management by the Brussels-based bureaucracy) of EU peacebuilding. This, however, lowers the chances for effective political accountability—both for $A_i$ and for $A_c$—at the EU level.

## 4. Interparliamentary Turf Wars

The analysis above has shown that neither national parliaments nor the EP have, on their own, the necessary competences and capacities to thoroughly scrutinize EU security and defence matters, in particular EU peacebuilding activities. At the national level, some parliaments are able to keep track of executive decision-making with regard to EU security and defence, including at times the right of approval and/or oversight of civilian or civil military dispatches. At the EU level, parliamentarians have some budgetary leverage over civilian missions and enjoy consultation and information rights, both of which enable MEPs to keep an eye on the Brussels-based crisis management bureaucracy. While scattered across policy levels, these parliamentary oversight functions are complementary. Joining parliamentary forces across levels would therefore considerably increase political accountability as it would allow for decisive scrutiny of strategic, budgetary, and operational aspects of civilian CSDP. However, parliamentary cooperation across policy levels has proved difficult in practice where competition seems to outweigh complementarity—to the detriment of political accountability.

The tensions between the different parliamentary players have been stirred by the Treaty of Lisbon, which profoundly changed the parliamentary landscape in the field of EU security and defence. Prior to 2009 parliamentary oversight regarding the CFSP/CSDP was potentially in the hands of (at least) three parliamentary bodies: (i) the Assembly of the Western European Union (WEU), (ii) the EP, and (iii) Member State parliaments.[164] With the incorporation of the operational dimension of the WEU into EU primary law, the organization was dissolved in 2011, including its Assembly which had wide-ranging competences and expertise in European security and defence.[165] This necessary rearrangement of oversight functions brought up the core question of how parliamentary activity across policy levels would be remodelled in the absence of the WEU parliamentary body, leaving the parliamentary field to the EP and national parliaments.

The two parliamentary players had, however, diverging agendas. On the one hand, national parliaments attempted to strengthen their position in EU security and defence and act as key figures.[166] While the influence of national parliaments over EU security and defence had de facto weakened since the 2000s, the CFSP/CSDP remained de jure an intergovernmental policy field with political accountability formally being exercised by national parliaments. The EP was thus regarded as a superfluous parliamentary player.[167] On the other hand, the EP aimed to become a hub for parliamentary cooperation.[168] The institution had managed to considerably increase its parliamentary involvement in CSDP matters (ie budget prerogatives for civilian missions and access-to-information arrangements) and had established direct contact with EU security and defence decision-makers. It was eager to see this de facto and partially de jure reaffirmed position reflected in the arrangements on interparliamentary cooperation. Therefore, the EP proposed that MEPs should scrutinize the EU executive, while national MPs should oversee their respective government representatives.[169] This illustrates that, instead of understanding the scrutiny of EU security and defence as a joint responsibility,

[164] In the broader European security landscape, there was/is obviously also the respective Parliamentary Assembly of the North Atlantic Treaty Organization (NATO) and the Organization for Security and Co-operation in Europe (OSCE).

[165] Stefan Marschall, 'Transnational Parliamentary Assemblies and European Security Policy' in Dirk Peters, Wolfgang Wagner, and Nicole Deitelhoff (eds), *The Parliamentary Control of European Security Policy* (ARENA 2008) 115–19.

[166] Herranz Surrallés (n 16) 968–69.

[167] Huff (n 4) 8; Herranz Surrallés (n 16) 969.

[168] Herranz Surrallés (n 16) 965.

[169] European Parliament resolution of 7 May 2009 on the development of the relations between the European Parliament and national parliaments under the Treaty of Lisbon (2008/2120(INI)) para 18. In a similar vein, see Note by Elmar Brok and Roberto Gualtieri on parliamentary scrutiny of EU external action, including the common foreign security policy (CFSP) and the common security and defence policy (CSDP), following the entry into force of the Lisbon Treaty, draft version (7 November 2010).

both parliamentary levels conceived of interparliamentary cooperation as a zero-sum game.[170] As a consequence, this meant that neither the intergovernmental nor the Europeanized aspects of civilian crisis management would be subject to thorough parliamentary scrutiny.

The inconclusive wording of the Treaty of Lisbon did not help the situation.[171] Of particular importance are the provisions contained in Protocol no 1 on the role of national parliaments annexed to the Treaties. Under Title II, the said protocol deals expressly with interparliamentary cooperation, including in the field of foreign, security, and defence policy. The pertinent provisions read as follows:

> *Article 9.* The European Parliament and national Parliaments shall together determine the organisation and promotion of effective and regular interparliamentary cooperation within the Union.
>
> *Article 10.* A conference of Parliamentary Committees for Union Affairs may submit any contribution it deems appropriate for the attention of the European Parliament, the Council and the Commission. That conference shall in addition promote the exchange of information and best practice between national Parliaments and the European Parliament, including their special committees. It may also organise interparliamentary conferences on specific topics, in particular to debate matters of common foreign and security policy, including common security and defence policy. Contributions from the conference shall not bind national Parliaments and shall not prejudge their positions.

While Article 9 puts the EP and national parliaments on an equal footing as regards interparliamentary cooperation (even if the EP is mentioned first), Article 10 attributes to national parliaments the lead role as it gives them the right of initiative concerning the organization of cross-level parliamentary encounters. The implementation of these provisions caused major friction and has resulted in disrupting instead of fostering interparliamentary cooperation.[172] Cautious to shield their respective prestige and legitimacy,[173] both national parliaments and the EP tried to impose themselves as the dominant partner in the negotiation process. As the details of the long and tortuous negotiation process have been set out elsewhere,[174] the following analysis focuses on two major points of

[170] Anna Herranz-Surralés ascribes this parliamentary conflict to the 'mismatch between formal constitutional authority and the actual *parliamentary capital* that the EP [European Parliament] and the NPs [national parliaments] enjoy'. These competitive dynamics over (overlapping) authority are exacerbated by a zero-sum logic in case 'the growing parliamentary capital of one level appears to challenge the political and constitutional mandate of the other'. Herranz Surralés (n 16) 961.

[171] Barbé and Herranz Surralés (n 92) 102.

[172] Herranz Surralés (n 16) 961.

[173] ibid.

[174] Herranz Surralés (n 16). See also Jan Wouters and Kolja Raube, 'Seeking CSDP Accountability Through Interparliamentary Scrutiny' (2012) 47 The International Spectator 149, 155–59.

disagreement in the final stages of the negotiations (ie after the entry into force of the Treaty of Lisbon).

The first contentious issue was the format of interparliamentary cooperation: a parliamentary *conference* or a parliamentary *assembly*, the two differing considerably in composition and institutionalization. Whereas the former is composed of national delegations of equal size, the delegations to the latter reflect the (population) size of member countries and political groupings of the respective national parliaments. Also, a parliamentary conference is organized along national lines, whereas a parliamentary assembly operates on the basis of transnational parliamentary groups with specialized committees. Another distinguishing feature is that a conference has no specialized secretariat (it is chaired by a rotating presidency), in contrast to an assembly, which has a permanent secretariat. Despite the wording of Protocol no 1 hinting in the direction of a parliamentary conference, the WEU Assembly advocated for the latter option.[175] It proposed the establishment of a bicameral parliamentary body to oversee the CSDP, with the EP as the first and the WEU Assembly as the second chamber.[176] This proposal, however, was not backed by MEPs who opined that the wording of the Treaty provisions did not envisage the establishment of a new autonomous parliamentary body.[177] In addition, national parliamentarians refused to accept a constellation privileging the EP.[178] Quite to the contrary, many national MPs wanted to preserve the intergovernmental blueprint of the CSDP, thus asserting their own control competences.[179] Telling in this regard is the 2011 report issued by the House of Commons, underlining that,

> [t]he inter-governmental nature of decision-making in the CFSP and CSDP means that parliamentary scrutiny of these policies should not be left to the European Parliament alone; the significance of the CFSP and CSDP activities to which national governments may agree in the European Council and EU Council means that national parliaments have an important role in holding national governments to account. Inter-parliamentary oversight of the CFSP and CSDP should be continued, *with national parliaments taking the lead* [and proposing that the meetings of the future interparliamentary conference] will, as a general rule, be held in Brussels, in the Council building or other suitable premises, or in the Presidency country, *but not in the European Parliament.*[180]

[175] Hilger (n 19) 141–42.
[176] Marschall (n 165) 128–29.
[177] ibid 129; Herranz Surralés (n 16) 969–70.
[178] Hilger (n 19) 138.
[179] Huff (n 4) 7. Similar findings are also presented in Herranz Surralés (n 16) 966–70.
[180] Emphasis added. House of Commons, Foreign Affairs Committee, 'Future interparliamentary scrutiny of EU foreign, defence and security policy', Report, together with formal minutes, and written evidence, First report HC 697 (2010–11) (18 January 2011) 5, 10.

Another examples is a 2016 report of the French Sénat dealing with parliamentary oversight of French deployments, including under the CSDP framework, the multilevel parliamentary constellation was not even alluded to.[181] The EP is mentioned in a footnote only, when its offensive access-to-sensitive-information policy is implicitly criticized. On a side note, it is interesting to realize that the stance of national legislative bodies to refrain from sharing responsibilities with or conferring powers to a Brussels-based parliamentary body resembles the reluctant attitude of Member State executives throughout the development of the CFSP/CSDP to formally confer functions to Brussels-based bureaucracies.

The compromise reached in 2012 brought about an interparliamentary conference modelled on the Conference of Parliamentary Committees for Union Affairs of Parliaments of the European Union (COSAC). Intended to provide a framework for the exchange of information and best practices in the CFSP/CSDP area, the Inter-Parliamentary Conference for the CFSP and the CSDP is programmed to meet every six months under the rotating presidency, either in the country of the presidency or at the EP.[182] Next to presiding the conference, the rotating presidency provides the conference secretariat 'in close cooperation with the European Parliament and with the previous and next Presidency Parliaments'.[183] But conference dynamics have (reportedly) been strained:[184] there is mistrust between the administrative services of the national parliaments and the EP in the organization of such events as both players fear interferences in their respective competences from the other player.[185]

The second contentious issue was the distribution of seats within the conference. In 2011 a proposal was on the table that gave the EP a third of the seats (fifty-four seats), whereas the remaining two-thirds of the seats went to national parliaments (108, which is four per Member State).[186] Yet, national parliaments collectively refused to allocate the EP delegation a bigger share of the seats than the one given to national parliaments. The two diametrically opposed visions were, of course, not easy to reconcile, even once the EP had accepted to reduce its delegation to twenty-seven seats.[187] In the end, national parliaments are represented in the conference with six members each and the EP with sixteen parliamentarians.[188] Candidate

[181] Gautier and others (n 57) 244.

[182] Art 3 Rules of procedure of the Inter-Parliamentary Conference for the Common Foreign and Security Policy and the Common Security and Defence Policy, adopted at its first meeting in Cyprus (9–10 September 2012), as amended at its meeting in Rome (5–7 November 2014).

[183] Art 3 and Art 6 ibid.

[184] Daniel Schade, 'Parlamentarische Kontrolle durch Vernetzung? Eine kritische Analyse der Rolle der Interparlamentarischen Konferenz für die GASP/GSVP' (2019) 42 integration 118, 126–29.

[185] Andreja Pegan and Anna-Lena Högenauer, 'The Role of Parliamentary Administrators in Interparliamentary Cooperation' in Nicola Lupo and Cristina Fasone (eds), *Interparliamentary Cooperation in the Composite European Constitution* (Hart Publishing 2016) 149.

[186] Herranz Surralés (n 16) 970.

[187] ibid.

[188] Art 2(1) Rules of procedure of the Inter-Parliamentary Conference.

countries and members of North Atlantic Treaty Organization (NATO) (not represented by the aforementioned national delegations) can also take part in the biannual meetings, with four observers respectively.[189]

Finally, then, the fundamental divergence as to the role of each parliamentary level in the field of EU security and defence could not be settled. Rather, the creation of the Inter-Parliamentary Conference for the CFSP and CSDP is an exemplary case of non-cooperation eventually leading to a situation where both are worse off. Presented with a chance to pool resources and competences, the players of the two parliamentary levels have chosen not to cooperate. Their strategy has therefore prevented them from receiving the 'reward for mutual cooperation' and has, on the contrary, engendered a 'punishment for mutual defection'.[190] As a result, the Interparliamentary Conference in place since 2012 is far less institutionalized and structured, allows for significantly lower scrutiny, and cannot issue binding decisions in comparison to its WEU predecessor.[191] Indeed, the new Conference does not directly interact with the EU security and defence executive,[192] but is confined to being a platform for (information) exchange and debate.[193] Therefore, $A_i$ and $A_c$ are out of sight. This weak stance absurdly corresponds to the job description the Conference has given itself: the Rules of Procedure unequivocally stress that the structure's primary function is informative and *not* inquisitive.[194] In addition, the administrative resources at the disposal of national parliaments to prepare interparliamentary conferences are often very restricted. All of these elements are indicative of a dysfunctional multilevel parliamentary field regarding CFSP/CSDP matters.

In parallel to—or because of—this weak interparliamentary cooperation mechanism, a fragmented transnational parliamentary dialogue has developed. First, there are regular encounters at the level of specialized parliamentary committees. Biannually, the committees of foreign affairs and defence of the national parliaments are invited by the AFET committee of the EP to discuss foreign policy and security matters. However, as theses joint meetings are organized by AFET (and

[189] Art 2(2) ibid.

[190] Robert Axelrod, *The Evolution of Cooperation* (Basic Books 1984) 8.

[191] Herranz Surrallés (n 16) 959; Wouters and Raube (n 174) 156.

[192] Hilger (n 19) 139; Herranz Surrallés (n 16) 959.

[193] The same conclusion was reached in Dirk Peters, 'Actor, Network, Symbol: The Inter-Parliamentary Conference on CFSP/CSDP' in Kolja Raube, Meltem Müftüler-Baç, and Jan Wouters (eds), *Parliamentary Cooperation and Diplomacy in EU External Relations. An Essential Companion* (Edward Elgar 2019) 165, 171.

[194] Para 1.1 Rules of procedure of the Inter-Parliamentary Conference. The Rules of Procedure reverberate the tenor of the 2011 Presidency Conclusions which envisaged that 'the goal of the ... structure 'is to ensure the monitoring of the CFSP/CSDP from a parliamentary point of view (*scrutiny*) rather than truly to control it (*control*), which would involve a competence of sanction'. (Emphasis in the original). Presidency Conclusions concerning the parliamentary scrutiny of the Common Foreign and Security Policy (CFSP) and Common Security and Defence Policy (CSDP), adopted at the Conference of the Speakers of the Parliaments of the EU, Brussels, 4–5 April 2011 para 3.

not SEDE), the debate mostly circles around foreign policy matters, in particular neighbourhood policy issues, while defence questions are of secondary importance.[195] EU peacebuilding activities are generally not a topic, except in the rare cases when a salient political dossier is tied to a mission. These meetings take place in addition to the joint meetings scheduled twice a year by the rotating presidency in the context of the Interparliamentary Conference. The framework is quite formal and parliamentarians are not invited to have informal chats.

Secondly, national legislative bodies resort to informal networks to receive timely and accurate information on EU security and defence dossiers. A focal point in this regard are the liaison offices of national parliaments in Brussels. Initially a Danish idea, twenty-six out of twenty-seven Member States nowadays keep up a parliamentary liaison office in Brussels.[196] Except for the German delegation, the liaison offices are hosted by the EP and are situated on the same corridor: in proximity of the EP's Directorate for Relations with National Parliaments.[197] The primary role of national parliamentary representatives is information-gathering on behalf of their parliament. In this role, national parliamentary representatives interact with EU institutions (EP and Commission) and other liaison officers.[198] Via their national parliamentary representatives in Brussels, national parliaments have higher chances of being in the loop when policy issues are prepared by the EU.[199] Yet, the intensity of information exchange depends much on the political priorities and resources of the respective parliamentary liaison office, which greatly vary. The reporting intensity on issues pertaining to civilian crisis management is very low, which once again is not conducive to improving the already weak political accountability mechanisms at the national level.

The consequences of this parliamentary dysfunctionality for the political accountability of civilian CSDP are grave: the lack of parliamentary synergies across levels makes it tremendously more difficult to get hold of the edifice of Europeanized intergovernmentalism. In a perfect world characterized by cooperation, national parliaments would take care of their governments and thus assume political accountability over big parts of the 'intergovernmental' dimension of civilian crisis management, whereas the EP would cover the Europeanized realities by keeping a close eye on the Brussels-based bureaucracies. Sadly, the absence of such constructive cooperation across parliamentary levels considerably weakens political accountability for both the intergovernmental and the Europeanized dimension of civilian CSDP.

[195] Barbé and Herranz Surralés (n 92) 102.

[196] Pegan and Högenauer (n 185) 149.

[197] Huff (n 4) 15; Born and others (n 26) 20; Pegan and Högenauer (n 185) 149.

[198] Pegan and Högenauer (n 185) 150–51; Huff (n 4) 15–16.

[199] On the role of the national parliament representatives for information-sharing, see, Huff (n 4) 15–16.

## 5. The Significance of Effective Supranational Parliamentary Scrutiny

This chapter started by underscoring the importance of parliamentary scrutiny in modern democracies, while acknowledging the difficulty of such scrutiny with regard to *domaine réservé* issues. After having thoroughly analysed de jure and de facto political accountability arrangements in EU civilian crisis management covering both accountability for information ($A_i$) and accountability for conduct ($A_c$), it is now time to recapitulate the findings and give conclusive responses to the questions posed at the outset.

First, what parliamentary function is desirable and practicable in the *domaine réservé*? As foreign policy or defence issues are rarely legislative but predominantly executive in nature, the core function of parliaments is to control the action of the executive in this policy field—instead of (co-)decision-making. This non-legislative control function presupposes sufficiently strong inquisitive powers and adequate provision of information to enable the political forum to kick off the three-stage accountability process. Information being a scare resource in security and defence, accountability is likely to circle around informational aspects ($A_i$), not least to substitute for fully fledged involvement in decision-making. That is because information can constitute a power resource, especially in a policy area marked by a structural shortage of information. Therefore, the line between parliaments' control of and influence on executive action in external affairs can be thin given the possible anticipatory moves of the executive with a view to pre-emptively conform to the expected stance of parliaments. In sum, parliamentary scrutiny taking place ex post does not impede on *domaine réservé* prerogatives and therefore does not represent an impediment to external action, but constitutes an inherent value in modern democratic systems.

This leads us to the second interrogation. How does parliamentary scrutiny of the CFSP/CSDP unfold across different governance levels? At the national level, there is no uniform European standard for the scope and intensity of parliamentary involvement in EU security and defence issues. But the formal powers of national parliaments to make their voices heard prior to or after an EU decision with external action/defence implications is taken, with some exceptions, is low across European countries. When parliaments are in the CSDP loop, their involvement is almost exclusively related to extraterritorial military deployments in the context of peace or security operations. Because of an interplay of several factors—namely reduced formal powers, insufficient information-sharing with the legislative, difficult intra-parliamentary divisions of labour, and a lack of political will—civilian CSDP activities generally fly under the national parliamentary radar. As a result, the overall framework for national parliamentary oversight of EU security and defence usually provides for scant levels of $A_i$ and also for very limited $A_c$. Supplementary channels of parliamentary dialogue may contribute to improving information flows and can potentially enhance accountability by national parliaments. Nonetheless, the parliamentary patchwork at Member State level for EU security and defence, combined with the recently established weak interparliamentary forum, is not conducive to accountability.

The situation is far less grim at the EU level. As the analysis of this chapter has shown, most formal and informal powers to keep the EU security and defence executive in check, especially for civilian crisis management, are in principle in the hands of MEPs. This is the result of several battles fought with the Council on budget issues and timely access to (sensitive) information. While the $A_c$ that the EP can exercise is mainly based on informal mechanisms—especially reputational blame and shame tactics—the EP has significantly increased its formalized powers to hold the EU executive to account for $A_i$ on civilian crisis management.

This brings us to the third question. How has the division of labour between national parliaments and the EP in this field evolved over time? Since the creation of the CFSP with the Treaty of Maastricht, the EP has continuously increased its formal and informal powers regarding EU foreign affairs, security, and defence. While initially this did not seem to bother national parliaments, a change of perspective occurred with the Treaty of Lisbon. The result of the lengthy negotiations on the creation of a new interparliamentary forum after the entry into force of the Treaty of Lisbon turned out to considerably deteriorate interparliamentary cooperation. Instead of using the vehicle of transnational parliamentary cooperation to enhance political accountability—for both information and conduct—the negotiations resulted in a mechanism which lacks the means to do so. The current arrangements providing for an Inter-Parliamentary Conference on CFSP/CSDP issues actually bolster executive dominance as they curtail transnational parliamentary interaction to formalized discursive encounters instead of allowing for real scrutiny.[200] Because of the dysfunctional multilevel parliamentary field, both $A_i$ and $A_c$ remain low in the area of civilian CSDP (and the situation is even worse when it comes to military matters). Hence, instead of bundling powers in the aftermath of the dissolution of the WEU Parliamentary Assembly, turf wars between national and European parliamentarians have considerably diminished political accountability across levels.

Finally, it is judicious to gauge to what extent the current division of parliamentary labour has adapted to the edifice of Europeanized intergovernmentalism. The day-to-day routine of EU civilian crisis management is much less intergovernmental than primary law suggests. Because of Europeanization, the centre of strategic and operational gravity of EU peacebuilding activities is in Brussels. It would therefore be paradoxical—not to say out of touch with reality—to channel parliamentary oversight (primarily) through national parliaments, as this would mean

[200] This conclusion is shared by other authors, such as Peters (n 193) 159.

that executive decision-makers could bypass political accountability. Therefore, effective parliamentary scrutiny is necessary at the EU level to capture EU civilian crisis management operating in Europeanized intergovernmentalism.

This corroborates the salience of scrutiny by the EP to avoid a 'double democratic deficit'.[201] The EP is indeed better situated to scrutinize EU security and defence than its national counterparts.[202] This is particularly true for EU peacebuilding activities, not least because MEPs have a say over budget issues and can, in addition, access sensitive information and interact directly with decision-makers as well as implementers of the crisis management bureaucracy, notably on the basis of IIAs and established practice. Even though EP scrutiny does not cover all aspects of civilian crisis management—above all, the 'intergovernmental' part escapes the oversight of MEPs, such as consensual decision-making by the Council/PSC—the EP has de facto turned into the primary forum for political accountability regarding the important Europeanized dimension of civilian CSDP, including operational and budgetary aspects.

So far, however, one cannot qualify the EP's scrutiny of civilian CSDP as zestful. Until now, civilian CSDP has clearly not been a political priority of the EP. The profile of EU peacebuilding activities is politically too low, institutionally and procedurally complex, and offers little potential to attract the attention of the electorate. Therefore, issues related to civilian missions are primarily discussed by the EP if they open up leverage against other political dossiers. In addition, there are insufficient bureaucratic resources to keep track of all civilian CSDP activities: the handful of staff in the SEDE-secretariat is mainly focussing on military operations and, more importantly, on the manifold (recent) developments in the security sector of the EU.

Finally, some words on the appropriateness of the political accountability mechanisms in EU civilian crisis management would be well placed. (A longer response to the appropriateness question is provided in Chapter 8 of this book.) In short, the perseverance of the EP has resulted in a positive finding. There are political accountability arrangements at the EU level covering the strategic and operational aspects of EU civilian crisis management (quantity). In addition, the EP has much improved its inquisitive and sanctioning powers (quality): it has formal means at its disposal to exercise accountability for information and through primarily informal channels can exercise accountability for conduct. Finally, the envisioned accountability capacity—parliamentary scrutiny of decisional and operational activity through discursive interaction resting on the provision of information and budget control—is in principle accomplished. The question is rather whether the EP has the resources and political will to make full use of its accountability potential.

[201] Hänggi (n 14) 4–8; Gourlay (n 34) 193.
[202] Gourlay (n 34) 189.

Hence, in order to render political accountability (more) effective, it is necessary to increase, in a first step, parliamentary awareness and processes, as well as content expertise regarding civilian CSDP at both the EU level and on the national plane. In a second step, then, it is judicious to strengthen political accountability by means of parliamentary oversight above all at the supranational level. At the same time, it is equally important to improve interparliamentary cooperation across levels to ensure that neither decision-making nor the implementation of civilian missions occurs without the appropriate accountability mechanisms in place.

# 6

# Legal Accountability: Beyond Jurisdictional Reach?

In democratic societies based on the rule of law, legal accountability fulfils an essential function: it ensures that the exercise of public power is subject to judicial review and that power-holders can be sanctioned in the event of non-observance of rules or regulations. Courts are thus vital accountability fora in power-limited constitutional systems.[1] In fulfilling their role, judicial bodies possess a rare attribute compared to other accountability fora: they have the capacity to inflict *formal* sanctions on actors, which is an important element for effective accountability.[2] This is because accountability, defined as a three-stage mechanism,[3] necessarily comprises consequences that the accountability forum can impose on the actor. In many cases, these consequences are informal in nature. Think, for instance, of the reputational damage incurred by an institution because of a corruption scandal subject to a public hearing or report. Courts, however, pronounce formal sentences. Especially vis-à-vis political actors, the formality attribute makes judicial bodies privileged accountability fora.

Legal accountability entails three 'foundational precepts'.[4] The first precept—legality—concerns the availability of judicial review. On the one hand, this availability depends on a court having the jurisdictional competence to hear a dispute and, on the other hand, on the (criteria for the) admissibility of a claim. The second precept—access to justice—is related to the *locus standi* of the aggrieved individual or entity. The third precept—monetary relief—is tied to the criteria for damages liability.

[1] On the conceptual underpinnings of power-limiting constitutional systems and the role of courts herein, see, Christoph Möllers, 'Verfassungsgebende Gewalt—Verfassung—Konstitutionalisierung' in Armin von Bogdandy and Jürgen Bast (eds), *Europäisches Verfassungsrecht: Theoretische und dogmatische Grundzüge* (2nd edn, Springer 2009) 234–38.

[2] On the primordial importance of courts for accountability in a democratic society, see, inter alia, Carol Harlow and Richard Rawlings, 'Promoting Accountability in Multilevel Governance: A Network Approach' (2007) 13 European Law Journal 542, 546–48; Richard Mulgan, *Holding Power to Account, Accountability in Modern Democracies* (Palgrave Macmillan 2003) 75–83.

[3] The accountability model used in this book consists of three stages, namely the provision of information by the actor (stage 1), scrutiny by the forum (stage 2), and consequences, implying formal or informal sanctions emanating from the forum (stage 3). See Mark Bovens, 'Analysing and Assessing Accountability: A Conceptual Framework' (2007) 13 European Law Journal 447, 450.

[4] Paul Craig, 'Accountability' in Anthony Arnull and Damian Chalmers (eds), *The Oxford Handbook of European Union Law* (Oxford University Press 2015) 440.

*Accountability in EU Security and Defence.* Carolyn Moser, Oxford University Press (2020). 
DOI: 10.1093/oso/9780198844815.001.0001

Against the backdrop of these three foundational precepts, the present chapter sets out to thoroughly explore legal accountability arrangements with regard to the multilevel and multi-actor environment of EU peacebuilding activities, which is an operational tool of the European Union's (EU) Common Security and Defence Policy (CSDP). Questions arise in two interrelated fields of research. First, which judicial body—national, European, or both—is competent to adjudicate on matters related to extraterritorial EU civilian missions? According to primary law, civilian CSDP remains an intergovernmental policy instrument, so that formal accountability is channelled through national institutions. But while the institutional and procedural foundations remain de jure intergovernmental, administrative and operational realities have de facto moved beyond intergovernmentalism and have become Europeanized. This implies that both decision-making and action capacity in EU civilian crisis management has been transferred from the national sphere to the European realm, notably from ministerial departments or national agencies to a specialized and independent bureaucracy in Brussels that prepares, steers, and implements civilian missions. EU peacebuilding activities thus take place in a setting of *Europeanized intergovernmentalism*.[5] Hence, one can inquire as to how legal accountability can be reconciled with Europeanized intergovernmentalism.

Secondly, how is legal accountability exercised, and in respect of which aspects and actors? This interrogation ties in with the scope, intensity, and nature of judicial review, and with the judicial benchmarks employed by courts. Can courts scrutinize only 'formal' CFSP decisions adopted in the intergovernmental sphere of the CSDP—acts of intergovernmental bodies codified by primary law—or can their judicial review extend to 'informal' derivative CSDP decisions taken in the Europeanized realm of civilian crisis management—day-to-day (administrative) choices made by seconded civil servants to implement or concretize formal decisions? Are actors at both the strategic and operational level amendable to judicial review? In addition, adjudication can circle around procedural or substantive matters, while the evaluation can be based on constitutional requirements, general principles, or jurisprudence. Is accountability for *conduct* ($A_c$) the primary focus or accountability for *information* ($A_i$), or both? In the first scenario, the forum's ability to assess and impose consequences for the actor's action or omission will be at the centre of the accountability attention, whereas in the second scenario, the focus will be on the inquisitive and sanctioning powers of the forum in relation to the timely and encompassing provision of information by the actor.

The responses to these interrogations, which will draw on both de jure and de facto elements, will feed into the overall research endeavour of this book, which tries to answer an overriding question: *to what extent has the transfer of powers by Member States to Brussels-based EU civilian crisis management structures been*

[5] For further details on Europeanized intergovernmentalism, see Chapter 2.

*matched with the establishment of appropriate accountability mechanisms at the European level*? Appropriateness bears three dimensions: quantity, quality, and capacity. The study of legal accountability arrangements in EU civilian crisis management attempts to evaluate (i) whether there are legal accountability mechanisms when and where power is exercised, that is, at the EU level (quantity criterion); (ii) whether courts have sufficient inquisitive and sanctioning powers to hold actors effectively to account, which boils down to the question of whether courts actually have jurisdiction (quality benchmark); and (iii) whether the capacity—safeguarding codified institutional and procedural arrangements and individual legal protection—is attained.

The chapter at hand first illustrates why and how judicial actors were kept at a safe jurisdictional distance from EU foreign policy and security matters. Building on this analysis, the second section sketches out the limited function of national judicial actors in adjudicating matters pertaining to the civilian dimension of the CSDP. Subsequently, the discussion of section 3 engages with the important role of the Court of Justice of the European Union (CJEU) with regard to foreign policy issues. In a first step, the assessment covers the role of the EU judicature as an accountability *facilitator*. In a second step, the study focuses on the CJEU as an accountability *forum*, legally holding different crisis management actors to account. Against this backdrop, section 4 measures the wider jurisdictional field, that is, the division of labour between the CJEU on the one hand, and national courts and the European Court of Human Rights (ECtHR) in Strasbourg on the other. The last section of the chapter (5) finally draws some conclusions on the evolution and current state of legal accountability in civilian CSDP.

## 1. Keeping the Judges at Arm's Length

Foreign policy together with defence are highly sensitive issues. Executive actors enjoy a wide discretion in these *domaine réservé* matters, while legislative and judicial institutions are traditionally less involved. The special nature—in terms of substance and procedure—of foreign affairs and defence issues has, at the EU level, led to a specific legal framework characterized by a low level of codification (meaning limited *juridification*) coupled with limited judicial review and thus limited judicial power (meaning limited *judicialization*).[6] Both aspects, in turn, impact on the three precepts of legal accountability, namely the availability of judicial review, access to justice, and damages.

[6] Christina Eckes, 'Common Foreign and Security Policy: The Consequences of the Court's Extended Jurisdiction' (2016) 22 European Law Journal 492, 493; Lars C Blichner and Anders Molander, 'Mapping Juridification' (2008) 14 European Law Journal 36.

That is because adjudication (judicialization) and law (juridification) are obviously entangled—not to say mutually reinforcing: if there is no provision setting out procedural requirements for public institutions or no stipulation granting rights to individuals against public power, it will be difficult for plaintiffs to make a case in court. If, however, there are legal grounds to bring a case to court, judges can interpret existing rules, and thereby shape conditions for legal accountability. Simply put, the scarcity of law leaves limited room for adjudication, and the absence of jurisprudence in turn is unlikely to improve framework conditions of legal accountability. Yet, if a case ever makes it to court in an environment of limited juridification and judicialization, judicial actors have a wide interpretative leeway: insufficient law, then, leaves ample room for judicial law-making.

### 1.1 Limited juridification

A look at EU Treaties reveals that there are only a few provisions codifying foreign affairs, security, and defence: in the Treaty on European Union (TEU) and the Treaty on the Functioning of the European Union (TFEU), which together count more than 400 articles, only twenty-four articles specifically deal with the Common Foreign and Security Policy (CFSP) and the CSDP. A key feature of matters with foreign, security, and defence implications at the EU level is undeniably the limited role of law: law is less pronounced in *high* politics (which is the area of the CFSP and the CSDP) than it is or has been in other fields of EU integration concerned with *low* politics (the former Community area, to be precise).[7]

What is more, since its incorporation into EU primary law in 1986, foreign policy—and later security and defence—has been granted a special legal treatment: built on essentially intergovernmental principles, the normative features of the Community legal order (or Community method[8]) would not apply. In short, the Council of the European Union (Council)—instead of the European Commission (Commission)—was put in charge of defining, conducting, and implementing the policy according to specific intergovernmental rules and procedures by using specific legal instruments.

In legal terms, this meant that EU foreign policy, security, and defence formed part of the corpus of EU law without, however, bearing the typical characteristics of supranational EU rules. This specificity made it difficult for legal scholars to capture

[7] Panos Koutrakos, 'The Role of Law in Common Security and Defence Policy: Functions, Limitations and Perceptions' in Panos Koutrakos (ed), *European Foreign Policy: Legal and Political Perspectives* (Edward Elgar 2011) 236.

[8] The *Community method* is the prevailing mode of cooperation and decision-making at the EU level, namely the ordinary legislative procedure. Characteristics of the Community method are (i) the sole right of legislative of the Commission, (ii) the Council and the EP acting as co-decide legislators, and (iii) voting in the Council taking place according to qualified majority.

the policy in the categories of the existing legal discourse. Indeed, for a long time, the CFSP and the CSDP have not received much attention by legal scholars as there was too little law to explore.[9] In political terms, the distinctive legal framework was (and still is) indicative of the limited inclination of Member States to integrate foreign affairs, security, and defence at the European level: limited law stands for limited integration, which in turn signifies limited delegation.[10]

This reluctance towards juridification has led to practice paving the way for law in many pivotal institutional and procedural matters. As a matter of fact, legal provisions in EU security and defence have often been preceded by informal arrangements between Member States, so that law has merely codified existing practice. The codification of the European Political Cooperation (EPC) is a telling example of this *(in)formality pattern*. After the failure of both the European Defence Community in 1954 and the rejection of the Fouchet plans in 1962,[11] security and defence were excluded from the realm of supranational European integration and remained outside the Treaties. Consequently, cooperation and integration between Member States in this area were based on informal consultation arrangements between governments. Once the time was ripe, these informal cooperation agreements and established practice were codified in EU primary law through the Single European Act (SEA) in 1986.

Another illustration of the (in)formality pattern is the establishment of the CSDP and the related Brussels-based crisis management bureaucracy. Faced with a manifest failure of European States to take political or military action in the Kosovo crisis, Heads of State and Government sensed an urgent need for reform. Initially ad hoc, the CSDP was established outside of formal treaty-making procedures at the European Council Summit in Cologne (1999).[12] The policy was only integrated into primary law (by the Treaty of Nice) once its bureaucracy had already been put in place. Hence, the first crisis management structures—including the Political and Security Committee (PSC), the European Union Military Committee (EUMC), the European Union Military Staff (EUMS), and the Committee for Civilian Aspects of Crisis Management (CIVCOM)—were set up at high-ranking intergovernmental meetings throughout 1999 and 2000. These structures were formalized only later through secondary law provisions and, only in the case of the PSC, incorporated

[9] Piet Eeckhout, *EU External Relations Law* (2nd edn, Oxford University Press 2011) 467.

[10] On the delegation patterns of CFSP/CSDP integration, see Chapter 2.

[11] For a detailed study of the EDC and its failure, see David Scannell, 'Third Time Luck: The Pre-History of the Common Security and Defence Policy' in Anthony Arnull and others (eds), *A Constitutional Order of States? Essays in EU Law in Honour of Alan Dashwood* (Hart Publishing 2011) 566–82. For more information on the two Fouchet plans, see Simon Duke, *The EU and Crisis Management: Development and Prospects* (European Institute of Public Administration 2002) 4–5; Jaap W de Zwaan, 'Foreign Policy and Defence Cooperation in the European Union: Legal Foundations' in Steven Blockmans (ed), *The European Union and Crisis Management: Policy and Legal Aspects* (TMC Asser Press 2008) 19.

[12] Presidency Conclusions of the Cologne European Council (2–4 June 1999), Annex III: Presidency Report on Strengthening of the common European policy on security and defence.

into primary law.[13] The incremental development of the law of European foreign affairs, security, and defence has thus to a great extent been shaped by irreversible policy choices, leading to day-to-day practice constructed outside of intergovernmental conferences where primary law provisions are negotiated and eventually determined.[14]

An additional element of (in)formality tied to limited juridification is the restricted codification of legal instruments available in the CFSP/CSDP field. Indeed, according to primary law, the only legal instrument available under the CFSP/CSDP next to 'general guidelines' are 'decisions', even if they fulfil different functions (Article 25(b) TEU).[15] These decisions are adopted by the European Council and the Council, in principle, on the basis of unanimity (Article 31(1) TEU). This implies that, from a legalistic point of view, only decisions taken at the highest political level count as 'decisions' in the primary law sense, whereas the bulk of day-to-day management choices at the sub-Council do not. Decision-making by the Brussel-based bureaucracy is thus not spelled out by Treaty law, except for the substitute decision-making activities by the PSC for the Council (Article 38). What is more, Treaty law (Article 297(2) TFEU) prescribes the mandatory publication of non-legislative acts—formal CFSP decisions—but remains, logically, silent as to the publication of 'informal' derivative CFSP acts adopted by the civilian crisis management bureaucracy. The latter acts are, in parts, listed in the online register of the European External Action Service (EEAS) (or the Council) but not necessarily accessible as they are subject to security regulations. As a result, the extensive (administrative) work of the Brussels-based bureaucracy remains largely below the threshold of formality (in the primary law sense) and visibility. This is because the adoption of formal CFSP decisions by the Council is the exception in EU peacebuilding, while the adoption of (informal) derivative acts related to administrative or operational matters at the sub-Council level is the rule.

But why is there so little law? Law—both in terms of Treaty provisions and the interpretation thereof made by judicial actors—has considerably shaped the European project, and has acted as a catalyst of supranational integration patterns. A key notion in this context is 'integration through law'.[16] Precisely to avoid

[13] Codification of the Political and Security Committee through Art 25 TEU (Nice).

[14] This understanding comes close to a structurationist view (as opposed to an intergovernmental or neo-institutional perspective) on the constitutional development of the EU—at least as concerns foreign policy, security, and defence issues. For a concise overview of the three perspectives, see Andreas Maurer, Daniela Kietz, and Christian Völkel, 'Interinstitutional Agreements in the CFSP: Parliamentarization through the Back Door?' (2005) 10 European Foreign Affairs Review 175, 179–82.

[15] For further details, see Panos Koutrakos, *The EU Common Security and Defence Policy* (Oxford University Press 2013) 35–37.

[16] Karen J Alter, 'The European Court and Legal Integration: An Exceptional Story or Harbinger of the Future?' in Keith E Whittington, Daniel R Kelemen, and Gregory A Caldeira (eds), *The Oxford Handbook of Law and Politics* (Oxford University Press 2008) 213.

supranationalization, codification has consciously been kept at a safe distance from foreign affairs, security, and defence at the EU level. The two-treaty pattern mentioned in section 1.1 is indicative hereof.[17] In addition, the few legal rules eventually adopted provide for a predominantly intergovernmental CFSP (and by extension CSDP). The lower level of codification coupled with an intergovernmental framework signifies limited (supranational) integration and, as a result, a reduced role for supranational institutions, including the EU's judicature. It was not only law, therefore, which was kept at a safe distance, but also the judicial actors who could interpret the law.

## 1.2 Limited judicialization

The limited juridification of EU security and defence thus went hand in hand with the limited judicialization of this policy field at the EU level. This situation has essentially remained unaltered since EU foreign affairs, security, and defence were first codified in the SEA. The second sub-paragraph of Article 24(1) TEU and the first paragraph of Article 275 TFEU indeed stipulate that the CJEU has no general jurisdiction with respect to the CFSP/CSDP. There are two exceptions to this general preclusion of jurisdiction: questions of policy delimitation (Article 40 TEU) and concerning sanctions—in other words, restrictive measures directed against legal and natural persons (second paragraph of Article 275 TFEU). The latter exception was introduced into primary law as a reaction to the famous *Kadi*-jurisprudence.[18] The pertinent provisions, constituting a 'procedural eye of a needle' for the EU judicature,[19] read as follows:

> *Article 24(1) TEU.* The common foreign and security policy is subject to specific rules and procedures.... The Court of Justice of the European Union shall not have jurisdiction with respect to these provisions, with the exception of its jurisdiction to monitor compliance with Article 40 of this Treaty and to review the legality of certain decisions as provided for by the second paragraph of Article 275 of the Treaty on the Functioning of the European Union.
>
> *Article 275 TFEU.* The Court of Justice of the European Union shall not have jurisdiction with respect to the provisions relating to the common foreign and security policy nor with respect to acts adopted on the basis of those provisions.

[17] See Chapter 2.

[18] Eeckhout (n 9) 498. On Kadi in politics, jurisprudence, and legal scholarship, see Nele Yang, *Zur Grundlegung eines Begriffs und seiner Erforschung im Unionsrecht anhand des EuGH-Urteils Kadi* (Springer 2017).

[19] Own translation from the original German text, reading '*prozessuales Nadelöhr*'. Matthias Kottmann, *Introvertierte Rechtsgemeinschaft. Zur richterlichen Kontrolle des auswärtigen Handels der Europäischen Union* (Springer 2014) 202.

> However, the Court shall have jurisdiction to monitor compliance with Article 40 of the Treaty on European Union and to rule on proceedings, brought in accordance with the conditions laid down in the fourth paragraph of Article 263 of this Treaty, reviewing the legality of decisions providing for restrictive measures against natural or legal persons adopted by the Council on the basis of Chapter 2 of Title V of the Treaty on European Union.

It can be inferred from the above Treaty stipulations that the first precept of legal accountability—that is, judicial review—is severely limited by this jurisdictional carve-out. Again, the rationale for keeping judicial review at a low level resided in the reluctance of Member States to supranationalize this policy field out of fear of (judicial) entrapment. The conflict of intergovernmental versus supranational institutional design and fears of sovereignty loss eventually resulted in Member States granting only very limited jurisdictional competences to the EU judicature.[20]

There are two more strands of arguments to explain why the CJEU's jurisdiction in CFSP matters is (still) so narrow.[21] The first argument consists of saying that judicial review is not necessary given the legal nature of acts adopted under the CFSP; that is, decisions and activities of a politico-diplomatic character without direct impact on individuals.[22] The sanctions policy implemented by the EU has demonstrated that this argument is erroneous. The second attempt at explanation rests on the consideration that the intergovernmental framework of the CFSP mirrors the executive dominance in foreign and security affairs existing at the national level. However, a closer look at the incremental development of European foreign affairs, security, and defence does not back up this reading: Member States have been influenced far more by the fear of losing sovereignty than by the (unconscious) effort at reproducing national solutions at the European level.[23] Therefore, it is fair to state that the fear of 'supranational infection'[24] was the primary rationale driving Member States to lay down in primary law that the EU judicature has very limited jurisdiction with respect to EU foreign policy, security, and defence. This construction has severely hampered legal accountability.

[20] The EU judicature used to be divided into a Court of First Instance (created in 1998), the European Court of Justice (ECJ), and the Civil Service Tribunal (CST, established in 2004). Nowadays, the CJEU comprises the General Court and the Court of Justice, while the CST ceased to exist in 2016 when its jurisdiction was transferred to the General Court.

[21] This is a summary of the analysis presented by Kottmann. See Kottmann (n 19) 163–75.

[22] The German Constitutional Court argued this way in the judgment on the Treaty of Maastricht. It stated that decisions under the CFSP would per se lack '*eine grundrechtserhebliche Verbindlichkeit für den Einzelnen*'. Bundesverfassungsgericht 12.10.1993, *Maastricht*, BVerfGE 89, 155 para 73.

[23] On this point, see the careful analysis of the incremental development of the CFSP/CSDP in Hylke Dijkstra, *Policy-Making in EU Security and Defence: An Institutional Perspective* (Palgrave Macmillan 2013) 46–77.

[24] Eeckhout (n 9) 467.

### 1.3 Limited legal accountability?

A glimpse at the literature indeed suggests that the three precepts of legal accountability—legality, access, and damages—are built on shaky grounds in the context of the CFSP/CSDP,[25] which is the analytical focus of the present study. The first precept—legality—concerns the availability of judicial review, which in the EU context implies the amenability of (acts of) EU institutions to judicial review according to EU law provisions or jurisprudence.[26] In EU security and defence, the scope of judicial review by the CJEU is, however, severely limited.

Despite the Treaty of Lisbon conferring on the Court in Luxembourg jurisdiction on the entire corpus of EU law,[27] the CFSP remains under a reversed rule–exception regime, the rule being that the Court can only *exceptionally* adjudicate on CFSP matters.[28] In addition, the standing of the aggrieved individual or entity—the second precept—has proved problematic in the field of EU foreign and security affairs, leading to a patchy regime of legal protection; the same finding applies to the third precept, namely (criteria for) damages liability.[29] In view of both the lack of a defined judicial procedure allowing for enforcement and limited remedies (ie legal protection) open to potential complainants, Advocate General (AG) Wahl qualified the law governing the CFSP as *lex imperfecta*.[30] In sum, the primary law framework gives the EU judicature in principle little room to exercise accountability for conduct ($A_c$) and, similarly, few opportunities to enforce accountability for information ($A_i$) on behalf of other European institutions.

## 2. Hurdles to Adjudication by National Courts

The constitutional fabric of the CFSP, and especially the CSDP, being fundamentally intergovernmental, legal accountability on decisions taken in this policy field is de jure in the hands of national judicial institutions. This division of jurisdictional labour is corroborated by Article 19(1) TEU, which reads as follows:

> The Court of Justice of the European Union shall include the Court of Justice, the General Court and specialised courts. It shall ensure that in the interpretation and application of the Treaties the law is observed. Member States shall provide

25 See the introduction to this chapter.

26 Case 294/83 *Parti écologiste 'Les Verts' v European Parliament* [1986] EU:C:1986:166 para 23.

27 Art 19 TEU; Art 256 TFEU; Art 263 TFEU; Art 267 TFEU.

28 Case C–455/14 *P H v Council and others* [2016] EU:C:2016:212, Opinion of AG Wahl of 7 April 2016 para 2; Case C–263/14 *European Parliament v Council* [2015] EU:C:2015:729, Opinion of AG Kokott of 28 October 2015 para 43.

29 Kottmann (n 19) 200–29.

30 Case C–455/14 P [2016], Opinion of AG Wahl of 7 April 2016 paras 38–45.

> remedies sufficient to ensure effective legal protection in the fields covered by Union law.

In other words, the jurisdiction of the EU judicature being exceptional (in cases related to policy delimitation and sanctions), national courts are formally the primary legal accountability fora for disputes arising from EU security and defence activities, including peacebuilding missions.

In theory, then, the legal scrutiny of disputes arising in the context of CFSP/CSDP activities not falling under the exceptions regime remains a national matter. This reading of primary law was emphasized by AG Kokott, who argued that jurisdiction lies with national courts or tribunals in the absence of a direct recourse to the CJEU, which is the predominant case in the field of the CFSP.[31] As primary law enables judicial review only for some types of decisions (most prominently restrictive measures), even if other decisions could be legally binding for other entities than EU institutions, individuals have only limited judicial remedies at the EU level. Therefore, AG Wahl argued that Member States must ensure the principle of effective judicial protection.[32] Similarly, Christophe Hillion maintained that, with a view to guaranteeing legal protection, national judicial authorities can exercise 'complementary judicial control over CFSP, where and as long as the Court of Justice is not allowed to exercise it itself'.[33] Yet, formal jurisdictional competence notwithstanding, there are only very few cases pertaining to CSDP matters before national courts.

In practice, however, there are different hurdles to national courts actually adjudicating cases related to EU security and defence, both for procedural and substantive matters. First and foremost, there is the issue of *justiciability*. National courts might find that disputes arising in the context of international relations or defence activities are not legal but political in nature—they are related to or stem from a political decision taken by the executive in conformity with the constitutionally embedded separation of powers—and as such not justiciable. There are indeed remarkable (and recent) national judgments following the *acte de Gouvernement*-doctrine.[34] The French Conseil d'État, for instance, found in 2000 that deployment decisions were not amenable to review: as they were inseparably linked to the conduct of the Republic's foreign policy, these decisions were declared not justiciable.[35] The same reasoning was applied some years later when an applicant asked for the suspension of the decision of the President of the Republic

[31] View of AG Kokott, delivered on 13 June 2014 [2014] EU:C:2014:2475, Opinion procedure 2/13 para 96.

[32] Case C–455/14 P [2016], Opinion of AG Wahl of 7 April 2016 paras 38–45.

[33] Christophe Hillion, 'Decentralised Integration? Fundamental Rights Protection in the EU Common Foreign and Security Policy' (2016) 1 European Papers 55, 65.

[34] In the USA, this is known as the political question doctrine. It was set out in *Marbury v Madison* [1803] and reaffirmed in *Baker v Carr* [1962].

[35] Conseil d'État, *Mégret*, 5 juillet 2000, n° 206303 et 206965, publié au recueil Lebon.

authorizing British and US airplanes to cross French air space on their way to Iraq.[36] And only recently, the court held that it lacked the competence to hear cases related to the repatriation of female French citizens in Syrian camps who had previously left France deliberately to join Daesh, as such repatriation would greatly depend on political negotiations.[37] Taking a similarly deferential stance, national courts might thus find themselves lacking jurisdiction *ratione materiae* for cases related to EU security and defence activities, including civilian crisis management. But even if the justiciability hurdle is taken, there are further issues ahead.

In the event of a *procedural review* of a CFSP measure undertaken by national courts, jurisdiction would be limited in several regards. First, the scope of review would be restricted for two interrelated reasons. On the one hand, national courts can only hold to account the national representatives of their respective Member State (*ratione personae*). On the other hand, the only action that can be taken in the field of the CFSP/CSDP according to primary law consists of 'general guidelines' or 'decisions' adopted pursuant to Articles 26 and 31 TEU, that is (in principle) on the basis of unanimity. This in turn makes it very difficult for national judicial bodies to disentangle the action of their representative from the action of the remaining twenty-six executive actors. Enforcing the $A_c$ of national executives for specific CFSP decisions in the context of EU peacebuilding activities is therefore improbable.

Secondly, most CFSP/CSDP decisions, including civilian crisis management, are taken by the Brussels-based bureaucracy. Whereas high-level CFSP decisions are codified by primary law, derivative CFSP decisions (primarily administrative acts) are not as mentioned in section 1.1. This is the result of concealed agencification: an informal vertical transfer of both governmental decision-making and action capacity from the national ministerial departments of Member State to a specialized Brussels-based bureaucracy. While actors exercise de facto power at the EU level, their power is not formalized. Legally scrutinizing these derivative decisions is therefore highly problematic: from a legalistic point of view, and stressing the principle of conferral, they do not exist as they are not laid down in primary law and, from a realistic stance, are also not part of the national legal order as they are produced by Europeanized structures. Hence, it is more likely that national courts will be called to adjudicate on procedural matters related to decision-making involving national representatives. Consequently, scrutiny would focus on respecting national requirements governing the participation of national institutions other than the executive in decision-making, which primarily boils down to adjudicating on national parliamentary involvement.

[36] Conseil d'État, *Comité contre la guerre en Irak*, 10 avril 2003, n° 255905, mentionné aux tables du recueil Lebon.

[37] Conseil d'État, Juge des référés, 23 avril 2019, n° 429668, 243669, 438674, 429701.

Yet, thirdly, there are not that many procedural arrangements providing for countervailing powers at the Member State level which national courts could uphold to enforce accountability for conduct: most national parliaments have very reduced formal powers in relation to EU civilian crisis management, both prior to and after deployment.[38] Only in a third of Member States must the legislative branch give prior consent to a Council decision on deployment. Parliamentary oversight after deployment is even less developed across Member States—and the same is true for information rights. In addition, the hands of national courts are tied with regard to enforcing $A_i$ on behalf of national institutions or individuals, as pertinent information is mostly contained in classified EU documents, the declassification and disclosure of which national courts cannot order.

In the event of a *substantive review* on the effects of a specific CFSP decision, there is also a range of obstacles to national judicial scrutiny. First, even if a complaint related to the CFSP/CSDP is considered justiciable, national courts might declare the case inadmissible for two reasons: (i) immunity (often tied to questions of legal personality or territoriality), and (ii) lack of interpretative competence. As for immunity issues, the Status of Mission Agreements (SOMAs) signed between the EU and the respective host State confer immunity from jurisdiction and from execution both to the mission and its international staff members,[39] but they attribute jurisdiction to national courts for national experts seconded by their government.[40] This means that a Dutch court could rule on the misconduct of a Dutch civil servant seconded to an EU civilian mission, but could not assess the conduct of a Spanish civil servant working in the same mission. In addition to this restriction *ratione personae*, the mission as such enjoys immunity. This can constitute an insurmountable jurisdictional obstacle to national courts. Immunity of missions before domestic courts has indeed been controversial. An exemplary case in this regard, which orbited around questions of immunity from jurisdiction and execution, involved the EU crisis management mission in Guinea-Bissau, with the courts being undecided on whether immunity should be granted or not.[41] What is more, civilian missions have for a long time lacked an explicit legal status (under EU law). Since 2014, however, mandates bestow all missions with the capacity 'to

[38] A detailed analysis of the parliamentary blind spot at the national level regarding civilian crisis management can be found in Chapter 5.

[39] See Art 3, Art 6(4), Art 6(5), Art 6(7), and Art 8 Model SOMA. For more details on the immunity regime in place, see the analysis developed in Chapter 7.

[40] That is because the judicial authorities of the seconding State retain competence (both during and after the deployment) over the seconded staff members—for criminal jurisdiction for all acts, and for civil and administrative jurisdiction for all official acts. See Art 3, Art 6(4), Art 6(5), Art 6(7), and Art 8 Model SOMA.

[41] Recommendation of the European Ombudsman in case OI/13/2014/JF on the European External Action Service's non-recognition of a third country court ruling: payment of compensation Made in accordance with Art 3(6) of the Statute of the European Ombudsman (23 September 2016); Proposal of the European Ombudsman for a solution in the own initiative inquiry OI/13/2014/JF concerning the European External Action Service (19 June 2015).

procure services and supplies, enter contracts and administrative arrangements, employ staff, hold bank accounts, acquire and dispose of assets, discharge its liabilities and be a party to legal proceedings'.[42] Civilian missions thus enjoy legal *capacity* under EU law, but they are not independent legal entities in their own right—as is the case for EU agencies—because this would presuppose legal *personality*.[43] As a consequence of their legal capacity under EU law, missions can appear before jurisdictions—it is, however, not specified if the capacity to take part in legal proceedings is limited to EU courts or also extends to the domestic court of host States. Moreover, a British court recently rejected the claim that an EU civilian mission also enjoys domestic legal personality in the jurisdiction of the sending State. The case at stake concerned claims raised by Maria Bamieh against the Commonwealth Office, the EU Rule of Law Mission in Kosovo (EULEX Kosovo), and some co-workers with the Employment Tribunal of London; both in the first instance and in the appeal phase, the tribunal in question decided that it had no territorial jurisdiction in relation to EULEX Kosovo as the latter was found to lack domestic legal personality.[44]

Secondly, regarding interpretative competence, it is crucial to underline that the conduct of peacebuilding missions is regulated by and produces *EU* law. This is, for instance, the case when a mission is set up by a Council decision. Adjudicating cases related to civilian missions would thus imply interpreting EU law. But according to the *Foto-Frost* jurisprudence of the EU judicature, only EU courts can scrutinize the legality and validity of acts adopted by EU institutions.[45] In the past, it had been questioned by some jurists whether this general principle of interpretation would apply to the CFSP, where the jurisdictional rule-exception relationship is reversed: as the jurisdiction of the EU judicature is generally excluded, national courts would naturally step in and adjudicate.[46] Yet, the Court of Justice has recently confirmed the applicability of the *Foto-Frost* reasoning—that is the interpretative supremacy of EU courts regarding EU acts—to certain CFSP matters.[47]

This is related to yet another question. In the past, it was unclear whether national courts could circumvent their interpretative impasse by referring a case in the field of the CFSP/CSDP to their Luxembourg colleagues for a preliminary ruling pursuant to Article 19(3) TEU and Article 267 TFEU. While some argued that primary law clearly precluded the CJEU from giving any preliminary ruling in

[42] This is a standard formulation of mission mandates which has been inserted in the stipulations on 'legal arrangements' since 2014.

[43] On the difference between (domestic/international) legal *personality* and *capacity*, see Carolyn Moser and Anne Peters, 'Legal Uncertainty and Indeterminacy: Immutable Characteristics of the OSCE?' in Mateja Steinbrück Platise, Carolyn Moser, and Anne Peters (eds), *The Legal Framework of the OSCE* (Cambridge University Press 2019) 9–16.

[44] See *Bamieh v Eulex (Kosovo) and others* [2018] UKEAT 0268/16 paras 29–73.

[45] Case C-314/85 *Foto-Frost v Hauptzollamt Lübeck-Ost* [1987] EU:C:1987:452 para 17.

[46] View of AG Kokott, *Opinion 2/13* [2014] para 100.

[47] Case C-72/15 *Rosneft v Her Majesty's Treasury* [2017] EU:C:2017:236 paras 76–79.

the sphere of the CFSP,[48] others claimed that national courts could ask the CJEU to interpret EU law or ascertain the validity of acts adopted by EU institutions, including EU foreign affairs, security, and defence.[49] In a relatively recent decision, the Luxembourg judges partly solved this question. In response to a British court, which had asked the CJEU for a preliminary ruling pertaining to sanctions (Case C–72/15, *Rosneft*), the Court of Justice held that it was competent to give preliminary rulings to determine the (in)validity of acts of EU institutions 'in the field of the CFSP where the Treaties confer the Court jurisdiction to review their legality'.[50] Whereas this opens the venue for preliminary rulings on subjects covered by the explicit jurisdiction of the Court, namely sanctions and policy delimitation, it does not imply—but does not preclude either—that the CJEU can also render such rulings on other CFSP decisions.[51] Be that as it may, the Court remains the sole interpreter of CFSP issues for which it is competent by virtue of primary law or on the basis of its own jurisprudence.

But even if national courts were to scrutinize CFSP/CSDP decisions taken in the context of EU peacebuilding activities, they could limit the application in the respective Member State, but would lack the power to invalidate the disputed acts.[52] What is more, the decision of a national court would not necessarily bind the EU or its institutions; there is, therefore, the danger of unenforceability.[53] And finally, EU institutions could not appear before national courts.[54] Thus, $A_c$ would be incomplete in scope and geographically compartmentalized. Consequently, this could lead to a jurisprudential patchwork across Member States regarding legal protection.[55]

The final aspect potentially limiting adjudication by national courts is the *locus standi* of plaintiffs. Access rules are 'not homogeneous but variable in national systems'.[56] And even if national courts declared themselves competent to hear a case and the admissibility threshold was reached, it would not be obvious that liability could be established or damages enforced.[57] Liability claims (death, injury, damage, and loss) are subject to a special regime laid down in SOMAs. The mission

[48] View of AG Kokott, *Opinion 2/13* [2014] paras 89, 100; Geert de Baere, *Constitutional Principles of EU External Relations* (Oxford University Press 2008) 187, 188.

[49] Case C–455/14 P [2016], Opinion of AG Wahl of 7 April 2016 para 91; Hillion (n 33) 65.

[50] Case C–72/15 [2017] para 78.

[51] The reflections of AG Wathelet point to the same direction. Case C–72/15 *Rosneft v Her Majesty's Treasury* [2016] EU:C:2016:381, Opinion of AG Wathelet of 31 May 2016 paras 70–71.

[52] Case C–455/14 P [2016], Opinion of AG Wahl of 7 April 2016 para 103. See further Joni Heliskoski, 'Responsibility and Liability for CSDP Operations' in Steven Blockmans and Panos Koutrakos (eds), *Research Handbook on the EU's Common Foreign and Security Policy* (Edward Elgar 2018) 147.

[53] Stian Øby Johansen, 'Accountability Mechanisms for Human Rights Violations by CSDP Missions: Available and Sufficient?' (2017) 66 International and Comparative Law Quarterly 181, 203–4.

[54] Harlow and Rawlings (n 2) 549; Martina Spernbauer, *EU Peacebuilding in Kosovo and Afghanistan. Legality and Accountability* (Martinus Nijhoff Publishers 2014) 357.

[55] Eckes (n 6) 515.

[56] Harlow and Rawlings (n 2) 548.

[57] Kottmann (n 19) 227–29.

or its members cannot be held liable 'for any damages to or loss of civilian or government property' occasioned by the fulfilment (or protection) of the mandate.[58] In addition, claims not covered by this exception from liability follow a three-step procedure, consisting of (i) the attempt to reach an amicable settlement, the lack thereof leading to (ii) a possible settlement by a specifically established claims commission, and if a settlement is not possible either, (iii) recourse to diplomatic means or to a claims tribunal is programmed. These arrangements do not, a priori, give national courts jurisdiction to hear liability cases.[59]

To recapitulate, while in theory national courts would be the primary legal accountability fora in the context of EU peacebuilding activities, there are in practice different hurdles rendering adjudication on these matters problematic. The little case law at the national level underlines this point, especially when compared to the significant amount of cases lodged with the European Ombudsman (potentially) qualifying for administrative jurisdiction.[60] As a result, there are in practice few opportunities to hold national actors at the strategic or operational level of civilian crisis management to account for their decisions in Brussels ($A_c$), or to exercise accountability for information ($A_i$) on behalf of national institutions.

## 3. The Dual Accountability Role of the CJEU

A look at the EU judicature offers a more nuanced accountability picture. Within the limited jurisdiction in CFSP/CSDP matters attributed to the EU judicature under primary law (Article 24(1) TEU and Article 275 TFEU), the CJEU fulfils two crucial accountability roles.[61] First, the EU judicature acts as an accountability *facilitator*. In this role, the Court backs the accountability role of other institutions, such as the European Parliament (EP), on the basis of existing institutional or procedural arrangements. Adjudication concerns the allocation of power or competences in the institutionally and procedurally intergovernmental realm of the CFSP/CSDP. Secondly, the CJEU can be an accountability *forum*. In this function, the Court itself holds actors of EU security and defence to account for their action (or omission). Much adjudication in this respect relates to the Europeanized dimension of civilian crisis management as cases circle around day-to-day issues or,

[58] Art 16 Model SOMA.

[59] A detailed study of the settlement of claims arising from damages incurred in the course of civilian CSDP missions and the role of (domestic) courts in this settlement procedure, see Carolyn Moser, 'Loin de l'Union, loin des juges?—Sur les voies de recours juridictionnelles dans le cadre des activités de sécurité et de défense extraterritoriales de l'Union européenne' in Layla Kristina Jaber, Stefanie Lüer, and Anne-Marie Thévenot-Werner (eds), *Wechselseitige Einflüsse zwischen Rechtsordnungen am Beispiel des Zugangs zum Gericht gegen das Handeln der Exekutive* (Springer forthcoming 2020).

[60] See Chapter 7.

[61] On the double accountability role of courts in general, see Harlow and Rawlings (n 2) 547.

differently put, derivative CFSP decisions. Section 3.1 discusses in detail the facilitator role, and the section 3.2 addresses the Court's function as arbiter.

## 3.1 The Court as an accountability *facilitator*

Despite its de jure limited jurisdiction on matters related to the CFSP/CSDP, the EU judicature has been able to exercise its role as an accountability *facilitator*, mostly in relation to the intergovernmental facet of civilian crisis management (ie competences or rights in the codified intergovernmental, institutional, and procedural setting). The Court's jurisprudence has indeed severally impacted the institutional and procedural framework within which EU security and defence unfolds.[62] First, the Court's jurisprudence has somewhat alleviated the strict secrecy rules applicable to security and defence documents by affirming a general right to access information, while safeguarding specific exceptions of non-disclosure. Secondly, the Luxembourg judges have made sure that the institutional balance between supranational (Commission, EP) and intergovernmental institutions (Council) is respected in decision-making and implementation. Thirdly, and more recently, the CJEU has also strengthened parliamentary rights with a view to permitting democratic scrutiny of EU foreign affairs, security, and defence. All of these litigation constellations allowed the Court to clarify general substantive and procedural standards applicable to the CFSP/CSDP. Therefore, the Court decisions discussed in this section indirectly affect decision-making in and implementation of EU peacebuilding as they impact on the overall legal and political framework within which civilian missions are carried out.

### 3.1.1 Access to sensitive documents: rights and limits

At the turn of the century, transparent modes of governance were high on the agenda.[63] Against this broader backdrop, several cases were lodged at the Court in Luxembourg to decide whether and to what extent access to sensitive documents had to be granted in the field of EU foreign and security policy. In *Svenska Journalistförbundet*, a case in which the Council had denied access to documents because of the duty of confidentiality,[64] the Court of First Instance held in 1998 that, according to the 1993 Council decision on public access to Council documents,[65] public access to Council documents included *all* Council documents,

[62] Marise Cremona and Anne Thies, 'Introduction' in Marise Cremona and Anne Thies (eds), *The European Court of Justice and External Relations Law. Constitutional Challenges* (Hart Publishing 2014) 2.

[63] See, for instance, COM(2001) 428 final, 'European Governance—a White Paper', OJ [2001] C287/1.

[64] Case T-174/95 *Svenska Journalistförbundet v Council* [1998] EU:T:1998:127 paras 13, 18.

[65] Council Decision 93/731/EC of 20 December 1993 on public access to Council documents [1993] OJ L340/43.

regardless of their content.[66] This meant that CFSP documents were *not* subject to a special transparency or access policy.[67]

One year later, in 1999, the Court of First Instance upheld this view in *Hautala*, a case concerning a Member of the European Parliament (MEP) who had requested information on the export of conventional arms from the Council.[68] Moreover, the Court of First Instance introduced in this context a considerate judicial review of access-to-documents cases: exceptions to the general rule of access could be made by the Council if the disclosure of the documents requested would negatively impact on the international relations of the EU; in this constellation, the review by the Court (of First Instance) would be limited 'to verifying whether the procedural rules have been complied with, the contested decision is properly reasoned, and the facts have been accurately stated, and whether there has been a manifest error of assessment of the facts or a misuse of powers'.[69] If only parts of the requested information were covered by the exception, the Council would have to consider granting partial access to those parts of the documents not falling under the exceptions regime,[70] and here the Court could exercise a full review 'to verify whether the Council was obliged to consider whether partial access could be granted'.[71] Shortly after, the Court of First Instance ruled in two related cases—*Kuijer I* and *Kuijer II*—that a refusal to grant access to a document needed to be reasoned on the basis of the content and context of the document in question.[72]

In sum, the jurisprudence of the CJEU created a framework in which the Council—and, by extension, other institutions handling classified CFSP information—can refuse access to documents if their disclosure could have negative repercussions for the international relations of the EU according to an evaluation of the documents' content and context. For those parts not covered by the exceptions regime, partial disclosure has to be considered. In addition, the Court found itself competent to scrutinize whether the procedural rules of (not) granting access had been abided by. This line of jurisprudence improved access to

[66] Case T-174/95 [1998] paras 81–84.

[67] ibid 84.

[68] Case T-14/98 *Heidi Hautala v Council* [1999] EU:T:1999:157 para 42.

[69] ibid 72.

[70] ibid 87. In a later case (Case C-266/05 *P Sison v Council* [2007] EU:C:2007:75), the Court clearly stressed that 'the refusal of access by the institution is mandatory where disclosure of a document to the public would undermine the interests which that provision protects' (para 46). The Court further stated that the Council enjoyed a 'wide discretion for the purpose of determining whether disclosure of a document to the public would undermine the interests protected by that provision' (para 64). It also found the brevity of the Council's statement of reasons was justified as it meant to protect sensitive interests (para 82). This deferential attitude has been criticized by scholars. See, for instance, de Baere (n 48) 175.

[71] Case T-14/98 [1999] para 76. The Court upheld the 1999 first instance decision in a judgment delivered in 2001. Case C-353/99 *P Council v Heidi Hautala* [2001] EU:C:2001:661 paras 22–31.

[72] Case T-188/98 *Aldo Kuijer v Council* [2000] EU:T:2000:101 paras 36–48. This reasoning was again unfolded and corroborated in a judgment delivered in 2002 Case T-211/00 *Aldo Kuijer v Council* [2002] EU:T:2002:30 paras 60–64.

sensitive documents of individuals and, in this way, paved the way for enhanced accountability regarding EU foreign affairs, security, and defence, which included peacebuilding activities. This holds both for $A_i$ exercised through individuals and including MEPs, and for $A_c$ exercised by the Court when reviewing the compliance with existing procedures. But it must be stressed that despite this somewhat attenuating judicial interpretation of existing secondary legislation on public access to documents, the mandatory and optional exceptions contained in the 2001 Regulation on public access to EU documents,[73] together with the restrictive internal security regulations of the Council and the EEAS, continue rendering public access to documents in (civilian) CSDP a complex endeavour.[74]

### 3.1.2 Institutional balance: from policy delimitation to democracy promotion

Another highly contentious subject area was (and still is) the delimitation of strands of external action, which is linked to the principle of institutional balance. Here, the Court had to repeatedly adjudicate which institution was competent to take external action. The key element in this regard is the choice of the appropriate substantive legal basis, which is to be selected in accordance with objective factors amenable to judicial review.[75] This choice is of 'constitutional significance',[76] as it ensures that EU institutions are acting on the basis of powers conferred to them. No less important is the significance of the substantive legal basis regarding institutional balance: the choice of the *substantive* legal basis determines the *formal* legal basis, namely the applicable decision-making procedures, and therefore impacts the extent to which different European institutions are involved in decision-making and policy implementation.[77]

To delineate external competences, the Court has developed the *centre of gravity test*, which consists in a thorough examination of the aim and the content of an adopted measure.[78] When a measure pursues several objectives or consists of several components, a distinction has to be made between the main or predominant

[73] Regulation (EC) 1049/2001 of the European Parliament and of the Council of 30 May 2001 regarding public access to European Parliament, Council and Commission documents [2001] OJ L145/43.

[74] Council Decision 2013/488/EU of 23 September 2013 on the security rules for protecting EU classified information [2013] OJ L274/1; Decision of the High Representative of the EU for Foreign Affairs and Security Policy of 19 September 2017 on the security rules for the European External Action Service ADMIN(2017) 10 OJ C126/1. For further details, see the accountability challenges discussed in Chapter 3.

[75] Case C–300/89 *Commission v Council* [1991] EU:C:1991:244 para 10; Case 45/86 *Commission v Council* [1987] EU:C:1987:163 para 11.

[76] *Opinion 2/00* of the Court of 6 December 2001 [2001] EU:C:2001:664 para 5; Case C–263/14 *European Parliament v Council* [2016] EU:C:2016:2436 para 42.

[77] Peter van Elsuwege, 'The Potential for Inter-Institutional Conflicts before the Court of Justice: Impact of the Lisbon Treaty' in Marise Cremona and Anne Thies (eds), *The European Court of Justice and External Relations Law. Constitutional Challenges* (Hart Publishing 2014) 115.

[78] ibid 117–19.

element and the incidental element—the former determining the legal basis. If objectives or components cannot be hierarchized because they are inextricably linked, the measure can, in principle, be based on several legal bases.[79] Scrutiny of the appropriate legal basis is a powerful tool to ensure that institutions act according to primary law provisions, and therefore helps the Court to enforce $A_c$.

Traditionally, litigation concerning policy delimitation was brought by the Commission against the Council to delineate development from security policies. But in recent years, court cases have been initiated by the EP against the Council with a view to defining the limits of security policy activities and the (external dimension of the) Area of Freedom, Security and Justice (AFSJ), the EP having far more participation rights in the latter. The litigation constellation in delimitation cases has thus changed since the entry into force of the Treaty of Lisbon.[80]

The most prominent pre-Lisbon litigation related to development/security delimitation was the *ECOWAS* case about the non-proliferation of small arms and light weapons (SALWs) in Africa, which opposed the Commission and the Council. In order to call a halt to the destabilizing accumulation and spread of SALWs, the Council had taken a decision,[81] implementing a Joint Action,[82] to 'offer a financial contribution and technical assistance to set up the Light Weapons Unit within the ECOWAS Technical Secretariat and convert the Moratorium into a Convention on small arms and light weapons between the ECOWAS Member States'.[83] The Commission brought an action before the CJEU for the annulment of the measures at stake, arguing that they had an invalid legal basis as they pursued development (instead of security) objectives. In short, the Commission's core claim was that both the Joint Action and the implementing decision fell within the scope of the shared competences on the basis of which the Community conducted its development policy. As these Community competences were protected through the non-affectation clause,[84] set out by then Article 47 TEU (Nice), the Council's measures were considered to violate the Community's competence in the area.[85] Article 47 TEU (Nice) stipulated that 'nothing in this Treaty shall affect the

[79] This approach was confirmed by several post-Lisbon rulings. See Case C-263/14 [2016] para 44; Case C-658/11 *European Parliament v Council* [2014] EU:C:2014:2025 para 43; Case C-130/10 *European Parliament v Council* [2012] EU:C:2012:472 paras 42–44.

[80] This observation was also made in Van Elsuwege (n 77) 119.

[81] Council Decision 2004/833/CFSP of 2 December 2004 implementing Joint Action 2002/589/CFSP with a view to a European Union contribution to ECOWAS in the framework of the Moratorium on Small Arms and Light Weapons [2004] OJ L395/65.

[82] Council Joint Action of 12 July 2002 on the European Union's contribution to combating the destabilising accumulation and spread of small arms and light weapons and repealing Joint Action 1999/34/CFSP [2002] L191/1.

[83] Art 1(2) Council Decision 2004/833/CFSP [2004] OJ L395/65.

[84] Peter van Elsuwege, 'EU External Action After the Collapse of the Pillar Structure: In Search of a New Balance Between Delimitation and Consistency' (2010) 47 Common Market Law Review 987, 1002–4.

[85] An analysis of the arguments provided by the Commission and the Council can be found in Christophe Hillion and Ramses A Wessel, 'Competence Distribution in EU External Relations after ECOWAS: Clarification or Continued Fuzziness?' (2009) 46 Common Market Law Review 551; Panos

Treaties establishing the European Communities or the subsequent Treaties and Acts modifying or supplementing them'. The Court followed the Commission's line of argument regarding the interpretation of this provision—shielding Community competences from encroachment—and annulled both Council measures.[86]

Meanwhile, the non-affectation clause has been substantially altered: it has turned into a *mutual* non-affectation clause.[87] Given this modified primary law framework, the significance of the existing jurisprudence (ie the *ECOWAS* case) is reduced under the new constitutional arrangements.[88] The current Treaty provision reads as follows:

> Article 40 TEU The implementation of the common foreign and security policy shall not affect the application of the procedures and the extent of the powers of the institutions laid down by the Treaties for the exercise of the Union competences referred to in Articles 3 to 6 of the Treaty on the Functioning of the European Union. Similarly, the implementation of the policies listed in those Articles shall not affect the application of the procedures and the extent of the powers of the institutions laid down by the Treaties for the exercise of the Union competences under this Chapter.

Hence, the *acquis communautaire*—former Community competences—is protected from encroachment by the stipulations of the first paragraph, just as the *acquis sécuritaire*[89]—under the CFSP—is shielded from impingement by supranational strands of external action by virtue of the second paragraph.[90]

Interestingly, after the entry into force of the Treaty of Lisbon, the Court refrained for several years from expressly mentioning Article 40 in judgments dealing with delimitation issues. The first reference to Article 40, however, was made in 2016, and only to its first paragraph, namely the protection of supranational competences from intergovernmental impingement. This is somewhat puzzling given

Koutrakos, 'The Nexus Between the European Union's Common Security and Defence Policy and Development', *A Constitutional Order of States? Essays in EU Law in Honour of Alan Dashwood* (Hart Publishing 2011) 600.

[86] Case C-91/05 *Commission v Council* [2008] EU:C:2008:288.

[87] Van Elsuwege (n 84) 1002–4.

[88] Alan Dashwood, 'Article 47 TEU and the Relationship between First and Second Pillar Competences' in Alan Dashwood and Marc Maresceau (eds), *Law and Practice of EU External Relations. Salient Features of a Changing Landscape* (Cambridge University Press 2008) 98–103; Koutrakos (n 15) 236–44.

[89] Term used by Steven Blockmans in Steven Blockmans, 'An Introduction to the Role of the EU in Crisis Management' in Steven Blockmans (ed), *The European Union and Crisis Management: Policy and Legal Aspects* (TMC Asser Press 2008) 3.

[90] AG Yves Bot, for instance, explicitly mentioned that the provisions of Article 40 TEU henceforth protected the *acquis sécuritaire* from supranational encroachment. See Case C-130/10 *European Parliament v Council* [2012] EU:C:2012:50, Opinion of AG Bot of 31 January 2012 para 67. The Court did, however, not include his reasoning in the final judgment.

that in the case at hand (discussed below) the EP challenged intergovernmental competences (CFSP) by advancing supranational competences pertaining to the AFSJ.[91]

This being said, the Treaty of Lisbon puts a strong emphasis on the consistency of external action (Article 21(3) TEU), although it does not impose a hierarchy of different forms of external action. Consequently, the status quo regarding the consistency requirement is that development and the (external dimension of the) AFSJ on the one hand, and the CFSP/CSDP on the other hand, are on an equal footing from a formal point of view.[92] This reading is consolidated by Article 1(3) TEU, stipulating the same legal value of the TEU and the TFEU. The new provisions contained in Article 40 TEU on the mutual non-affectation of the CFSP—and implicitly the CSDP—and external activities undertaken under other policy fields also corroborate this formal equality. The Court has to determine why, in certain constellations, one strand of external policy takes priority over another, especially as they pursue common objectives according to Article 21(2) TEU.

This is precisely what the CJEU had to do with regard to a series of cases related to AFSJ/CFSP delimitation, which has been at the core of post-Lisbon cases on institutional balance, all initiated by the EP against the Council. In addition, the CJEU strengthened the role of the EP as a political accountability forum. While taking into consideration the institutional prerogatives and procedural arrangements laid down by the Treaty drafters, the EU judicature gave existing procedural requirements a parliamentary-friendly reading.

The first contentious case was related to the imposition of restrictive measures in the fight against terrorism.[93] The EP had brought an action to the CJEU to annul a Council Regulation imposing such restrictive measures,[94] claiming that the Regulation had been adopted on the incorrect substantive legal basis, namely under Article 215(2) TFEU falling under the CFSP and not under Article 75 TFEU falling under the AFSJ. The Court, sitting in its Grand Chamber composition, repeated that a recourse to a dual legal basis was not possible if the procedures linked to the respective legal bases were incompatible with each other—which was the case with Article 215(2) TFEU and Article 75 TFEU: the two legal bases could not be cumulated as they laid down a very different degree of involvement for the EP.[95] In view of the aim, content, and context of the contested Regulation, the Court found that Article 215(2) TFEU constituted 'the appropriate legal basis

[91] Case C–263/14 [2016] para 42.

[92] Jörg Monar, *The External Dimension of the EU's Area of Freedom, Security and Justice. Progress, Potential and Limitations after the Treaty of Lisbon* (Swedish Institute for European Policy Studies 2012) 28.

[93] Case C–130/10 [2012].

[94] Council Regulation (EU) 1286/2009 of 22 December 2009 amending Regulation (EC) 881/2002 imposing certain specific restrictive measures directed against certain persons and entities associated with Usama bin Laden, the Al-Qaida network and the Taliban [2009] OJ L346/42.

[95] Case C–130/10 [2012] paras 45–49.

for measures ... directed to addressees implicated in acts of terrorism who, having regard to their activities globally and to the international dimension of the threat they pose, affect fundamentally the Union's external activity',[96] and eventually dismissed the action.[97] Moreover, the Court stated that the limited de jure role of the EP in the CFSP could not determine the choice of the (substantive) legal basis favouring a parliamentary-friendly (formal) legal basis.[98] At the same time, the judges also emphasized that the restricted involvement of the EP in CFSP matters was 'the result of the choice made by the framers of the Treaty of Lisbon'.[99] The Luxembourg judges recalled on this occasion that,

> participation by the Parliament in the *legislative process* is the reflection, at Union level, of the fundamental democratic principles that the people should participate in the exercise of power through the intermediary of a representative assembly.[100]

The second contentious case—*Mauritius Agreement*—concerned the conclusion of an international agreement in the context of the EU's anti-piracy activities off the Somali coast. On behalf of the EU, the Council (without consultation or prior consent of the EP) had in 2011 decided to sign and conclude an agreement with the Republic of Mauritius to regulate the conditions of the transfer of suspected pirates (and their post-transfer conditions), including any associated seized property, from the EU-led naval force to the Republic of Mauritius.[101] The contested international agreement included aspects of judicial cooperation in criminal matters and police cooperation, and therefore raised questions of policy delimitation. The Court found, however, that to warrant a (single) legal basis on the ground of the AFSJ—and not the CFSP—the measures implemented under Articles 82 TFEU (judicial cooperation in criminal matters) and 87 TFEU (police cooperation) necessarily needed to be linked to the fostering of security *within* the EU and that, in the given case, measures had been taken with a view to strengthening international security *outside* the EU.[102] This take, which stressed the salience of CFSP/CSDP activities (including its civilian dimension), however, is not necessarily in line with operational realities and political desires both of which point to increased CSDP/AFSJ cooperation outside the EU.[103] This said, the Court found the substantive legal basis chosen by the Council (Article 37 TEU, triggering the procedures set

[96] ibid 78.
[97] ibid 112.
[98] ibid 79.
[99] ibid 82.
[100] Emphasis added, ibid 81.
[101] Council Decision 2011/640/CFSP of 12 July 2011 on the signing and conclusion of the Agreement between the European Union and the Republic of Mauritius on the conditions of transfer of suspected pirates and associated seized property from the European Union-led naval force to the Republic of Mauritius and on the conditions of suspected pirates after transfer [2011] OJ L254/1.
[102] Case C-658/11 [2014] para 35.
[103] On this issue, see Chapter 2.

out in Article 218(5) and 218(6) TFEU) to be correct, even though it annulled the decision for procedural reasons while maintaining its effects.[104]

As in the first post-Lisbon delimitation case (C–130/10), the Luxembourg judges referenced the democratic principles underpinning the EU. This time the Court stated that,

> the Parliament's involvement in the *decision-making process* is the reflection, at EU level, of the fundamental democratic principles that the people should participate in the exercise of power through the intermediary of a representative assembly.[105]

It is noteworthy that the linguistic pendulum swung from *legislative* process to *decision-making* process, the latter leaving a far broader room for parliamentary involvement given the preclusion of legislative acts in the CFSP area. What is more, the CJEU found that the 'Treaty of Lisbon has even enhanced the importance of that rule in the treaty system', and that it could not be inferred from primary law provisions that 'the Parliament has no right of scrutiny in respect of that EU policy'.[106] Precisely because primary rules confer to Parliament a very limited role in relation to the CFSP, the Court reasoned, the provision of information was essential for the EP to be:

> in a position to exercise *democratic scrutiny* of the European Union's external action and, more specifically, to verify that its powers are respected precisely in consequence of the choice of legal basis for a decision concluding an agreement.[107]

Crucial with regard to the information and consultation rights of the EP was the Court's interpretation of Article 218(10) TFEU which stipulates that '[t]he European Parliament shall be *immediately* and *fully* informed [by the Council] at all stages of the procedure'.[108] The Court held that this provision set out an *information requirement* that, in turn, constituted an *essential procedural requirement*.[109] Furthermore, the judges made clear that this obligation applied to *any* procedure for the conclusion of international agreements, including those agreements relating

[104] Case C–658/11 [2014] paras 87, 91.

[105] Emphasis added, ibid 81.

[106] ibid 82, 84.

[107] Emphasis added, ibid 80. A similar reflection is developed in ibid 83–86.

[108] Emphasis added. In addition to primary law, this obligation had been underlined by policy documents. See European Parliament legislative resolution of 8 July 2010 on the proposal for a Council decision establishing the organisation and functioning of the European External Action Service (08029/2010 – C7-0090/2010 – 2010/0816(NLE)), P7_TA(2010)0280, Annex: Declaration by the High Representative on political accountability para 2.

[109] AG Bot argued that Art 218(10) TFEU contained an information *obligation* for the Council. Case C–658/11 *European Parliament v Council* [2014] EU:C:2014:41, Opinion of AG Bot of 30 January 2014 para 143.

exclusively to the CFSP.[110] Hence, even in the event of the Council adopting a decision concluding an international agreement, for which neither the consultation nor the prior consent of the EP is necessary as it exclusively relates to CFSP matters (Article 218(6) TFEU), the institution has to comply with this essential procedural requirement and inform the EP in time. For the agreement with Mauritius, the Council had kept the MEPs informed about the negotiation of the agreement, but had communicated the contested decision allowing for the conclusion of the agreement taken in July 2011 to the EP by letter in October 2011 only, four months after its adoption. The Court considered the publication of the decision in the Official Journal in September 2011 not sufficient to fulfil the Council's obligations toward the EP. Therefore, the Court of Justice found that, regardless of the period in question having included the summer recess, an infringement of the information requirement had occurred.[111] The contested decision was consequently annulled, but its effects maintained.

The third litigious case opposing the EP and the Council concerned, again, the conclusion of an international agreement in the context of anti-piracy measures, this time with the United Republic of Tanzania. In *Tanzania Agreement*, the EP argued that the agreement did not exclusively relate to the CFSP but equally pursued AFSJ objectives. Therefore, the agreement should not have been based on Article 37 TEU only but likewise on Articles 82 and 87 TFEU.[112] The EP thus tried to move from a single legal basis in the TEU, excluding the institution from the negotiation, to a double legal basis granting parliamentarians far more consultation rights. The Court, however, upheld its reasoning of the almost identical *Mauritius Agreement* case, and found that the contested agreement fell predominantly within the scope of the CFSP, warranting Article 37 TEU as a single legal basis (leading to the procedure set out in Article 218(6) TFEU).[113] The contested Council decision to conclude the agreement was eventually annulled, while its effects were maintained.[114] Even though the Court cautiously avoided entering the difficult terrain of a (potential) dual legal basis,[115] AG Kokott in her Opinion argued that the jurisprudence of the Court would not rule out a dual legal basis for CFSP/CSDP matters, provided the aim, content, and context of the decision would warrant a CFSP and an additional AFSJ legal basis.[116]

In addition, the EU judicature further extended the information rights of the EP with regard to CFSP matters. The Court of Justice stressed in its Grand Chamber

[110] Case C–658/11 [2014] para 85.

[111] Argument made by the Council. See ibid 67.

[112] Case C–263/14 [2016] para 26.

[113] ibid 51, 55.

[114] ibid 85, 89.

[115] Soledad R Sánchez-Tabernero, 'The Choice of Legal Basis and the Principle of Consistency in the Procedure for Conclusion of International Agreements in CFSP Contexts: Parliament v. Council (Pirate-Transfer Agreement with Tanzania)' (2017) 54 Common Market Law Review 899, 910–12.

[116] Case C–263/14 [2015], Opinion of AG Kokott paras 52–59.

judgment that the participation of the EP in the legislative process—the pendulum swung back from *decision-making* to *legislative* process—mirrored the fundamental democratic principles, and found that:

> [a]s regards the procedure for negotiating and concluding international agreements, the information requirement laid down in Article 218(10) TFEU is the expression of that democratic principle, on which the European Union is founded.[117]

The Court opined that, whereas the Council did not have to reveal international preparatory processes to fulfil this information requirement, the institution could not solely inform the EP on those stages leading to formal Council decisions. On the contrary, in order to *fully* inform, intermediate negotiation results needed to be communicated to the EP at the time they were shared with the foreign counterpart, including 'the text of the draft agreement and the text of the draft decision approved by the Council's Foreign Relations Counsellors who are responsible for the negotiations'[118] to make sure that the EP was in a position to exercise its scrutiny powers. The Court also held that the EP needed to be informed without delay—a lapse of time of nine days (seven working days) was judged too long to comply with the obligation set out by primary law, stipulating that the EP had to be informed *immediately*.[119]

To conclude, regarding accountability for *conduct* ($A_c$) the jurisprudence of the CJEU on institutional balance matters contributed to foster accountability, notably by the Council. By scrutinizing compliance with primary law arrangements on competences and procedures (ie choice of legal basis and related procedures), the CJEU ensured that power-wielders exercised their functions within the limits of the powers conferred by Member States. So far, disputed decisions have not concerned civilian crisis management missions. But given the conceptual and operational overlap of certain development activities and civilian missions on the one hand, and measures adopted under the AFSJ and civilian crisis management on the other hand, it is not unlikely that the CJEU will hear cases related to the delimitation of EU peacebuilding and other external activities in the future. There is, indeed, a progressively starker operational overlap of civilian missions and activities undertaken under the AFSJ umbrella.[120] It is uncertain whether (and how much) the jurisprudence on incompatible legal bases—forged by *Tanzania*

[117] Case C-263/14 [2016] para 70.

[118] ibid 77. See also Case C-263/14 [2015], Opinion of AG Kokott para 86.

[119] Case C-263/14 [2016] para 81.

[120] See on this overlap, inter alia, Gregory Mounier, 'Civilian Crisis Management and the External Dimension of JHA: Inceptive, Functional and Institutional Similarities' in Sarah Wolff, Nicole Wichmann, and Gregory Mounier (eds), *The External Dimension of Justice and Home Affairs: A Different Security Agenda for the European Union?* (Routledge 2010) 44.

and *Mauritius*—will be upheld by the Court in view of cases deriving from the intensifying CSDP/AFSJ operational and institutional interaction, in particular in the civilian CSDP remit.[121]

Concerning accountability for *information* ($A_i$), the jurisprudence of the CJEU strengthened the information rights of the EP on the grounds that the provision of information was the prerequisite of the little democratic scrutiny of the EU's external action under the given primary law framework. As AG Juliane Kokott wrote in her 2016 Opinion in the *Tanzania Agreement* case:

> [d]emocratic control is not limited to the exercise of formal rights to have a say, and the purpose of informing the Parliament is not only to prepare for the exercise of such rights. Rather, the transparency created by informing the Parliament immediately and fully at all stages of the procedure is in itself an element of democratic control which is not to be underestimated and therefore has *inherent* value.[122]

Seemingly inspired by a similar line of reasoning, the jurisprudence of the Court in Luxembourg significantly enhanced $A_i$ of the Council vis-à-vis the EP. In the same vein, accountability mechanisms were furthered by the obligation to keep the EP unremittingly informed about steps taken. This is not without consequences. As information is a power resource, enhancing the obligation for the Council (actor) to share information with the EP (forum) eventually leads to a de facto changed allocation of power.[123] It remains to be seen whether the operationalization of the far-reaching information rights granted to the MEPs will eventually modify the initially intended institutional balance. The jurisdictional backing of parliamentary scrutiny of EU external action out of democratic considerations might, in any event, increase the Council's willingness to communicate information to the EP in this policy field. In order to avoid or attenuate interinstitutional friction, potentially leading to further court cases, the Council might adopt a more proactive stance in this respect. Yet, the immediate impact of this jurisprudence on information-sharing regarding international agreements signed in the context of civilian CSDP should not be overestimated. That is because international agreements relating to civilian CSDP—such as SOMAs or accords with contributing third States—are drafted on the basis of template documents. They essentially contain standard clauses which do not change from one agreement to another.

[121] On the increasing CSDP/AFSJ overlap, not to say interweaving, see Chapter 2. Similar concerns were, moreover, voiced in Paula García Andrade, 'EU External Competences in the Field of Migration: How to Act Externally When Thinking Internally' (2018) 55 Common Market Law Review 157, 182–85.

[122] Emphasis added. Case C–263/14 [2015], Opinion of AG Kokott para 78.

[123] On the significance of information for accountability and its nature as a power resource, see Chapter 3.

Imposing an information-sharing obligation on the Council is, hence, rather symbolic in nature. But even symbolic gestures can in the long run have substantial effects.

## 3.2 The Court as an accountability *forum*

Besides the Court's role as an accountability facilitator, the CJEU also increasingly acts as arbiter in the CSDP. While in the first constellation judicial review is largely procedural, scrutiny shifts to more substantial matters in the latter situation where the Court acts as an accountability *forum*. Indicative hereof are two judgments of the CJEU on cases related to civilian crisis management, handed down in November 2015 and July 2016 respectively. The first proceeding, *Elitaliana* (C–439/13 P), concerned procurement in the context of the Rule of Law Mission (EULEX) in Kosovo, whereas the second dispute, *H v Council and others* (C–455/14 P), related to human resources choices within the police mission EUPM in Bosnia and Herzegovina. Both cases gave the EU judicature, that is both the General Court and in particular the Court of Justice, the opportunity to clarify two paramount issues, namely jurisdiction and attribution.

### 3.2.1 Adjudicating Europeanized intergovernmentalism

The two issues—*jurisdiction* and *attribution*—are inseparably bound up with the sui generis edifice of Europeanized intergovernmentalism. For jurisdiction, primary law considerably restricts supranational judicial review of the CFSP/CSDP. This jurisdictional carve-out mirrors the de jure intergovernmental character of the CFSP, which was left unaltered by the latest Treaty revision,[124] and also highlights the deeply rooted fear of (some) Member States causing them to shield EU foreign affairs, security, and defence from judicial review by the Luxembourg judges.[125] Yet, civilian crisis management de facto takes place in a Europeanized administrative and operational setting, even if it de jure unfolds within an institutionally and procedurally intergovernmental framework. To steer and implement civilian missions, civilian crisis management actors take numerous derivate CFSP decisions that are not, however, (explicitly) laid down in primary law as a result of concealed agencification as outlined in section 1.1. Their publication, therefore, is not mandatory and only a few of them are traceable in the online register of the EEAS or the Council. The Brussels-based actors thus operate largely below the threshold of formality (and visibility), so that their actions are in principle difficult to legally scrutinize or oppose.

[124] View of AG Kokott, *Opinion 2/13* [2014] para 90.

[125] Kottmann (n 19) 172–75; Eileen Denza, *The Intergovernmental Pillars of the European Union* (Oxford University Press 2002) 312.

The second issue—attribution—is equally linked to the intricate administrative and operational set-up of EU peacebuilding. Given the complex de jure and de facto environment resulting from concealed agencification,[126] it was (and in some respects still is) unclear to which body or institution a disputed decision could be imputed. The Court opted to pragmatically deal with the (in)formal ramifications of concealed agencification and Europeanized intergovernmentalism: the decisive criterion for attribution was not the *institutional* anchorage of the different civilian crisis management actors, but their *functional* nexus with EU institutions for specific tasks due to the chain of command or supervision requirements.

The two issues of jurisdiction and attribution were addressed in the abovementioned 2015 and 2016 judgments. The new case law declared certain operational actions by civilian crisis management actors—namely decisions with financial implications as well as day-to-day management choices at the theatre level—amendable to judicial review by the EU judicature, and furthermore clarified to which EU institution these actions could be attributed. The CJEU found that decisions with financial implications were attributable to the Commission, whereas day-to-day management choices at theatre level could be imputed to the Council.[127] As a result, executive prerogatives were narrowed down and legal protection substantially enhanced: the initially unaccountable crisis management apparatus can henceforth be called to account for its actions via the CJEU. As the following analysis shows, the administrative and operational specificities of peacebuilding were pivotal in this respect as they allowed the Luxembourg judges to embed the sui generis edifice of civilian crisis management into the broader legal and institutional EU context, and to extend their own judicial scrutiny of the CFSP/CSDP by virtue of *implied* and *contingent* jurisdictional competences. In this way, the Court adjusted the scope of its judicial scrutiny to Europeanized intergovernmentalism. The limited juridification and judicialization of (civilian) CSDP has left the judges with ample interpretative leeway for jurisdictional aspects.[128] Cleverly using this interpretative room for manoeuvre, and through its jurisprudence related to civilian crisis management activities, the EU judicature has caused a breach in the preclusion of judicial review regarding CFSP/CSDP matters set out in primary law.

[126] A definition and detailed analysis of the process of concealed agencification can be found in Chapter 2.

[127] The European Ombudsman has proposed a slightly different *démarche*. While the Commission was equally identified as the institution to be addressed for issues relating to budget implementation, the High Representative of the EU for Foreign Affairs and Security Policy (HR) was found to be the initial contact point for all other allegations of maladministration—mainly because the Council had demonstrated very little will to deal with inquiries of the Ombudsman in civilian CSDP. See Decision of the European Ombudsman closing the own-initiative inquiry OI/12/2010/(BEH)MMN concerning the Council of the European Union, the European Commission and the High Representative/European External Action Service (30 August 2013). For further information, see Chapter 7.

[128] On this issue, see Chapter 6.

### 3.2.2 Implied jurisdiction for budget issues

The first proceeding, *Elitaliana* (C–439/13 P), related to procurement in the context of the rule of law mission EULEX Kosovo.[129] A restricted public contract award procedure had been opened in autumn 2011 to provide EULEX Kosovo with helicopter support. In December 2011, the then EULEX Head of Mission (HoM) asked the Italian company Elitaliana SpA (hereafter referred to as Elitaliana or the applicant) to take part in the tendering procedure, which shortly after submitted a bid. In March 2012, Elitaliana was informed by a letter signed by the director of the EULEX administration that its bid had been placed second. In April 2012, the applicant sought access to documents of the tendering procedure (ie the bid of the company placed first) but was refused access by a letter signed by the HoM. In reaction, Elitaliana lodged an application at the General Court in May 2012, claiming that the general principles of transparency, proportionality, equal treatment, and effective competition had been infringed upon in the said tendering procedure. In addition, an application for interim relief was simultaneously lodged, but dismissed shortly after. A Court order of the General Court dated June 2013 mainly dealt with three interrelated legal questions: (i) the capacity of EULEX to be a defendant, (ii) the procedural requirement incumbent upon the applicant to identify the party against which action should be directed, and (iii) the attribution of the disputed decision.[130]

The General Court declared that the disputed decision—a refusal by the HoM to grant the applicant access to documents from the tendering procedure—was attributable to the Commission, given the financial arrangements existing between EU peacebuilding activities (ie the civilian mission in Kosovo) and the Commission for the implementation of the mission's budget, notably procurement procedures.[131] According to the rules in place, the HoM could conclude procurement contracts only with the approval of the Commission. The Commission was therefore regarded by the Court as the delegating institution to which measures adopted pursuant to delegated powers could in principle be attributed. Thus, the decisive element for attribution was the functional link, forged by reporting requirements and supervision arrangements for budgetary questions between the HoM and the Commission. In the concrete case, however, the action of Elitaliana was considered inadmissible because the judges did not concur with the applicant that, in the absence of EULEX Kosovo having legal capacity to be a defendant, they should identify the party against which the action could be pursued. Elitaliana had brought an action against EULEX Kosovo, claiming that the latter was a body, office, or agency of the EU within the meaning of the first paragraph of Article 263

[129] The mission was launched in 2008 by the Council Joint Action 2008/124/CFSP of 4 February 2008 on the European Union Rule of Law Mission in Kosovo, EULEX KOSOVO [2008] OJ L42/92.

[130] Case T–213/12 *Elitaliana SpA v EULEX Kosovo* [2013] EU:T:2013:292.

[131] Case C–439/13 *P Elitaliana SpA v EULEX Kosovo* [2015] EU:C:2015:753 paras 55–66; Case T–213/12 [2013] paras 29–34.

TFEU, that is, an entity intended to produce legal effects vis-à-vis third parties.[132] The General Court, however, held that EULEX Kosovo did *not* constitute such a body, office, or agency, and could therefore not be a defendant.[133] It declared that the applicant's error was not excusable as the case law at the time the application was made already clearly underlined that civilian missions could not be regarded as a body, office, or agency of the EU.[134] The action of Elitaliana was therefore considered inadmissible.[135]

Notwithstanding the inadmissibility in the *Elitaliana* case, the decision implies that budget-related decisions with implications for third parties taken by members of the crisis management bureaucracy (ie the HoM) are attributable to the Commission and can be heard by the EU judicature, provided the applicant identifies the right parties to the dispute, namely the Commission—and, for incidents having taken place after 2014, potentially also the respective mission as mandates have since then provided missions with the legal capacity to appear in court.[136]

The case then went to the appeal stage, giving the Court of Justice the opportunity to discuss questions of legal status, attribution, and jurisdiction in its 2015 judgment.[137] The Firth Chamber upheld the General Court's assessment that EULEX Kosovo was not a body, office, or agency of the EU and could not be a party to the proceedings as it lacked legal capacity.[138] The innovative qualification of EULEX as a 'temporary interinstitutional cooperative structure and not a body with legal existence of its own' proposed by AG Jääskinen in his Opinion of May 2015 was not taken on by the Court.[139] But in line with the Opinions of AG Jääskinen of December 2014 and May 2015,[140] the judges underlined that the measures adopted in the context of the public procurement procedure in question were attributable to the Commission, given the financial arrangements in place.[141] In the end, the action for appeal was declared inadmissible in its entirety.

[132] Case T-213/12 [2013] para 39.

[133] ibid 26, 35.

[134] ibid 38–39, 43, 45–46.

[135] ibid 45–46.

[136] Since 2014, a standard formulation has been inserted in mission mandates in the stipulations on 'legal arrangements stating that missions can 'be a party to legal proceedings' (see section 2). In 2017 a first application regarding procurement matters was lodged against both the Commission and a civilian mission (EUBAM Libya). Even though the action was dismissed, the Court did in its judgment not question the proper identification by the applicant of the two defendant parties. See Case T-206/17 *Argus Security Projects Ltd v Commission and EUBAM Libya* [2018] EU:T:2018:288.

[137] Case C-439/13 P [2015].

[138] ibid 58–59.

[139] Case C-439/13 *P Elitaliana SpA v EULEX Kosovo* [2015] EU:C:2015:341, Opinion of AG Jääskinen of 21 May 2015 para 53.

[140] Case C-439/13 P [2015], Opinion of AG Jääskinen; Case C-439/13 *P Elitaliana SpA v EULEX Kosovo* [2014] EU:C:2014:2416, Opinion of AG Jääskinen of 4 December 2014.

[141] Case C-439/13 P [2015] paras 60–66.

In addition to the interrelated questions of legal status and attributability, the crucial point of the Court's jurisdiction was raised in the appeal phase. The administrative arrangements regarding financial matters played a paramount role in this regard. A key vector was a 'constitutional oddity',[142] introduced by the Treaty of Maastricht, according to which supranational funds can be disbursed for intergovernmental activities conducted under the CSDP. Indeed, Article 41(1)–(2) TEU stipulates that both administrative and operating expenditure without military and defence implications arising from CFSP/CSDP activities are charged to the EU budget. This, in turn, signifies that the Council and the EP have to find an agreement on the budget appropriations allocated to the CFSP, including civilian crisis management, and that this budget is eventually implemented by the Commission (first paragraph of Article 317 TFEU, together with the pertinent financial rules).[143] As the Commission performs central administrative functions in civilian crisis management—though this is not explicitly spelled out in the Treaty provisions on foreign policy—the financial rules pertaining to the general EU budget are applicable.[144]

In this respect, in his Opinion dated 21 May 2015 AG Jääskinen demonstrated that the abovementioned constitutional oddity ascribed to the Commission the final responsibility for the budget administration of CFSP funds, according to rules and procedures applicable to the EU budget. As the Court can hear cases related to the EU budget and financial administration, AG Jääskinen regarded its jurisdiction in the present as established.[145] Without explicitly referring to the Opinion of AG Jääskinen, the Court developed the same reasoning in its judgment,[146] and declared itself competent.[147] The Court thus asserted jurisdiction on the basis of its *implied jurisdictional competences*.

The Court had, indeed, convincing legal arguments to declare itself competent to hear cases related to financial CFSP matters on the basis of implied jurisdiction. The constitutional oddity codified by primary law creates a jurisdictional loophole—the Commission is responsible, and the jurisdiction of the Court is not explicitly excluded—which the Court cleverly used to extend its jurisdictional competences. The Court's implied competence was rendered explicit by the *Elitaliana* case. It remains to be seen in how far this might lead to indirectly

[142] Jörg Monar, 'The Finances of the Union's Intergovernmental Pillars: Tortuous Experiments with the Community Budget' (1997) 35 Journal of Common Market Studies 57, 59.

[143] For further details on the (implementation of the) CFSP budget, see Günter Sautter, 'The Financing of Common Foreign and Security Policy—on Continuity and Change' in Hermann-Josef Blanke and Stelio Mangiameli (eds), *The European Union after Lisbon: Constitutional Basis, Economic Order and External Action* (Springer 2012).

[144] At the point in time when the disputed decision was adopted, the Financial Rules of 2002 were in place. See Council Regulation (EC, Euratom) 1605/2002 of 25 June 2002 on the Financial Regulation applicable to the general budget of the European Communities [2002] OJ L248/1.

[145] Case C-439/13 P [2015], Opinion of AG Jääskinen paras 41, 59.

[146] Case C-439/13 P [2015] paras 56–66.

[147] ibid 48–50.

attributing the Commission a bigger say over civilian crisis management because of financial micro-management manoeuvres. Already, the Commission fulfils essential supervisory tasks regarding budget implementation. With the amount of expenditure (and thus budgetary supervision) significantly increasing over the years, the day-to-day implication of the Commission—that is its Service for Foreign Policy Instruments (FPI)—has steadily augmented in CSDP activities. While the Commission might tighten its financial supervision because of its jurisdictionally underscored administrative responsibilities, the decision-making power regarding the annual budget of civilian crisis management remains with the Council and the EP, and the implementation takes place in close coordination with the respective missions and the Headquarters in Brussels (ie the Civilian Planning and Conduct Capability (CPCC)). The Court's *Elitaliana* decision, however, certainly reinforces a constitutional disequilibrium that was already judged irreconcilable with 'all traditions of democratic governance'[148] prior to the CSDP going operational: while the Commission can be held (i) politically accountable by the EP in the course of the discharge procedure, and (ii) legally accountable by the EU judicature for financial decisions related to civilian CSDP, the Commission has no decision-making power in this policy field. Accountability is therefore not the corollary to exercising power, but the result of another actor holding power. This leads to a paradoxical situation where the Commission as '"cashier" of intergovernmental co-operation [is] deprived of political responsibility',[149] but nonetheless carries political and legal accountability for the implementation of decisions taken by other EU players.

That said, the legal construct of civilian CSDP missions is less neat than the EU judicature suggests, both regarding institutional affiliation and functional aspects. As to institutional anchorage, the chain of command points from the field mission to Brussels-based structures, namely the PSC (exercising political control and strategic direction) reporting directly to the Council, and the Civilian Operation Commander (exercising command and control) who is institutionally affiliated with the EEAS. In financial matters, however, the HoM is in direct contact with the Commission. It is surely not an easy exercise for a company in the business of helicopter services to figure out these complexities and to bring an action against the right party.

Moreover, regarding functional matters, the assessment of the Court that EULEX Kosovo does not constitute a body, office, or agency of the EU within the meaning of Article 263 TFEU is questionable. According to its mandate, EULEX Kosovo contains a strengthening objective (provision of advice, training, etc) and an executive dimension (prosecution, investigation, adjudication of war crimes, terrorism, corruption cases, etc). The mission can thus produce legal effects

[148] Monar (n 142) 78.
[149] ibid.

vis-à-vis third parties. A functional assessment of crisis management realities also reveals that these missions are de facto more than diplomatic missions, even if they are de jure labelled as such. Even though they are in principle limited in time, they fulfil a certain mandate, have dedicated staff, administer their own budget, and have certain decision-making powers, and therefore operate agency-like. In another litigious case (discussed in section 3.2.3), AG Wahl therefore argued that the HoM could act as an EU body.[150] The Court's interpretation, however, was limited to a rather legalistic examination of the law—in short, that the mission had not formally been established as an EU body, office, or agency—with little attention being paid to the realities revealing concealed agencification. In light of these elements, the reasoning of the Court could have been more applicant-friendly. However, from a jurisdictional point of view, it is more plausible to attribute the mission's activities to an EU institution instead of arguing in favour of a stand-alone liability and identifying the competent judicial body.

As a matter of fact, *Elitaliana* is a precedent as it extends the jurisdiction of the EU judicature to review cases related to financial matters on the basis of *implied* jurisdictional competences. In this way, accountability for conduct ($A_c$) of civilian crisis management exercised through the CJEU improved considerably. Indeed, this novel jurisdictional competence might bring a number of cases to the CJEU. Annual commitments for civilian crisis management missions generally amount to some EUR 300 million, and procurement is a significant share of this budget. The implementation of financial allocations might potentially trigger several legal disputes, especially over procurement. Yet, plaintiffs might also refrain from launching (lengthy) judicial procedures for a procurement issue against the powerful Commission (and the respective mission). Thus, the fact that the Court attributed financial decisions to the Commission might, paradoxically, reduce the number of cases being brought to Luxembourg.

### 3.2.3 Contingent jurisdiction for acts of staff management

The CJEU also managed to assert and extend its jurisdiction on operational actions in *H v Council and others* (C-455/14 P). The litigation in this case revolved around an action for annulment and compensation brought by H against a staff management decision taken in the context of an EU civilian mission, namely the EU's Police Mission to Bosnia and Herzegovina (EUPM).[151] As AG Wahl put it, '[t]he present case offer[ed] to the [Court] one of the first opportunities to determine the scope of its jurisdiction with regard to the CFSP'.[152] And the members of the Grand Chamber (gladly) seized the opportunity to propose a new reading of

[150] Case C-455/14 P [2016], Opinion of AG Wahl of 7 April 2016 paras 94–99.

[151] The mission was launched by Council Joint Action 2002/210/CFSP of 11 March 2002 on the European Union Police Mission [2002] OJ L70/1.

[152] Case C-455/14 P [2016], Opinion of AG Wahl of 7 April 2016 para 3.

Treaty provisions, extending their jurisdiction on the basis of *contingent jurisdictional competences*. The Grand Chamber ruling in the *H* case indeed has the potential to profoundly impact the accountability environment of EU peacebuilding activities as it enhances accountability for conduct of the Europeanized bureaucracy. As a matter of fact, the *H* ruling is now frequently cited in case law pertaining to CFSP issues when asserting the jurisdiction of the Court. Civilian crisis management has thus served as a unique window of jurisdictional opportunity for the EU judicature to recalibrate the scope and intensity of its otherwise tightly restricted judicial control over the CFSP, of which it ingeniously took advantage.

H was seconded to the headquarters of EUPM in Sarajevo by decree of the Italian Minister of Justice in October 2008, indicating that she was to act as 'Criminal Justice Unit Adviser' from November 2008 onwards. Her secondment was prolonged twice (in April and December 2009) to extend until December 2010 in order for her to perform the duties of 'Chief Legal Officer'. In a letter to the HoM dated March 2010, H reported that some irregularities in the management of the mission had allegedly taken place, without the mission administration following up on her reporting. On 7 April 2010, then, H was redeployed to the regional office of Banja Luka to act as 'Criminal Justice Adviser—Prosecutor' by a decision signed by the Chief of Personnel of the mission. Dissatisfied with this decision, H contacted the Italian authorities. She also lodged a complaint, to which the HoM responded in late April by stating that he himself had decided to redeploy her out of operational reasons, given the need for prosecutorial advice in the local office. In June, H filed an action against EUPM before the Regional Administrative Court in Lazio (Italy), and shortly after lodged an application with the Registry of the General Court for annulment of the contested decisions and for an award of damages. H also lodged an application for interim measures, which was dismissed for lack of urgency by Court order in July 2010.[153] In 2014 the General Court issued an order holding that it lacked jurisdiction to hear the case, which was dismissed as inadmissible.[154] H appealed against this order and in 2016, the case was adjudicated on appeal, this time by the Court's Grand Chamber.[155]

In its judgment of 19 July 2016, the first pressing question for the Grand Chamber to address was the legal nature of the contested decision of redeployment. The Court of Justice refuted the claim of the applicant that the contested decision constituted a restrictive measure in the sense of the second paragraph of Article 275 TFEU, providing for its jurisdiction under the fourth paragraph of Article 263 TFEU.[156] The applicant had, furthermore, argued that the redeployment decision was an administrative act, which did not qualify as an act referred

[153] Case T-271/10 *H v Council and others* [2010] EU:T:2010:315.
[154] Case T-271/10 *H v Council and others* [2014] EU:T:2014:702.
[155] Case C-455/14 *P H v Council and others* [2016] EU:C:2016:569.
[156] ibid 30.

to in Article 24(1) TEU, and therefore was not subject to the jurisdictional exceptions regime.[157] The Commission, for its part, put forward that the provisions on the CFSP contained in the TEU implicitly distinguished between 'acts of sovereign policy' (*actes de Gouvernement*) not subject to judicial review and 'acts of implementation' subject to judicial review. According to the Commission, the actions of a CFSP mission belonged to the latter category and, hence, fell under the jurisdiction of the CJEU.[158] The Council strongly opposed the Commission's reading of the Treaties, stating that *all* acts, regardless of them being strategic or operational in nature, were covered by the exception of jurisdiction laid down in Article 24(1) TEU.[159]

The Court concluded that the contested decision was an operational action of the EU, qualifying the decision under review as an 'act of staff management relating to staff members seconded by the Member States'.[160] The qualification of the contested decision as operational action and, more precisely, as an act of staff management, laid the foundation for the Court's reasoning on jurisdictional aspects. With a view to determining jurisdictional competences, the Court explored matters of human resources management and institutional affiliation of staff, including jurisdiction over staff. A central point was the legal arrangements regarding the different types of staff working side-by-side in civilian missions, in particular seconded *national experts* and seconded *EU officials*.

The Court of Justice showed that both types of personnel were subject to the same rules regarding the performance of their duties at the theatre level: both EU staff and national experts were under the strategic and operational command of Brussels-based bodies (the Civilian Operations Commander), and at the theatre level had to follow the instructions of the HoM.[161] According to the pertinent secondary rules, namely stipulations of the mission's mandate and Staff Regulations, the EU judicature could hear cases related to seconded EU officials but lacked jurisdiction with respect to claims emanating from seconded national experts, as they remained under the disciplinary responsibility of the sending State.[162] Therefore, at the theatre level the two types of civilian personnel were equal in duties, but not in law. In addition, the Court underlined that it had been granted jurisdictional competences by the Council regarding seconded national personnel for two agencies or agency-like bodies in the field of EU foreign affairs, security, and defence: the European Defence Agency and the EEAS.[163] Its jurisdiction with respect to seconded national experts could, therefore, not per se be dismissed—a finding which

[157] ibid 29.
[158] ibid 32, 34, 35.
[159] ibid 35.
[160] ibid 42, 55.
[161] ibid 51–53.
[162] ibid 50, 55–57.
[163] ibid 56.

was in stark contrast to the Court's own case law, according to which disciplinary measures concerning seconded national experts were, by virtue of the applicable regulations, undoubtedly a matter for the authorities of the sending state.[164] In *H*, however, the judges argued that the absence of jurisdictional competence of the EU judicature to hear cases involving seconded national experts would lead to legal inequality and a lack of the rule of law, which would be incompatible with the values and principles of the EU set out in Articles 2 TEU and with the objectives of external action contained in Article 21 TEU.[165] In view of remedying this de jure–de facto discrepancy, the judges declared themselves competent to hear, by virtue of EU Staff Regulations cases, related to seconded EU staff, including those seconded to EUPM.[166] In other words, the Court extended its competence regarding CFSP/CSDP matters based on already existing *contingent* jurisdiction. It is noteworthy that AG Wahl had, in contrast, concluded that even when facing the *lex imperfecta* in the CFSP field, the Court could not 'interpret the rules set out in the Treaties to widen its jurisdiction beyond the letter of those rules or to create new remedies not provided therein'.[167]

In the end, the judges declared themselves competent—so to say, by legal analogy—to hear cases emanating from seconded national experts for issues occurring at the theatre level of CSDP activities,[168] stressing that the contested decision was *not* subject to the exceptions regime.[169] On the contrary, the Court of Justice found that the contested act could not be subtracted from its judicial review, and affirmed its jurisdiction to review the legality of acts under Article 263 TFEU and, for non-contractual liability of the EU, under Article 268 TFEU (read in conjunction with Article 340 TFEU).[170] As source for its jurisdictional competences, the Court also listed Article 19(1) TEU on jurisdiction and legal protection, and Article 47 of the Charter of Fundamental Rights of the European Union (hereafter referred to as Charter) on the rights to an effective remedy and to a fair trial. In this way, the Court squared the circle: it adjusted its own jurisdictional competences in the CFSP to the codified imperative of effective judicial remedies.[171]

Eventually, the Grand Chamber referred the case back to the General Court for judgment on the substance, while clarifying that the contested decisions were imputable to the Council *only* given the chain of command.[172] The judges thus followed the same functional attribution logic as in the *Elitaliana* case. The Court

[164] Case T–383/13 *Chatzianagnostou v Council and others* [2015] EU:T:2015:246 para 41.
[165] Case C–455/14 P [2016] para 41.
[166] ibid 44.
[167] Case C–455/14 P [2016], Opinion of AG Wahl of 7 April 2016 para 49.
[168] Case C–455/14 P [2016] paras 55, 59.
[169] ibid 59.
[170] ibid 58.
[171] Christophe Hillion, 'A Powerless Court? The European Court of Justice and the Common Foreign and Security Policy' in Marise Cremona and Anne Thies (eds), *The European Court of Justice and External Relations Law. Constitutional Challenges* (Hart Publishing 2014) 54.
[172] Case C–455/14 P [2016] paras 68, 71.

demonstrated that, for theatre level decisions, the reporting line ran from the HoM over the CPCC to the PSC (and over the High Representative of the EU for Foreign Affairs and Security Policy), and ended at the Council. The chain of command followed precisely the inverse order, starting at the Council and ending at the HoM.[173] Again, the Court construed attribution on the grounds of functional connectivity—instead of institutional anchorage—of the civilian crisis management bureaucracy with the EEAS.

In light of the above, the Grand Chamber judgment surely constitutes a landmark decision as it redefines the scope of judicial review of CFSP acts: it enlarged judicial review from 'formal' CFSP decisions codified in primary law adopted in the intergovernmental sphere of civilian CSDP to 'informal' derivative CFSP decisions taken by Europeanized structures. Hence, the judgment at hand significantly improves the legal protection of individuals for operational matters and thereby contributes to closing the gap of individual legal protection which manifestly exists with respect to the CFSP.[174] But while this jurisprudential development is desirable with a view to strengthening the protection of individuals, it is not unambiguous.

The first ambiguity has to do with the extension of judicial competence in the CFSP field, which encroaches upon the constitutionally enshrined intergovernmental character of EU foreign affairs, security, and defence. The EU judicature has no general jurisdiction in this field, but can adjudicate on clearly defined exceptions.[175] In the words of AG Juliane Kokott, '[o]nly *highly exceptionally* do the Courts of the EU have jurisdiction in relation to the CFSP'.[176] The second paragraph of Article 275 TFEU indeed explicitly states that the CJEU has jurisdiction neither with regard to the primary law of this policy field, nor with regard to acts adopted on the basis of those provisions—and the absence of a definite article insinuates that *any* act adopted on the basis of those provisions is what is meant. This reading of primary law—precluding jurisdiction on implementation measures based on a CFSP legal basis adopted by the Council or by a (derivative) entity—was also defended by AG Wahl,[177] and equally by AG Wathelet.[178] The jurisdictional carve-out regarding CFSP/CSDP acts is the result of a particular integration rationale governing foreign affairs, security, and defence.[179] A look at the drafting history of Article 275 TFEU provides valuable insights: it has been the evident will of the Treaty drafters to exclude *all* CFSP acts—except for policy delimitation and sanctions—from the CJEU's jurisdiction, including derivative acts. This was submitted by the Council in the *H* case, and was furthermore echoed in

173 See the figures on reporting lines provided in Chapter 3.
174 On the existing legal gap regarding individual protection see Kottmann (n 19) 200–29.
175 See on this point section 1 of this chapter.
176 Emphasis added. View of AG Kokott, *Opinion 2/13* [2014] para 84.
177 Case C-455/14 P [2016], Opinion of AG Wahl of 7 April 2016 para 58.
178 Case C-72/15 [2016], Opinion of AG Wathelet of 31 May 2016 para 49.
179 See section 1 of this chapter.

the panoply of arguments presented in the context of the 2014 Opinion on the EU's accession to the European Convention on Human Rights.[180]

In its *Opinion 2/13* of 2014, the Court had indeed acknowledged this jurisdictional carve-out by emphasizing that it had only very limited competence in the CFSP field, opening up judicial review to certain CFSP acts only.[181] In the Grand Chamber judgment in *H v Council*, however, the Court set aside these considerations protecting an intergovernmental setting by giving the rule–exception regime a new reading: the Court's jurisdiction is considered general according to Article 19(1) TEU, while the derogation to this general jurisdiction contained in Article 24(1) TEU cannot be read so extensively as to exclude decisions pertaining to the 'theatre level' of CSDP activities. Whereas it is true that the derogation from the general principle of jurisdiction set out in Article 24(1) TEU has to be construed narrowly,[182] it is difficult to construe it so narrowly as to turn around the rule–exception regime. As AG Kokott stressed in her view regarding the accession to the European Convention on Human Rights (ECHR) of June 2014:

> [T]he authors of the founding Treaties of the EU consciously refrained from setting up a supranational structure and renounced the uniform and autonomous interpretation of EU law by a judicial institution of the EU itself in a particular area—in this case, in the field of the CFSP.[183]

While the *H* judgment does not question the intergovernmental institutional and procedural set-up of the CFSP, it strengthens the single supranational legal order created by the Treaty of Lisbon. This does not per se prompt a fully fledged supranationalization of the CFSP, but it brings essential parts of CSDP activities under supranational judicial control.

The new reading of the Court's jurisdiction proved indeed to a big step in the direction of supranationalization, as recent jurisprudence on staff management incidents in the CFSP field exemplifies. By analogy to the contingent jurisdiction logic underpinning the *H* proceedings, the General Court reasoned in *SatCen*—a case that concerned a staff-management dispute between a (former) staff member and their (former) employer, the European Union Satellite Centre (SatCen)—that its jurisdiction to review the legality of acts extended to derivative CFSP acts if those acts were in terms of content, objectives, and procedure identical to acts for which the EU judicature would otherwise have competence.[184] According to the General Court, this is because the absence of its jurisdiction on such derivative acts would 'amount to excluding the staff members of an EU body covered by the CFSP

[180] *Opinion 2/13* of the Court of 18 December 2014 [2014] EU:C:2014:2454 paras 128–40.
[181] ibid 249–50, 252.
[182] Case C–455/14 P [2016] para 40.
[183] View of AG Kokott, *Opinion 2/13* [2014] para 193.
[184] Case T–286/15 *KF v SatCen* [2018] EU:T:2018:718 para 96.

from the system of judicial protection offered to EU staff members, in breach of the principle of equal treatment'.[185] In other words, the EU judicature stated that, with a view to upholding the principle of equal treatment, it would in its legality review disregard the CFSP nature of an entity (or its acts).[186] And so, in the case at hand, all contested decisions were annulled by the General Court, and SatCen was ordered to pay the applicant the sum of EUR 10,000 as compensation for the non-material harm she had sustained because of a flawed disciplinary investigation leading eventually to her removal. For CFSP entities, in turn, the judgment in *SatCen* is a game changer: it means that the general exclusion of the CJEU from the CFSP no longer shields them from a judicial review of their derivative decisions (bearing a staff management character). It is not surprising, therefore, that SatCen has formed an appeal against the decision to put a halt to this line of jurisprudence, which steadily enlarges the EU judicature's judicial control over CFSP matters.[187] Notwithstanding these recent supranationalization tendencies drawing on the *H* precedent, it is important to stress at this juncture that the *H* case adapted judicial scrutiny by the CJEU to Europeanized intergovernmentalism.

This leads us to the second ambiguity. The interpretation of what kind of CFSP decisions (or acts) fall under the jurisdiction of the EU judicature—and what kind of decisions do not—is indeed debateable. Treaty provisions do not differentiate between politico-strategic choices and theatre level decisions: they codify the former (CFSP decisions) and remain silent as to the latter (derivative acts). This is why AG Wahl had clearly underlined in his Opinion concerning the *H* case that 'neither a literal nor a systematic reading of the relevant Treaty provisions supports the argument ... which suggests distinguishing between different categories of CFSP acts, depending on their nature and content'.[188] It seems that, by labelling the contested decision as a reviewable act of staff management, the Court followed the aforementioned logic proposed by the Commission to differentiate between acts of sovereign policy and acts of implementation without, however, making this explicit. Indeed, the Court's approach discreetly introduces a typology of different CFSP 'acts' that is not spelled out in primary law, where only CFSP 'decisions' taken by the Council are codified (Articles 26 and 31 TEU), and derivative CFSP decisions for implementation purposes taken by the PSC are mentioned (Article 38 TEU). In her view on the accession of the EU to the ECHR, AG Kokott distinguished the Court's jurisdictional competence regarding *Rechtsakte* and *Realakte*.[189] So far, it

185 ibid 97.

186 In this vein, see ibid 83.

187 Appeal brought on 10 January 2019 by the European Union Satellite Centre (SatCen) against the judgment of the General Court (Ninth Chamber, Extended Composition) delivered on 25 October 2018 in Case T–286/15 *KF v SatCen* (Case C–14/19 P).

188 Case C–455/14 P [2016], Opinion of AG Wahl of 7 April 2016 para 57. See also para 72.

189 AG Kokott opposed the interpretation of Art 275 TFEU put forward by the Commission, namely that the Court had jurisdiction not only for decisions within the meaning of Art 263 TFEU having binding legal effect (*Rechtsakte*), but also with respect to mere 'material acts' (*Realakte*) without legal effect. See View of AG Kokott, *Opinion 2/13* [2014] paras 86, 88.

is argued here, only codified decisions—namely Council decisions pertaining to policy delimitation and sanctions (*Rechtsakte*)—were justiciable. Derivative CFSP decisions taken at the sub-Council level related to steering, implementing, and co-ordination (mostly *Realakte*) were not codified by primary law and therefore escaped judicial review as they remained below the threshold of formality (in the primary law sense). The *H* judgment, though, extends the Court's jurisdiction to the latter category of acts, which means that the Court can henceforth review the bulk of administrative decisional matters in a predominantly intergovernmental setting. Yet, the contours of what other types of acts fall under the 'operational action' category remain vague.

To arrive at this result, the Court had to strike a balance between the principle of judicial remedy on the one hand, and the principle of conferred powers on the other. The Grand Chamber found that '[t]he very existence of effective judicial review designed to ensure compliance with provisions of EU law is inherent to the existence of the rule of law'.[190] This is in strong contrast to the finding of the General Court, which had held that 'it should be remembered that, according to the case-law, the absence of other possibilities for a judicial remedy cannot in itself give rise to jurisdiction of the judicature of the European Union in a legal system based on the principle of conferred powers'.[191] The two court instances obviously diverged, with the second instance eventually favouring the principle of the rule of law over the principle of conferred powers. This jurisprudence, which aligns Treaty provisions with the rule of law principle, is not uncontested. Some might ask in how far this is compatible with the Court's duty to 'ensure that in the interpretation and application of the Treaties the law is observed' (Article 19(1) TEU). It is, however, questionable whether the conflict programmed by the Treaties—primary law only exceptionally granting judicial review and, thus, offering very little legal protection—could have been solved otherwise in the absence of a Treaty revision. Nonetheless, this reasoning nourished the (seemingly justified) fear of a jurisdictional snowball effect: in the name of legal protection and equal treatment, the carve-out regarding CFSP matters laid down in primary law is progressively filled with principle-based jurisprudence affirming the jurisdiction of EU Courts. This incursion into the intergovernmental policy field is viewed by some authors as highly problematic.[192]

It is furthermore remarkable that the Court exclusively focused its analysis on seconded EU officials and seconded national experts. Two further types of personnel—namely international contracted experts and local contracted civilians—were not mentioned at all in the judgment. This is surprising as the

[190] Case C-455/14 P [2016] para 41.

[191] Case T-271/10 [2014] para 56.

[192] See, by way of illustration, Luigi Lonardo, 'The Political Question Doctrine as Applied to Common Foreign and Security Policy' (2017) 22 European Foreign Affairs Review 571, 587.

Court has, since 2014, been the jurisdictional forum identified in the dispute settlement clauses inserted in the contracts of international contracted personnel. What is more, numbers show that there are by far more international contracted experts working in EU missions than seconded EU officials, barely any of whom were or are deployed.[193] The parallel the Court drew between seconded national experts and seconded EU experts is accurate in theory but less relevant in practice—in reality seconded national experts work side by side with international contracted civilians, while only the latter can bring their cases to Luxembourg. Therefore, it could have been advantageous to extend the 'equal in duties but unequal in law' argument in the *H* case on the conferral of jurisdictional competence to cases pertaining to contracted international staff—for which the Court has jurisdiction (since 2014)—instead of basing the comparison solely on the numerically less significant seconded EU officials.

Indeed, a look at recent jurisprudence stresses the broader (jurisdictional) relevance of claims brought on the basis of settlement clauses inserted in the work contracts of international contracted staff. The applicant in *PY v EUCAP Sahel Niger* was the first staff member of an EU peacebuilding mission to receive a financial compensation (amounting to EUR 10,000) for non-material damage suffered from the mission's omission to follow its own internal rules and investigate in a reasonable time the complaints of harassment brought forward by the applicant.[194]

What is more, in its decision in *Jenkinson v Council and others* of July 2018, the Court of Justice made another daring jurisdictional move in the field of civilian CSDP (and the CFSP, more generally), partly reviewing its own jurisprudence. The case at hand concerned Mr Jenkinson, an international contracted employee of EULEX Kosovo (who had previously also worked in other civilian missions), whose last fixed-term contract was not renewed. He brought an action to recategorize his long-standing contractual relationships (in total fifteen years) as an 'employment contract of an indefinite duration', and furthermore claimed compensation for the supposedly abusive use of consecutive fixed-term contracts and for discrimination. In contrast to the first instance judgment of January 2017,[195] the appeals decision of October 2018 stipulates that the CJEU can hear applications that contain claims arising under previous employment contract(s)—explicitly conferring jurisdiction on the Brussels labour tribunal—in the event that the application equally entails claims under the contract containing the arbitration clause, or under the condition that there is a direct connection between the obligations arising from the contract

[193] Of the currently roughly 2,000 deployed staff, one half of the personnel are internationals (out of which two thirds are seconded national experts, and a third international contracted civilians), and the other half of the staff are locally hired employees. This staff-ratio is based on own research (mainly EEAS website) and on the numbers contained in Annalisa Creta and others, 'Civilian and Military Personnel in CSDP Missions and Operations', *EP/EXPO/B/SEDE/2016/02* (European Parliament 2017) 14.

[194] Case T–763/16 *PY v EUCAP Sahel Niger* [2018] EU:T:2018:181.

[195] Case T–602/15 *Jenkinson v Council and others* [2016] EU:T:2016:660.

conferring jurisdiction to the Court in Luxembourg.[196] In the case at hand, the Court opined—following the reasoning of AG Szpunar[197]—that the applicant's multiple, consecutive fixed-term contracts constituted one single and continuous employment, so that the claims he brought *also* arise under the contract granting jurisdiction to the EU judicature.[198] In other words, if an international contracted staff member was employed by a mission before and after 2014 (the year in which the arbitration clause started to be inserted in contracts) on the basis of consecutive fixed-term contracts, and in the event he or she wishes to lodge an application whose claims also relate to the period before 2014, the jurisdictional forum for *all* claims is henceforth in Luxembourg (and not in Brussels). Interestingly, in a previous case against EULEX Kosovo dating back to 2014, which concerned, inter alia, the supposedly unequal treatment of seconded and contracted staff regarding the prolongation of their contracts by the mission, the General Court had found that there was no instance of unjustified unequal treatment and, further, that it manifestly lacked jurisdiction, as the Brussels tribunals were competent according to the work contracts of the plaintiffs.[199] That said, the numerous (pending) cases lodged by international contracted staff in Luxembourg and also before national courts has prompted the EEAS to draft an internal assessment report, which, inter alia, discusses possible legal consequences of forthcoming judgments.[200] Indeed, if all those international contracted staff, who for years worked in civilian missions on the basis of consecutive fixed-term contracts, were found to be entitled to a contract with indefinite duration and/or a compensation for discrimination, this would trigger an unprecedented avalanche of very costly claims. The *Jenkinson* ruling of 2018 could thus engender a nerve-racking and costly judicial snowball effect for the EEAS and the concerned missions.

The third and last ambiguity of the Grand Chamber judgment in *H v Council* is that the decision implies a new and also contested jurisdictional paradigm. In previous judgments relating to CFSP matters, the Luxembourg judges decided on policy procedures (ie choice of the legal basis or information obligations) while showing some deference to external policy choices, including in security and defence matters.[201] In *H v Council*, however, the *substance* of the disputed decision mattered (an act of staff management) not its *form*—a derivative CFSP decision, informal under primary law, taken by a member of the crisis management bureaucracy at operational level, and not explicitly subject to judicial review. This is

[196] Case C–43/17 *P Jenkinson v Council and others* [2018] EU:C:2018:531 para 45.

[197] ibid 47.

[198] ibid 47–48.

[199] Case T–410/13 *Bitiqi and others v Commission and others* [2014] EU:T:2014:871 paras 27, 35.

[200] Information contained in the reply of the EEAS dated 28 August 2019 (EEAS reference: eeas.sg.affg en.2(2019)6028746), denying an access-to-documents request concerning the internal analysis of recent jurisprudence and ongoing court cases (namely document EEAS(2019)809 of 17 July 2019) lodged on 6 August 2019 (request reference 2019/145).

[201] In a similar vein, see Cremona and Thies (n 62) 2–3.

unchartered territory that the Court has continued to explore, in particular in the *SatCen* case. Here, the General Court reasoned that it had contingent jurisdiction to adjudicate on the contested measures given that they

> constitute[d] purely acts of staff management which, in light of their grounds and objectives, and of the context in which they were adopted, were not indented to support the conduct, definition or implementation of the CFSP within the meaning of Article 24(2) TEU, or, more specifically, to fulfil the missions of SatCen falling within the CFSP.[202]

In other words, as the disputed acts do not fall under the category of *actes de Gouvernement*, the EU judicature can review them—a distinction the Court had already implicitly followed in the *H* case.

Now that the three ambiguities of the *H* ruling of 2016 have been outlined—namely (i) a potential jurisdictional supranationalization of the CFPS/CSDP; (ii) the legal uncertainty generated by the enlarged but imprecise scope of judicial review as regards derivative CFSP acts; and (iii) the equivocal shift from procedural to substantive review of foreign policy measures—let us focus once more on the *H* ruling and recapitulate its jurisdictional added value. As a matter of fact, the decision represents a crucial improvement in legal protection. Initially, the application against a staff management decision taken in the context of an EU civilian mission seemed to be a lost cause, given the tight jurisdictional competences of the CJEU in this policy field. Bringing theatre level decisions issued in the context of EU peacebuilding activities under the jurisdiction of the Court considerably broadens the scope of judicial review. Currently, there are some 2,000 civilian experts working in ten ongoing civilian missions on behalf of the EU, of which at least a third constitutes seconded national experts. The judgment implies that the CJEU can henceforth review human resources decisions taken with regard to all these seconded national experts. Cases like the one of Maria Bamieh could henceforth be heard by the Court.[203] Based on the *H* precedent, the Court of Justice has in *Jenkinson* subsequently enlarged its jurisdictional competence to applications of international contracted staff containing claims that even predate the insertion of the arbitration clause conferring jurisdiction on the CJEU. As a result, the *H* precedent constituted the crucial first step on the long road to strengthening accountability for conduct ($A_c$) in civilian CSDP.

But while the scope of judicial review was enhanced, the *H* judgment also leads to legal uncertainty as it sets a precedent that potentially modifies existing Treaty law, not least because the judgment is not conclusive in delineating which derivative CFSP decisions apart from human resources choices would fall into the

[202] Case T-286/15 *KF v SatCen* [2018] EU:T:2018:718 para 91.
[203] For further details on this incident, see Chapter 1.

category of 'operational actions'. Moreover, $A_c$ could be weakened by the reaction of the Council and of Member States to the said judgment. The interpretation of rules in the *domaine réservé* by supranational institutions in favour of a supranational judicial review is likely to prompt an intergovernmental backlash, especially in times where security concerns are high on the agenda. Member States have always been worried that supranational actors, including the Court in Luxembourg, could become power hungry and intrude into intergovernmental policy fields.[204] Recent adjudication might stir up their seemingly warranted fear and even revive executive tendencies in civilian crisis management (and European security questions more broadly). Again, the *SatCen* case reaffirms existing worries about creeping supranationalization. The General Court's judgment of autumn 2018 explained that 'EU Courts have jurisdiction to hear actions relating to the management by CSDP missions of their staff, *even* where such management concerns "field" operations'.[205] It is argued here that the 'even' implies two things. First, CFSP activities are situated on a high politics spectrum, with field operations located at the higher end of that spectrum. Secondly, if the EU judicature can adjudicate on derivative decisions taken at the higher end of the *domaine réservé* spectrum, the CJEU can obviously also handle claims arising from activities at the lower end of the foreign policy spectrum (ie *SatCen*). Consequently, this signifies that except for *domaine réservé* core business—that is, in the words of the Court, 'decisions … indented to support the conduct, definition or implementation of the CFSP within the meaning of Article 24(2) TEU'[206]—the Luxembourg judges will henceforth scrutinize CFSP (derivative) acts. It is not clear from the judgment, however, which acts would fall under the conduct, definition, or implementation categories if an act of staff management does not qualify as an act intended to support the implementation of a CFSP activity.

Also beyond civilian CSDP, it is possible that the Court's move towards broader CFSP adjudication will lead national governments to resort increasingly to international law solutions in sensitive policy areas, as they did in the context of the financial crisis. This would lead to a decline of judicial control, and would thus negatively impact on $A_c$. In addition, the *H* precedent together with the more recent CFSP-related jurisprudence of the CJEU might have operational repercussions. Member States will most probably find a way to diminish the margin of judicial review by, for instance, labelling more CSDP actions as military activities. Hence, civilian missions would be components of military operations. This legal construct would make it more difficult for the Court to assert jurisdiction. Moreover, governments could decide to deploy more civilian missions under the framework of the Organization for Security and Co-operation in Europe (OSCE), where judicial

[204] Kottmann (n 19) 172–75; Denza (n 125) 312.
[205] Emphasis added. Case T-286/15 *KF v SatCen* [2018] EU:T:2018:718 para 53.
[206] ibid 91.

review is fairly absent given its informal framework. Ironically, then, the assertion and extension of jurisdiction of the EU judicature for civilian missions could, by that very assertion and extension, undermine the operational dimension of civilian missions and eventually lead to a reduced scope of judicial review and limited $A_c$.

It is worth mentioning that both the *H* proceedings and the *Elitaliana* case related to incidents that had taken place before civilian missions were endowed with legal capacity.[207] Therefore, it is somewhat unclear whether and how the conferral of legal capacity to civilian missions could or would essentially modify the Court's jurisprudence. Since 2014 the missions have legal *capacity* under EU law, allowing them to appear before (EU and potentially domestic) jurisdictions, but they are not independent legal entities in their own right—as it is for EU agencies—as this would presuppose legal *personality*.[208] As the Court based its judgments on functional parameters (eg lines of reporting and delegation arrangements) instead of the legal construction underpinning the missions, it is unclear to what extent the conferral of legal capacity to civilian crisis management missions could alter attribution schemes in the future. The modified legal status has not changed operational realities—including reporting obligations, supervision requirements, and chains of command. Therefore, the upgraded legal status of civilian missions is likely to have the effect of dual attribution: first, to the missions, because of their relative legal independence; and secondly, to the respective EU institution, in light of their unaltered role as supreme administrative and strategic authority. This dual attribution, in turn, would engender dual legal accountability, according to which it would be possible to hold both the Council or the Commission, *and* the respective mission, to account before the CJEU.

## 4. Measuring the Wider Jurisdictional Field

The recent jurisprudence of the CJEU on CFSP matters—notably the decisions in *Elitaliana* (2015), *H v Council* (2016), *Rosneft* (2017), *Jenkison* (2018), and *SatCen* (2018)—is not without an impact on the wider jurisdictional field. These decisions affect the parameters of complementary and competing adjudication and thereby recalibrate jurisdictional competences on CFSP matters, including both vertical

[207] As mentioned in section 2, a standard provision on legal arrangements has been inserted in mission mandates since 2014 stating that, as required to implement the respective decision, the mission 'shall have the capacity to procure services and supplies, enter into contracts and administrative arrangements, employ staff, hold bank accounts, acquire and dispose of assets, discharge its liabilities and be a party to legal proceedings'. Interestingly, the Council opted for the narrower legal *capacity* instead of broader legal *personality* for civilian missions, the Commission and the Court of Auditors having advocated for the latter. See C(2012)4052 final (26 June 2012) (Administrative Decision), 'Rules for the Financial Management of the Common Foreign and Security Policy Missions' 6; Special report of the Court of Auditors No 18/2012, 'European Union assistance to Kosovo related to the rule of law' 7.

[208] On the difference between (domestic/international) legal *personality* and *capacity*, see Moser and Peters (n 43) 9–16.

and horizontal aspects. In section 4.1, a closer look at the division of labour between national courts and the EU judicature illustrates that the jurisprudential leeway of the former has been reduced by and to the favour of the latter. Similar conclusions can be drawn with regard to the ECtHR in Strasbourg as outlined in section 4.2.

## 4.1 Revised vertical division of labour

Primary law sets out a clear rule–exception regime with regard to CFSP matters: the *rule* is that the CJEU has no jurisdiction over CFSP matters, with the *exception* of matters pertaining to policy delimitations and sanctions (Article 24(1) TEU and Article 275 TFEU). Because of this jurisdictional carve-out, jurisdiction in the CFSP field primarily rests with national courts that, however, cannot declare that act invalid.[209] It is thus up to the EU institution concerned to remedy shortcomings identified by national courts in relation to CFSP matters not covered by the abovementioned exceptions.[210]

Yet, recent case law of the CJEU has shaken the initially codified division of labour. Recalling that the jurisdictional carve-out had to be construed narrowly,[211] the Court declared itself competent to hear cases related to both CFSP implementing acts with financial implications (*Elitaliana*), and to CFSP acts of staff management at the theatre level (*H v Council*). What is more, the Court significantly enlarged its competence *ratione temporis* when it comes to applications lodged on the basis of the arbitration clause inserted in the work contracts of international contractual staff since 2014. In *Jenkinson*, the Court of Justice indeed held that its jurisdiction was, under certain conditions, also retrospective—to the detriment of domestic courts.[212] Especially in the second and third constellations—the *H* and *Jenkinson* cases—the Court's jurisprudence constitutes a clear encroachment on existing arrangements allocating jurisdiction to national courts: the provisions both of the SOMAs and the mission mandates leave no doubt that national courts are in charge of adjudicating human resources cases concerning seconded national experts;[213] likewise, the conferral of jurisdiction on the Brussels labour tribunal is unequivocal for disputes arising under contracts signed with international contracted staff up to 2014. This encroachment leads to a situation of competing

[209] On this point, see section 2 of this chapter.

[210] Case C-455/14 P [2016], Opinion of AG Wahl of 7 April 2016 para 103.

[211] Case C-455/14 P [2016] para 40.

[212] For a discussion of the case, see the analysis in section 3 of this chapter.

[213] That is because the judicial authorities of the seconding State retain competence (both during and after the deployment) over the seconded staff members—for criminal jurisdiction for all acts, and for civil and administrative jurisdiction for all official acts. See Art 3, Art 6(4), Art 6(5), Art 6(7), and Art 8 Model SOMA.

jurisdiction, in particular in the case of seconded personnel: the law in the books directs potential claimants to their respective national courts—and there is proof of at least two cases before domestic courts[214]—while CJEU case law invites them to lodge a case in Luxembourg. One might argue that the extension of the CJEU's jurisprudence to adjudicate staff management matters pertaining to seconded national experts is a means to ensure equality between mission personnel. As such, the enlargement of jurisdiction constitutes a somewhat natural consequence of the attribution of jurisdiction (since 2014) over staff management matters pertaining to international contracted civilians. But even though this competence parallelism is in theory judicious, it creates in practice jurisdictional distortions and legal uncertainty. To whom do individuals now actually have to turn? This open issue is not without repercussions on effective legal accountability and could also hamper $A_c$. However, the broader application of the logic underpinning the *H* case—that the EU judicature has jurisdiction in the name of the principle of equality (between staff members), even if primary or secondary law does *not* expressly confer jurisdiction on the Court in Luxembourg—to other CFSP staff management cases, as it happened in *SatCen*, poses serious legal problems because it undermines both legal certainty and the principle of conferral. What is more, the argument underpinning *H*, namely that jurisdiction by the EU courts was needed to ensure equality *within* a CFSP entity (ie a civilian mission), was significantly broadened in *SatCen*: it was stretched *beyond* the CFSP. Indeed, according to the ruling, the principle of equality would no longer concern employees of the same CFSP entity only, but implied that employees of a CSFP entity and employees of *non*-CFSP entities needed to be treated equally regarding adjudication.[215] In other words, when it comes to staff management, the Court underlined that there is only one EU legal order—the consequence being that any CFSP differentiation or limitation in terms of access to the EU judicature will be struck down by the Luxembourg judges, again to the detriment of the jurisdiction of national courts.

In addition, the CJEU underlined the applicability of the *Foto-Frost* doctrine to CFSP matters not covered by the jurisdictional carve-out in its *Rosneft* decision. This means that the EU judicature is the only judicial institution competent to evaluate the validity of acts emanating from EU institutions, including in the CFSP realm. But as the carve-out in the CFSP field is being incrementally narrowed down by CJEU case law, it seems that national courts will sooner or later have to ask for preliminary rulings for a whole range of CFSP-related issues. Already, they have to do so regarding sanctions and policy delimitation, and—potentially—certain derivative (implementing) decisions with financial and staff management implications as a consequence of the *H* and *Elitaliana* judgments.

[214] Bamieh (in the UK) and H (in Italy).

[215] Case T–286/15 *KF v SatCen* [2018] EU:T:2018:718 paras 96–97.

Yet, there is a debate whether national courts could, in line with the *Solange* dictum, step in when the CJEU does not exercise its jurisdictional competences.[216] However, it needs to be stressed that, in EU peacebuilding, decisions do not in principle engender acts with direct effect for EU citizens, which is different when sanctions are adopted. And when decisions have direct effect, which is most likely the case with mission members working in civilian crisis management, the road to Luxembourg is open for most plaintiffs. EU seconded personnel can bring cases according to Article 91 of the EU Staff Regulations and Article 270 TFEU—provided that internal remedies have been exhausted—and the same remedies are open to HoMs. In addition, international contracted personnel can lodge cases with the CJEU on the basis of a dispute settlement clause inserted in their work contracts since 2014.[217] Furthermore, according to the *H v Council* judgment of 2016, seconded national experts can henceforth also have recourse to the EU judicature in cases related to staff management.[218] Gradually, then, these jurisdictional developments reverse the initial vertical allocation of jurisdiction, conferring the CJEU de facto jurisdictional priority over national courts.

## 4.2 Strasbourg calling: legal protection in horizontal juxtaposition

Similar patterns can be observed in relation to the horizontal allocation of jurisdictional competences at the European level.[219] Undeniably, many of the recent rulings on CFSP issues—including *Elitaliana, H v Council and others, Rosneft, Jenkinson*, and *SatCen*—can be read against the backdrop of *Opinion 2/13* of December 2014 on the draft agreement on the accession of the EU to the ECHR. In the said Opinion, the limited scope of judicial review by the EU judicature regarding the CFSP was identified by the CJEU as a major impediment to the EU's accession to the Convention. The discussion on the specific characteristics of jurisdiction with respect to the CFSP indeed left no doubt that the Luxembourg judges were uneasy with Treaty law curtailing their say in this policy field.[220] In short, the Court declared that there ought not to be an EU policy without an EU judge—especially if the alternative to the EU judicature was to be a non-EU jurisdiction. Hence, the

[216] Eckes (n 6) 497. As for the *Solange II* case, see Bundesverfassungsgericht 22.10.1986, *Solange II*, BVerfGE 73, 339. This reasoning—the protection of individuals and their rights for want of other remedies—is also a crucial argument put forward by the CJEU in the *H v Council* case. See Case C-455/14 P [2016] para 58.

[217] Not least the applications in *Jenkinson* and *PY* were lodged on the basis of the arbitration clause. See, for instance, Case T-602/15 [2016]; Case T-763/16 [2018].

[218] Case C-455/14 P [2016].

[219] Takis Tridimas, 'The ECJ and the National Courts: Dialogue, Cooperation, and Instability' in Anthony Arnull and Damian Chalmers (eds), *The Oxford Handbook of European Union Law* (Oxford University Press 2015) 411.

[220] *Opinion 2/13* [2014] paras 249–57.

different CFSP cases analysed in section 3 have proved a salutary window of opportunity for the Court to expand its own jurisdiction on a range of matters potentially qualifying for proceedings in Strasbourg.[221]

The rationale behind this jurisdictional move is rather simple: 'The higher the protection of fundamental rights offered by the ECJ, the less the need to go to Strasbourg.'[222] According to Article 6(3) and Articles 52(3), as well as 53 of the Charter of Fundamental Rights, the fundamental rights enshrined in the ECHR constitute general principles of EU law, the interpretation and application of which is to be monitored by the CJEU (Article 19(1) TEU).[223] Importantly, the Grand Chamber of the ECtHR held in its 2005 *Bosphorus* dictum that, as the EU offered a standard of protection equivalent to that of the Convention regarding both substantive and procedural aspects, the Strasbourg Court would limit its adjudication to specific cases where the particular circumstances would undermine the presumed equal protection standard: the protection of Convention rights would be 'manifestly deficient'.[224]

The horizontal allocation of jurisdiction at the European plane is thus embedded in a construction that rests on two interdependent pillars, namely (i) the role of the CJEU as the guardian of human rights standards in the EU legal order, and (ii) the *Bosphorus* presumption of equal protection. This, in turn, creates a dilemma for the EU judicature as regards the CFSP: the presumption of equal protection stands and falls with the very existence of effective judicial remedies, which are, however, severely limited in the CFSP both at the EU level and at the Member State level.[225] How would the CJEU be able to fulfil the *Bosphorus* requirement to provide for equal protection in the field of the CFSP/CSDP if it lacked general jurisdiction to uphold Charter or Convention rights in this very policy field?

In light of the intertwined protection regimes, it is not surprising that the CJEU has tried to advance legal protection under EU law—in particular by enlarging the scope of its own judicial review—to pre-empt proceedings in Strasbourg. This reasoning in favour of the principle of effective judicial protection—to the detriment of the principle of conferred powers—is present in the *H* case, and particularly articulated in *Rosneft*. Stressing the importance of the principle of effective judicial protection under Article 47 of the Charter, the Grand Chamber judgment in *Rosneft* states that, whereas the said Charter Article 'cannot confer jurisdiction on

[221] It is fair to stress that individual legal protection before the Strasbourg Court is underdeveloped in CFSP issues and in CFSP-like constellations. On this point, see, for instance, the analysis provided by Daniel Engel. Daniel Engel, *Der Beitritt der Europäischen Union zur EMRK* (Mohr Siebeck 2015) 91, 98, 106.

[222] Tridimas (n 219) 411.

[223] On the difficult co-existence of the Convention and the Charter, see Engel (n 221) 23–33.

[224] Judgment of 30 June 2005 in *Bosphorus Hava Yolları Turizm ve Ticaret AS v Irland*, application no 45036/98 paras 155–56.

[225] Kottmann (n 19) 200–29; Christophe Hillion and Ramses A Wessel, '"The Good, the Bad and the Ugly": Three Levels of Judicial Control over the CFSP' in Steven Blockmans and Panos Koutrakos (eds), *Research Handbook on the EU's Common Foreign and Security Policy* (Edward Elgar 2018) 76.

the Court, where the treaties exclude it, the principle of effective judicial protection nonetheless implies that the exclusion of the Court's jurisdiction in the field of the CFSP should be interpreted strictly'.[226] The Court thus explicitly puts forward effective judicial protection considerations, citing Article 47 of the Charter, to assert its jurisdictional competences in CFSP matters.[227] Effective judicial protection was also at the heart of the argument in *Jenkinson* and *SatCen*.[228] The carve-out in primary law notwithstanding, the Court in *SatCen* made its adjudicatory claim over CFSP decisions explicit by stating that 'the fact that the contested decisions fall within the framework of the functioning of a body operating in the field of the CFSP cannot, in itself, mean that the EU judicature lacks jurisdiction to rule on this dispute', not least because 'the principle of effective judicial protection nonetheless implies that the exclusion of the EU judicature's jurisdiction in the field of the CFSP should be interpreted narrowly'.[229]

In principle, then, $A_c$ has been strengthened by the CJEU with a view to reinforcing legal protection. However, the invocation of Article 47 of the Charter has so far not necessarily been of imminent help for the respective complainants: in the *Elitaliana* case, the Court declared the case inadmissible, and in the *Rosneft* Opinion, the judges found that the disputed restrictive measures were valid. The latest ruling in the *H* case, handed down in April 2018, is particularly striking: the plaintiff's five pleas in law were all rejected and the action for annulment dismissed in its entirety.[230] Even though many legal questions were discussed by the Sixth Chamber in its ruling, the core issue—namely that the plaintiff had been redeployed and downgraded after having reported on irregularities within the EU Police Mission (EUPM)—was only marginally noticed.[231] This is astonishing given the broader context sketched out by the Court. The plaintiff H had not reported alone on irregularities within the mission but she had done so jointly with a mission colleague. While H was redeployed after having raised her criticism, the colleague was dismissed. And while H decided to bring the case to court, the colleague lodged an application with the European Ombudsman who, in 2015, stated that the decision to dismiss the complainant could well be understood as a sanction for complaining about irregularities, and therefore concluded that an instance of maladministration had occurred.[232] Interestingly, the Court in Luxembourg did not come to this conclusion with regard to H: it interpreted the letter of complaint and the redeployment as a matter of correlation instead of causality.[233]

[226] Case C-72/15 [2017] para 74.

[227] ibid 73–74, 81; Case C-455/14 P [2016] para 58.

[228] Case C-43/17 *P Jenkinson v Council and others* [2018] EU:C:2018:531 para 41; Case T-286/15 *KF v SatCen* [2018] EU:T:2018:718 paras 33, 85–86.

[229] Case T-286/15 *KF v SatCen* [2018] EU:T:2018:718 paras 83, 85.

[230] Case T-271/10 *RENV H v Council* [2018] EU:T:2018:180.

[231] ibid paras 142–51.

[232] Decision of the European Ombudsman closing the inquiries into complaints 26/2011/DK and 1307/2012/DK against the European External Action Service (4 June 2015).

[233] Case T-271/10 RENV [2018] paras 147–49.

What is more, the Court's expansive reading of its jurisdiction on foreign affairs issues, including the broad interpretation of Article 47 of the Charter in this field, did not last too long. When the Luxembourg judges were called to decide on applications lodged by asylum seekers against the European Council in the context of the EU–Turkey deal of March 2016,[234] the General Court denied jurisdictional competence regarding the said deal in a first instance order of early 2017.[235] The applicants had challenged the legality of the deal on measures to be implemented in order to reduce the number of asylum seekers crossing the Turkish–Greek border, inter alia, because of its alleged incompatibility with fundamental rights. The Court held that it lacked jurisdiction as the concluded agreement had not been adopted by an EU institution and had not produced reviewable EU law. Instead, the deal was said to represent an international agreement concluded by Member States not subject to judicial review by the EU judicature.[236] The judges furthermore clarified in paragraph 74 of their order(s) that 'Article 47 of the Charter of Fundamental Rights of the European Union is not intended to change the system of judicial review laid down by the Treaties'.

It is difficult to imagine that this difference in judgment regarding judicial review between the *H, Rosneft, Jenkinson*, and *SatCen* cases and the EU–Turkey deal decision can be explained by the mere fact that the latter actions were, according to the CJEU's classification scheme, brought under the AFSJ and not the CFSP (as in the former). But, more importantly, it is difficult to square this jurisprudence with the case law of the ECtHR on the horizontal allocation of jurisdictional competences. The lack of judicial remedies for individuals concerned by the effects of the EU–Turkey agreements clearly undermines the *Bosphorus* presumption.[237] It also runs contrary to the *Matthews* decision of 1998, according to which parties to the ECHR can be held accountable for consequences of an international agreement concluded (in the EU context) as they continue to be responsible for securing the rights enshrined in the Convention.[238]

This reasoning, hampering judicial review—and thus accountability for conduct in EU security matters—was not challenged by the Court of Justice in the appeals

[234] EU–Turkey European Council Statement of 18 March 2016 after the meeting of EU Heads of State or Government with Turkey. For detailed information on the content of the EU–Turkey agreements, see Commission factsheet on the EU–Turkey Agreement of 18 March 2016 titled 'EU–Turkey Agreement: Questions and Answers'.

[235] Case T-192/16 *NF v European Council* [2017] EU:T:2017:128; Case T-193/16 *NG v European Council* [2017] EU:T:2017:129; Case T-257/16 *NM v European Council* [2017] EU:T:2017:130.

[236] The 'compacts' which the EU set out to conclude with a range of third countries (ie Ethiopia, Jordan, Lebanon, Niger, Mali, Nigeria, and Senegal) with a view to reducing the number of migrants coming to Europe would suffer the same jurisdictional sort given their informal nature. For further information on the compacts, see Commission factsheet on the 'Partnership Framework' with third countries under the European Agenda on Migration dated 7 June 2016.

[237] See, in this context, the analysis developed by Martina Spernbauer on the subsidiary responsibility of Member States in cases where the *Bosphorus* presumption does not apply. Spernbauer (n 54) 372–77.

[238] Judgment of 18 February 1999 in *Matthews v the United Kingdom*, application no 24833/94 paras 32–33.

phase. In 2018 the appellants' appeals were dismissed as manifestly inadmissible as they lacked 'any legal argument to demonstrate how the General Court allegedly erred in law' and therefore primarily expressed the appellants' discontentment with the court's assessment of the fasts.[239] As this leaves the claimants (and persons in a similar situation) both de jure and de facto without remedies, the Court in Strasbourg might see itself confronted with a number of cases related to a range of current and future EU foreign policy decisions having direct effect on individuals. This would accentuate the competitive relationship between the Luxembourg Court and the Strasbourg Court to allow for $A_c$ regarding CSDP activities.

## 5. Coping with the *lex imperfecta*

This chapter commenced by portraying a framework that is not in principle conducive to legal accountability: a low level of codification coupled with restricted jurisdiction leaves few prospects for judicial review. Indeed, in light of limited juridification and judicialization of the CFSP/CSDP, courts have (had) a hard time ensuring legal accountability regarding EU peacebuilding activities. Across all levels, the three foundational precepts of legal accountability—legality, access to justice, and damages—are built on shaky grounds. Yet, the EU judicature in particular managed to extend legal accountability for information ($A_i$) and accountability for conduct ($A_c$) to actors at both the strategic and operational level of EU civilian crisis management.

This brings us to the first set of questions the chapter at hand attempted to answer. Which judicial body—national, European, or both—is competent to adjudicate on matters related to extraterritorial EU civilian missions? And further, how is legal accountability exercised, and with respect to which aspects and actors? There are potentially three (groups of) judicial players: national courts, the EU judicature, and the ECtHR. In theory, judicial review in the de jure intergovernmental realm of foreign affairs and security policy would be channelled through national judicial bodies. Yet, jurisdictional activity, both in terms of scope and intensity, at the Member State level faces several procedural and substantive hurdles, including obstacles related to the justiciability and admissibility of claims, immunity and confidentiality issues, limited interpretative authority of national courts regarding EU law, and at times difficult *locus standi* rules. In practice, then, national courts have relatively few means to hold national actors to account—both high-level representatives and Eurocrats—for their action in the CFSP domain ($A_c$), and they equally have little jurisdictional leeway to enforce accountability for information ($A_i$) on behalf of citizens or national institutions.

[239] Joined Cases C-208/17 P to C-210/17 P *NF, NG and NM v European Council* [2018] EU:C:2018:705 paras 21, 29.

This lack of legal accountability at the national level was countered by the EU judicature, which significantly fostered accountability for both conduct and information at the EU level. First, the CJEU supported the role of other accountability fora, notably the EP, to hold executive actors to account, in particular for the provision of information ($A_i$). The parliamentary-friendly reading of the information-sharing requirement incumbent upon the Council in the context of the conclusion of international CFSP agreements is indicative hereof. Secondly, the CJEU claimed jurisdiction for a range of CFSP issues going beyond the exceptions laid down in primary law and, consequently, 'further eroded the immunity from jurisdiction for acts adopted in the field of CFSP'.[240] Next to adjudicating sanctions and policing policy delimitation, the Court affirmed its competence for derivative CFSP decisions, and, more specifically, for implementation acts in civilian crisis management relating to financial matters (*Elitaliana*) and staff management relating to seconded national experts (*H v Council*). The EU judicature furthermore held that it had, under certain circumstances, retroactive jurisdictional competence to hear human resources incidents involving international contractual staff that predated the express conferral of jurisdiction to the EU judicature by the insertion of an arbitration clause into the work contracts (*Jenkinson*). In addition, the Court confirmed that it could deliver preliminary rulings on certain CSFP topics (*Rosneft*), thereby endorsing its position as a primary interpreter of EU law. This expansive jurisdictional stance of the CJEU is to a large extent a reaction to the *lex imperfecta* governing the CFSP: primary law provides little judicial remedies, resulting in a weak legal protection regime—and thus little $A_c$.

Closing this legal protection gap has a double rationale for the CJEU: it sensibly improves effective judicial remedies in the EU legal order and, simultaneously, cuts off possible procedures in Strasbourg as (stronger) legal protection is necessary to fulfil the ECtHR's *Bosphorus* presumption of equal protection. This consolidates the role of the CJEU as a legal accountability forum for CFSP and CSDP matters, including peacebuilding, at the European level. The case law of the CJEU pertaining to civilian crisis management has indeed limited the jurisdictional room for manoeuvre of the Court in Strasbourg. It remains open whether or not this allocation of horizontal jurisdictional competences will be upheld in future cases related to external action. There seems to be a pattern according to which the General Court is reluctant to assert jurisdiction over CFSP/CSDP matters, whereas the Court of Justice has a more proactive stance. It is also unclear how Member States—many of which are proponents of an intergovernmental scheme with lax or no judicial review of CFSP decisions—will react to the new line of jurisprudence developed by the CJEU, which increasingly insists on exercising jurisdiction over (derivative) CFSP decisions well beyond civilian CSDP (as in *SatCen*).

[240] Sara Poli, 'The Common Foreign Security Policy after Rosneft: Still Imperfect but Gradually Subject to the Rule of Law' (2017) 54 Common Market Law Review 1799, 1800.

This leads us to the second interrogation, which is tied to the specific edifice of civilian crisis management: How can legal accountability be reconciled with Europeanized intergovernmentalism? The key aspect here is the scope of judicial review by the EU judicature in relation to the Europeanized aspects of civilian crisis management, despite the codified preclusion of judicial review (except for sanctions and policy delimitation). In the *Elitaliana* and *H* cases handed down respectively in 2015 and 2016, the EU judicature attempted to remodel the jurisdictional carve-out set out in the Treaties: the judges extended the scope of their judicial review by virtue of *implied* and *contingent* jurisdictional competences. As a consequence, judicial review henceforth entails both 'formal' CFSP decisions adopted by the Council (or the PSC) in the intergovernmental sphere of the CSDP covered by the exceptions regime, *and* derivative CFSP decisions (mostly administrative acts) taken in the Europeanized realm of civilian crisis management by members of the Brussels-based bureaucracy or field personnel in the implementation of civilian missions.

This jurisdictional move substantially contributed to reconciling legal accountability with Europeanized intergovernmentalism. By stretching its own jurisdiction to operational matters, the CJEU considerably improved the $A_c$ of influential Europeanized bureaucratic actors in civilian crisis management, who had so far escaped judicial oversight despite the considerable decision-making and executive powers they had acquired by concealed agencification. Likewise, actors at the strategic level, in particular the Council, can no longer hide behind the intricate administrative edifice of civilian CSDP to eschew attribution of (derivative) decisions. Judicial review has thus been strengthened both at the strategic level, namely the Council and the PSC, and at the operational level, notably bureaucratic supra-structures in Brussels and personnel in the field. Moreover, a shift from a procedural review to a more substantive review can be discerned in the recent case law. This leads to the conclusion that the EU judicature has through its jurisprudence de facto relocated jurisdiction on civilian CSDP vertically from the national to the EU level. This shift in jurisdiction follows the shift in governance to the EU level: the informal vertical transfer of decision-making and action capacity.

This brings us to the question of the appropriateness of current accountability arrangements. The overall evaluation of all three appropriateness criteria—quantity, quality, and capacity—is positive. This is only the case because the CJEU applied an expansive reading regarding operational matters, and thereby adapted the scope of jurisdiction to the scope of Europeanized decision-making and action. Today, legal accountability at the EU level covers both strategic and operational aspects of civilian crisis management (quantity). In addition, the CJEU has equipped itself with the necessary inquisitive and sanctioning powers for effective legal accountability by declaring itself competent to adjudicate both on 'formal' CSFP decisions and on derivative CFSP decisions, that is administrative acts (quality). Finally, this jurisdictional move brought the initially accountability-unfriendly de jure environment much closer to the capacity-benchmark as it allows for judicial review of constitutionally enshrined, institutional and procedural arrangements and improves legal protection.

To conclude, the CJEU has made a big step forward in ensuring legal accountability for conduct and information both at the strategic and operational level of civilian crisis management. An important element in this development was that the Court has progressively adapted the jurisdictional landscape on operational matters with a view to adjusting judicial review to the edifice of Europeanized intergovernmentalism. It will be interesting to see whether the Court will manage to maintain its positive record as an accountability facilitator, and whether it will be able to keep the ambitious jurisdictional promises it has made to individuals as an accountability forum.

# 7
# Administrative Accountability: Separate but Complementary Fora

EU peacebuilding activities unfold within a patchy administrative framework. This is, to a large extent, due to the particular integration trajectory and institutionalization pattern of (the civilian dimension of) the Common Security and Defence Policy (CSDP) of the European Union (EU): against the backdrop of a rudimentarily codified intergovernmental framework of EU foreign affairs, security, and defence, bureaucratic structures were created *ex nihilo* in the 2000s to speedily provide for operational capacity. The administrative arrangements underpinning these increasingly Europeanized bureaucratic structures were mostly put in place and further developed once the policy had gone operational—that is *ex post facto*. Hence, the development of civilian CSDP was characterized by 'underthematisation, conceptual looseness and rapidity',[1] and therefore left little room for building administrative sub- or supra-structures. As a result, reporting requirements and procedural arrangements, including disciplinary measures and appeal mechanisms, were relatively volatile, lacked transparency, and took time to be unified and consolidated. Individuals therefore ran into difficulties when they had to identify either complaint mechanisms or bodies responsible for access-to-documents issues.

In addition, the administrative procedures and arrangements eventually established did not envisage external administrative scrutiny—that is, scrutiny outside of the civilian crisis management apparatus. Because of the sensitive character of security and defence matters, it was far from obvious to Member States why administrative control should be set up at the EU level for policy issues that largely escaped administrative review at the national level.[2] However, over the years the crisis management bureaucracy has acquired considerable administrative decisional and executive competences: Brussels-based actors autonomously plan, implement, and oversee all civilian CSDP activities.

[1] Giovanni Faleg, *The EU's Common Security and Defence Policy—Learning Communities in International Organizations* (Palgrave Macmillan 2017) 89.

[2] Indicative of this attitude are, for instance, the responses of the Council to inquiries of the European Ombudsman, which rarely exceed(ed) four to five lines when refuting the competence of the Council to deal with such issues. See, inter alia, Decision of the European Ombudsman closing the own-initiative inquiry OI/12/2010/(BEH)MMN concerning the Council of the European Union, the European Commission and the High Representative/European External Action Service (30 August 2013) para 29.

*Accountability in EU Security and Defence.* Carolyn Moser, Oxford University Press (2020). © Carolyn Moser.
DOI: 10.1093/oso/9780198844815.001.0001

Indeed, EU civilian crisis management—also referred to as EU peacebuilding activities—nowadays operates in a context of *Europeanized intergovernmentalism*: while the de jure framework is intergovernmental, bureaucratic realities have become de facto Europeanized.[3] This means that decision-making and action capacity along the entire policy cycle and implementation process of civilian crisis management has been vertically transferred from Member States (eg ministerial departments, agencies) to a specialized Brussels-based bureaucracy. This scheme is characteristic of agencification. Yet, in civilian CSDP the transfer of functions has taken place informally, so that agencification is concealed.

The repercussions of *concealed agencification* leading to Europeanized intergovernmentalism in accountability matters are twofold. First, some parts of the administrative edifice of civilian CSDP are intergovernmental, whereas others are Europeanized. This schizophrenic setting obviously does not facilitate administrative accountability. Secondly, de facto administrative power is exercised in civilian crisis management, while there is a de jure lack of clearly defined rules and procedures underpinning or limiting the exercise of this power.

In the absence of clearly defined rules and procedures in Europeanized intergovernmentalism, it is not surprising that in peacebuilding, like in other EU external activities, 'administrative power is frequently exercised in a non-linear manner; in a discretionary fashion; and informally which is often the synonym of legally invisible'.[4] This state of affairs, though, is difficult to reconcile with the principle of the rule of law laid down in EU primary law, which mandates the oversight of administrative EU decisions and acts.[5] This poses questions in terms of accountability because there are many de facto administrative hands at work with very few de jure administrative eyes watching.[6]

Following the call to accord more attention to the administrative external competences of EU institutions and bodies,[7] the present chapter sets out to disentangle administrative accountability in the context of EU peacebuilding activities conducted under the CSDP. Accountability is defined as a three-stage

3 On this point, see the analysis provided in Chapters 1 and 2.

4 Illaria Vianello, 'Guiding the Exercise of Union's Administrative Power in the EU Wider Neighbourhood. The Rule of Law from Paper to Operationalisation', *EUI Working Paper LAW 2015/08* (EUI 2015) 1. This statement was made in relation to the Stabilisation and Association Process and the European Neighbourhood Policy, but equally applies to civilian CSDP, not least because the underlying patterns and dynamics are very similar.

5 Gerard C Rowe, 'Administrative Supervision of Administrative Action in the European Union' in Herwig CH Hofmann and Alexander H Türk (eds), *Legal Challenges in EU Administrative Law: Towards an Integrated Administration* (Edward Elgar 2009) 179.

6 This statement is inspired by the writings of Thompson and Bovens. See Dennis F Thompson, 'Moral Responsibility of Public Officials: The Problem of Many Hands' (1980) 74 American Political Science Review 905; Mark Bovens, 'Analysing and Assessing Accountability: A Conceptual Framework' (2007) 13 European Law Journal 447, 455–57.

7 Herwig CH Hofmann and Alexander H Türk, 'Legal Challenges in EU Administrative Law by the Move to an Integrated Administration' in Herwig CH Hofmann and Alexander H Türk (eds), *Legal Challenges in EU Administrative—Law Towards an Integrated Administration* (Edward Elgar 2009) 372.

mechanism—consisting of (i) the provision of information by an actor, (ii) scrutiny by a forum, and (iii) potential formal or informal consequences imposed by the forum on the actor[8]—which can either focus on conduct (accountability for *conduct*, $A_c$) or on the provision of information (accountability for *information*, $A_i$). The assessment focuses on quasi-judicial and financial accountability arrangements at both the national and EU level. Proceedings in court relating to administrative disputes (eg labour law cases, disciplinary matters) are only tackled in an ancillary manner in this chapter. Jurisdictional aspects tied to administrative matters are discussed in detail in Chapter 6 on legal accountability given that the nature of the forum (not of the matter under scrutiny) is in this book the qualifying parameter for accountability types.

That said, the chapter at hand addresses a set of interrelated questions. (i) To what extent has the legal and procedural framework of civilian crisis management enabled administrative accountability? (ii) What is the role of administrative fora? Do they tackle cross-cutting administrative questions or solve individual cases? How has their role evolved over time? (iii) And in how far are the existing de jure and de facto administrative accountability arrangements aligned with Europeanized intergovernmentalism? Against the backdrop of the overarching research question of this book—*to what extent has the transfer of powers by Member States to Brussels-based EU civilian crisis management structures been matched with the establishment of appropriate accountability mechanisms at the European level?*—the quest for answers is guided by three dimensions of appropriateness: (i) quantity, (ii) quality, and (iii) capacity. As for quantity, the study explores whether there are administrative accountability mechanisms at the EU level, which is the level where administrative decisions are actually taken. Concerning the quality criterion, the inquisitive and sanctioning powers regarding both $A_i$ and $A_c$ are taken into account. Finally, capacity implies that (i) individuals have redress options, including complaints mechanisms, and that (ii) there is effective financial control, both for compliance and performance aspects.

The chapter unfolds in five steps. First, section 1 decorticates the administrative environment of civilian CSDP. The scrutiny covers institutional, legal, and procedural components (reporting lines and attribution schemes, disciplinary arrangements, etc). The second section of this chapter outlines the small role national authorities play in administrative accountability. Thirdly, the assessment concentrates on the role of the European Ombudsman (also referred to as Ombudsman) as a quasi-judicial accountability forum for both individual complaints and overall administrative questions. The evaluation of the Ombudsman's role in section 3 is followed in section 4 by a study of the dual function of the European Court of Auditors (ECA), which simultaneously fulfils an auditing and a consultative

[8] Bovens (n 6) 450.

function. Finally, the complementarity of these two institutions—the Ombudsman and the ECA—is discussed (section 5).

## 1. Administrative Bits and Pieces

The Europeanized administrative structure of civilian CSDP came into being bit by bit as a response to practical questions. Form followed function. The result of this demand-driven and sliced construction of the administrative framework is twofold: first, reporting lines differ according to different tasks; secondly, members of civilian missions operate under a variety of contractual and disciplinary regimes.[9] Both aspects—reporting lines and staff regimes (including disciplinary arrangements)—considerably impact on administrative accountability. Clear and transparent administrative (including disciplinary) regimes ensure that actors can be held to account for their action or omission according to standing rules, and enable personnel concerned to launch a complaint or an appeal against a decision directed against them. While the first instance of disciplinary procedures tends to unfold within the structure concerned, the appeal phase can involve external (quasi-)judicial actors, who then hold to account the institution for its (in)action.

### 1.1 Diverging reporting lines and varying attribution schemes

Reporting requirements together with chains of command or delegation constitute the pillars of each accountability edifice as they are decisive for determining the attribution of administrative decisions.[10] Regarding EU peacebuilding activities, there are two broad reporting schemes according to different activities (and responsibilities), schematically outlined in Figure 7.1.

When it comes to *general administrative and operational business* (ie day-to-day management) the highest authority of decision-making and reporting is the Council of the EU (Council), in particular in its Foreign Affairs Council (FAC) composition—that is national foreign ministers and, on defence issues, defence ministers. The chain of command thus starts at the Council and consecutively runs through the Political and Security Committee (PSC), to whom the Council can delegate certain decision-making tasks. The chain of command then continues with the Civilian Operations Commander (CivOpsCdr) and ends at the Head of

[9] Another consequence of this sliced institutionalization is that continuous organizational/experiential learning constitutes a main characteristic of the bureaucratic apparatus in charge of civilian missions. See Michael E Smith, *Europe's Common Security and Defence Policy. Capacity-Building, Experiential Learning, and Institutional Change* (Cambridge University Press 2017); Raphael Bossong, 'EU Civilian Crisis Management and Organizational Learning' (2013) 22 European Security 94.

[10] Rowe (n 5) 191.

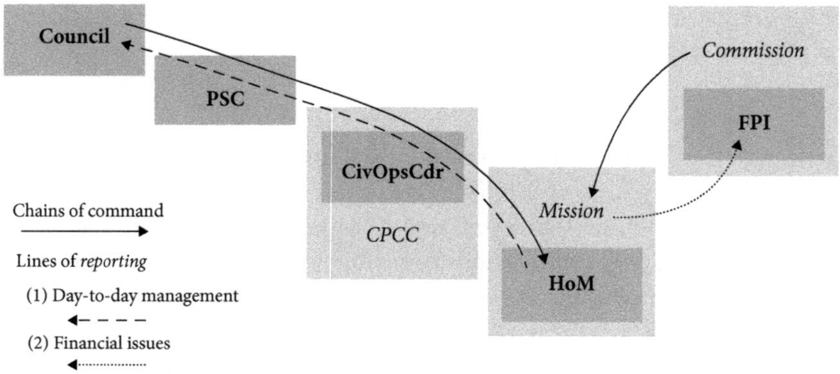


**Figure 7.1** Simplified scheme of command and reporting arrangements

Mission (HoM). The formal line of reporting mirrors the inverted course of the chain of command.[11]

In contrast, the European Commission (Commission) is the supreme administrative authority for *financial issues* given the budgetary arrangements in place: the spending of EU money for civilian missions is under the supervision of the Commission.[12] Both ex ante and ex post financial control is in the hands of the Commission's Service for Foreign Policy Instruments (FPI), which is entitled to conduct internal audits to verify the correct disbursement for and by civilian missions. This is because the Commission entrusts the mission by a delegated act with the implementation of the appropriations of the Common Foreign and Security Policy (CFSP) contained in Chapter 19.03 of the EU budget,[13] while the mission administers the funds in compliance with principles of sound financial management,[14] and concludes the necessary contracts (eg procurement of personnel and services) in consultation with Brussels-based structures. Reporting on financial issues is thus between the mission and the FPI, while the Civilian Planning and Conduct Capacity (CPCC), affiliated with the European External Action Service (EEAS), is also in the loop for coordination purposes.

These diverging reporting schemes for day-to-day management decisions, on the one hand, and for financial issues, on the other, have two interrelated effects

[11] Eg Council Doc 9919/07 of 1 February 2007, 'Draft Guidelines for Command and Control Structure for EU Civilian Operations in Crisis Management' RESTREINT EU; Council Doc 11277/07 of 28 June 2007, 'Standard language for planning documents and legal acts for civilian ESDP operations' LIMITE.

[12] See in particular Chapters 2 and 5.

[13] Article 58(1)(c) Regulation (EU, EURATOM) 2015/1929 of the European Parliament and of the Council of 28 October 2015 amending Regulation (EU, Euratom) No 966/2012 on the financial rules applicable to the general budget of the Union [2015] OJ L286/1.

[14] This includes the duty to prevent, detect, correct, and notify irregularities and fraud to the Commission, and to carry out ex ante and ex post controls. Art 60(3) ibid.

on administrative accountability. First, different lines of reporting and chains of command or delegation give rise to different attribution schemes. Given the intricate Europeanized administrative framework of civilian crisis management, there was confusion about the attributability of specific derivative decisions, which are (often administrative) decisions taken by crisis management actors with a view to implementing civilian missions. According to primary law, only acts adopted by the Council (or the PSC) count as 'decisions' in the sense of a formal legal CFSP act that is attributable to their originator—the Council or the PSC respectively; other decisions or measures adopted by the Brussels-based bureaucracy or personnel in the field (eg HoM) are not expressly mentioned in primary law, and their 'informality' makes attribution difficult in the context of Europeanized intergovernmentalism. The EU judicature sorted out this open issue in two judgments rendered in 2015 and 2016 respectively. Basing attribution on a functional nexus, according to reporting lines and obligations, the Court of Justice of the European Union (CJEU) held in *H v Council* that acts of staff management—in other words day-to-day management decisions at the theatre level—were attributable to the Council.[15] In view of the existing budgetary arrangements, the CJEU in its *Elitaliana* decision endorsed that administrative decisions with financial implications (ie procurement, including employment contracts) were attributable to the Commission.[16]

Both Court decisions concerned, however, incidents that had taken place before the Council started in 2014 to endow civilian missions with the capacity 'to procure services and supplies, enter contracts and administrative arrangements, employ staff, hold bank accounts, acquire and dispose of assets, discharge its liabilities and be a party to legal proceedings'.[17] The operational realities of peacebuilding, such as responsibilities or reporting requirements, have not been altered by the missions' modified legal status. The conferral of legal capacity has, above all, been a great relief for HoMs who had previously been personally responsible and liable for budgetary matters because of an *ad personam* budget delegation arrangement with the Commission.[18] Could attribution therefore be fundamentally different after the conferral of legal capacity to civilian missions if the realities—and the overall framework—have not changed? Most probably, the reasoning which motivated the Court's decision would lead to dual attribution, as attribution was based on the existing functional nexus. Concretely, this would mean that acts of staff management

[15] Case C–455/14 *P H v Council and others* [2016] EU:C:2016:569. See the detailed case analysis provided in Chapter 6.

[16] Case C–439/13 *P Elitaliana SpA v EULEX Kosovo* [2015] EU:C:2015:753. See the detailed case analysis provided in Chapter 6.

[17] This is a standard formulation in mission mandates, which has been inserted since 2014 in the stipulations on 'legal arrangements'.

[18] C(2009)9502/1 (30 November 2009) (Administrative Decision), 'Specific Rules for Special Advisers of the Commission entrusted with the implementation of operational CFSP actions and contracted international staff'. See also C(2012)4052 final (26 June 2012) (Administrative Decision), 'Rules for the Financial Management of the Common Foreign and Security Policy Missions'.

would be attributable both to the Council and the mission at stake, and that acts with financial implications would be attributable both to the Commission and the respective mission.[19]

That being said, the European Ombudsman in 2013 reached a similar conclusion to that of the CJEU as regards attribution: an own-initiative inquiry into accountability for maladministration in CSDP activities identified the Commission as an interlocutor for matters pertaining to budget implementation, and the High Representative of the EU for Foreign Affairs and Security Policy (HR) as the contact point for all other allegations of maladministration—mainly because the Council had demonstrated very little will to deal with inquiries of the Ombudsman in civilian CSDP.[20]

Secondly, and this ties in with questions of attribution, both the Council and the Commission have a dual accountability role regarding administrative matters: they are simultaneously accountability fora *and* actors. On the one hand, the Council and the Commission constitute the supreme institutional authority for specific tasks within the crisis management structures, respectively for day-to-day management (Council) and financial matters (Commission). On the other hand, the Council and the Commission are accountability actors who, because of attribution schemes, have to give an account to other EU institutions and entities—such as the European Parliament (EP), the European Ombudsman, or the ECA—on their (in)action in civilian crisis management. This dual accountability role is crucial because *external* scrutiny concerns, to a large proportion, the way in which the respective institution *internally* exercises administrative authority along the line of reporting or, differently put, the chain of delegation. In other words, the performance of the two institutions as an accountability *forum* is decisive for their position as an accountability *actor*. Again, it is unclear if and how the conferral of legal capacity to civilian missions would change the situation of a dual accountability role given that the CJEU attributed specific acts on the basis of functional connectivity and not on the basis of institutional anchorage, including legal status. Instead of discharging the Council or the Commission from their respective responsibilities because of the conferral of legal capacity to missions, a double accountability regime is likely, rendering it possible to attribute acts both to the missions (because of their relative independence) *and* to the respective EU institution (because of their unaltered role as a supreme administrative and strategic authority).

[19] In 2017 a first application regarding procurement matters was lodged at the CJEU against the Commission *and* a civilian mission (EUBAM Libya). Even though the action was dismissed, the Court did in its judgment not question the proper identification by the applicant of the two defendant parties. See Case T-206/17 *Argus Security Projects Ltd v Commission and EUBAM Libya* [2018] EU:T:2018:288. In addition, in the event that the EEAS was closely associated with adoption of the disputed act (which is particularly probable in disciplinary procedures), attribution could additionally concern the EEAS.

[20] Decision closing the own-initiative inquiry OI/12/2010/(BEH)MMN [2013] para 53. A detailed analysis of this own-initiative inquiry can be found in this chapter (section 3).

## 1.2 A disparate legal and disciplinary regime for mission personnel

In addition to the complexities regarding reporting and attribution, the administrative framework of EU peacebuilding activities sets out a disparate legal and disciplinary regime for mission personnel (a summary of which is provided at the end of this section in Table 7.1). This disparity is engendered, to a large degree, by

**Table 7.1** Legal and disciplinary regimes for staff of civilian missions

| | **Seconded EU personnel** | **Seconded national experts** | **HoM** | **International contracted civilians** | **Local contracted civilians** |
|---|---|---|---|---|---|
| *Applicable staff regulations* | | | | | |
| EU Staff Regulations | Applicable | –/– | Partly applicable | –/– | –/– |
| CEOS | –/– | Not applicable | Partly applicable | Not applicable | Not applicable |
| *Disciplinary matters* | | | | | |
| Disciplinary control | DHoM | DHoM | CPCC | DHoM | DHoM |
| Disciplinary action | Seconding EU institution | Seconding national authority | Seconding national authority | HoM | HoM |
| *Complaint mechanism* | | | | | |
| Availability | Yes | Yes | Yes | Yes | Yes |
| Legal basis | EU Staff Regulations (Art 90) | Code of conduct | CEOS and EU Staff Regulations (Art 90) | Code of conduct | Code of conduct |
| *Judicial review* | | | | | |
| Competent court(s) | CJEU | CJEU | CJEU | CJEU | Host State Courts |
| Legal basis | EU Staff Regulations (Art 91) | CJEU case law vs mission mandate and SOMA | EU Staff Regulations (Art 91) | Dispute settlement clause | Mission mandate and SOMA |
| *Social and labour laws* | | | | | |
| EU law | Yes | –/– | Yes | –/– | –/– |
| National law(s) | –/– | Seconding Member State or third State | Seconding Member State or third State | Home country/ country of fiscal residency | Host State of civilian mission |

**Figure 7.2** Distribution of mission personnel per staff type

the differences between mission personnel. There are two categories of staff with two sub-categories each. First, mission staff consist of seconded personnel, either (i) from EU institutions or (ii) from national authorities (from Member States or third States). The HoM fall under the second sub-category but enjoy a specific legal status, which will be outlined below. Secondly, mission staff include contracted personnel, namely (iii) international contracted civilians and (iv) local contracted civilians. All missions taken together, the biggest share of staff is locally hired personnel (almost half of the personnel), followed by seconded civil servants (roughly a third) and international contracted staff (one sixth), as can be seen in Figure 7.2 on the distribution of mission personnel per staff type.[21] While the ratio of internationals to locals varies considerably from mission to mission—being 50:50 in Kosovo but 70:30 in Mali—there is a common trait across missions, namely that there is barely any seconded EU official working in current civilian missions.

Staff belonging to these different categories largely operate under different conditions, except for some essential similarities. These similarities (or differences) have so far not been outlined in the academic literature. Up to now, one had to study pertinent—and not necessarily directly accessible—internal Council and EEAS documents together with the recent but growing case law of the CJEU, as well as a number of complaints lodged with the European Ombudsman to understand the specificities of the different regimes at work. The following concise overview of co-existing legal and disciplinary arrangements in civilian crisis management is thus a valuable addition to the literature, not least because it lays open for a wider public the intricate setting that has until now only been known in detail to a few insiders. Even complainants lodging cases with the European Ombudsman, for instance, are not always aware of all administrative or procedural details.

[21] This distribution of staff types—49% local contracted staff, 35% seconded experts, and 16% international contracted staff—is based on Annalisa Creta and others, 'Civilian and Military Personnel in CSDP Missions and Operations', *EP/EXPO/B/SEDE/2016/02* (European Parliament 2017) 14. According to the information on deployed personnel displayed on the EEAS website, the share of international staff is slightly higher: instead of a 51:49 ratio (international–locals), the ratio indicated is 54:46.

Let us first turn to the similarities, which primarily concern *behavioural standards*. The 2016 Code of Conduct and Discipline for EU civilian missions explicitly applies to *all* types of mission personnel.[22] The Code specifies the competent bureaucratic structure(s) for disciplinary procedures, whose precise course it also regulates. The Code of Conduct and Discipline was primarily drafted in reaction to the 2015 Jacqué report, which outlined a number of institutional as well as systemic weaknesses in civilian crisis management.[23] While the Code of Conduct and Discipline codifies largely existing but disparate practice (behavioural matters were previously addressed in the Operations Plan of each mission), it also presents some improvements, for instance, as regards the categorization of wrongdoings or the course of disciplinary proceedings. Since its entry into force in 2016, the new Code has regularly been applied to disciplinary cases. Likewise, the Upgraded Generic Standards of Behaviour for CSDP Missions and Operations of 2018,[24] which replaced the Generic Standards of Behaviour for CSDP activities of 2005,[25] apply to all staff members.[26] The said Upgraded Generic Standard concretizes desired professional conduct and behaviour (respectful attitude and tolerance vis-à-vis co-workers and locals, commitment, integrity, discretion, etc) and defines punishable actions and omissions (sexual exploitation and abuse, trafficking in human beings, harassment, and corruption). Equally applicable to all staff members, regardless of their contractual regime, are the Standard Operating Procedures (SOPs) on Whistleblowing in civilian crisis management introduced in 2015. The document clearly states that all staff members can voice concerns internally (to the HoM and, if necessary, to the Brussels-based bureaucracy) and, if appropriate, externally to the European Ombudsman or the European Anti-Fraud Office (OLAF).[27] Whistleblowing matters were also addressed by the Jacqué report, and the codification of procedures had been suggested by the European Ombudsman.[28]

[22] Article 1(1) Council Doc 12076/16 of 9 September 2016, 'Code of Conduct and Discipline for EU civilian CSDP Missions'.

[23] Jean-Paul Jacqué, 'Review of the EULEX Kosovo Mission's Implementation of the Mandate with a Particular Focus on the Handling of the Recent Allegations' Report commissioned by the High Representatives and released (with annexes) on 31 March 2015 <https://eulex-kosovo.eu/eul/repository/docs/150331_jacque-report_en.pdf> and <https://eulex-kosovo.eu/eul/repository/docs/150331_jacque-report-annexes_en.pdf> both accessed 18 February 2020. For more information, see Chapter 1.

[24] Council Doc 6877/18 of 7 March 2018, 'Upgraded Generic Standards of Behaviour for CSDP Missions and Operations', as endorsed by the Council on 22 January 2018.

[25] Council Doc 8373/3/05 of 18 May 2005, 'Generic Standards of Behaviour for ESDP Operations'.

[26] Para 12 Upgraded Generic Standards of Behaviour.

[27] Civilian Operations Commander Instruction, 'Standard Operating Procedures on Whistleblowing', Ref Ares (2015)5643835 of 7 December 2015 para 5.

[28] Decision of the European Ombudsman closing the own-initiative inquiry OI/15/2014/PMC into the way in which the European External Action Service (EEAS) handles allegations of serious irregularities involving the EU Rule of Law Mission (EULEX) in Kosovo (4 December 2014) para 31.

Yet, the differences between staff types are far more numerous than the similarities. They concern, first, *budgetary arrangements*. While salary-related costs for seconded personnel, both from EU institutions and national authorities, continue in principle to be paid by the seconding institution, the salaries of contracted personnel, both international and local, are charged to the EU budget. Mission costs (eg travel expenses and daily subsistence allowances) are charged to the EU budget for all staff types, whereas the seconding authority is to cover costs for installation, housing, high-risk insurance, compensation for working abroad or in an insecure environment (hardship and risk allowances), and reimbursement of regular trips to the country of permanent residence of seconded personnel.[29]

These differing budgetary arrangements are tied to the second aspect, namely diverging *contractual regimes* of different staff types, including the applicable social and labour legislation (eg annual and special leave, contract termination, social security insurance including sickness and pensions, and liability aspects). There are five different contractual regimes co-existing in civilian missions. Regime (i) concerns personnel seconded by EU institutions, to whom the Staff Regulations of Officials of the European Communities (hereafter referred to as EU Staff Regulations) are applicable, as is EU social and labour law. Regime (ii) relates to personnel seconded by national authorities, who continue to have a contract with their respective seconding State authority. They are neither subject to the EU Staff Regulations, nor to the Conditions of Employment of Other Servants of the EU (CEOS).[30] In addition, their contracts are governed by the applicable social and labour laws of the respective seconding Member State. Heads of Mission are subject to contractual regime (iii). Their appointment depends on the Council, but their contractual arrangements are with the Commission as they act as Special Advisers for CFSP questions.[31] Accordingly, certain provisions of the CEOS apply, making reference to EU Staff Regulations. Regime (iv) applies to international contracted civilians, whose contracts are established with the respective civilian mission.[32] The CEOS are not applicable. The

[29] Council Doc 7291/09 of 10 March 2009, 'Guidelines for allowances for seconded staff participating in EU civilian crisis management missions'. The Court of Auditors in 2001 identified that, in practice, the treatment regarding seconded experts varied according to the action and/or the seconding authority. Special report of the Court of Auditors No 13/2001 on the management of the common foreign and security policy (CFSP), together with the Council's replies and the Commission's replies [2001] OJ C338/01 para 58.

[30] On a side note, it is worth mentioning that the situation is different for national experts directly seconded to the civilian crisis management structures within the EEAS: in this constellation, seconded national experts are regarded as temporary agents of the EU to whom the CEOS apply. See Case F–2/15 *Gergő Pasqualetti v Commission* [2016] EU:F:2016:64.

[31] 3a. Specific Rules for Special CFSP Advisers.

[32] Prior to the conferral of legal capacity from 2014 onwards, the contracts of international contracted staff were signed by the staff member and the HoM in his/her role as administrator of the budget allocations. See ibid 4.

contracts are in principle subject to the applicable social and labour laws of their home country or of the country of (permanent) fiscal residency of the contracted person prior to taking up duties in the mission—that is, potentially twenty-seven Member State legislations, plus the laws of cooperating countries such as Norway or Switzerland—but in practice there is a lack of clarity about these arrangements.[33] Local contracted civilians, under regime (v), sign contracts with the mission (prior to 2014 with the HoM), which are subject to the applicable national social and labour laws of the mission's host country. The CEOS are not applicable. This enumeration undeniably underlines that the uneven contractual arrangements of different staff types co-existing in the missions has led to a complex and opaque administrative patchwork.

Thirdly, *immunity* is the same for all international mission personnel but differs for locally hired staff. Each time the EU decides to deploy a civilian mission, a Status of Mission Agreement (SOMA) is signed between the EU and the host State to govern the status and the privileges and immunities of both the civilian mission and the civilian personnel deployed. An important reference in this regard is the Vienna Convention on Diplomatic Relations (VCDR) of 1961, which codifies customary rules on diplomatic relations. The said Convention regulates the status and the privileges as well as immunities of both diplomatic missions and their personnel. Crucial in this respect is the principle of inviolability, which includes the mission's premises (Article 22 VCDR), archives and documents (Article 24 VCDR), correspondence (Article 27 VCDR), and its diplomatic agents (Article 30 VCDR). Based on the rules laid down in the said Convention, the EU developed a Model SOMA.[34] The Model SOMA grants international mission personnel, regardless of their rank, all privileges and immunities accorded to diplomatic agents under the VCDR.[35] Thus, all international staff members of civilian missions enjoy in principle absolute immunity from criminal jurisdiction and execution, and functional civil as well as administrative immunity from jurisdiction and execution in the host State.[36] Accordingly, the judicial authorities of the seconding State or authority retain jurisdictional competences

[33] On the complexity—not so say opacity—of different contractual regimes existing in parallel in civilian mission, programming the application of different national and social laws to contracted personnel, see Decision of the European Ombudsman on complaint 3008/2005/OV against the European Commission (26 July 2007).

[34] Council Doc 17141/08 of 15 December 2008, 'Draft Model Agreement on the Status of the European Union Civilian Crisis Management Mission in a Host State (SOMA)', endorsed by the Council on 18 September 2007. A thorough analysis of the coming into being of the (Model) SOMA, see Aurel Sari, 'Status of Forces and Status of Mission Agreements under the ESDP: The EU's Evolving Practice' (2008) 19 European Journal of International Law 67.

[35] According to Article 1(e) VCDR, the denomination *diplomatic agent* is applicable to the head of the mission and to members of the diplomatic staff of the mission.

[36] For further information on privileges and immunities granted to mission personnel, see Sari (n 34) 91–92; Panos Koutrakos, *The EU Common Security and Defence Policy* (Oxford University Press 2013) 199–200.

during and after the deployment of the seconded staff members—for criminal jurisdiction for all acts, and for civil and administrative jurisdiction for all official acts.[37] Immunity from jurisdiction or from execution has to be waived by the respective sending authority (EU, Member State, or third State) for seconded personnel, and by the mission for contracted personnel. Yet, local contracted personnel enjoy privileges and immunities according to the authorization of the host State, which shall exercise its jurisdiction over such personnel. Thus, there are two different immunity regimes, one for international staff (seconded and contracted) offering the highest level of protection and one for local staff providing for a lower level of protection.

Fourthly, these different contractual and immunity regimes, and institutional affiliations also impact on *disciplinary procedures*. Given the number of staff deployed in civilian missions (some 2,000 personnel), disciplinary procedures are frequent. As it is commonly the case in peace operations, many procedures revolve around traffic issues (minor infringements), but also cover some cases of serious misconduct (eg sexual abuse). A differentiation needs to be made between disciplinary control and disciplinary action. While the former—disciplinary *control*—entails the capacity to launch and conduct disciplinary investigations, to propose appropriate measures, and to help implement these measures, the latter—disciplinary *action*—has to do with the capacity to take the actual decision imposing disciplinary measures. In addition, disciplinary action comprises, if required, the competence to lift immunity from both jurisdiction and execution.[38] For international and local contracted civilians, both disciplinary control and action are in the hands of the Deputy Head of Mission (DHoM). For seconded EU and national experts, the DHoM (in coordination with the CPCC) is in charge of disciplinary control; the final disciplinary action, however, depends on the approval of the proposed disciplinary measures by the seconding authority (EU institution or competent authority of the seconding State). These disciplinary arrangements are set out by the Code of Conduct and Discipline (2016),[39] and correspond to the clauses contained in various SOMAs and mission mandates. As previously outlined, the SOMAs accord jurisdiction to the judicial bodies of the seconding State over the deployed personnel for all criminal matters and most civil as well as administrative proceedings.

Fifthly, differences exist concerning *complaint mechanisms and legal remedies*. According to Article 90(1)–(2) of the EU Staff Regulations, personnel seconded by

[37] See Art 3, Art 6(4), Art 6(5), Art 6(7) and Art 8 Model SOMA.

[38] Immunity for the entire civilian mission needs to be waived by the EEAS. See Recommendation of the European Ombudsman in case OI/13/2014/JF on the European External Action Service's non-recognition of a third country court ruling: payment of compensation Made in accordance with Article 3(6) of the Statute of the European Ombudsman (23 September 2016).

[39] Art 2(3) Code of Conduct.

EU institutions can file complaints against administrative decisions taken against them with the competent authority within a time limit of three months. Moreover, the EU judicature is according to Article 91 of the EU Staff Regulations (echoed by Article 270 of the Treaty on Functioning of the European Union (TFEU)) competent to hear cases related to disputes arising between the EU and any person subject to the EU Staff Regulations, provided that internal remedies have been exhausted (ie complaint according to the abovementioned Article 90(2) of the EU Staff Regulations). The same disciplinary and judicial arrangements are relevant for HoMs under the regime of Special Adviser applicable to them; their contracts activate clauses of the CEOS, which refer, inter alia, to complaint and review stipulations of the EU Staff Regulations.[40] According to the law as it now stands, international contracted personnel have standing at the CJEU to bring disciplinary cases. While Belgian courts used to be the jurisdictional fora identified by the work contracts of international contracted personnel, the dispute settlement clause inserted in such contracts since 2014 refers cases to the CJEU. In the recent *Jenkinson* case, the General Court ruled that its jurisdictional competence to hear cases involving international contracts staff was under certain circumstances retrospective, meaning that it could deal with claims predating the insertion of the clause.[41] In addition, the 2016 Code of Conduct and Discipline lays down a standard (non-judicial) appeal procedure against disciplinary measures.[42] Somewhat unclear is the situation for seconded national experts. According to primary and secondary rules, the EU judicature cannot hear their cases, but the Code of Conduct and Discipline provides for non-judicial remedies. Yet, the Grand Chamber decision of July 2016 in the *H v Council and others* case opened judicial review to seconded national experts at the CJEU for acts of staff management.[43] The judgment leads to a situation where the de jure framework (an intergovernmental institutional and procedural setting precluding jurisdiction for derivative decisions) diverges form jurisdictional developments (reviewable administrative acts produced by Europeanized structures) which adds to the complexity of the already intricate administrative framework of civilian crisis management, summarized in Table 7.1.

[40] In particular Article 124 CEOS declares applicable Arts 90 and 91 of the Staff Regulations which concern appeals procedures (including the seizure of the CJEU). 3b. Specific Rules for Special CFSP Advisers.

[41] Prior to 2014, the Brussels labour tribunal was the jurisdictional authority to which claims of international contracted staff had to be submitted. The CJEU has, however, ruled in *Jenkinson* that it could, under certain conditions (ie the existence of a connection between claims), retrospectively extend its review to claims covering the period before 2014. Case C–43/17 *P Jenkinson v Council and others* [2018] EU:C:2018:531 paras 47–48.

[42] Art 36–40 Code of Conduct.

[43] Case C–455/14 P [2016].

## 2. Faraway National Authorities

While there is much to say about the patchy administrative framework at the EU level, the following analysis regarding administrative functions of national authorities will be rather short. This is because national administrative or quasi-judicial bodies act de jure and de facto as subsidiary accountability fora in civilian crisis management. This division of labour underlines that the Europeanized momentum of EU peacebuilding activities is considerably more developed than the intergovernmental facet of the policy tool.

Concerning disciplinary measures, national authorities play a residual role, as the 2016 Code of Conduct and Discipline exemplifies. Given that the seconding States retain 'full command and control' over seconded personnel, they in principle constitute the authority responsible for imposing disciplinary action. But as operational command and control is delegated to the HoM, the DHoM is vested with disciplinary control. This means that the initiative to open (preliminary) disciplinary investigations and to propose measures rests with the civilian missions, while only the final approval of measures to be implemented—again by the mission hierarchy—has to be given by the seconding authority upon recommendation of the crisis management bureaucracy. This arrangement leaves prima facie little leeway to national administrative bodies, and therefore lowers the prospects for $A_c$.

As mentioned in section 1.2, jurisdictional activities at the national level is low. Indeed, national judicial bodies of Member States were attributed only a minor role for labour law cases. There used to be a dispute settlement clause in the work contracts of international contracted staff ascribing jurisdictional competence to the labour tribunal of Brussels.[44] Yet, since civilian missions have been conferred legal capacity from 2014 onwards, administrative disputes relating to work contracts are to be submitted to the CJEU.[45] National administrative or (quasi-)judicial authorities are therefore fairly absent from EU peacebuilding activities, except for the jurisdictional aspects tied to immunity stipulations—that is legal accountability of seconded national experts, especially for criminal matters. Indeed, in relation to seconded national experts, only two applications lodged with national courts are known.[46] Another context in which national judicial bodies (potentially) become active is when OLAF finds sufficient ground to believe that fraud or other misconduct has happened and should be pursued by national bodies. These cases, however, are rare.[47] The chances of $A_c$ through national tribunals are equally low.

44 See Case T–410/13 *Bitiqi and others v Commission and others* [2014] EU:T:2014:871.

45 See, inter alia, Case T–763/16 *PY v EUCAP Sahel Niger* [2018] EU:T:2018:181; Case T–602/15 *Jenkinson v Council and others* [2016] EU:T:2016:660.

46 One case was filed by Maria Bamieh with the London Employment Tribunal, UK, and the other application concerned the Regional Administrative Court of Lazio, Italy, in the *H* case.

47 Reported cases concern incidents involving the rule of law and capacity building missions deployed to the Palestinian Territories (EUPOL COPPS), Afghanistan (EUPOL Afghanistan) and Niger (EUCAP Sahel Niger), and—on an individual level—the former head of the CPCC, Kenneth

Concerning administrative accountability for financial matters, the hands of national institutions are also tied: civilian crisis management missions are financed through the EU budget, and therefore fall under the financial supervision of the ECA. Yet, some costs are born by national budgets as the staff-related expenditure for seconded national experts are paid for by the respective national authorities. While this in theory presents a tiny opportunity for national players to be (or become) administrative fora in civilian crisis management and enforce accountability for conduct, in practice it has proved irrelevant.

In addition, quasi-judicial activity is low at the national level for two reasons. First, there is not a guaranteed quasi-judicial institution to which aggrieved personnel could address their complaints. In Germany, for instance, the institution of the Parliamentary Commissioner for the Armed forces (*Wehrbeauftragter*) deals with complaints of soldiers deployed in peace operations in their function as ombudsman of the armed forces.[48] While any member of the armed forces can report to the *Wehrbeauftragter*, civilian experts deployed in civilian missions cannot, and there is no alternative complaint route for members of civilian missions. Secondly, even if appropriate quasi-judicial institutions existed in Member States, they would likely lack competence. In fact, complaints concern decisions taken by members of the crisis management bureaucracy (eg HoM or DHoM) in the context of EU security and defence policy and *not* by actors operating in the framework of national regulations. National quasi-judicial fora are, however, not allowed to hear cases related to administrative acts emanating from EU institutions or bodies. It is the European Ombudsman's tasks to deal with complaints of this nature. This again reduces the already small prospects for $A_c$ and, by extension, $A_i$ exercised by national administrative fora.

In sum, the Europeanized administrative edifice of civilian crisis management leaves limited administrative oversight powers to national players. This subsidiary role of national administrative bodies regarding civilian CSDP provides little prospect of $A_c$ or $A_i$ at the national level. Yet, at the EU level, the situation looks less

Dean. Nicolas Gros-Verheyde, 'Le SEAE dans la tourmente. L'OLAF pourrait saisir le parquet dans une affaire impliquant les missions civiles de crises' [2019] Bruxelles2 <https://club.bruxelles2.eu/2019/08/le-seae-dans-la-tourmente-lolaf-pourrait-saisir-le-parquet-dans-laffaire-k-d/> accessed 18 February 2020; Nicolas Gros-Verheyde, 'Les limiers de l'OLAF enquêtent sur un Britannique, ancien numéro 2 de la PSDC. Des dérives graves en cause' [2019] Bruxelles2 <http://club.bruxelles2.eu/2019/03/les-limiers-de-lolaf-enquetent-sur-un-britannique-ancien-numero-2-de-la-psdc-derives-graves-en-cause/> accessed 18 February 2020; Nicolas Gros-Verheyde, 'Y-a-t-il un problème de commandement dans les missions civiles de l'UE ?' [2017] Bruxelles2 <https://club.bruxelles2.eu/2017/06/y-a-t-il-un-probleme-de-commandement-dans-les-missions-civiles-de-lue/> accessed 18 February 2020.

[48] The Parliamentary Commissioner for the Armed Forces (*Wehrbeauftragter*) operates as a subsidiary body of the Bundestag to protect fundamental rights of military personnel (Article 45b Grundgesetz). On their own initiative as well as on the basis of complaints received, the *Wehrbeauftragter* investigates incidents which potentially imply violations of human dignity or freedom of opinion, or which cause harm to the legal protection of service personnel.

grim: both the European Ombudsman and the ECA intervene as administrative accountability fora, as the following sections 3 and 4 demonstrate.

## 3. The European Ombudsman: At the Core of Administrative Redress

The European Ombudsman has been a proactive administrative (and (quasi-)judicial) accountability forum regarding EU peacebuilding missions. The Ombudsman managed to be a 'machinery for accountability',[49] including CFSP/CSDP matters. As the following study shows, the European Ombudsman (hereafter also referred to as Ombudsman) has (acquired) the inquisitive and sanctioning powers to foster both $A_c$ and $A_i$ regarding administrative matters in civilian CSDP.

This accountability role was initially not programmed but evolved through practice. When civilian crisis management went operational in 2003, the EU edifice still rested on three pillars, the CFSP/CSDP being the second, non-communitarized pillar. The mandate of the Ombudsman covered acts of Community institutions and bodies, and therefore did not *stricto sensu* include CFSP/CSDP matters.[50] This restrictive approach, though, has never been followed by the European Ombudsman. As early as 2003, when the first mission was launched in Bosnia and Herzegovina, the Ombudsman got involved in issues related to peacebuilding activities.[51] Even though the Council—the institution concerned at that time—denied being responsible for the alleged instances of maladministration, the competence of the Ombudsman to deal with complaints arising from CFSP/CSDP activities was not challenged. In 2009 the creation of one legal order by the Treaty of Lisbon formally extended the maladministration review from '*Community* institutions and bodies' to henceforth include '*Union* institutions, bodies, offices and agencies'. Because of the extension of the mandate to the entire corpus of EU law, EU security and defence activities now explicitly fall within the remit of the Ombudsman's competences[52]—a fact that the Ombudsman was keen to stress after the entry into force of the new Treaty.[53] The institutions and bodies active in civilian crisis management are the Council, the Commission, and the EEAS; the missions themselves are not established under the heading of 'body' or 'agency'.

[49] Carol Harlow and Richard Rawlings, 'Promoting Accountability in Multilevel Governance: A Network Approach' (2007) 13 European Law Journal 542, 546.

[50] Alexandros Tsadiras, 'The Ombudsman' in Paul Craig (ed), *EU Administrative Law* (Oxford University Press 2006) 835.

[51] Decision of the European Ombudsman on complaint 1200/2003/OV against the Council (19 December 2003).

[52] Julia Haas, *Der Ombudsmann als Institution des Europäischen Verwaltungsrechts. Zur Neubestimmung der Rolle des Ombudsmanns als Organ der Verwaltungskontrolle auf der Grundlage europäischer Ombudsmann-Einrichtungen.* (Mohr Siebeck 2012) 253; Tsadiras (n 50) 835.

[53] European Ombudsman, 2009 Annual Report 2010 23, 25.

The involvement of the European Ombudsman in CFSD/CSDP matters has definitely increased under the new Treaty: more than twenty investigations have been carried out by the Ombudsman in relation to civilian missions since 2010. The particular nature and approach of the entity have allowed the Ombudsman to foster accountability both in specific cases and with regard to the overall administrative framework of EU peacebuilding activities.

## 3.1 A polyvalent accountability forum

The function of the European Ombudsman is to review maladministration at the EU level: both actions and omissions giving rise to instances of maladministration. This broad job description enables the Ombudsman to deal with questions of redress in individual complaint cases on the one hand, and with general principles and arrangements shaping the overall administrative framework on the other.[54] The legal basis for the Ombudsman's activities are Article 228(1) TFEU read in conjunction with Article 24(2) TFEU and Article 43 of the Charter of Fundamental Rights of the European Union,[55] the Statute approved by the EP,[56] and finally the implementing provisions adopted by the Ombudsman.[57]

The European Ombudsman is simultaneously a parliamentary body and a court-like institution, combining 'instruments of parliamentary scrutiny and [a] judicial role'.[58] The Ombudsman thus operates like a parliamentary inquiry committee, but pursues a legal instead of a political focus.[59] This hybrid nature allows the Ombudsman to 'reconcile executive delegation with parliamentary democracy',[60] which is a crucial attribute in the particular policy context of EU security and defence, where (informal) executive governance is strong and (formal) parliamentary involvement weak. Key in this regard is that the logic underpinning the work of the Ombudsman is not adversarial but guided by a 'conciliatory ethos'.[61] The activity of the Ombudsman unfolds in three steps—information gathering, evaluation of the facts, proposals for solutions/decisions—and therefore embodies

[54] Paul Magnette, 'Between Parliamentary Control and the Rule of Law: The Political Role of the Ombudsman in the European Union' (2003) 10 Journal of European Public Policy 677, 681; Katja Heede, 'Enhancing the Accountability of Community Institutions and Bodies: The Role of the European Ombudsman' (1997) 3 European Public Law 587, 588.

[55] Hereafter referred to as the Charter of Fundamental Rights or Charter.

[56] European Parliament Decision 94/262/ECSC, EC, Euratom of 9 March 1994 on the regulations and general conditions governing the performance of the Ombudsman's duties [1994] OJ L113/15, as amended by European Parliament Decision 2008/587/EC, Euratom of 18 June 2008 [2008] OJ L189/25.

[57] Decision of the European Ombudsman adopting Implementing Provisions of 1 September 2016 [2016] OJ C231/1.

[58] Magnette (n 54) 678.

[59] Heede (n 54) 603.

[60] Magnette (n 54) 677.

[61] Tsadiras (n 50) 845.

the three-phased accountability process model sketched out by Bovens,[62] which is used in this book.

Both the competences of the Ombudsman—*scope* of review—and its evaluation benchmark—*criteria* of review—are tied to maladministration, which entails two dimensions, namely (i) legality and (ii) rules and procedures.[63] While primary law makes reference to maladministration (Articles 24 and 41 TFEU, Article 43 of the Charter), Treaty provisions leave the precise meaning and content of maladministration undefined. This is why the Ombudsman's practice has been pivotal in determining and delimiting what constitutes an instance of maladministration. An important reference in this respect is the European Code of Good Administrative Behaviour (ECGAB), which sets out essential procedural requirements. Endorsed by the EP in 2001, the ECGAB concretizes actions and omissions which constitute instances of maladministration.[64] The code lists, for example, lawfulness, the absence of discrimination, proportionality, the absence of abuses of power, impartiality as well as independence, a reasonable time limit for taking decisions, and the duty to state the grounds of decisions as essential ingredients of good administrative behaviour.[65] This non-exhaustive list covers not only unlawful (and justiciable) conduct but equally improper (non-justiciable) behaviour.[66] In the absence of a regulation on good administration binding upon all EU institutions, the EP, with which the Ombudsman is institutionally affiliated (even though functionally independent),[67] tasked the European Ombudsman to fulfil their duties based on the European Code of Good Administrative Behaviour.[68] The ECGAB has no legal value as such, but indirectly derives validity from the Charter as it is tied to the rights enshrined therein: since 2009, good administration has been recognized as a fundamental right of EU citizens and residents (Article 41 of the Charter). This right comprises several components, such as the right of having one's affairs being handled impartially, fairly and within a reasonable time, the right of being heard, the right to access one's file, the right to receive reasons for decisions made by public administrations, or the right to damages. In addition, the Charter identifies access to documents as an important right of EU citizens and residents in its Article 43.

[62] E Madalina Busuioc, *European Agencies: Law and Practices of Accountability* (Oxford University Press 2013) 224–28.

[63] Tsadiras (n 50) 849.

[64] European Parliament resolution on the European Ombudsman's Special Report to the European Parliament following the own-initiative inquiry into the existence and the public accessibility, in the different Community institutions and bodies, of a Code of Good Administrative Behaviour (C5-0438/2000—2000/2212 (COS)) [2002] OJ C72E/331.

[65] Art 4–8, Arts 17–18 ibid.

[66] Hans P Nehl, 'Good Administration as Procedural Right and/or General Principle?' in Herwig CH Hofmann and Alexander H Türk (eds), *Legal Challenges in EU Administrative Law: Towards an Integrated Administration* (Edward Elgar 2009) 340.

[67] Tsadiras (n 50) 832.

[68] Art 26 of the endorsed ECGAB.

The investigations of the European Ombudsman can be complaint-based or result from an own-initiative inquiry.[69] Own-initiative inquiries allow the Ombudsman to address administrative problems of a broader scope or of a systemic nature, and therefore constitute an important tool of agenda-setting.[70] The Ombudsman has proactively used this agenda-setting tool in the past, including in the context of EU peacebuilding activities.[71] In either constellation (complaint-triggered or own-initiative inquiry), information is crucial to the work of the Ombudsman. The provisions contained in the Statute of the Ombudsman ensure that EU institutions and bodies concerned are bound to cooperate with the Ombudsman by sharing requested information or giving access to pertinent files.[72] This also applies to classified information for which the Ombudsman agrees with the institution or body concerned in advance on the conditions for treatment.[73] In addition, the Ombudsman can organize visits on the spot and interview members of the administrative structures, which provides the Ombudsman with valuable factual and operational insights. With regards to the admissibility of complaints, the most important requirement is that complainants need to have made appropriate administrative approaches to the EU institution concerned prior to addressing the Ombudsman,[74] or, when work relationships are at stake, they need to have exhausted internal remedies (requests or complaint mechanisms).[75] In short, then, the existing information-sharing arrangements endow the Ombudsman with sufficient inquisitive power to pursue accountability demands—both with regard to information and to conduct.

The privileged outcome of an investigation confirming an instance of maladministration is a friendly solution acceptable to both the complainant and the institution(s) concerned.[76] Friendly solutions are proposed when the instance of maladministration can still be remedied. If no friendly solution is reached (or accepted), the Ombudsman has two more redress options. First, the Ombudsman can close a case by making a critical remark to the EU entity concerned.[77] These remarks are the 'most important vehicle for the Ombudsman's active rule formulation',[78] as they denounce the instance of maladministration—and as such constitute an informal sanction in the accountability model used in this study—and

[69] Art 228(2) TFEU; Art 3(1) Statute of the European Ombudsman.
[70] Magnette (n 54) 683.
[71] See, in particular, Decision closing the own-initiative inquiry OI/15/2014/PMC [2014]; Decision closing the own-initiative inquiry OI/12/2010/(BEH)MMN [2013]; Recommendation of the European Ombudsman in case OI/13/2014/JF [2016].
[72] Art 3(2) Statute of the European Ombudsman.
[73] Art 3(2) ibid.
[74] Art 2(4) ibid.
[75] Art 2(8) ibid.
[76] Art 3(5) ibid. See also Art 5 Implementing provisions.
[77] Art 3(6) Statute of the European Ombudsman. See further Art 6 Implementing provisions.
[78] Peter G Bonnor, 'The European Ombudsman: A Novel Source of Soft Law in the European Union' (2000) 25 European Law Review 39, 44.

can include a follow-up. Secondly, the Ombudsman can issue a draft recommendation to the EU entity concerned, proposing steps to be taken to remedy the identified instance of maladministration. The affected EU institution or body then has to reply to the Ombudsman's draft recommendations in a detailed opinion within three months.[79] In the event that the Ombudsman is dissatisfied with the response or the follow-up, a special report can be issued to the EP (which is very rarely done).[80] Regardless of the remedial powers eventually employed, the procedures lodged with the Ombudsman lead to a published decision; therefore, the accountability process does not stop at the scrutiny of facts, but results in a publicly accessible positive or negative evaluation regarding alleged instances of maladministration. Thus, there are potential reputational—that is informal—consequences for the actor. This gives the Ombudsman an important sanctioning power as an accountability forum.

This is true even though decisions by the Ombudsman are *not* legally binding, nor do they create enforceable rights or obligations for the complainant or the institution concerned. This lack of legal bindingness is, however, not an obstacle to the work of the Ombudsman but constitutes a source of their 'diffuse power',[81] rendering the European Ombudsman a 'magistrate of influence'.[82] In reality, the institutional nature—a hybrid between a parliamentary body and a court—and the employed method—a solution-oriented approach—have contributed to establishing the European Ombudsman as an 'alternative route to administrative litigation'.[83] This alternative route is used to foster both $A_c$ and $A_i$, while the former constitutes the far bigger share in civilian crisis management as section 3.2 illustrates.

Indeed, the Ombudsman plays a complementary role to the EU judicature as it allows several limits of judicial review at the EU level to be overcome.[84] Four elements are crucial in this regard. First, the European Ombudsman offers more procedural flexibility, not least because he or she does not follow an adversarial logic. Secondly, the threshold of accessibility is lower. Standing is tied to EU citizenship or residence in the EU without there being a need for an own interest or affectation to launch a complaint. These arrangements are much laxer than the *locus standi* requirements of the CJEU.[85] In addition, in the context of civilian CSDP, the Ombudsman has launched several own-initiative inquiries to circumvent the

[79] Art 3(6) Statute of the European Ombudsman. See further Art 6 Implementing provisions.

[80] Art 3(7) Statute of the European Ombudsman. See further Art 7 Implementing provisions.

[81] Magnette (n 54) 682.

[82] ibid 681.

[83] Tsadiras (n 50) 829.

[84] Busuioc (n 62) 221.

[85] See Decision of the European Ombudsman closing the own-initiative inquiry concerning EULEX Kosovo OI/1/2017/NF (5 April 2017); Recommendation of the European Ombudsman in case OI/13/2014/JF [2016]; Decision of the European Ombudsman closing the own-initiative inquiry OI/1/2010/(BEH)MMN concerning EUPOL COPPS (29 November 2011).

citizenship–resident requirement. What is more, aggrieved individuals can submit their complaint to the Ombudsman up to two years after the alleged maladministration occurred. Thirdly, the review criteria are broader than those of a court as the assessment of maladministration goes beyond the restricted scrutiny of lawfulness or legality. And finally, the financial costs incurred by the complainants are much lower than for proceedings in court.[86] However, there is a caveat to this 'cheap, flexible and accessible from of redress for individual grievances':[87] time for processing has in the past been quite long (between two to three years). Recently, though, decisions have been rendered within the span of a year or so, which is meaningfully faster than adjudication through courts.

### 3.2 Privileged administrative venue for human resources cases

The biggest share of Ombudsman files concerning peacebuilding activities are individual complaints, which almost exclusively relate to alleged irregularities concerning acts of staff management. Three categories are particularly prominent, namely (i) contractual matters (dismissal of staff, renewal or termination of contracts, etc), (ii) employment conditions (grading, allowances, disciplinary proceedings, etc), and (iii) recruitment (selection criteria, procedures, etc). Given the nature of complaints, the Ombudsman primarily fosters $A_c$ in civilian CSDP. Request for information was at the core of only one complaint (in the early days of EU peacebuilding), and access to one's file was raised in two complaints lodged with the European Ombudsman—in one case as a 'subsidiary' claim, that is, in combination with a complaint about an alleged wrongful dismissal. The non-disclosure of the outcome of a disciplinary investigation was the object of the complaint in another case. This starkly contrasts with other policy areas, where access-to-document requests, falling under the category of $A_i$, constitute a crucial segment of the Ombudsman's work.[88] The nature of the complaints lodged with the Ombudsman underscores that, in civilian CSDP, aggrieved persons turn to the Ombudsman as an arbitrator and not as a mediator, as they are looking for an alternative to judicial review.[89]

Especially when compared to the EU judicature, a considerable part of the Ombudsman's attractiveness resides in its more context-sensitive (and therefore often more applicant-friendly) approach. Indeed, it can be more advantageous—in

[86] These comparative advantages are discussed in detail in Busuioc (n 62) 222–24.

[87] Heede (n 54) 588.

[88] In general, see Petia Kostadinova, 'Improving the Transparency and Accountability of EU Institutions: The Impact of the Office of the European Ombudsman' (2015) 53 Journal of Common Market Studies 1077, 1080–81, 1088; regarding access to documents in the context of agencies, see Busuioc (n 62) 234–39.

[89] This is in line with what suggested Katja Heede with regard to recruitment and staff matters in general. Heede (n 54) 601.

terms of substance—to turn to the Ombudsman and not to the EU judicature. Telling in this regard are two parallel cases concerning the EU Police Mission (EUPM) in Bosnia, one of which landed on the docket of the CJEU in Luxembourg, while the other was handled by the Ombudsman. Both cases have their origin in 2010, when two EUPM colleagues, C and H, signal serious irregularities concerning the functioning of the mission to the mission hierarchy. C, an international contracted staff, is informed of the termination of his employment contract eight days after his report. His colleague, H, a seconded national expert, is shortly after her report redeployed to a regional office of the same mission. Both colleagues unsuccessfully appeal the decisions, which are respectively addressed at them. Finally, C decides to complain to the Ombudsman,[90] while H lodges an action for annulment of the redeployment decision with the Court in Luxembourg.[91] This means that both the CJEU and the Ombudsman had to deal with staff management decisions taken by the EUPM that were allegedly triggered by the same joint complaint of C and H. The different procedures of the two fora notwithstanding, their diverging findings regarding the (circumstances of the) disputed decisions are remarkable.

As for C's application, the Ombudsman saw a possible link between the signalling of irregularities and the termination of the contract, conferring onto the dismissal a potentially punitive character; the Ombudsman therefore concluded that an instance of maladministration—of a particularly serious nature—had occurred and proposed an *ex gratia* payment (of EUR 2,000).[92] The CJEU, for its part, questioned the punitive character of the redeployment decision in the *H* case and, consequently, decided to dismiss the action.[93] In other words, confronted with the same context, the Ombudsman suggested a possible causal link between the applicant's action (report about irregularities) and the administrative reaction (C's dismissal), whereas the Court inferred a simple correlation of facts between the signalling of irregularities on the one hand, and the redeployment of H on the other. Faced with these diverging interpretations of the context (and facts), one might be tempted to believe that it is more advantageous for applicants who seek redress for disputed administrative measures to take their complaint to Strasbourg and not to Luxembourg.

The increasing appeal that the Ombudsman has for aggrieved staff members is confirmed by a look at the numbers. As Table 7.2 illustrates, the Ombudsman received in the time period from 2003 to 2009 six complaints related to EU peacebuilding activities, three of which were settled prior to the entry into force

[90] Complaint 26/2011/DK opened on 24 March 2011.

[91] Application lodged at the Court Registry on 16 June 2010, leading to Case T-271/10 *H v Council and others*.

[92] Decision of the European Ombudsman closing the inquiries into complaints 26/2011/DK and 1307/2012/DK against the European External Action Service (4 June 2015) paras 17, 19, 23.

[93] Case T–271/10 *RENV H v Council* [2018] EU:T:2018:180 paras 142–51.

**Table 7.2** Overview of European Ombudsman cases regarding civilian missions

| Case number [Year of closure] | Mission/institution | Subject matter |
|---|---|---|
| *1200/2003/OV [2003]* | EUPM BiH | Alleged wrongful dismissal |
| *471/2004/OV [2005]* | EUPM BiH | Alleged wrongful dismissal |
| *1875/2005/GG [2005]* | Council | Alleged failure to grant access to documents |
| *3008/2005/OV [2007]* | EUPOL Proxima | Contractual arrangements regarding international contracted experts (grading, allowances, social security, etc) |
| *3328/2008/(ELB)FOR [2011]* | EUMM Georgia | Alleged wrongful grading |
| *OI/1/2010/(BEH)MMN [2011]* | EUPOL COPPS | Alleged departure from terms of the vacancy notice |
| *3177/2008/(JDG)OV [2012]* | EUMM BiH | Alleged wrongful dismissal after reporting on irregularities |
| *532/2011/(FOR)CK [2013]* | EULEX Kosovo | Alleged age discrimination regarding renewal of contract |
| *OI/12/2010/(BEH)MMN [2013]* | Commission/ Council/EEAS/all missions | Inquiry into accountability for instances of maladministration in CFSP/CSDP activities |
| *OI/15/2014/(PMC) [2014]* | EULEX Kosovo | Irregularities affecting EULEX Kosovo (ie corruption) |
| *1239/2013/NF [2015]* | EULEX Kosovo | Contractual dispute (provision of services) |
| *26/2011/DK & 1307/ 2012/DK [2015]* | EUPM BiH | Alleged wrongful dismissal and access to documents |
| *OI/2/2015/MG [2016] & 13 underpinning complaints* | EULEX Kosovo | Review of internal staff selection procedures |
| *OI/13/2014/JF [2016]* | EUSSR Guinea-Bissau | Alleged failure to lift immunity as required by local court |
| *928/2016/JF [2016] & 1396/2016/JF [2016]* | EUCAP Nestor | Alleged administrative irregularities triggering personal liability of HoMs for ineligible expenses |
| *969/2016/JN [2017]* | EUAM Ukraine | Alleged problems with review of selection procedure |
| *OI/1/2017/NF [2017]* | EULEX Kosovo | Alleged failure to provide information on internal staff selection procedure |
| *247/2016/AMF [2017]* | EUCAP Sahel Niger | Alleged irregularities concerning granting leave for travel time |
| *134/2016/AMF [2017]* | EUCAP Sahel Niger | Alleged irregularities concerning granting leave |

(*Continued*)

Table 7.2 *Continued*

| Case number [Year of closure] | Mission/institution | Subject matter |
|---|---|---|
| *1756/2016/MDC [2017]* | EULEX Kosovo | Alleged failure to reply to a report concerning the Code of Conduct and Discipline |
| *OI/12/2017/TE [2018]* | EULEX Kosovo | Alleged failure to disclose the outcome of a disciplinary investigation |
| *586/2016/AMF [2018]* | EUCAP Sahel Niger | Alleged unfairness in granting daily allowances |
| *564/2018/TM [2018]* | EULEX Kosovo | Alleged failure to reply answer correspondence concerning medical expenses |
| *1708/2018/NH [2019]* | EUCAP Sahel Mali | Alleged failure to reply to the complaint about the administrative notice on travel days |
| *736/2019/NH [pending]* | EUCAP Somalia | Alleged problems with the handling of the staff recruitment procedure |

of the Treaty of Lisbon (2009) and the creation of the CPCC (in 2007). In recent years, the number of cases lodged has considerably increased: next to six own-initiative inquiries, more than a dozen applications have been lodged since 2010 (not counting an additional thirteen cases underpinning the most recent own-initiative inquiry). These numbers underscore that the European Ombudsman has become the major administrative forum for human resources matters related to EU peacebuilding activities.

A common thread in many human resources cases is the contestation by complainants of the broad administrative discretion given to the crisis management bureaucracy. This contestation, in turn, triggers procedures for accountability for conduct ($A_c$). Complaints are primarily submitted by (international) contracted staff who are directly employed by the mission (previously by the HoM). Two entities are of particular importance in this regard, namely HoMs and the CPCC. HoMs enjoy considerable decision-making prerogatives at the theatre level, including personnel issues. Prior to the establishment of the CPCC in 2007 and the conferral of legal capacity to the missions from 2014 onwards, ending the *ad personam* delegation of budget appropriations,[94] these prerogatives lacked a bureaucratic superstructure in Brussels overseeing administrative matters. This meant that, in the first years of operational action, complainants were at a loss when attempting to identify another interlocutor for administrative issues than the

[94] C(2012)4052 final (26 June 2012) (Administrative Decision), 'Rules for the Financial Management of the Common Foreign and Security Policy Missions'.

respective HoM who, in general, had taken the decision the complainants wanted to contest. Since 2007, though, many human resources issues have been channelled through or handled by the CPCC, such as calls for applications, terms and conditions of selection procedures, or the adoption of general administrative rules, including disciplinary codes or behavioural standards. Hence, while in the early days of civilian crisis management the wide decisional margin at mission level was not matched with sufficient administrative oversight and review procedures, the incremental institutionalization and professionalization of civilian crisis management has brought about a more solid administrative set-up: the theatre level has been supplemented by an administrative layer in Brussels.

This layered administrative set-up was, however, still in its infancy when the Ombudsman started to investigate complaints related to peacebuilding missions in 2003. This implied, first, that the institution or actor responsible had to be identified and, secondly, that applicable procedures and rules governing administrative (including disciplinary) matters had to be found. Both issues proved complicated. Concerning procedures, there was a great unsteadiness within and across missions, not least because decisions were primarily taken on an ad hoc basis by HoMs (and other higher-ranking staff members). There was much experimentation and improvisation to meet a range of operational demands.[95] Regarding institutions, both the Council and the Commission tried to pass the buck to the respective HoMs, who were neither institutions, bodies, nor agencies under EU law and therefore escaped (administrative) review. In the first case dealt with by the European Ombudsman, the Council argued that its (administrative) accountability was precluded for day-to-day management decisions as these decisions were taken by the HoM without the knowledge of the General Secretariat of the Council.[96] In another early case, the Commission put forward that the HoM constituted the contracting authority (under the *ad personam* delegation scheme of budget allocations), and therefore no maladministration could be attributed to the Commission.[97]

This unsettled—not to say opaque—distribution of responsibilities, due to concealed agencification, prompted the European Ombudsman in 2010 to open an own-initiative inquiry into the fundamental issue of accountability in and for CSDP activities. This own-initiative inquiry brings us to the second category of Ombudsman activities in civilian CSDP, namely overarching administrative questions impacting both on $A_c$ and $A_i$.

[95] Bossong (n 9) 102.

[96] Exemplary in this regards were the submissions by the Council in October 2003 and January 2004 in the first Ombudsman investigation into a human resource complaint arising from a member of a civilian mission. Decision of the European Ombudsman on complaint 471/2004/OV against the Council of the European Union (31 May 2005); Decision closing the inquiry into complaint 1200/2003/OV [2003].

[97] Decision closing the inquiry into complaint 3008/2005/OV [2007].

### 3.3 Fostering accountability arrangements in the overall framework

The 2010 own-initiative inquiry on accountability regarding CSDP activities marked an important step: it aimed at disentangling administrative accountability arrangements in the intricate Europeanized administrative edifice of civilian crisis management, which had so far invited involved actors to eschew accountability for conduct ($A_c$).

Exemplary of the institutional strategy to avoid accountability in the context of Europeanized intergovernmentalism was a case of alleged wrongful dismissal after reporting on irregularities, which occurred in 2007 in the Monitoring Mission in Bosnia and Herzegovina (EUMM). The Council stated that allegations related to work relationships fell under the competences of the Commission in the context of the latter's financial supervision obligations.[98] The Commission explained that the HoM acted under his own responsibility—even if in accordance with Commission rules on financial and employment issues—and therefore was to be considered the right interlocutor for the Ombudsman.[99] The HoM, however, had left the mission and had in the meantime taken up an ambassadorial assignment abroad for his Member State. At a later stage of the inquiry, the Commission refuted accountability for disciplinary matters arising from contractual arrangements, and referred the complainant to the recently created EEAS, and more precisely to the CPCC.[100] This meant that four years after having first contacted the Commission on the matter, the complainant was advised to start from scratch with another institution. The Commission's suggestion was considered 'completely inappropriate' by the Ombudsman who also found the advice revealing in that the institution was 'avoiding its responsibility'.[101] The Ombudsman characterized this administrative back-and-forth as a '*Kafkaesque situation*'[102]—engendering, eventually, the lack of administrative remedies for the aggrieved staff member. The attitude of the institutions concerned seriously undermined $A_c$. In fact, not even the first stage of the accountability process—the provision of information—could be kicked off, not to talk about scrutiny in the second phase. Against this backdrop, the European Ombudsman invited all involved institutions—the Council, the Commission, and the HR/EEAS—to clarify accountability matters in the context of the abovementioned own-initiative inquiry.

But instead of resolving the issue, the opinions submitted by the different institutions underscored the existing accountability problem stirred up by Europeanized

[98] Decision of the European Ombudsman on complaint 3177/2008/(JDG)OV against the European Commission (20 September 2012) para 7.

[99] ibid 8.

[100] ibid 62–63.

[101] ibid 70.

[102] ibid 72.

intergovernmentalism. The Council communicated in two lines that it had referred the inquiry to the HR as it concerned CSDP matters. In other words, the Council reiterated that accountability issues arising from alleged maladministration in CSDP activities were none of its business. The Commission in its submission stated that it could be held accountable, through the HoM, for instances of maladministration occurring *only* in relation to budget implementation and sound financial management, and explicitly denied accountability for instances of maladministration occurring outside of financial management (eg disciplinary matters arising from contractual arrangements). The then HR Catherine Ashton submitted two separate opinions. In her first communication, the HR found that civilian missions themselves could not be held to account given their lacking legal personality. After contrary reflections on the role of the Commission in her first submission, the HR underscored in her second submission that the Commission's role in civilian crisis management was limited to budget implementation and did not extend to other issues. In the same vein, the HR could not be held legally accountable for acts of maladministration in CSDP activities either. Nonetheless, the HR proposed to act as a contact point for all non-financial issues arising from civilian missions, that is, to confirm receipt of complaints, request the relevant departments of the institutions concerned to deal with the complaint, and to forward the responses to the Ombudsman.

In addition to the sobering submissions in the context of the own-initiative inquiry launched in 2010, the first civilian crisis management complaint with the Ombudsman involving the EEAS—opened in 2011 and still pending when the own-initiative inquiry was pursued—proved to be an equally difficult undertaking for the Ombudsman. The final evaluation of the Ombudsman was phrased in uncommonly sharp language, stating that 'the EEAS did not engage with him in a constructive dialogue and missed an opportunity to correct the instances of maladministration identified in his proposal for a friendly solution'.[103] It is not surprising then that the office closed the case with two critical remarks, finding an instance of maladministration committed by the EEAS and attributing to the EEAS a behaviour contrary to the principles of good administrative behaviour.[104]

In view of the submissions in the context of the own-initiative inquiry (and certainly with the cumbersome cooperation with the EEAS in mind), the Ombudsman concluded in its own-inquiry on accountability for CFSP/CSDP activities that, in the absence of an institution declaring itself responsible or accountable for CSDP acts, the encountered situation was 'highly unsatisfactory', not least because the situation did not square with the review requirement according to EU law.[105] In the

[103] Decision of the European Ombudsman on complaint 532/2011/(FOR)CK against the European External Action Service (2 May 2013) para 34.

[104] Decision closing the inquiry into complaint 532/2011/(FOR)CK [2013].

[105] Decision closing the own-initiative inquiry OI/12/2010/(BEH)MMN [2013] para 56.

end, the Ombudsman determined that the Commission was the appropriate interlocutor for complaints linked to financial issues, while the EEAS would constitute the focal point for all other inquiries and channel requests of the Ombudsman to the appropriate entity (that is the respective HoM).[106] The Ombudsman, however, noted that 'it [was] by no means obvious that these arrangements [were] sufficient to ensure the fundamental right to good administration contained in Article 41 of the Charter',[107] and therefore reserved for himself the right to take up the matter again if need be.

So far, the proposed arrangement has worked out—maybe also because of the harsh conclusions of the Ombudsman, both in the abovementioned staff-case concerning the EEAS and in the own-imitative inquiry, going hand in hand with the announcement that there was a possibility to reopen the case again as a matter of principle. Indeed, a constructive *modus operandi* could be found with the Commission (FPI) and the EEAS. Indicative hereof, for example, is the clarification of procedures within the EEAS: the parliamentary affairs division, after having been contacted by the European Ombudsman, channels requests for information or demands for opinions to the relevant missions, whose response is sent to the European Ombudsman after internal approval by the CPCC. Hence, the own-initiative inquiry of the European Ombudsman on accountability issues in CSDP activities did not only trigger a reflection on the issue of accountability, but has likewise increased awareness of and cooperation on a subject matter that was, until this point, consciously ignored—or at best neglected—by the acting institutions. A sign of the politico-administrative salience of the Ombudsman's inquiries is that, within the EEAS, Ombudsman requests are now supervised at the directorial level, while they used to be dealt with at the departmental level. The assertive stance of the Ombudsman with regard to CFSP/CSDP dossiers thus sensibly improved the framework conditions for accountability for conduct ($A_c$) regarding civilian crisis management.

In addition to this major achievement, the Ombudsman managed to foster $A_c$ in the overall administrative framework in two more instances, both of which concerned staff-related rules. First, the Ombudsman had underlined in the own-initiative inquiry regarding EULEX Kosovo (2014) that internal rules (ie Code of Conduct and Discipline) did not provide for an external reporting channel on alleged irregularities, posing a dilemma for potential whistleblowers. As outlined in section 1.2, SOPs on Whistleblowing were eventually adopted in late 2015 in reaction to the shortcomings on external reporting identified by the European Ombudsman, which were echoed in the 2015 Jacqué report.[108] The SOPs on

[106] ibid C.

[107] ibid.

[108] Decision closing the own-initiative inquiry OI/15/2014/PMC [2014] para 31; Jacqué report (n 23).

Whistleblowing explicitly mention the European Ombudsman as a route for external reporting (as a measure of last resort if internal reporting has not been effective).[109]

Secondly, the proactive stance of the Ombudsman certainly helped to confirm the validity of the European Code of Good Administrative Behaviour (ECGAB) for civilian missions.[110] While the legal value of the ECGAB generally derives from the rights enshrined in the Charter, its applicability was explicitly recognized in the field of civilian crisis management: in the section on general principles of behaviour and discipline, the 2016 Code of Conduct and Discipline stresses that 'all mission members shall have regard to and act in conformity with the currently applicable versions of ... the European Code of Good Administrative Behaviour'.[111] Even though there have been some hiccups with the unlimited applicability (and bindingness) of the ECGAB,[112] it is against the backdrop of the provisions of the ECGAB and the Charter that the Ombudsman can assess alleged instances of maladministration in the context of civilian crisis management, both for redress in individual cases and concerning overall administrative questions.

Finally, the activity of the Ombudsman is an important vector for improving access to information in the sensitive field of EU security and defence, and consequently, for enhancing $A_i$. This is tied, first, to the 'case law' of the Ombudsman facilitating access to information. In 2005 the European Ombudsman was approached by a complainant who had tried to access all documents related to the (elaboration of the) Status of Force and Status of Mission Agreements signed between the EU and the host State. Most documents in the CFSP realm are classified, and therefore covered by the exceptions regime to public access laid down in the pertinent 2001 Regulation and the internal security regulations of the Council (and the EEAS).[113] Jurisprudence of the CJEU has, however, questioned the restrictive character of mandatory and optional exceptions from disclosure, so that next to giving reasons for (non-)disclosure, the grant of partial access to non-sensitive parts of a classified or confidential document has to be considered.[114] In the Ombudsman case at hand, though, this *modus operandi* did not work out. In short, the Council granted partial access to some of the preparatory documents but failed to properly investigate—upon the explicit demand of the complainant—whether other documents were relevant to the access-to-document application. It

[109] SOPs on whistleblowing para 5.

[110] Art 4(3) Code of Conduct.

[111] Art 4(3) ibid.

[112] In an investigation concerning EUCAP Sahel Niger, the applicability of the code to (all) mission members was put into question by a letter of a HoM forwarded by the EEAS. Finally, the validity of the Code was underlined by the European Ombudsman and acknowledged by the EEAS. See Decision of the European Ombudsman on complaint 134/2016/AMF against the European External Action Service (10 November 2017) para 17.

[113] For further information on the classification scheme and restricted access to secret documents in the CFSP area, see Chapter 3.

[114] See the analysis developed in Chapter 6.

appeared that, in the case at stake, the Council was not able (or not willing) to chase up documents in its own administration or register. The Ombudsman considered that this attitude did not merely constitute a 'clerical error', as the Council had argued, but was a serious issue. The Ombudsman found that maladministration had occurred because the Council had not properly and carefully dealt with the access-to-documents request.[115] The Ombudsman closed the case with a critical remark, and pointed to the fact that new Council internal rules on the handling of documents would preclude similar problems from happening, that is, the untraceability of documents labelled *limité* or, at the time, *SN* (meaning *sans numéro*).[116] In two more instances, the Ombudsman dealt with access-to-information requests related to the complainants' own files,[117] and in one application addressed the non-disclosure applied to the outcomes of a disciplinary procedure.[118] It is interesting to note that, in the most recent access-to-information case, the involvement of the European Ombudsman proved key in resolving the problem: while the EEAS had, without giving reasons, refused to provide the requested information to the complainant in the first place, it granted access to information shortly after the Ombudsman had intervened.[119] The course of action was somehow similar for the second case, an own-investigation inquiry into the refusal to disclose information on the closure of a disciplinary investigation: in the course of the Ombudsman's inquiry, the applicant received the information from EULEX Kosovo she had initially requested.[120] These cases underscore that the Ombudsman acts as an information *facilitator*, and thus improves $A_i$ on behalf of complainants.

Secondly, the proactive disclosure policy of the Ombudsman increases the information available on CSDP activities, rendering the institution an information *multiplier*. The final decisions of the Ombudsman are made public—in cases treated confidentially in an anonymized version. These final decisions contain much relevant information: they state the grounds of the complaint, summarize the opinions and observations submitted by the involved institution(s), present an assessment of the Ombudsman on the alleged instances of maladministration, and outline the outcome of the investigation (friendly solution, draft recommendation,

[115] Decision of the European Ombudsman on complaint 1875/2005/GG against the Council of the European Union (9 November 2005) para 1.7.

[116] Documents qualified *limité* or *SN* (*sans numéro*) are documents internal to the Council (and other EU institutions) not automatically made public as their disclosure could have adverse repercussions on decision-making procedures. For further information on the matter, see Council Doc 11336/11 of 9 June 2011, 'Handling of documents internal to the Council'.

[117] Decision closing the own-initiative inquiry OI/1/2017/NF [2017]; Decision of the European Ombudsman closing the inquiries into complaints 26/2011/DK and 1307/2012/DK against the European External Action Service (4 June 2015).

[118] Decision of the European Ombudsman closing the own initiative inquiry OI/12/2017/TE on the refusal by the European Union Rule of Law Mission in Kosovo to disclose the outcome of a disciplinary investigation (22 March 2018).

[119] Decision closing the own-initiative inquiry OI/1/2017/NF [2017] para 5.

[120] Decision of the European Ombudsman closing the own initiative inquiry OI/12/2017/TE [2018] paras 6, 15–16.

or critical remarks). This information, which is accessible online, enables a broader audience to keep track of the investigations on instances of maladministration conducted by the Ombudsman, both for individual redress issues and overarching administrative questions. Considering that information in EU security and defence is generally scarce given the regulations on classified information,[121] the decisions (and other information) published by the Ombudsman act as a multiplier of information and therefore help to facilitate (further) accountability claims, in particular for conduct ($A_c$). In addition, by increasing third-party transparency, which the EU entities concerned cannot control, the Ombudsman stimulates norm-compliance and improves the behavioural standards of the institutions, as the latter will be tempted to pre-emptively abide by the rules given that non-compliance could be rendered public.[122] Again, the potential reputational risk engendered by an investigation on maladministration—regardless of the outcome—confers the Ombudsman important (informal) sanctioning powers.

To the benefit of the wider public, the European Ombudsman has further strengthened third-party transparency by improving the visibility of files related to civilian CSDP, seemingly following up on an earlier recommendation submitted to the Ombudsman.[123] While formerly users of the Ombudsman's online search engine needed to be familiar with the intricate institutional set-up of civilian crisis management to find all relevant case files (for instance, by entering the name of the respective missions), it nowadays suffices to search for 'civilian mission' or 'CSDP' to find (almost) all closed and pending Ombudsman cases pertaining to civilian CSDP. This change significantly improves the accessibility of the Ombudsman's 'jurisprudence' by potential applicants or interested citizens.

Additional steps in the direction of a more visible 'jurisprudence' could be taken in the future. It has been argued that Ombudsmen in general create 'quasi-judicial "case-law"' through their decisions, which eventually add up to a series of precedents.[124] In CSDP-related cases, however, the European Ombudsman does not consistently make reference to or use of precedents, even though the problems touched upon by the different complaints result from similar causes or patterns. Reference to previous decisions has, so far, primarily been made in relation to the own-initiative inquiry determining the appropriate interlocutors for complaints covering different CSDP topics. Yet, more often citing arguments previously made

[121] Decision of the High Representative of the EU for Foreign Affairs and Security Policy of 19 September 2017 on the security rules for the European External Action Service ADMIN(2017) 10 OJ C126/1; Council Decision 2013/488/EU of 23 September 2013 on the security rules for protecting EU classified information [2013] OJ L274/1; Regulation (EC) 1049/2001 of the European Parliament and of the Council of 30 May 2001 regarding public access to European Parliament, Council and Commission documents [2001] OJ L145/43.

[122] Albert Meijer, 'Transparency' in Mark Bovens, Robert E Goodin, and Thomas Schillemans (eds), *The Oxford Handbook of Public Accountability* (Oxford University Press 2014) 517.

[123] Carolyn Moser, *EU Civilian Crisis Management—Law and Practice of Accountability* (PhD thesis 2018) 279.

[124] Bonnor (n 78) 46.

or refuted by the Ombudsman could help to consolidate a stronger stance on CFSP/CSDP matters.

These elements notwithstanding, the Ombudsman has become a major forum for administrative redress in individual cas*es* related to civilian CSDP, thereby fostering $A_c$. It is currently unclear, however, whether seconded national experts would henceforth have to exhaust internal remedies—administrative requests and complaints in accordance with Article 90(1)–(2) of the EU Staff Regulations—before turning to the Ombudsman. In its *H v Council* decision of 2016, the CJEU granted seconded national experts the right to seize the Court in Luxembourg—by legal analogy to its jurisdictional competences regarding EU officials in accordance with Article 91 of the EU Staff Regulations—to provide for more legal protection in the sphere of the CFSP.[125] Yet, according to the EU Staff Regulations, the Court can in principle only be seized in staff cases after steps under Article 90(1)–(2) have been taken. Did the judgment therefore indirectly impose the obligation on seconded national experts to exhaust internal remedies prior to seizing the Court? And would this obligation need to be considered if the aggrieved person decided to turn to the Ombudsman? It is argued here that the answer is negative. In its *H v Council* decision, the CJEU aimed at closing the existing gap of legal protection for individuals. It would be counterintuitive in light of the rule of law spirit of that decision to deprive individuals from taking an alternative route to administrative redress with the Ombudsman as a result of an improved legal protection regime.

It should not be forgotten that the administrative accountability role of the Ombudsman, which has steadily increased over the last years, is essential in the intricate Europeanized administrative framework of civilian crisis management, where legal protection is generally weak.[126] The European Ombudsman constitutes in some cases the only forum for administrative quasi-litigation, and in others the only affordable redress option. New developments in the legal and jurisdictional environment of EU peacebuilding activities should therefore not limit but help to strengthen this important alternative route to administrative redress.

## 4. The European Court of Auditors: Between Auditor and Consultant

Next to the European Ombudsman, the second important administrative accountability forum in EU peacebuilding is the ECA. Whereas the Commission is in charge of implementing the EU budget (Article 317 TFEU), and the EP is the discharge authority (Article 319 TFEU), the ECA acts as the external auditor

[125] Case C–455/14 P [2016].

[126] Matthias Kottmann, *Introvertierte Rechtsgemeinschaft. Zur richterlichen Kontrolle des auswärtigen Handels der Europäischen Union* (Springer 2014) 200–29.

verifying all EU revenues and expenditures (Article 287(1) TFEU). According to the Financial Regulation, the audit activities of the ECA extend to EU revenues and expenditures in external action, and include the EEAS.[127] Hence, the ECA undeniably plays a central role as a financial accountability forum each time EU money is spent. This equally holds true for civilian missions for which the stipulations of the Financial Regulation apply.[128] While initially, it was not obvious to all involved actors why CFSP/CSDP accounts should be audited by the ECA, given the intergovernmental character of the policy and parts of its expenditure (certain positions of the operating expenditure are paid for by the Member States, eg the salaries of seconded national experts), the role of the ECA is no longer contested. Interaction between the Luxembourg-based auditors and the Brussels-based players are smooth.

## 4.1 Auditing compliance and performance

The financial accountability function of the ECA is exercised through two types of audit exercise, both of which aim at accountability for *conduct*. First, the ECA carries out statement of assurance audits. The assessment, which circles around compliance issues, covers the reliability of accounts—the correctness of the numbers—and the regularity as well as legality of transactions according to the financial laws and regulations in place. The annual financial and compliance audit is primarily based on the randomized testing of transaction samples of revenues and expenditures of all policy fields, and on evaluating existing systems allowing for supervision and control. The results of this type of audit are included in the annual reports of the ECA.

Secondly, the ECA undertakes performance audits, in which it measures the value for money (spent by the EU)—a branch of audit activity that has significantly increased over the last decade. Here, the ECA gauges the quality of EU revenue or spending, and the compliance with principles of sound financial management. The result of these performance audits—assessing the economy, efficiency, and effectiveness in the use of EU spending along the entire policy cycle (from inception and implementation to outcome)—are published in special reports. These special reports deal with cross-cutting topics of political and financial salience, which are chosen by the ECA while taking into account the interests of the EP.

In the context of civilian CSDP, the ECA primarily carries out performance audits, which appraise the planning of missions, their implementation, and their results; financial as well as compliance audits are less probable given the randomized

[127] Arts 167 and 184 Financial Regulation.

[128] The competence of the ECA is not reiterated in the decisions establishing a mission. Therefore, the general rules contained the Financial Regulations apply. See Art 58(3) ibid.

selection of sample transactions and the comparatively small amount of EU money spent on civilian missions.[129] The primary interlocutor of the ECA when preparing a statement of assurance audit is the FPI of the Commission, and for performance audits the CPCC (and to a lesser degree the CMPD, now the Directorate Integrated Approach for Security and Peace (ISP)). Trips to the civilian mission(s) concerned are part of the performance audit exercise in order to draw valuable insights from practice through the interaction with mission staff. During these trips, EU delegations in the respective host State are also consulted to evaluate the coordination and consistency of EU external activities on the ground.

This illustrates that, in the context of civilian CSDP, the ECA does not limit is assessment to exploring the numbers, but builds essential parts of its analysis on contextual elements, including information gathered in interviews with crisis management actors. One can therefore state that the approach of the ECA related to EU peacebuilding activities is well suited to the three-step accountability process described by Bovens: upon the provision of information by the actor (FPI or EEAS), the forum (ECA) scrutinizes the actor's conduct, including dialectic interaction, and finally issues a judgment (special report).

So far, the ECA has published six special reports dealing with or touching upon EU peacebuilding activities, covering, inter alia, the EU Capacity Building Missions in the Sahel region (EUCAP Sahel Mali and EUCAP Sahel Niger), the EU Advisory Mission in Ukraine (EUAM Ukraine), the EU Police Missions in Afghanistan (EUPOL Afghanistan) and Congo (DRC) (EUPOL Kinshasa and EUPOL DRC), the EU Security Sector Reform Mission in Congo (EUSEC DRC), and the EU Rule of Law Mission in Kosovo (EULEX Kosovo).[130] These special reports, which are publicly available on the website of the ECA, are not only the product of the accountability process regarding conduct ($A_c$), but furthermore bring to the public domain otherwise scarce information about crisis management realities—that is managerial and structural strengths and weaknesses. Therefore, the publication of special reports on civilian CSDP can be understood as a multiplier of information, similar to the publication of decisions by the Ombudsman. This multiplication function is, however, less developed than for the Ombudsman for two reasons. First, there are far fewer ECA special reports

[129] Since 2013, per annum budget appropriations and payments regarding civilian crisis management missions have been relatively stable: they level at EUR 300 million with some yearly variation. Appropriations are generally somewhat higher than payments which vacillate between EUR 270 and EUR 290 million. The amount dedicated to civilian crisis management thus corresponds to roughly 3% of the 'Global Europe'–heading, and to approximately 0.2% of the overall annual EU budget.

[130] Special report of the Court of Auditors No 15/2018, 'Strengthening the capacity of the internal security forces in Niger and Mali: only limited and slow progress'; Special report of the Court of Auditors No 32/2016, 'EU assistance to Ukraine'; Special report of the Court of Auditors No 7/2015, 'The EU police mission in Afghanistan: mixed results'; Special report of the Court of Auditors No 9/2013, 'EU support for governance in the Democratic Republic of the Congo'; Special report of the Court of Auditors No 18/2012, 'European Union assistance to Kosovo related to the rule of law'; Special report of the Court of Auditors No 13/2001 (CFSP).

than Ombudsman decisions regarding civilian CSDP. Secondly, the restricted thematic scope of special reports (eg rule of law assistance, police cooperation) at times renders the extrapolation of findings to other contexts difficult.

## 4.2 Improving conditions for sound financial management

Over the years, the ECA has acted simultaneously as an *auditor* evaluating the accounts and as a *consultant* making suggestions for improving the overall administrative framework of civilian CSDP. Indeed, through its diverse audit activities (ie annual reports, special reports, opinions), the ECA has impacted the administrative framework within which civilian missions are deployed. The ECA has done so by spotting general weaknesses in the implementation (and administration) of the budget, especially in the early days of the CFSP/CSDP—that is prior to the CSDP going operational in 2003. In this way, the ECA prepared the terrain for sound financial management regarding civilian missions, and thereby set out clear (procedural) benchmarks for $A_c$.

First, the ECA repeatedly dealt with the incorrect classification of expenses, namely administrative and operating expenditure. The differentiation between administrative and operating expenses, introduced by the Treaty of Maastricht, gave rise to different budgetary procedures. While operating expenditure arising from the implementation of the policy was subject to parliamentary control according to the normal budget procedure,[131] the Council's administrative expenditure could be charged to the Community budget without any involvement of the EP due to a gentlemen's agreement reached in 1970.[132] To avoid parliamentary scrutiny, Member States tried to label as much CFSP expenditure as possible as 'administrative' Council expenditure.[133] The ECA detected this manoeuvre in several publications (1996, 1997, 2001), in which it criticized that certain operational expenses resulting from the policy's implementation—primarily preparatory works and launching expenses for a mission, including travel expenses, per diems, or logistic support—had incorrectly been labelled as administrative expenses of the Council, leading to a lack of budgetary transparency and consistency.[134] The

[131] Art J.11 and K.8 TEU (Maastricht).

[132] Esther Barbé and Anna Herranz Surralés, 'The Power and Practice of the European Parliament in Security Policies' in Dirk Peters, Wolfgang Wagner, and Nicole Deitelhoff (eds), *The Parliamentary Control of European Security Policy* (ARENA 2008) 84–87; Jörg Monar, 'The Finances of the Union's Intergovernmental Pillars: Tortuous Experiments with the Community Budget' (1997) 35 Journal of Common Market Studies 57, 59–60.

[133] Barbé and Herranz Surralés (n 132) 84.

[134] Special report of the Court of Auditors No 13/2001 (CFSP) paras 35, 62–65; Avis n°1/1997 de la Cour des Comptes sur les conditions régissant l'exécution des dépenses dans le cadre de la politique étrangère et de sécurité commune (PESC) paras 27, 47; Special report of the Court of Auditors No 2/1996 concerning the accounts of the Administrator and the European Union Administration, Mostar (EUAM) accompanied by the replies of the Commission and the Administrator of Mostar paras 42–45.

criticism voiced by the ECA put a halt to this disguised technique of incorrectly labelling preparatory works and launching expenses as administrative costs of the Council's General Secretariat: after the Council practice had been highlighted by the ECA in 1996 and 1997, a specific budget item was introduced in 1998 to cover preparatory costs.[135] In its recent audit activities, the ECA has detected no errors (or instances of fraud) related to CFSP accounts. Even though some operational expenses are paid for directly by Member States, such as salaries of seconded national experts, the accounts at present clearly indicate the source of the finances. It is thus possible to differentiate between administrative as well as operating expenditure, and between EU funds and contributions by Member States. This helps the ECA to carry out its work and ensure $A_c$ for financial management with regard to current civilian missions.

Secondly, the ECA outlined procedural weaknesses and asked for the Commission's involvement to be clarified. As for procedural inconsistency, the ECA found that certain staff-related costs regarding seconded staff were, depending on the mission and the seconding authority, charged to the EU budget, even though these costs should have been paid for by the respective seconding authority.[136] In addition, accounts were judged inadequate and reports were handed in late.[137] Nowadays, there are no more irregularities when it comes to accounting or reporting to the ECA. Concerning the unclear role of the Commission,[138] many administrative points raised by the ECA were addressed: over the years, procedural arrangements were put in place, and a specific *modus operandi* was found for the Commission Services to interact with other Brussels-based actors (ie the CPCC), as well as personnel in the field. Yet, it is worth mentioning at this juncture that one fundamental politico-institutional issue remains unresolved, namely the role of the Commission in civilian CSDP: while the Commission is in control of administering the CFSP expenditure charged to the EU budget, the Council continues to be the sole decision-maker. Metaphorically, the work of the ECA has helped to tidy up some but not all of the disorderly rooms in the intricate edifice of Europeanized intergovernmentalism.

Thirdly, the ECA advocated for the conferral of legal personality to civilian missions. Echoing claims made by the Commission,[139] the ECA in its 2012 special report on rule of law assistance to Kosovo qualified the absence of legal personality as a 'significant handicap' as it made the implementation of the mandate—including the administration of the budget ensuing from the *ad personam* delegation to the HoM—dependent on one single person: the HoM. This, in turn, implied very high

[135] Special report of the Court of Auditors No 13/2001 (CFSP) paras 63–64, 67.
[136] ibid 58.
[137] ibid 59–60.
[138] ibid 66; Avis n°1/1997 de la Cour des Comptes (PESC) para 49.
[139] C(2012)4052 final (26 June 2012) (Administrative Decision), 'Rules for the Financial Management of the Common Foreign and Security Policy Missions'.

stakes for the respective HoM as he or she was personally responsible and legally liable for actions taken in the context of the mission. In addition, the fact that the mission could not enter into a contractual relationship with a third party—only the HoM could sign contracts on their own behalf—prevented the conclusion of important agreements.[140] From 2014 onwards, civilian missions have been endowed with the capacity 'to procure services and supplies, enter into contracts and administrative arrangements, employ staff, hold bank accounts, acquire and dispose of assets, discharge its liabilities and be a party to legal proceedings'.[141] Interestingly, the Council did not go for legal personality—preferred by the Commission and recommended by the ECA—but instead opted for the conferral of legal capacity. What might seem like a minor nuance is in reality a crucial legal difference: legal *capacity* confers a person or entity, inter alia, legal standing in court, but it does *not* create an independent legal entity in its own right—as the conferral of legal *personality* does, for instance, in the case of EU agencies.[142] Nonetheless, the conferral of legal capacity has, to some extent, rendered the Europeanized dimension of the civilian crisis management apparent: the legal construct of civilian missions has outgrown its tight intergovernmental corset in order to adapt to Europeanized realities. As a result, this is an important vector for $A_c$.

## 4.3 Remaining challenges

There are, however, some remaining challenges for the ECA to ensure accountability for conduct in administrative matters related to civilian CSDP. Some challenges pertain to implementation issues, whereas others derive from framework conditions.

Exemplary of the challenges related to implementation are the findings and recommendations made by the ECA in its 2015 report on EUPOL Afghanistan, all of which were confirmed by the most recent special report on the EUCAP Sahel missions in Niger and Mali released in 2018. To start with, staffing proved problematic. As for other missions, there was a considerable delay in filling positions as Member States did not follow up on their commitment regarding seconded national experts.[143] The fact that positions remained vacant for a long period did not only pose operational problems, but created budgetary distortions as the planned appropriations did not correspond to the disbursed funds.

[140] Special report of the Court of Auditors No 18/2012 (EULEX Kosovo) paras 92–93.

[141] As mentioned in section 1.1, this is a standard formulation of mission mandates, which has been inserted in the stipulations on 'legal arrangements' since 2014.

[142] On the difference between (domestic/international) legal *personality* and *capacity*, see Carolyn Moser and Anne Peters, 'Legal Uncertainty and Indeterminacy: Immutable Characteristics of the OSCE?' in Mateja Steinbrück Platise, Carolyn Moser, and Anne Peters (eds), *The Legal Framework of the OSCE* (Cambridge University Press 2019) 9–16.

[143] Special report of the Court of Auditors No 7/2015 (EUPOL Afghanistan) para 15, 31.

Therefore, these staffing bottlenecks overshadowed any performance evaluation and, hence, automatically impacted negatively on $A_c$: in the absence of staff, the mission could not fulfil its mandate and therefore use funds effectively. Staffing problems were again deplored by the ECA in its 2018 special report on the civilian missions deployed to the Sahel region (EUCAP Sahel Niger and EUCAP Sahel Mali)—as was the insufficient pre-deployment training leading to inefficiency on the ground.[144] Staffing and training are thus persistent problematic companions of civilian missions.

Then, the ECA observed that the mission's mandate contained only vague and broad objectives, which did not lend themselves to a performance evaluation. Indeed, in the absence of a clearly determined operational target, it was unclear which activities could or should be developed and implemented. With respect to EUPOL Afghanistan, the mission managed after several years of activity, characterized by great operational disparity, to pin down the mission's mandate and to develop activities according to identified indicators. In this way, mission funds could be spent in a consistent and effective way, and activities could be evaluated against a pre-determined benchmark. The latest special report paints a similar picture of the peacebuilding efforts undertaken in the Sahel region. Notwithstanding the fact that both EUCAP Sahel missions had developed procedures allowing for the documentation and monitoring of (some) activities and outputs, they both lacked an appropriate operating evaluation system.[145] The absence of independent external evaluation was also critically noted.[146]

Finally, the ECA pointed to procedural shortcomings and weaknesses regarding institutional memory. For a long time, there were no standardized CSDP guidelines or procedures regarding the implementation of mission mandates.[147] This, in turn, had repercussions on (evaluating) $A_c$: how can one hold actors to account if the purpose of their conduct is not clear, and thus their activity not spelled out? In addition, good practices were not disseminated between the missions, which had two implications. First, EUPOL Afghanistan spent much time working on elaborating procedural standards and producing templates for a range of administrative procedures instead of getting operational work done. Secondly, in the absence of a superposed (Brussels-based) mechanism for storing or sharing best practices, procedural and administrative arrangements developed by one mission did not benefit other missions. This seriously hampered performance, and therefore frustrated effective budget spending. These problems persist. Therefore, the ECA came to a very similar conclusion with regard to the Sahel mission, stating that, in the absence of operational guidance from the EEAS Headquarters, '[e]ach

144 Special report of the Court of Auditors No 15/2018 (Sahel) paras 25–27, 31–33.
145 ibid 57, 60.
146 ibid 60.
147 Special report of the Court of Auditors No 7/2015 (EUPOL Afghanistan) 21.

EUCAP Sahel Mission spent considerable time and resources on defining and setting up its own procedures, which were not always operationally efficient'.[148]

In sum, staffing continues to be problematic across missions. Recruitment procedures have been harmonized (and are now channelled through the CPCC), but the lack of qualified staff remains an issue.[149] In addition, there is an increasing tendency to hire international contracted staff instead of employing seconded national experts.[150] Yet, only the latter receive training prior to deployment, which generates a lack of technical expertise on the ground.[151] In addition to staffing shortages, there is also a shortfall of training. Indirectly, recruitment and training impasses impact on the missions' performance and, consequently, balance sheet. As for objectives, work on clearer mandates and defined indicators has been undertaken, but further progress in this respect needs to be made while 'taking into account cost-efficiency and resources implications'.[152] Yet, EU peacebuilding activities are carried out in difficult and often volatile contexts, implying that (output) flexibility is required. Finally, progress has been made on structuring review and reporting processes (especially in 2008–9), but organizational learning cycles fostering institutional memory have reportedly stagnated since the coming into being of the EEAS.[153] The three major hurdles to effective $A_c$—staffing and training, benchmarking, and institutional memory—thus remain topical.

Another big challenge for (ensuring) effective accountability are the specific rules for accessing, processing, and using sensitive information in the field of civilian CSDP. According to the stipulations of the Financial Regulation, EU institutions and bodies have to grant the ECA access to information (Articles 159(2) and 161). In principle, these provisions create conditions that are beneficial to kick off the first stage of the accountability process (the provision of information), and to carry out thorough scrutiny (stage 2). Yet, a lot of information on EU peacebuilding activities is classified, engendering a specific manner of handling and processing documents. This has to do with the internal rules on classified EU documents adopted by the Council and the EEAS.[154] While access to and the processing of classified or confidential information used to be smooth—in the context

[148] Special report of the Court of Auditors No 15/2018 (Sahel) para 30.

[149] Faleg (n 1) 154.

[150] In the Civilian CSDP Compact of 2018, Member States committed to reverse this trend. Henceforth, 70% of the staff of civilian mission should be constituted by seconded national experts (instead of the current share of 50–60% across missions). Conclusions of the Council and of the Representatives of the Governments of the Member States, meeting within the Council, on the establishment of a Civilian CSDP Compact, as adopted by the Foreign Affairs Council at its meeting held on 19 November 2018, Council Doc 14305/18 5.

[151] Faleg (n 1) 154.

[152] Council Conclusions on Common Security and Defence Policy, adopted by the Foreign Affairs Council on 1 December 2011 para 30.

[153] Bossong (n 9) 99–107. On the institutionalization of lessons-learned processes in civilian crisis management, see also Faleg (n 1) 147–52.

[154] Council rules for protecting EU classified information; EEAS security rules.

of the 2015 EUPOL Afghanistan report, for example, auditors could consult considerable amounts of material without difficulty and store data on protected USB keys—the stricter application of security rules henceforth seemingly complicates access and processing. As the applicable internal security rules prevent the EEAS from transmitting classified or confidential information to the ECA without the latter having in place the required security infrastructure,[155] an ad hoc solution for information-sharing had to be found for the latest special report: the relevant files were sent (by the EEAS) to a secured Commission room in Luxembourg, where the auditors could then consult the documents. Even though the Commission building and the headquarters of the ECA are not situated far from one another in the Kirchberg area, this arrangement was somewhat cumbersome. In addition, there is a tendency of over-classification which has been criticized in the past,[156] implying that much financially relevant information labelled 'restricted' or 'confidential' can frequently be found in other publicly available sources (eg policy or budget documents of the Commission). For other documents required for the drafting of the special report on the Sahel missions, special requests for ad hoc releases had to be made by the ECA for classified documents originating in the General Secretariat of the Council.[157]

Another issue is the way in which the ECA can publicly report on classified or confidential information without breaching security rules or compromising classified information (eg by disclosure to unauthorized persons or entities).[158] The non-disclosure rules applying to sensitive information pose the risk of diminishing the ECA's capacity to act as information multiplier as it might render public reporting more difficult. These restrictions, both for access to and the processing of sensitive information, hamper the ability of the ECA to foster $A_c$—an ability that the ECA has undeniably had in the past. This is because the auditing of accounts implies more than a mere checking of numbers; it equally entails an evaluation of the circumstances of the spending. This latter dimension gives the ECA a powerful tool to address institutional and procedural shortcomings, such as staffing shortages or the lack of clear benchmarks and objectives, and thereby contributes to holding crisis management actors administratively to account. Cumbersome access to and restricted use of sensitive information, however, render the accountability process difficult, especially the first and second stages (ie the provision of information by the actor and scrutiny by the forum).

Despite the remaining hurdles, the ECA has so far done a good job in (i) ameliorating the conditions for accountability, and (ii) holding administrative actors

[155] See, inter alia, Annex A (Art 8), Annex III, and Annex IV to the EEAS security rules.

[156] Guri Rosén, 'Secrecy versus Accountability. Parliamentary Scrutiny of EU Security and Defence Policy', *ARENA Working Paper 1/2014* (ARENA Centre for European Studies 2014) 15.

[157] See, for instance, Council Doc 7790/17 of 29 March 2017, 'Ad hoc release of classified documents to the Court of Auditors'.

[158] Art 8 EEAS security rules.

to account in civilian crisis management. The future stance of the ECA as an administrative forum in civilian CSDP will depend to a large degree on information-sharing and disclosure arrangements regarding sensitive CSDP documents and information. Should the ECA have difficulties in consulting documents or statistics pertinent for a performance audit, this would necessarily negatively impact its inquisitive powers. Likewise, if the final report could not contain information labelled as 'sensitive', this would reduce the ECA's sanctioning power.

## 5. Many Hands Overseen by Some Vigilant Eyes

As the first section of this chapter illustrated, administrative arrangements in EU civilian crisis management were crafted bit by bit as a response to operational and institutional needs, resulting in a patchy administrative framework with many operationally interrelated Europeanized structures. It is against this backdrop that the in-depth study of de jure and de facto arrangements providing for administrative accountability—both for information ($A_i$) and for conduct ($A_c$)—in civilian CSDP unfolded.

The first question the chapter set out to answer was to what extent the legal and procedural framework of civilian crisis management has enabled administrative accountability. Civilian CSDP constitutes a sui generis administrative edifice: while the institutional and procedural framework is, according to primary law, intergovernmental, the day-to-day operational realities and administrative set-up is Europeanized. Although the blueprint of civilian CSDP is intergovernmental, administrative oversight at the national level was (and still is) weak. And because of concealed agencification, administrative oversight at the EU level was initially not envisaged. This de facto–de jure discrepancy engendered by Europeanized intergovernmentalism led to a situation where many primarily Brussels-based actors and high-ranking mission personnel exercised administrative power without clear rules and procedures guiding or restraining their exercise of administrative power. This left ample room for administrative discretion while offering few options for (external) administrative oversight. At the outset, then, there were many administrative hands framing and implementing peacebuilding activities, but very few administrative eyes overseeing their actions.

Despite these initially unfavourable conditions for administrative accountability, EU administrative bodies have in practice gotten a good hold of civilian CSDP as the analysis presented in this chapter has demonstrated. Both the European Ombudsman and the ECA have managed to become important administrative accountability fora, which have a double function: first, they scrutinize administrative action in particular cases; and, secondly, they address general administrative shortcomings. In this way, they have an impact on the overall administrative framework within which EU peacebuilding activities take place.

This finding is already hinting at some answers to the second set of questions asked in this chapter. What is the role of administrative fora? Do they tackle cross-cutting administrative questions or solve individual cases? And how has their role evolved over time? In the Europeanized set-up of civilian crisis management, the European Ombudsman and the ECA fulfil separate but complementary accountability roles. In both cases, the fora had, in a first phase, to create or improve the necessary framework conditions for administrative accountability in order to be able, in a second phase, to exercise their respective function. Today, both entities foster—in their own field—accountability for *conduct* of the Brussels-based crisis management bureaucracy and high-ranking mission personnel.

The European Ombudsman, on the one hand, constitutes an essential alternative route to administrative litigation in courts with complaints relating almost exclusively to human resources issues (in particular contractual matters, work conditions, and recruitment procedures). At the same time, the Ombudsman's work strengthens overarching accountability vectors, for instance, by clarifying the appropriate institutional interlocutor for administrative decisions taken by crisis management actors. The ECA, on the other hand, through performance audits, ensures compliance with financial management standards in terms of the economy, efficiency, and effectiveness of EU funds spent on civilian crisis management. The ECA furthermore (continuously) contributes to sharpening benchmarks for conduct, for example, when underlining the importance of clearly defined mission objectives that can be translated into concrete activities on the ground.

Additionally, the activity of the Ombudsman and the ECA generate publicly available information on crisis management realities. Both the Ombudsman's decisions and the special reports of the ECA contain valuable information, for example on procedures, shortcomings, institutional reactions, and organizational changes. The publication of this information in a policy field where information is generally scarce is an important contribution to fostering accountability, as there cannot be accountability without information. The accountability focus is thus on $A_c$, while there are also ancillary positive effects on $A_i$.

The question now is whether this scope and content of administrative scrutiny fits the context. In other words: in how far are the existing de jure and de facto administrative accountability arrangements aligned with Europeanized intergovernmentalism? The bad news in this regard is that national administrative fora are largely absent from EU peacebuilding activities—both de jure and de facto—given the Europeanized character of the policy tool. This implies that there needs to be scrutiny at the EU level to avoid a power–accountability gap. The good news, however, is that administrative accountability exercised by the European Ombudsman and the ECA covers essential parts of the Europeanized setting. Nevertheless, this activity is not comprehensively spelled out in law but derived, to a considerable extent, from (institutional) practice.

In how far are the existing arrangements appropriate? As explained in the introduction to this chapter, appropriate accountability entails three dimensions, namely (i) quantity, (ii) quality, and (iii) capacity. Regarding the first dimension—quantity—there are administrative accountability arrangements at the EU level, primarily covering operational aspects, which is logical in administrative matters. When it comes to quality, the assessment is also positive. Both the European Ombudsman and the ECA have sufficient inquisitive and sanctioning powers to effectively hold actors to account for conduct and for information. Finally, the proactive stance of both the Ombudsman and the ECA regarding civilian crisis management helped to bring peacebuilding realities closer to the capacity-criterion: there are (i) redress options, including complaints mechanisms—ensured by the Ombudsman—and (ii) effective financial control—carried out by the ECA. In line with the constitutional perspective on accountability, one can thus conclude that there are appropriate administrative checks and balances around civilian crisis management structures.

In sum, then, the combination of the two administrative accountability fora provides for a considerable amount of administrative accountability arrangements keeping the involved actors—in Brussels and in field missions—in check. Especially regarding $A_c$, the many administrative hands have been complemented by some vigilant administrative eyes at the EU level.

# 8
# Civilian Crisis Management in an Accountability Crisis?

The point of departure of this book was the finding of a de jure–de facto discrepancy regarding peacebuilding activities carried out under the Common Security and Defence Policy (CSDP) of the European Union (EU): while the formal institutional and procedural features of EU peacebuilding are fundamentally intergovernmental, its realities have become Europeanized. This Europeanization is the result of several interrelated factors. The reluctance of Member States—not to say resistance—to integrate and formalize security and defence at the EU level led to little codification. This low level of juridification, in turn, left the doors wide open to informal arrangements and practices that, eventually, resulted in concealed agencification—an informal vertical transfer of both governmental decision-making and action capacity from national ministerial departments to a specialized Brussels-based bureaucracy. Concealed agencification, on its part, considerably contributed through practice to Europeanizing the initial intergovernmental design. In the end, EU peacebuilding takes place in a setting of Europeanized intergovernmentalism.

This reshuffle has obviously impacted the allocation of power. The centre of strategic and operational gravity of EU peacebuilding activities is in Brussels and not in Member State capitals as primary law provisions—translating an intergovernmental blueprint—suggest. Indeed, a specialized Brussels-based bureaucracy autonomously runs the entire crisis management process from planning to implementation. But as Treaty provisions only regulate the intergovernmental facet of EU civilian crisis management, the (informal) Europeanized structures that, however, carry out the bulk of decisional and operational work remain largely invisible and potentially unaccountable. This book therefore set out to assess *to what extent the transfer of powers by Member States to Brussels-based EU civilian crisis management structures has been matched with the establishment of appropriate accountability mechanisms at the European level.*

Understanding accountability as a corollary to exercising public power, the study unfolded from a constitutional perspective. The analysis thus focused on processes allowing for countervailing power(s) and covered the peacebuilding cycle from deployment onwards, that is, once the decision to launch a civilian mission has been adopted. Accountability was conceptualized as a three-stage mechanism involving an actor and a forum, in which the actor has to provide the forum

*Accountability in EU Security and Defence.* Carolyn Moser, Oxford University Press (2020). © Carolyn Moser.
DOI: 10.1093/oso/9780198844815.001.0001

with information (stage 1), which the forum can then scrutinize (stage 2) and impose both formal and informal consequences on the actor for his or her conduct or performance (stage 3).[1] The study thoroughly assessed three types of accountability relationships—political, legal, and administrative arrangements—to gauge whether the considerable decision-making and action capacity exercised in the context of EU civilian crisis management was mirrored by an equally important accountability capacity at both the strategic and the operational level of the exercise of public power in civilian CSDP. Key in this regard was the differentiation between accountability finalities; that is, accountability for the provision of information (accountability for *information*, $A_i$) and accountability for the actor's action or omission (accountability for *conduct*, $A_c$). In the former scenario, the provision of information and the ability of the forum to sanction informational noncompliance are at the core of the accountability process. In the second scenario, the scope of the accountability process is larger: it concerns the (in)action of the actor in general and, hence, the ability of the forum to impose formal or informal sanctions for conduct judged unsuitable.

## 1. Appropriateness: A Matter of Perspective

The overarching research question of this inquiry circled around accountability appropriateness. But what is appropriate or inappropriate? The appropriateness of existing de jure and de facto accountability arrangements in EU peacebuilding was evaluated on the basis of three criteria: (i) quantity, (ii) quality, and (iii) capacity. The first two criteria were rather 'formal' (the density of the accountability web, and the intensity of accountability mechanism) while the third benchmark (aiming at an optimal configuration allowing for countervailing powers) entailed substantive elements.

In terms of quantity, the book defined as appropriate the existence at the EU level of political, legal, and administrative accountability arrangements on both the strategic and the operational plane of civilian crisis management. As for quality, the respective forum should be able to (i) require information from the actor allowing for substantive scrutiny, and to (ii) sanction either for the absence or incomplete provision of information ($A_i$) or for (mis)conduct ($A_c$). Finally, capacity was determined in accordance with the specificities of *domaine réservé* issues—that is, on the one hand, the traditional absence of accountability mechanisms and, on the other hand, the high level of secrecy and informality. Political accountability was deemed appropriate in the presence of parliamentary scrutiny of decisional and operational activity (of executive actors), including budgetary aspects. The

[1] Mark Bovens, 'Analysing and Assessing Accountability: A Conceptual Framework' (2007) 13 European Law Journal 447, 450.

capacity yardstick of legal accountability entailed (i) the safeguarding of constitutionally enshrined institutional and procedural arrangements by the judiciary, and (ii) sufficient individual legal protection. Administrative accountability was considered appropriate if there were (i) redress routes and complaint options (for individuals), and (ii) financial oversight, both for compliance and performance.

On the basis of a thorough assessment of de jure and de facto accountability mechanisms of a political, judicial, and administrative nature at the national level, the EU level, and across levels in EU civilian crisis management, the answer to the overarching research question of this book is twofold.

## 1.1 Sobering in-law accountability

A look at the primary rules governing the Common Foreign and Security Policy (CFSP) and by extension the CSDP reveals that the de facto shift in governance to the EU level has *not* been followed by a de jure shift in accountability mechanisms, which corresponds to a general trend in international relations.[2] Contrary to the proliferation of accountability regimes observed in relation to other (mostly supranational) EU policies,[3] this book illustrated that de jure accountability mechanisms are a scarce phenomenon in EU security and defence. That is because 'Europeanizing' policies in this sensitive domain has not led to the application of the supranational Community method.

As the constitutional fabric of EU peacebuilding activities is predominantly shaped by intergovernmental features, there is formally little room for mutual dependencies between institutional actors. It is indeed difficult to locate in primary law traditional countervailing powers (eg parliamentary involvement and judicial scrutiny) at the level where formal decisions are actually taken and implemented, that is in Brussels where the centre of strategic and operational gravity of civilian crisis management is undoubtedly situated. What is more, according to the legal framework in place, mirroring an intergovernmental construction, accountability is hypothetically channelled through domestic bodies: national representatives are in charge of decision-making and implementation, and national institutions are supposed to hold the relevant actors to account. Yet, the influential Brussels-based peacebuilding bureaucracy works underneath the threshold of formality—and transparency—and is consequently at a safe distance from parliamentary control or judicial review, both on the national plane and at the EU level. Planning,

[2] James N Rosenau, 'Change, Complexity, and Governance in Globalizing Space' in Jon Pierre (ed), *Debating Governance: Authority, Steering, and Democracy* (Oxford University Press 2000) 192; Deirdre Curtin and André Nollkaemper, 'Conceptualizing Accountability in International and European Law' (2005) 36 Netherlands Yearbook of International Law 3, 6.

[3] Mark Bovens, Deidre Curtin and Paul 't Hart (eds), *The Real World of EU Accountability* (Oxford University Press 2010) 176–79.

steering, and implementation are, therefore, formally not covered by appropriate accountability mechanisms—neither at the European nor at the national level. In sum, there are almost no codified accountability arrangements at the EU level (quantity), the scope and intensity of the few formally existing accountability processes is weak (quality), and the de jure power of the respective fora to ensure their role as a counterweight to the power-holder is almost entirely absent (capacity). Consequently, when focusing on the institutional and procedural framework set out by law, the accountability glass is at best half empty. Piet Eeckhout called this situation 'unacceptable in a polity governed by the rule of law'.[4] The circumvention of accountability in a Union based on the rule of law is puzzling given the far-reaching strategic and operational powers exercised by the Brussels-based bureaucracy.[5] This poses serious questions in terms of (democratic) legitimacy and accountability, both within and outside the EU.

## 1.2 Promising in-practice accountability

Yet, a closer look at peacebuilding practice brings to the fore a range of de facto accountability arrangements in civilian CSDP. Indeed, the bottom-line of the comprehensive study of political, legal, and administrative accountability developed in Chapters 5 through 7 is that the fundamentally intergovernmental institutional and procedural framework of civilian CSDP has not prevented EU institutions in charge of political, (quasi-)judicial, or administrative oversight to get their foot into the door and hold actors effectively to account at both the strategic and operational level of EU peacebuilding activities. This de facto adjustment, which confirms the finding that accountability regimes generally take shape once a new governance setting has materialized,[6] allows for countervailing powers, or, differently put, ensures a certain level of legal, political, and administrative accountability in EU civilian crisis management. The glass is therefore at least half-full when glancing at accountability in the context of EU peacebuilding activities from a practice-angle: the verdict on the quantity, quality, and capacity of accountability is positive.

Chapter 5 on *political accountability* illustrated that national parliaments have little power or will to scrutinize (civilian) CSDP—a situation that is not

[4] Piet Eeckhout, *EU External Relations Law* (2nd edn, Oxford University Press 2011) 500. Other scholars share this view. See, for instance Peter van Elsuwege, 'Upholding the Rule of Law in the Common Foreign and Security Policy: H v. Council' (2017) 54 Common Market Law Review 841, 858.

[5] The first reference to the 'Union based on the rule of law' was made in Case C–550/09 *Criminal proceedings against E and F* [2010] EU:C:2010:382 para 44. The analogous notion 'community based on the rule of law' was first used in 1986 in Case 294/83 *Parti écologiste 'Les Verts' v European Parliament* [1986] EU:C:1986:166 para 23.

[6] Gijs Jan Brandsma, Eva Heidbreder, and Ellen Mastenbroek, 'Accountability in the Post-Lisbon European Union [Introduction to the Theme Issue]' (2016) 82 International Review of Administrative Sciences 621.

improved by the largely dysfunctional parliamentary cooperation across levels. The European Parliament (EP), on the contrary, enhanced both the accountability for conduct ($A_c$) and accountability for information ($A_i$) of the Council of the EU (Council) and other Brussels-based crisis management actors. The EP ameliorated its standing regarding CFSP/CSDP matters by employing four successful strategies, namely budget pressure, access to information, litigation, and parliamentary outreach. Indeed, the EP has managed to become in principle the main political accountability forum for civilian crisis management. But there is an important caveat to this success story: in its parliamentary routine, the EP displays little interest and disposes of few resources to thoroughly scrutinize civilian CSDP. The lack of political interest in EU peacebuilding activities—both at the EU and at the national level—hampers effective parliamentary scrutiny of civilian CSDP, as does the lack of trans-parliamentary cooperation.

Chapter 6 on *legal accountability* elucidated the important role played by the Court of Justice of the European Union (CJEU) in strengthening accountability, acting both as an accountability facilitator and an accountability forum. This applies both to accountability for information ($A_i$), where the Court fostered accountability on behalf of other institutions, and to accountability for conduct ($A_c$). Furthermore, this study demonstrated that the proactive stance of the CJEU recalibrated legal accountability, both vertically (between the EU judicature and national courts) and horizontally (between the CJEU and the European Court of Human Rights) to its own advantage. Despite the jurisdictional carve-out laid down in primary law, the EU judicature significantly broadened its judicial review on the basis of implied and contingent jurisdiction, and thus strengthened its accountability capacity. However, the expansionist case law, giving the Court an increasing say over CFSP/CSDP matters, might in the end impair legal protection. It remains to be seen how executive actors will react to the recent case law of the EU judicature on operational CSDP activity, which include the *Elitaliana* case[7] and, notably, the *H v Council* precedent,[8] whose importance as a jurisdictional gate of entry is not to be underestimated as a look at *Jenkinson* and *SatCen* shows.[9] Instead of consolidating fewer intergovernmental patterns—including oversight mechanisms and remedies—the recent judgments, especially in the *H v Council* and *Jenkinson* cases, might in reality result in slowing down or even reversing the positive accountability pattern as Member States rediscover their fear of (supranational) integration through case law.

Chapter 7 on *administrative accountability* underscored that EU peacebuilding activities take place in an intricate and patchy administrative framework, which

[7] Case C-439/13 *P Elitaliana SpA v EULEX Kosovo* [2015] EU:C:2015:753.

[8] Case C-455/14 *P H v Council and others* [2016] EU:C:2016:569.

[9] Case C-43/17 *P Jenkinson v Council and others* [2018] EU:C:2018:531; Case T-286/15 *KF v SatCen* [2018] EU:T:2018:718.

renders administrative accountability a challenging endeavour. The study demonstrated that, despite these unfavourable circumstances, both the European Ombudsman and the European Court of Auditors (ECA) have successfully striven to improve accountability—especially for conduct ($A_c$)—in civilian crisis management, and have, in this way, positively impacted the overall administrative framework of civilian CSDP. However, there are also some attenuating elements—not because of the performance of the fora, but because of difficult framework conditions. On the one hand, the input on structural and managerial matters of the ECA is sporadic given the limited scope of its auditing activity, both in terms of numbers of reports and topics covered. On the other hand, the European Ombudsman is frequently and increasingly solicited as a forum: the office has become a major instance of administrative redress for individuals working in civilian missions. While this is a notable achievement, the Ombudsman might become a victim of its own success. As the statistics show, the workload of the Ombudsman tied to civilian CSDP is growing, and it is unlikely that this trend will soon be reversed. The rising number of cases might, at some point, overburden the Ombudsman and lead to backlogs. In addition, more thorough administrative scrutiny might cause unease among administrative actors, especially those in the field, whose focus is understandably on delivering stability and security in crisis areas and not in ensuring (often burdensome) extraterritorial administrative correctness. The fear of being involved in time-consuming (external) administrative procedures might lead these actors to adopt a defensive stance, including on information disclosure. Ironically, then, the relative success of administrative accountability arrangements could eventually undermine administrative accountability.

In light of the above, EU peacebuilding is, for the time being, still prone to executive governance, albeit to a lesser degree than previously. The current situation is surely imperfect, though it has already much improved in terms of the quantity, quality, and capacity of accountability. The EP, the CJEU, the European Ombudsman, and the ECA have together successfully managed to 'accountabilize' civilian CSDP. However, this has not been a smooth or automatic process, but the result of institutional stamina.

There is indeed a positive (but fragile) trend towards more accountability at the EU level, especially from those actors entrusted with operational functions in EU peacebuilding. This means that the unfavourable de jure accountability setting has de facto gradually been adapted to mirror the Europeanized intergovernmentalism of civilian CSDP, as depicted in Figure 8.1. In sum, then, the transfer of powers by Member States to Brussels-based EU civilian crisis management structures has incrementally been matched with the establishment of appropriate accountability mechanisms at the European—not through law, but through practice.

This overall positive verdict of accountability in civilian CSDP quashes the received wisdom about a (general) lack of accountability in and of the EU. Many observers indeed attest that the EU has a deficient governance system, leading to

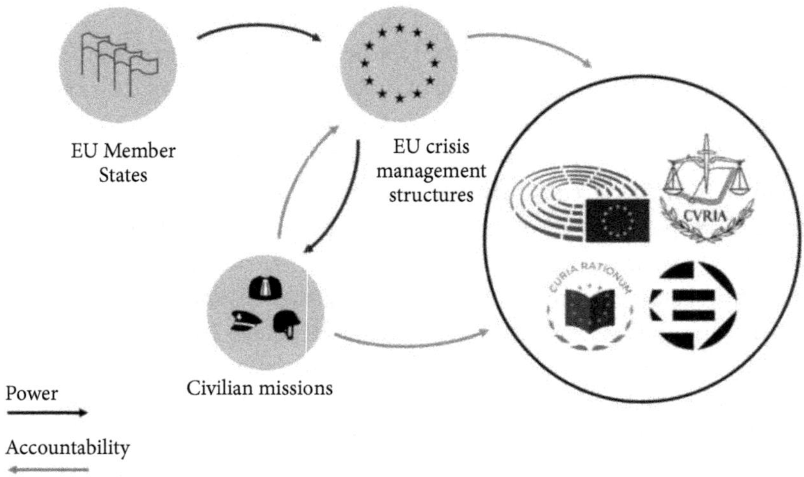


**Figure 8.1** Accountability arrangements in peacebuilding

a democratic deficit or, even worse, missing legitimacy. Though, this study has proved that, when it comes to accountability in peacebuilding, the EU actually scores higher than Member States: there is more parliamentary oversight, more judicial review, and more administrative scrutiny at the EU level than in most of the Member State systems. It must be stressed that, at the national level, the dominance of executive players in security and defence—especially in civilian crisis management—is hardly ever challenged. To (EU) sceptics it might come as a surprise that the comparatively low level of codified countervailing powers in CSDP matters allowing for accountability at the EU level is higher than what one can find in the constitutional frameworks of most Member States. What is more, the weak de jure framework has been enriched by an accountability-fostering practice at the EU level, while such practice is fairly absent on the national plane. This book has therefore demonstrated that the EU is better than her reputation when it comes to accountability in sensitive policy areas.

## 2. Implications for Theory and Practice

Let us now turn to the implications of this study. What do the findings suggest with regard to accountability in civilian crisis management? There are two major implications, both of which are connected to (in)formality. Let us first look at formalization prospects. The analysis presented in this book brings to the fore that the existing de jure regime of EU civilian crisis management is not prone to accountability: Treaty drafters have successfully shielded security and defence issues at the EU level from (too restrictive) parliamentary scrutiny, judicial control, and administrative overview. Some believe that this weakness needs to be remedied first and foremost by amending primary rules so as to allow for more countervailing powers (at the EU level). This book comes to a different conclusion and argues, mainly for pragmatic reasons, that the safest and fastest way to consolidate the de facto accountability acquis is to renounce, for the time being, the normative gold standard of codification by Treaty law. Given, on the one hand, the realities of Treaty revision—that is a lengthy and tortuous process with an unclear outcome—and considering, on the other hand, the progressive development of accountability mechanisms at the EU level through practice, consolidation at the working level would be more judicious both from an institutional and individual perspective. This could be done by (i) broadening and improving intra-institutional regulations and administrative rules related, for instance, to the disclosure of documents or the handling of internal complaints, and (ii) concluding or updating interinstitutional agreements, for example, on access to and use of sensitive information by the EP or the ECA. The currently limited juridification (and judicialization) of the CSDP and, by extension, civilian crisis management would be a great advantage to this consolidation endeavour through secondary law and administrative agreements as limited law leaves much room for interpreting existing rules and setting new standards.

This leads to another comment on (in)formality, which relates to the question of accountability-*makers* and accountability-*takers*. The positive accountability trend regarding EU peacebuilding activities underscores that Treaty drafters cannot prevent accountability from spilling over to sensitive EU policies—even to those that are fundamentally intergovernmental and touch upon *domaine réservé* issues. Indicative hereof is that the increased de facto accountability in EU peacebuilding emerged because of, and not in spite of, a handful of EU actors: it was due to the perseverance of several EU players—notably the EP, the CJEU, the European Ombudsman, and the ECA—that accountability arrangements incrementally developed notwithstanding the unfavourable accountability conditions set out by national governments. In addition, the civilian crisis management structures themselves have—in part due to outside pressure—modified internal processes and institutional arrangements to improve framework conditions, in particular for administrative issues. In other words, this book revealed that EU actors have through practice closed considerable accountability gaps that Member State executives had conceded in the de jure setting of civilian CSDP. This development leaves Treaty drafters and, more generally, involved intergovernmental actors with two (future) formalization options: they can either continue to defend the intergovernmental character of EU peacebuilding while facing the continuous resistance of other EU institutions, or they can embrace the Europeanized realities of the policy tool with the opportunity of proactively shaping the accountability regime in place jointly with other EU institutions. It seems that over the past years, the Brussels-based crisis management structures have opted for the second solution. The adoption of internal behavioural rules and the clarification of disciplinary rules (including complaint mechanisms) are indicative hereof. This more accountability-accommodating stance is a positive development that should be maintained.

Furthermore, one can ask what lessons can be learned for accountability theory and practice beyond civilian crisis management. The short answer to this question is that this inquiry brought to light novel insights on a generally understudied topic. Very little is known about the legal, institutional, and procedural aspects of civilian crisis management. Most analyses cover the policy *context* (the international security environment) or the policy *area* (CFSP/CSDP issues) but only marginally deal with the policy *tool*. If attention is drawn to operational CSDP aspects, then military operations clearly rank first. This study, on the contrary, brought into view the civilian dimension of the CSDP and, most importantly, shed light on the strengths and weaknesses of existing de jure and de facto accountability mechanisms regarding EU peacebuilding activities. This is an important contribution to the literature. Moreover, the book makes available information on administrative and procedural aspects, in particular related to disciplinary matters, that are otherwise difficult to access. This might help individuals as well as institutions in their (future) quest for accountability.

The longer answer to the question is twofold. The first lesson is related to conceptualization(s). The EU is a complex construct, and it is not always possible—or desirable—to employ traditional analytical or conceptual instruments to come to grips with the de jure and de facto complexities of the polity. The law and practice approach of this book allowed both a disciplinary and a conceptual divide to be overcome, which then paved the way for innovative findings. Combining the law in the books (static component) with an assessment of practice (dynamic elements) has indeed made it possible to leave behind the entrenched dichotomy between supranationalism and intergovernmentalism. EU peacebuilding activities do not fit these traditional categories, and hanging on to them would be detrimental to studying or fostering accountability.[10] In contrast, approaching EU civilian crisis management under the headings of Europeanized intergovernmentalism and concealed agencification brought to the analytical forefront the *content* of the policy tool (ie day-to-day business) instead of its *context* (ie the nature of the framework). Also beyond EU peacebuilding activities, the concept of Europeanized intergovernmentalism can be a useful tool. In the aftermath of the financial crisis, for instance, decision-making and action capacity was bundled together at the EU level for a series of dossiers that had previously been dealt with primarily along (inter)governmental lines. What has

[10] According to Piet Eeckhout, '[t]he focus of the debate should not continue to be the well-worn battle between supranationalism and intergovernmentalism, but should turn to issues of accountability'. Piet Eeckhout, *EU External Relations Law* (2nd edn, Oxford University Press 2011) 500.

been described as a 'post-crisis method'[11] of economic governance—a mixture of supranational and intergovernmental institutional as well as procedural features related to decision-making and implementation aspects—could in many, though not in all, instances turn out to be a form of Europeanized intergovernmentalism and/or concealed agencification. The same holds true for many policy issues of the former third pillar (ie Justice and Home Affairs), such as migration or internal security, where a primarily intergovernmental mode is enriched by (informal) Europeanized elements.[12] Similar governance and accountability interrogations arise thus in relation to other policy issues, and this could serve as a reference for exploring policies or policy tools that are intergovernmental in form but Europeanized in substance.

This brings us to the second lesson, which is tied to the operationalization of accountability. This analysis underscored that it is judicious to construe accountability in line with the actual allocation of power as accountability is essentially about keeping (the exercise of) power in check. Hence, accountability arrangements will look differently in traditional nation-state contexts, where the triad of legislative, executive, and judicial power is well entrenched, than for internationalized policy settings, where executive governance is prevalent and countervailing powers are fairly absent. In other words, particular governance characteristics necessitate particular accountability features if accountability is to be effective. This is where the differentiation between accountability for *information* ($A_i$) and accountability for *conduct* ($A_c$) comes into play. Information is the *sine qua non* prerequisite of accountability. What is more, information is a power resource—and sharing information means changing the allocation of power. In policy areas where executive predominance is the rule and not the exception, and where chronic information-shortage seriously hampers accountability demands, it is paramount to oblige (executive) actors to provide timely and encompassing information about their decisions and measures. Think, for instance, of the (draft) free-trade agreement with the United States (Transatlantic Trade and Investment Partnership (TTIP)): once the content and scope of certain clauses of the draft agreement became public (ie investor–state dispute settlement), the EU negotiators were obliged to revisit their position on TTIP. Specifically in internationalized constellations, information—or the absence thereof—is the linchpin of the governance equation. It is at this central informational element that accountability must set in. Accountability for information is thus not the lame version of accountability for conduct: it is an accountability dimension in its own right. Accountability for information is indeed

[11] Mark Dawson, 'The Legal and Political Accountability Structure of "Post-Crisis" EU Economic Governance' (2015) 53 Journal of Common Market Studies 976.

[12] See, for instance, the operational realities of the European Asylum Support Office in Greece. Catharina Ziebritzki and Robert Nestler, '"Hotspots" an der EU-Außengrenze. Eine rechtliche Bestandsaufnahme. Arbeitspapier', *MPIL Research Paper No 2017-17* (Max Planck Institute for Comparative Public Law & International Law 2017).

an important vehicle to control the executive, particularly in an internationalized environment where traditional checks and balances, such as parliaments or courts, are not institutionalized. If on top of or in parallel to accountability for information there is accountability for conduct, then this is all for the better. But targeting $A_i$ in the first place nonetheless remains crucial. The analytical distinction between $A_i$ and $A_c$ is therefore salient beyond (civilian) CSDP, where *domaine réservé* issues with a traditionally low level of accountability go hand in hand with a high level of informality and secrecy.

## 3. Outlook on Accountability in (Civilian) CSDP

The final part of this work is dedicated to an outlook on CSDP and accountability. How could different types of accountability develop? What are the most salient issues? Bearing these questions in mind, this book closes by elaborating on three central elements and their potential effect(s) on accountability in (civilian) CSDP.

First, there is an increase in (quasi-)legal accountability demands in civilian crisis management. Most of these demands centre around operational issues, mainly theatre level decisions of an administrative (including disciplinary) nature. Now that the bureaucratic structures of civilian crisis management have matured, there is a growing quest for accountability from within. Indicative hereof is that more and more mission staff ask for a review of administrative decisions affecting them. This trend is not likely to ebb. On the contrary, many future accountability issues will relate to—if not stem from—the patchy administrative framework within which EU peacebuilding missions unfolds. Much depends therefore on the will and capacity of crisis management *actors*—the Brussels-based bureaucracy and (senior) field personnel—to consolidate administrative procedures and streamline complaints. There have been significant efforts in the past, for instance, with regard to behavioural standards or whistleblowing regulations, but there is still work ahead. On the *forum* side, two institutions will play a paramount role, namely the EU judicature and the European Ombudsman. The European Ombudsman already has an impressive track-record in this regard (even though the jurisprudential line could still be clearer), but might become overburdened by an ever-increasing number of cases lodged by staff members of civilian missions. The CJEU, for its part, has been keen on asserting its jurisdiction for theatre-level choices in civilian CSDP: in addition to its jurisdiction for seconded EU personnel and international contracted staff, which can bear a retroactive facet under certain circumstances according to recent jurisprudence (*Jenkinson*), the CJEU declared itself competent to hear cases concerning seconded national experts (*H*). It remains to be seen how this expansionist reading of jurisdictional competences will be met by actual adjudication on (informal) administrative decisions. Recent case law rendered by the General Court (in *SatCen*) suggests that the Court is eager to expand its adjudicatory power to derivative CFSP decisions beyond civilian CSDP. Furthermore, it will be interesting to see how the two fora will simultaneously deal with administrative redress matters arising from the same EU peacebuilding activities.

Secondly, (access to) information will be a key thread regarding EU peacebuilding activities. The current disclosure policy, including the institutional rules on handling classified or sensitive information, is problematic in two ways: it is often not necessary in relation to civilian CSDP, where no defence secrets are at stake, and additionally frustrates transparency. What is more, there seems to have been a negative trend regarding openness since the incident of 2014 concerning the EU's rule of law mission in Kosovo (EULEX). The general deletion of names prior to public release of the 2015 external report on the incident is indicative: this redaction manoeuvre seriously impaired the understanding of the facts and the analysis contained in the report. Likewise, the problems the ECA encountered in the work on the latest special report on the EU's Capacity Building Missions EUCAP Sahel in Niger and Mali are telling: accessing and processing CSDP documents or information proved complicated given the stricter enforcement of security regulations on classified information by the EEAS. Improving access to and disclosure of information will certainly be an important aspect of prospective CSDP accountability.

Finally, as regards future integration patterns or prospects, an intergovernmental backlash in civilian crisis management is implausible, given the already achieved level of (in)formal integration and the recent cooperation thrust in EU security and defence. Supranationalization, in turn, is unlikely to happen in view of the persistent reluctance of Member States to supranationalize *domaine réservé* issues. In the end, Europeanized intergovernmentalism will most probably continue to shape the edifice of civilian CSDP. Will there be codification of this edifice? Even though lawyers would be delighted to see more law, the response is likely to be negative, at least in the medium term. With Brexit having dominated the political agenda for many months, Member States have (had) other priorities than undergo a tortuous revision of primary law provisions on the CFSP/CSDP. However, the Europeanized facet of the CSDP in general is likely to become more prominent and visible in practice, both in institutional and operational terms. On 13 November 2017, almost all Member States signed a joint notification on a future Permanent Structured Cooperation (PESCO) to boost EU defence integration.[13] After approval by the Foreign Affairs Council on 11 December 2017,[14] twenty-five participating Member States will in the future extend their cooperation on defence

[13] Council Conclusions on security and defence in the context of the EU Global Strategy, adopted by the Foreign Affairs Council on 13 November 2017.

[14] Council Decision (CFSP) 2017/2315 of 11 December 2017 establishing permanent structured cooperation (PESCO) and determining the list of participating Member States [2017] OJ L331/57. Initially twenty-three Member States committed to PESCO, namely Austria, Belgium, Bulgaria, Croatia, Cyprus, Czech Republic, Estonia, Finland, France, Germany, Greece, Hungary, Italy, Latvia, Lithuania, Luxembourg, the Netherlands, Poland, Romania, Slovakia, Slovenia, Spain, and Sweden. In the meantime, Ireland and Portugal have also joined.

issues as programmed in primary law.[15] This novel CSDP integration endeavour—resting on intergovernmental cooperation through Europeanized structures—would be a tremendous new research subject for studying accountability in the context of Europeanized intergovernmentalism, this time in relation to military CSDP. And a similar finding applies to the strategic and operational rapprochement of CSDP actors and agencies of the Area of Freedom, Security and Justice (eg Frontex or Europol). The increased synergy of the two intergovernmental policy fields under one common Europeanized roof, envisaged in the name of an integrated approach to crisis management, will sooner or later also prompt questions of accountability.

[15] Art 42(6) TEU; Art 46 TEU; Protocol no 10 on permanent structured cooperation established by Article 42 of the Treaty on European Union.

# Bibliography


Abazi V, *Official Secrets and Oversight in the European Union* (Oxford University Press 2019)

Allen D, '"Who Speaks for Europe?" The Search for an Effective and Coherent External Policy' in John Peterson and Helene Sjursen (eds), *A Common Foreign Policy for Europe? Competing Visions of the CFSP* (Routledge 1998)

Alter K J, 'The European Court and Legal Integration: An Exceptional Story or Harbinger of the Future?' in Keith E Whittington, Daniel R Kelemen, and Gregory A Caldeira (eds), *The Oxford Handbook of Law and Politics* (Oxford University Press 2008)

Anghel S and others, 'National Parliamentary Oversight of ESDP Missions' in Dirk Peters, Wolfgang Wagner, and Nicole Deitelhoff (eds), *The Parliamentary Control of European Security Policy* (ARENA 2008)

Antolovic Tovornik N, 'CSDP Civilian Capability Development' in Thierry Tardy (ed), *Recasting EU civilian crisis management* (European Union Institute for Security Studies 2017)

Attar F, 'Supranational', *Dictionnaire des relations internationales de 1945 à nos jours* (Éditions du Seuil 2009)

Axelrod R, *The Evolution of Cooperation* (Basic Books 1984)

Balzacq T, 'The Policy Tools of Securitization: Information Exchange, EU Foreign and Interior Policies' (2008) 46 Journal of Common Market Studies 75

Barbé E and Herranz Surralés A, 'The Power and Practice of the European Parliament in Security Policies' in Dirk Peters, Wolfgang Wagner, and Nicole Deitelhoff (eds), *The Parliamentary Control of European Security Policy* (ARENA 2008)

Biscop S, *European Strategy in the 21st Century. New Future for Old Power* (Routledge 2019)

Blandin A, 'Article 35 de la Constitution: état de l'information du Parlement sur les interventions militaires à l'étranger' [2016] Revue française de droit constitutionnel 3

Blichner L C and Molander A, 'Mapping Juridification' (2008) 14 European Law Journal 36

Blockmans S, 'An Introduction to the Role of the EU in Crisis Management' in Steven Blockmans (ed), *The European Union and Crisis Management: Policy and Legal Aspects* (TMC Asser Press 2008)

——and Hillion C (eds), *EEAS 2.0—A Legal Commentary on Council Decision 2010/427/EU Establishing the Organisation and Functioning of the European External Action Service* (Centre for European Policy Studies 2013)

Blokker N, 'Proliferation of International Organizations: An Exploratory Introduction' in Niels Blokker and Henry Schermers (eds), *Proliferation of International Organizations. Legal Issues* (Kluwer Law International 2001)

Bonnor P G, 'The European Ombudsman: A Novel Source of Soft Law in the European Union' (2000) 25 European Law Review 39

Bono G, 'Challenges of Democratic Oversight of EU Security Policies' (2006) 15 European Security 431

Born H and Hänggi H (eds), *The Use of Force Under International Auspices: Parliamentary Accountability and 'Democratic Deficits'* (Ashgate 2004)

—— and Hänggi H, 'The Use of Force under International Auspices: Strengthening Parliamentary Accountability', *DCAF Policy Paper No 7* (Geneva Centre for the Democratic Control of Armed Forces (DCAF) 2005)

—— and others, 'Parliamentary Oversight of Civilian and Military ESDP Missions: The European and National Levels', *Study PE 348.610* (European Parliament 2007)

Bossong R, 'EU Civilian Crisis Management and Organizational Learning' (2013) 22 European Security 94

Böttcher C, 'The Compact Roadmap: Towards a New Level or Professionalization in Civilian CSDP', *DGAPkompakt n°11/2019* (Deutsche Gesellschaft für Auswärtige Politik 2019)

Bovens M, 'Analysing and Assessing Accountability: A Conceptual Framework' (2007) 13 European Law Journal 447

——, 'Two Concepts of Accountability: Accountability as a Virtue and as a Mechanism' (2010) 33 West European Politics 946

——, Curtin D, and 't Hart P, 'Studying the Real World of EU Accountability: Framework and Design' in Mark Bovens, Deidre Curtin and Paul 't Hart (eds), *The Real World of EU Accountability* (Oxford University Press 2010)

——, Curtin D, and 't Hart P (eds), *The Real World of EU Accountability* (Oxford University Press 2010)

——, Schillemans T, and Goodin RE, 'Public Accountability' in Mark Bovens, Robert E Goodin, and Thomas Schillemans (eds), *The Oxford Handbook of Public Accountability* (Oxford University Press 2014)

Brandsma G J, *Controlling Comitology: Accountability in a Multi-Level System* (Palgrave Macmillan 2013)

——and Moser C, 'Accountability in a Multi-Jurisdictional Order' in Miroslava Scholten and Alex Brenninkmeijer (eds), *Controlling EU Agencies. The Rule of Law in a Multi-jurisdictional Legal Order* (Edward Elgar 2020)

—— and Schillemans T, 'The Accountability Cube: Measuring Accountability' (2013) 23 Journal of Public Administration Research and Theory 953

——, Heidbreder E, and Mastenbroek E, 'Accountability in the Post-Lisbon European Union [Introduction to the Theme Issue]' (2016) 82 International Review of Administrative Sciences 621

Burke E, *Reflections on the Revolution in France: And on the Proceedings in Certain Societies in London Relative to That Event. In a Letter Intended to Have Been Sent to a Gentleman in Paris* (J Dodsley 1790)

Busuioc E M, *European Agencies: Law and Practices of Accountability* (Oxford University Press 2013)

—— and Lodge M, 'The Reputational Basis of Public Accountability' (2015) 29 Governance 247

Chesterman S, 'Rule of Law', *The Max Planck Encyclopedia of Public International Law*, vol VIII (Oxford University Press 2012)

Chivvis C S, *EU Civilian Crisis Management—The Record So Far* (RAND Corporation 2010)

Costas M, *The Accountability Gap in EU Law* (Routledge 2017)

Craig P, 'Accountability' in Anthony Arnull and Damian Chalmers (eds), *The Oxford Handbook of European Union Law* (Oxford University Press 2015)

Cremona M, 'The European Neighbourhood Policy: Partnership, Security and the Rule of Law' in Nathaniel Copsey and Alan Mayhew (eds), *European Neighbourhood Policy and Ukraine* (University of Sussex European Institute 2005)

——, 'The Two (or Three) Treaty Solution: The New Treaty Structure of the EU' in Andrea Biondi, Piet Eeckhout, and Stefanie Ripley (eds), *EU Law After Lisbon* (Oxford University Press 2012)

——, 'Structural Principles and Their Role in EU External Relations Law' (2016) 69 Current Legal Problems 35

—— and Thies A, 'Introduction' in Marise Cremona and Anne Thies (eds), *The European Court of Justice and External Relations Law. Constitutional Challenges* (Hart Publishing 2014)

Creta A and others, 'Civilian and Military Personnel in CSDP Missions and Operations', *EP/EXPO/B/SEDE/2016/02* (European Parliament 2017)

Crum B and Fossum J E, 'The Multilevel Parliamentary Field: A Framework for Theorizing Representative Democracy in the EU' (2009) 1 European Political Sciences Review 249

Curtin D, 'Holding (Quasi-)Autonomous EU Administrative Actors to Public Account' (2007) 13 European Law Journal 523

——, 'Challenging the Executive Dominance in European Democracy' (2014) 77 The Modern Law Review 1

——, 'Overseeing Secrets in the EU: A Democratic Perspective' (2014) 52 Journal of Common Market Studies 684

—— and Nollkaemper A, 'Conceptualizing Accountability in International and European Law' (2005) 36 Netherlands Yearbook of International Law 3

—— Papadopoulos Y, and Mair P, 'Positioning Accountability in European Governance: An Introduction' (2010) 33 West European Politics 929

Dann P, 'Accountability in Development Aid Law: The World Bank, UNDP and Emerging Structures of Transnational Oversight' (2006) 44 Archiv des Völkerrechts 381

Dashwood A, 'Article 47 TEU and the Relationship between First and Second Pillar Competences' in Alan Dashwood and Marc Maresceau (eds), *Law and Practice of EU External Relations. Salient Features of a Changing Landscape* (Cambridge University Press 2008)

Dawson M, 'The Legal and Political Accountability Structure of "Post-Crisis" EU Economic Governance' (2015) 53 Journal of Common Market Studies 976

de Baere G, *Constitutional Principles of EU External Relations* (Oxford University Press 2008)

de Schoutheete P, *La coopération politique européenne* (Editions LABOR 1980)

de Zwaan J W, 'Foreign Policy and Defence Cooperation in the European Union: Legal Foundations' in Steven Blockmans (ed), *The European Union and Crisis Management: Policy and Legal Aspects* (TMC Asser Press 2008)

Dehousse R, 'Misfits: EU Law and the Transformation of European Governance' in Christian Joerges and Renaud Dehousse (eds), *Good Governance in Europe's Integrated Market* (Oxford University Press 2002)

Dekker I F, 'Making Sense of Accountability in International Institutional Law' (2005) 36 Netherlands Yearbook of International Law 83

Denza E, *The Intergovernmental Pillars of the European Union* (Oxford University Press 2002)

Deutsch K W, *Political Community at the International Level—Problems of Definition and Measurement* (Doubleday & Company Inc 1954)

——, *The Analysis of International Relations* (3rd edn, Prentice-Hall 1988)

Devuyst Y, 'The European Council and the CFSDP after the Lisbon Treaty' (2012) 17 European Foreign Affairs Review 327

Di Mauro D, Krotz U, and Wright K, 'EU's Global Engagement: A Database of CSDP Military Operations and Civilian Missions Worldwide', *Version 2.0* (European University Institute 2017) <doi:10.2870/14148>

Dieterich S, Hummel H, and Marschall S, 'Parliamentary War Powers: A Survey of 25 European Parliaments', *DCAF Occasional Paper No 21* (Geneva Centre for the Democratic Control of Armed Forces (DCAF) 2007)

Diez T, 'Normative Power as Hegemony' (2013) 48 Cooperation and Conflict 194.
——, 'Speaking Europe, Drawing Boundaries: Reflections on the Role of Discourse in EU Foreign Policy and Identity' in Caterina Carta and Jean-Frédéric Morin (eds), *EU Foreign Policy through the Lens of Discourse Analysis. Making Sense of Diversity* (Ashgate 2014)
Dijkstra H, 'The Council Secretariat's Role in the Common Foreign and Security Policy' (2008) 13 European Foreign Affairs Review 149
——, 'EU External Representation in Conflict Resolution: When Does the Presidency or the High Representative Speak for Europe?' (2011) 15 European Integration Online Papers 1
——, 'The Influence of EU Officials in European Security and Defence' (2012) 21 European Security 311
——, *Policy-making in EU Security and Defence: An Institutional Perspective* (Palgrave Macmillan 2013)
Dubnick M J, 'Seeking Salvation for Accountability' (2002) <mjdubnick.dubnick.net/papersrw/2002/salv2002.pdf> [accessed 18 February 2020]
Duke S, *The EU and Crisis Management: Development and Prospects* (European Institute of Public Administration 2002)
—— and Courtier A, 'EU Peacebuilding: Concepts, Players and Instruments', *The European Union and Peacebuilding: Policy and Legal Aspects* (TMC Asser Press 2008)
—— and Vanhoonacker S, 'Administrative Governance in the CFSP' (2006) 11 European Foreign Affairs Review 163
Dyrberg P, 'Accountability and Legitimacy: What Is the Contribution of Transparency' in Anthony Arnull and Daniel Wincott (eds), *Accountability and Legitimacy in the European Union* (Oxford University Press 2002)
Eckes C, 'Common Foreign and Security Policy: The Consequences of the Court's Extended Jurisdiction' (2016) 22 European Law Journal 492
——, *EU Powers under External Pressure* (Oxford University Press 2019)
Eeckhout P, *EU External Relations Law* (2nd edn, Oxford University Press 2011)
——, 'The EU's Common Foreign and Security Policy After Lisbon: From Pillar Talk to Constitutionalism' in Andrea Biondi, Piet Eeckhout, and Stefanie Ripley (eds), *EU Law After Lisbon* (Oxford University Press 2012)
——, 'A Normative Basis for EU External Relations? Protection Internal Values Beyond the Single Market' in Markus Krajewski (ed), *Services of General Interest Beyond the Single Market. External and International Law Dimensions* (Springer 2015)
Engel D, *Der Beitritt der Europäischen Union zur EMRK* (Mohr Siebeck 2015)
Epstein D and O'Halloran S, *Delegating Powers: A Transaction Cost Politics Approach to Policy Making under Separate Powers* (Cambridge University Press 1999)
Erkelens L and Blockmans S, 'Setting Up the European External Action Service: An Institutional Act of Balance', *CLEER Working Papers 2012/1* (Centre for the Law of the EU External Relations (CLEER) 2012)
Faleg G, *The EU's Common Security and Defence Policy—Learning Communities in International Organizations* (Palgrave Macmillan 2017)
Farrall J M, 'Rule of Accountability or Rule of Law? Regulating the UN Security Council's Accountability Deficits' (2014) 19 Journal of Conflict and Security Law 389
Galloway D, 'Classifying Secrets in the EU' (2014) 52 Journal of Common Market Studies 668
García Andrade P, 'EU External Competences in the Field of Migration: How to Act Externally When Thinking Internally' (2018) 55 Common Market Law Review 157
Gautier J and others, 'Interventions extérieures de la France: renforcer l'efficacité militaire par une approche globale coordonnée', *Rapport d'information n°794* (Sénat 2016)

General Secretariat of the Council of the European Union, 'Interview with Javier Solana, Secretary General of the Council, High Representative for the CFSP' [2005] ESDP newsletter 10

Geuijen K and others, *The New Eurocrats: National Civil Servants in EU Policy-making* (Amsterdam University Press 2008)

Gosalbo-Bono R, 'The Significance of the Rule of Law and Its Implications for the European Union and the United States' (2010) 72 University of Pittsburgh Law Review 229

Gourlay C, 'Parliamentary Accountability and ESDP: The National and the European Level' in Hans Born and Hans Hänggi (eds), *The 'Double Democratic Deficit'. Parliamentary Accountability and the Use of Force Under International Auspices* (Ashgate 2004)

Grant R W and Keohane R O, 'Accountability and Abuses of Power in World Politics' (2005) 99 American Political Science Review 29

Gros-Verheyde N, 'Y-a-t-il un problème de commandement dans les missions civiles de l'UE ?' [2017] Bruxelles2 <https://club.bruxelles2.eu/2017/06/y-a-t-il-un-probleme-de-commandement-dans-les-missions-civiles-de-lue/> [accessed 18 February 2020]

——, 'Les limiers de l'OLAF enquêtent sur un Britannique, ancien numéro 2 de la PSDC. Des dérives graves en cause' [2019] Bruxelles2 <http://club.bruxelles2.eu/2019/03/les-limiers-de-lolaf-enquetent-sur-un-britannique-ancien-numero-2-de-la-psdc-derives-graves-en-cause/> [accessed 18 February 2020]

——, 'Le SEAE dans la tourmente. L'OLAF pourrait saisir le parquet dans une affaire impliquant les missions civiles de crises' [2019] Bruxelles2 <https://club.bruxelles2.eu/2019/08/le-seae-dans-la-tourmente-lolaf-pourrait-saisir-le-parquet-dans-laffaire-k-d/> [accessed 18 February 2020]

Haas J, *Der Ombudsmann als Institution des Europäischen Verwaltungsrechts. Zur Neubestimmung der Rolle des Ombudsmanns als Organ der Verwaltungskontrolle auf der Grundlage europäischer Ombudsmann-Einrichtungen* (Mohr Siebeck 2012)

Haine J-Y, 'The European Security Strategy Coping with Threats. Is Europe Secure?' in Sven Biscop and Jan Joel Andersson (eds), *The EU and the European Security Strategy. Forging a Global Europe* (Routledge 2008)

Hänggi H, 'The Use of Force Under International Auspices: Parliamentary Accountability and "Democratic Deficits"' in Hans Born and Hans Hänggi (eds), *The 'Double Democratic Deficit'. Parliamentary Accountability and the Use of Force Under International Auspices* (Ashgate 2004)

Harlow C, *Accountability in the European Union* (Oxford University Press 2002)

——, 'Accountability and Constitutional Law', *The Oxford Handbook of Public Accountability* (Oxford University Press 2014)

—— and Rawlings R, 'Promoting Accountability in Multilevel Governance: A Network Approach' (2007) 13 European Law Journal 542

Haroche P, 'Supranationalism Strikes Back: A Neofunctionalist Account of the European Defence Fund' (2019) 26 Journal of European Public Policy <doi:10.1080/13501763.2019.1609570>

Heede K, 'Enhancing the Accountability of Community Institutions and Bodies: The Role of the European Ombudsman' (1997) 3 European Public Law 587

Heliskoski J, 'Responsibility and Liability for CSDP Operations' in Steven Blockmans and Panos Koutrakos (eds), *Research Handbook on the EU's Common Foreign and Security Policy* (Edward Elgar 2018)

Henderson C, 'Authority without Accountability? The UN Security Council's Authorization Method and Institutional Mechanisms of Accountability' (2014) 19 Journal of Conflict and Security Law 489

Henökl T, 'How Do EU Foreign Policy-Makers Decide? Institutional Orientations within the European External Action Service' (2015) 38 West European Politics 679

——, 'Conflict and Continuity in European Diplomatic Cultures: Accountability, Scrutiny and Control in EU External Affairs' (2016) 4 International Relations and Diplomacy 324

Herranz Surralés A, 'The EU's Multilevel Parliamentary (Battle)Field: Inter-Parliamentary Cooperation and Conflict in Foreign and Security Policy' (2014) 37 West European Politics 957

Hilger M, 'An Insider's View. Perspectives for Interparliamentary Cooperation of European Security Policy' in Dirk Peters, Wolfgang Wagner, and Nicole Deitelhoff (eds), *The Parliamentary Control of European Security Policy* (ARENA 2008)

Hillebrandt M, *Living Transparency. The Development of Access to Documents in the Council of the EU and Its Democratic Implications (Doctoral Thesis)* (University of Amsterdam 2017)

——, Curtin D, and Meijer A, 'Transparency in the EU Council of Ministers: An Institutional Analysis' (2014) 20 European Law Journal 1

Hillion C, 'A Powerless Court? The European Court of Justice and the Common Foreign and Security Policy' in Marise Cremona and Anne Thies (eds), *The European Court of Justice and External Relations Law. Constitutional Challenges* (Hart Publishing 2014)

——, 'Decentralised Integration? Fundamental Rights Protection in the EU Common Foreign and Security Policy' (2016) 1 European Papers 55

—— and Wessel R A, 'Competence Distribution in EU External Relations after ECOWAS: Clarification or Continued Fuzziness?' (2009) 46 Common Market Law Review 551

—— and Wessel R A, '"The Good, the Bad and the Ugly": Three Levels of Judicial Control over the CFSP' in Steven Blockmans and Panos Koutrakos (eds), *Research Handbook on the EU's Common Foreign and Security Policy* (Edward Elgar 2018)

Hofmann H C H and Türk A H, 'Legal Challenges in EU Administrative Law by the Move to an Integrated Administration' in Herwig CH Hofmann and Alexander H Türk (eds), *Legal Challenges in EU Administrative—Law Towards an Integrated Administration* (Edward Elgar 2009)

Hofmann S C, 'CSDP: Approaching Transgovernmentalism?' in Xymena Kurowska and Fabian Breuer (eds), *Explaining the EU's Common Security and Defence Policy* (Palgrave Macmillan 2010)

Howorth J, *European Integration and Defence: The Ultimate Challenge?* (WEU Institute on Security Studies 2000)

——, 'The CESDP and the Forging of a European Security Culture' (2002) 4 Politique européenne 88

——, 'Decision-making in Security and Defense Policy: Towards Supranational Intergovernmentalism?' (2012) 47 Cooperation and Conflict 433

Huff A, 'Executive Privilege Reaffirmed? Parliamentary Scrutiny of the CFSP and CSDP' (2015) 38 West European Politics 396

——, 'Problems and Patterns in Parliamentary Scrutiny of the CFSP and CSDP', *OPAL Online Paper Series 14/2013* (Observatory of Parliaments after the Lisbon Treaty)

Hyde-Price A, 'Decision-Making under the Second Pillar' in Anthony Arnull and Daniel Wincott (eds), *Accountability and Legitimacy in the European Union* (Oxford University Press 2002)

Jacqué J-P, 'Review of the EULEX Kosovo Mission's Implementation of the Mandate with a Particular Focus on the Handling of the Recent Allegations' Report commissioned by the High Representative and released (with annexes) on 31 March 2015 <https://www.

eulex-kosovo.eu/eul/repository/docs/150331_jacque-report_en.pdf> and <https://www.eulex-kosovo.eu/eul/repository/docs/150331_jacque-report-annexes_en.pdf> [both accessed 18 February 2020]

Jakobsen P V, 'Small States, Big Influence: The Overlooked Nordic Influence on the Civilian ESDP' (2009) 47 Journal of Common Market Studies 81

Johansen S Ø, 'Accountability Mechanisms for Human Rights Violations by CSDP Missions: Available and Sufficient?' (2017) 66 International and Comparative Law Quarterly 181

Juncos A E, 'Civilian CSDP Missions: "The Good, the Bad and the Ugly"' in Steven Blockmans and Panos Koutrakos (eds), *Research Handbook on the EU's Common Foreign and Security Policy* (Edward Elgar 2018)

——, 'The European Union and the Western Balkans: Enlargement as a Security Strategy' in Spyros Economides and James Sperling (eds), *EU Security Strategies—Expanding the EU System of Security Governance* (Routledge 2018)

Juncos A E and Pomorska K, 'Secretariat, Facilitator or Policy Entrepreneur? Role Perceptions of Officials of the Council Secretariat' (2010) 14 European Integration Online Papers 1

——, 'Invisible and Unaccountable? National Representatives and Council Officials in EU Foreign Policy' (2011) 18 Journal of European Public Policy 1096

——, 'Manufacturing Esprit de Corps: The Case of the European External Action Service' (2014) 52 Journal of Common Market Studies 302

Juncos A E and Reynolds C, 'The Political and Security Committee: Governing in the Shadow' (2007) 12 European Foreign Affairs Review 127

Keohane R O, *After Hegemony: Cooperation and Discord in the World Political Economy* (Princeton University Press 1984)

——, 'Global Governance and Democratic Accountability', Miliband Lecture at the London School of Economics <doi:10.1.1.610.6432>

——, 'Accountability in World Politics' (2006) 29 Scandinavian Political Studies 75

—— and Nye J S, *Power and Independence: World Politics in Transition* (Little, Brown and Company 1977)

Keukeleire S and MacNaughtan J, *The Foreign Policy of the European Union* (Palgrave Macmillan 2008)

Khol R, 'Civil-Military Co-Ordination in EU Crisis Management' in Agnieszka Nowak (ed), *Civilian crisis management—The EU way* (Institute for Security Studies 2006)

Kingsbury B, Krisch N, and Steward R B, 'The Emergence of Global Administrative Law' (2005) 68 Law and Contemporary Problems 15

Kluth M and Pilegaard J, 'The Making of the EU's External Action Service: A Neorealist Interpretation' (2012) 17 European Foreign Affairs Review 303

Koppell J G, 'Pathologies of Accountability: ICANN and the Challenge of "Multiple Accountabilities Disorder"' (2005) 65 Public Administration Review 94

Koskenniemi M, 'International Law Aspects of the Common Foreign and Security Policy' in Martti Koskenniemi (ed), *International Law Aspects of the European Union* (Martinus Nijhoff Publishers, Kluwer Law International 1998)

Kostadinova P, 'Improving the Transparency and Accountability of EU Institutions: The Impact of the Office of the European Ombudsman' (2015) 53 Journal of Common Market Studies 1077

Kottmann M, *Introvertierte Rechtsgemeinschaft. Zur richterlichen Kontrolle des auswärtigen Handels der Europäischen Union* (Springer 2014)

Koutrakos P, 'The External Dimension of the AFSJ and Other EU External Policies. An Osmotic Relationship', *The External Dimension of the European Union's Area of Freedom, Security and Justice* (PI E Peter Lang 2011)

——, 'The Nexus Between the European Union's Common Security and Defence Policy and Development', *A Constitutional Order of States? Essays in EU Law in Honour of Alan Dashwood* (Hart Publishing 2011)

——, 'The Role of Law in Common Security and Defence Policy: Functions, Limitations and Perceptions' in Panos Koutrakos (ed), *European Foreign Policy: Legal and Political Perspectives* (Edward Elgar 2011)

——, *The EU Common Security and Defence Policy* (Oxford University Press 2013)

——, 'The European Union in the Global Security Architecture' in Bart van Vooren, Steven Blockmans, and Jan Wouters (eds), *The EU's Role in Global Governance—The Legal Dimension* (Oxford University Press 2013)

——, 'The Nexus between the CFSP/CSDP and the Area of Freedom, Security and Justice' in Steven Blockmans and Panos Koutrakos (eds), *Research Handbook on the EU's Foreign and Security Policy* (Edward Elgar 2018)

Lembcke O W, 'Balancing Law and Politics—The Contribution of Political Theory' in Stephan Kirste and others (eds), *Interdisciplinary Research in Jurisprudence and Constitutionalism* (Franz Steiner Verlag 2012)

Ley I, *Opposition im Völkerrecht—Ein Beitrag zur Legitimation internationaler Rechtserzeugung* (Springer 2014)

Lonardo L, 'The Political Question Doctrine as Applied to Common Foreign and Security Policy' (2017) 22 European Foreign Affairs Review 571

Lord C, 'The Political Theory and Practice of Parliamentary Participation in the Common Security and Defence Policy' (2011) 18 Journal of European Public Policy 1133

Magnette P, 'Between Parliamentary Control and the Rule of Law: The Political Role of the Ombudsman in the European Union' (2003) 10 Journal of European Public Policy 677

Manners I, 'Normative Power Europe: A Contradiction in Terms?' (2002) 40 Journal of Common Market Studies 235

——, 'The Normative Ethics of the European Union' (2008) 84 International Affairs 45

Marschall S, 'Transnational Parliamentary Assemblies and European Security Policy' in Dirk Peters, Wolfgang Wagner, and Nicole Deitelhoff (eds), *The Parliamentary Control of European Security Policy* (ARENA 2008)

Maurer A, Kietz D, and Völkel C, 'Interinstitutional Agreements in the CFSP: Parliamentarization through the Back Door?' (2005) 10 European Foreign Affairs Review 175

Meijer A, 'Understanding the Complex Dynamics of Transparency' (2013) 73 Public Administration Review 429

——, 'Transparency' in Mark Bovens, Robert E Goodin, and Thomas Schillemans (eds), *The Oxford Handbook of Public Accountability* (Oxford University Press 2014)

Menon A and Sedelmeier U, 'Instruments and Intentionality: Civilian Crisis Management and Enlargement Conditionality in EU Security Policy' (2010) 33 West European Politics 75

—— and Weatherill S, 'Legitimacy, Accountability, and Delegation in the European Union' in Anthony Arnull and Daniel Wincott (eds), *Accountability and Legitimacy in the European Union* (Oxford University Press 2002)

Mérand F, *European Defence Policy beyond the Nation State* (Oxford University Press 2008)

Merket H, *The EU and the Security-Development Nexus* (Brill/Nijhoff 2016)

Möllers C, 'Verfassungsgebende Gewalt—Verfassung—Konstitutionalisierung' in Armin von Bogdandy and Jürgen Bast (eds), *Europäisches Verfassungsrecht: Theoretische und dogmatische Grundzüge* (2nd edn, Springer 2009)

Mölling C and Von Voss A, 'The Role of EU National Parliaments in Defence Affairs. A Comparison of Decision-Making Powers across Europe Concerning International Troop Deployments and Procurement Processes', *SWP Working Paper FG03-WP No 01* (Stiftung Wissenschaft und Politik 2015)

Monar J, 'The Finances of the Union's Intergovernmental Pillars: Tortuous Experiments with the Community Budget' (1997) 35 Journal of Common Market Studies 57

——, *The External Dimension of the EU's Area of Freedom, Security and Justice. Progress, Potential and Limitations after the Treaty of Lisbon* (Swedish Institute for European Policy Studies 2012)

——, 'Expending Experimentalist Governance: The External Dimension of the EU's Area of Freedom, Security and Justice' in Jonathan Zeitlin (ed), *Extending Experimentalist Governance? The European Union and Transnational Regulation* (Oxford University Press 2015)

Moravcsik A, 'Why the European Union Strengthens the State: Domestic Politics and International Cooperation', *CES Working Paper No 52* (Harvard University, Centre for European Studies 1994)

Moreno-Lax V, *Accessing Asylum in Europe* (Oxford University Press 2017)

Moser C, 'Frieden durch Recht aus französischer Perspektive' in Sarah Jäger and Wolfgang S Heinz (eds), *Frieden durch Recht. Rechtstraditionen und Verortungen* (Springer 2020)

——, 'Loin de l'Union, loin des juges?—Sur les voies de recours juridictionnelles dans le cadre des activités de sécurité et de défense extraterritoriales de l'Union européenne' in Layla Kristina Jaber, Stefanie Lüer, and Anne-Marie Thévenot-Werner (eds), *Wechselseitige Einflüsse zwischen Rechtsordnungen am Beispiel des Zugangs zum Gericht gegen das Handeln der Exekutive* (Springer forthcoming 2020)

——, '¿Union de Droit, Union de Sécurité? Sobre La Interacción Entre Actuación Interior y Exterior Respecto a Los Valores y Normas de La UE' in JI Ugartemendia, A Saiz Arnaiz, and M Morales Antoniazzi (eds), *La jurisdicción constitucional en la tutela de los Derechos Funda-mentales de la Unión Europea* (Instituto Vasco de Administración Pública; MPIL 2017)

——, *EU Civilian Crisis Management—Law and Practice of Accountability* (PhD thesis 2018)

——, 'Conceptualising Accountability in the Legal and Institutional Framework of the OSCE' in Mateja Steinbrück Platise, Carolyn Moser, and Anne Peters (eds), *The Legal Framework of the OSCE* (Cambridge University Press 2019)

——, 'Two Become One? On the Civil–Military Amalgamation of the CSDP' (*Verfassungsblog.com*, 30 March 2019) <https://verfassungsblog.de/two-become-one-on-the-civil-military-amalgamation-of-the-csdp/> [accessed 18 February 2020]

—— and Peters A, 'Legal Uncertainty and Indeterminacy: Immutable Characteristics of the OSCE?' in Mateja Steinbrück Platise, Carolyn Moser, and Anne Peters (eds), *The Legal Framework of the OSCE* (Cambridge University Press 2019)

Mounier G, 'Civilian Crisis Management and the External Dimension of JHA: Inceptive, Functional and Institutional Similarities' in Sarah Wolff, Nicole Wichmann, and Gregory Mounier (eds), *The External Dimension of Justice and Home Affairs: A Different Security Agenda for the European Union?* (Routledge 2010)

Mulgan R, '"Accountability": An Ever-Expanding Concept?' (2000) 78 Public Administration 555

——, *Holding Power to Account, Accountability in Modern Democracies* (Palgrave Macmillan 2003)

Mungiu-Pippidi A, 'Contextual Choices in Fighting Corruption: Lessons Learned' (Norwegian Agency for Development Cooperation (NORAD) 2011) Study Report 4/2011

Naert F, 'The International Responsibility of the Union in the Context of Its CSDP Operations' in Malcolm Evans and Panos Koutrakos (eds), *The International Responsibility of the European Union—European and International Perspectives* (Hart Publishing 2013)

Nehl H P, 'Good Administration as Procedural Right and/or General Principle?' in Herwig CH Hofmann and Alexander H Türk (eds), *Legal Challenges in EU Administrative Law: Towards an Integrated Administration* (Edward Elgar 2009)

Norheim-Martinsen P M, 'Beyond Intergovernmentalism: European Security and Defence Policy and the Governance Approach' (2010) 48 Journal of Common Market Studies 1351

——, 'Managing the Civil-Military Interface in the EU: Creating an Organisation Fit for Purpose' in Sophie Vanhoonacker, Hylke Dijkstra, and Heidi Maurer (eds), *Understanding the Role of Bureaucracy in the European Security and Defence Policy* (European Integration Online Papers (EIoP) 2010)

——, *The European Union and Military Force: Governance and Strategy* (Cambridge University Press 2013)

Nothelle A, 'The Parliamentary Assembly: Driving Reform', *OSCE Yearbook 2006*

Nowak A (ed), *Civilian Crisis Management—The EU Way* (European Union Institute for Security Studies 2006)

Nuttall S J, *European Political Co-Operation* (Clarendon Press 1992)

Nye J S, *Soft Power: The Means to Success in World Politics* (PublicAffairs 2004)

Oeter S, 'Article 21 [The Principles and Objectives of the Union's External Action]' in Hermann-Josef Blanke and Stelio Mangiameli (eds), *The Treaty on European Union (TEU). A Commentary* (Springer 2013)

Paine T, *Droits de l'homme: en réponse à une attaque de M. Burke sur la Révolution française* (François Soulès tr, F Buisson 1791)

——, *Rights of Man* (edited with introduction and notes by Gregory Claeys, Hackett Publishing Company 1992)

Papadopoulos Y, 'Problems of Democratic Accountability in Network and Multilevel Governance' (2007) 13 European Law Journal 469

Patil S V, Vieider F, and Tetlock PE, 'Process versus Outcome Accountability' in Mark Bovens, Robert E Goodin, and Thomas Schillemans (eds), *The Oxford Handbook of Public Accountability* (Oxford University Press 2014)

Pegan A and Högenauer A-L, 'The Role of Parliamentary Administrators in Interparliamentary Cooperation' in Nicola Lupo and Cristina Fasone (eds), *Interparliamentary Cooperation in the Composite European Constitution* (Hart Publishing 2016)

Peters A, 'Towards Transparency as a Global Norm' in Andrea Bianchi and Anne Peters (eds), *Transparency in International Law* (Cambridge University Press 2013)

Peters D, 'Actor, Network, Symbol: The Inter-Parliamentary Conference on CFSP/CSDP' in Kolja Raube, Meltem Müftüler-Baç, and Jan Wouters (eds), *Parliamentary Cooperation and Diplomacy in EU External Relations. An Essential Companion* (Edward Elgar 2019)

Peters D, Wagner W, and Deitelhoff N, 'Parliaments and European Security Policy. Mapping the Parliamentary Field' in Dirk Peters, Wolfgang Wagner, and Nicole Deitelhoff (eds), *The Parliamentary Control of European Security Policy* (ARENA 2008)

—— (eds), 'The Parliamentary Control of European Security Policy', *RECON Report No 6* (ARENA 2008)

Philp M, 'Delimiting Democratic Accountability' (2009) 57 Political Studies 28

Piris J-C, *The Lisbon Treaty: A Legal and Political Analysis* (Cambridge University Press 2010)

Pirozzi N, 'The European Union and Civilian Crisis Management after Lisbon' (2015) 20 European Foreign Affairs Review 287

——, 'The Civilian CSDP Compact—A Success Story for the EU's Crisis Management Cinderella?', *EUISS Brief 9/2018* (European Union Institute for Security Studies 2018)
Poli S, 'The Common Foreign Security Policy after Rosneft: Still Imperfect but Gradually Subject to the Rule of Law' (2017) 54 Common Market Law Review 1799
Pollack M A, 'Delegation, Agency, and Agenda Setting in the European Community' (1997) 51 International Organization 99
Pozen D E, 'Deep Secrecy' (2010) 62 Stanford Law Review 257
Princen S, *Agenda-setting in the European Union* (Palgrave Macmillan 2009)
Putnam R D, 'Diplomacy and Domestic Politics: The Logic of Two-level Games' (1988) 42 International Organization 427
Raube K, Müftüler-Baç M, and Wouters J (eds), *Parliamentary Cooperation and Diplomacy in EU External Relations. An Essential Companion* (Edward Elgar 2019)
Reinisch A, 'Securing the Accountability of International Organizations' (2001) 7 Global Governance 131
Rijpma J J and Cremona M, 'The Extra-Territorialisation of EU Migration Policies and the Rule of Law', *EUI Working Papers* (European University Institute, Department of Law 2007)
Rittberger B, '"No Integration without Representation!" European Integration, Parliamentary Democracy, and Two Forgotten Communities' (2006) 13 Journal of European Public Policy 1211
Rosén G, 'Secrecy versus Accountability. Parliamentary Scrutiny of EU Security and Defence Policy', *ARENA Working Paper 1/2014* (ARENA Centre for European Studies 2014)
——, 'EU Confidential: The European Parliament's Involvement in EU Security and Defence Policy' (2015) 53 Journal of Common Market Studies 383
Rosenau J N, 'Governance in the Twenty-First Century' (1995) 1 Global Governance 13
——, 'Change, Complexity, and Governance in Globalizing Space' in Jon Pierre (ed), *Debating Governance: Authority, Steering, and Democracy* (Oxford University Press 2000)
Rowe G C, 'Administrative Supervision of Administrative Action in the European Union' in Herwig C H Hofmann and Alexander H Türk (eds), *Legal Challenges in EU Administrative Law: Towards an Integrated Administration* (Edward Elgar 2009)
Sánchez-Tabernero S R, 'The Choice of Legal Basis and the Principle of Consistency in the Procedure for Conclusion of International Agreements in CFSP Contexts: Parliament v. Council (Pirate-Transfer Agreement with Tanzania)' (2017) 54 Common Market Law Review 899
Sari A, 'Status of Forces and Status of Mission Agreements under the ESDP: The EU's Evolving Practice' (2008) 19 European Journal of International Law 67
Sautter G, 'The Financing of Common Foreign and Security Policy—on Continuity and Change' in Hermann-Josef Blanke and Stelio Mangiameli (eds), *The European Union after Lisbon: Constitutional Basis, Economic Order and External Action* (Springer 2012)
Scannell D, 'Third Time Luck: The Pre-History of the Common Security and Defence Policy' in Anthony Arnull and other (eds), *A Constitutional Order of States? Essays in EU Law in Honour of Alan Dashwood* (Hart Publishing 2011)
Schade D, 'Parlamentarische Kontrolle durch Vernetzung? Eine kritische Analyse der Rolle der Interparlamentarischen Konferenz für die GASP/GSVP' (2019) 42 integration 118
Schedler A, 'Conceptualizing Accountability' in Andreas Schedler, Larry Diamond, and Marc F Plattner (eds), *The Self-Restraining State: Power and Accountability in New Democracies* (Lynne Rienner Publishers 1999)
Schimmelfennig F, 'Rule of Law Promotion Policies in Comparison of Major Western Powers' in Michael Zürn, André Nollkaemper, and Randy Peerenboom (eds), *Rule of Law Dynamics: In an Era of International and Transnational Governance* (Cambridge University Press 2014)

Senden L and Van den Brink T, 'Checks and Balances of Soft EU Rule-Making', *Study PE 462.433* (European Parliament 2012)

Sjursen H, 'Not so Intergovernmental after All? On Democracy and Integration in European Foreign and Security Policy' (2011) 18 Journal of European Public Policy 1078

——, 'The EU's Common Foreign and Security Policy: The Quest for Democracy' (2011) 18 Journal of European Public Policy 1069

Skordas A, 'The European Union as a Post-National Realist Power' in Steven Blockmans and Panos Koutrakos (eds), *Research Handbook on the EU's Common Foreign and Security Policy* (Edward Elgar 2018)

Smith M E, 'The New Intergovernmentalism and Experiential Learning in the Common Security and Defence Policy' in Christopher J Bickerton, Dermot Hodson, and Uwe Puetter (eds), *The New Intergovernmentalism: States and Supranational Actors in the Post-Maastricht Era* (Oxford University Press 2015)

——, *Europe's Common Security and Defence Policy. Capacity-Building, Experiential Learning, and Institutional Change* (Cambridge University Press 2017)

Spernbauer M, *EU Peacebuilding in Kosovo and Afghanistan. Legality and Accountability* (Martinus Nijhoff Publishers 2014)

Stein E, 'European Political Cooperation (EPC) as a Component of the European Foreign Affairs System' (1983) 43 Zeitschrift für ausländisches öffentliches Recht und Völkerrecht (ZaöRV) 49

Strøm K, 'Delegation and Accountability in Parliamentary Democracies' (2000) 37 European Journal of Political Research 261

Tallberg J, 'Delegation to Supranational Institutions: Why, How, and with What Consequences?' (2002) 25 West European Politics 3

Tan C, 'Mandating Rights and Limiting Mission Creep: Holding the World Bank and the International Monetary Fund Accountable for Human Rights Violations' (2008) 2 Human Rights and International Legal Discourse 79.

Tardy T, *CSDP in Action—What Contribution to International Security?* (European Union Institute for Security Studies 2015)

——, *Recasting EU Civilian Crisis Management* (European Union Institute for Security Studies 2017)

——, 'The New Forms of Civilian Crisis Management' in Thierry Tardy (ed), *Recasting EU civilian crisis management* (European Union Institute for Security Studies 2017)

Thompson D F, 'Moral Responsibility of Public Officials: The Problem of Many Hands' (1980) 74 American Political Science Review 905

Thym D, 'Beyond Parliament's Reach? The Role of the European Parliament in the CFSP' (2006) 11 European Foreign Affairs Review 109

——, 'Auswärtige Gewalt' in Armin von Bogdandy and Jürgen Bast (eds), *Europäisches Verfassungsrecht: Theoretische und dogmatische Grundzüge* (2nd edn, Springer 2009)

——, *Holding Europe's CFSP/CSDP Executive to Account in the Age of the Lisbon Treaty* (CEU Ediciones 2011)

——, 'The Intergovernmental Constitution of the EU's Foreign, Security & Defence Executive' (2011) 7 European Constitutional Law Review 453

——, 'GASP und äußere Sicherheit' in Andreas von Arnauld (ed), *Europäische Außenbeziehungen* (Nomos 2014)

Tondral J, 'Agencification' (2014) 74 Public Administration Review 545

Tridimas T, 'The ECJ and the National Courts: Dialogue, Cooperation, and Instability' in Anthony Arnull and Damian Chalmers (eds), *The Oxford Handbook of European Union Law* (Oxford University Press 2015)

Tsadiras A, 'The Ombudsman' in Paul Craig (ed), *EU Administrative Law* (Oxford University Press 2006)

Türk A, 'The Concept of the "Legislative" Act in the Constitutional Treaty' (2005) 6 German Law Journal 1554

van Elsuwege P, 'EU External Action After the Collapse of the Pillar Structure: In Search of a New Balance Between Delimitation and Consistency' (2010) 47 Common Market Law Review 987

——, 'The Potential for Inter-Institutional Conflicts before the Court of Justice: Impact of the Lisbon Treaty' in Marise Cremona and Anne Thies (eds), *The European Court of Justice and External Relations Law. Constitutional Challenges* (Hart Publishing 2014)

——, 'Upholding the Rule of Law in the Common Foreign and Security Policy: H v. Council' (2017) 54 Common Market Law Review 841

van Vooren B, 'A Legal-Institutional Perspective on the European External Action Service' (2011) 48 Common Market Law Review 475

van Wagenen RW, *Research in the International Organization Field: Some Notes on a Possible Focus* (Princeton University Press 1952)

van Zyl A, 'How Civil Society Organizations Close the Gap between Transparency and Accountability' (2014) 27 Governance 347

Vianello I, 'Guiding the Exercise of Union's Administrative Power in the EU Wider Neighbourhood. The Rule of Law from Paper to Operationalisation', *EUI Working Paper LAW 2015/08* (EUI 2015)

von Achenbach J, 'Informationsrechte von Bundestagsabgeordneten über Rüstungsexporte' (2015) 70 Juristenzeitung 96

von Bogdandy A, Dann P, and Goldmann M, 'Developing the Publicness of Public International Law: Towards a Legal Framework for Global Governance Activities' in Armin von Bogdandy and others (eds), *The Exercise of Public Authority by International Institutions: Advancing International Institutional Law* (Springer 2010)

Wagner W, 'Parliamentary Control of Military Missions: Accounting for Pluralism', *DCAF Occasional Paper No 12* (Geneva Centre for the Democratic Control of Armed Forces (DCAF) 2006)

Wessel R A, 'Good Governance and EU Foreign, Security and Defence Policy' in Deirdre M Curtin and Ramses A Wessel (eds), *Good Governance and the European Union: Reflection on Concepts, Institutions and Substance* (Intersentia 2005)

——, 'Lex Imperfecta: Law and Integration in European Foreign and Security Policy' (2016) 1 European Papers 439

—— and Den Hertog L, 'EU Foreign, Security and Defence Policy: A Competence-Responsibility Gap' in Malcolm Evans and Panos Koutrakos (eds), *The International Responsibility of the European Union: European and International Perspectives* (Hart Publishing 2013)

Whitman R G, 'Norms, Power and Europe: A New Agenda for Study of the EU and International Relations' in Richard G Whitman (ed), *Normative Power Europe: Empirical and Theoretical Perspectives* (Palgrave Macmillan 2011)

Wincott D, 'The Governance White Paper, the Commission and the Search for Legitimacy' in Anthony Arnull and Daniel Wincott (eds), *Accountability and Legitimacy in the European Union* (Oxford University Press 2002)

Wolfers A, *Discord and Collaboration* (The Johns Hopkins Press 1962)

Wolff S, Wichmann N, and Mounier G, 'The External Dimension of Justice and Home Affairs: A Different Security Agenda for the EU?' in Sarah Wolff, Nicole Wichmann, and Gregory Mounier (eds), *The External Dimension of Justice and Home Affairs: A Different Security Agenda for the European Union?* (Routledge 2010)

Wouters J and Raube K, 'Seeking CSDP Accountability Through Interparliamentary Scrutiny' (2012) 47 The International Spectator 149.

Yang N, *Zur Grundlegung eines Begriffs und seiner Erforschung im Unionsrecht anhand des EuGH-Urteils Kadi* (Springer 2017)

Ziebritzki C and Nestler R, '"Hotspots" an der EU-Außengrenze. Eine rechtliche Bestandsaufnahme. Arbeitspapier', *MPIL Research Paper No 2017-17* (Max Planck Institute for Comparative Public Law & International Law 2017)

## Official Documents and Reports

### Council of the European Union

Conclusions of the Council and of the Representatives of the Governments of the Member States, meeting within the Council, on the establishment of a Civilian CSDP Compact, as adopted by the Foreign Affairs Council at its meeting held on 19 November 2018, Council Doc 14305/18.

Council Conclusions on Common Security and Defence Policy, adopted by the Foreign Affairs Council on 1 December 2011

Council Conclusions on ESDP, adopted by the Council on 17 November 2009, Council Doc 16500/09, Annex (23 November 2009)

Council Conclusions on security and defence in the context of the EU Global Strategy, adopted by the Foreign Affairs Council on 13 November 2017.

Council Conclusions on strengthening civilian CSDP, adopted by the Foreign Affairs Council on 28 May 2018, Council Doc 9288/18

Council Conclusions on the Integrated Approach to External Conflicts and Crises, adopted by the Council on 22 January 2018, Council Doc 5413/18

Council Doc 10684/12 of 4 June 2012, 'Breakdown of documents by security classification levels' LIMITE

Council Doc 11277/07 of 28 June 2007, 'Standard language for planning documents and legal acts for civilian ESDP operations' LIMITE

Council Doc 11336/11 of 9 June 2011, 'Handling of documents internal to the Council'

Council Doc 11716/1/08 REV1 of 3 February 2009, 'EU Concept for Civil-Military Co-operation (CIMIC) for EU-led Military Operations', declassified version of Council Doc 11716/08 of 11 July 2008

Council Doc 11807/18 of 4 September 2018, 'Civilian Capabilities Development Plan'

Council Doc 12076/16 of 9 September 2016, 'Code of Conduct and Discipline for EU civilian CSDP Missions'

Council Doc 14392/16 of 14 November 2016, 'Implementation Plan on Security and Defence', Annex

Council Doc 14457/03 of 7 November 2003, 'Paper on EU Civil Military Co-ordination (CMCO)'

Council Doc 14513/02 of 19 November 2002,' Comprehensive EU concept for missions in the field of Rule of Law in crisis management, including annexes'

Council Doc 14823/07 of 19 November 2007, 'Civilian Headline Goal 2010', approved by the ministerial Civilian Capabilities Improvement Conference and noted by the General Affairs and External Relations Council on 19 November 2007.

Council Doc 15343/12 of 23 October 2012, 'Access by the European Parliament to classified information in the area of the Common Foreign and Security Policy' [proposal by the HR on a draft Arrangement]

Council Doc 15863/04 of 7 December 2004, 'Civilian Headline Goal 2008', endorsed by the European Council on 7 December 2004

Council Doc 16858/11 of 14 November 2011, 'A strategic framework for the Horn of Africa, Annex to the Annex of Council Conclusions on the Horn of Africa', as adopted by the Council on 14 November 2011

Council Doc 17141/08 of 15 December 2008, 'Draft Model Agreement on the Status of the European Union Civilian Crisis Management Mission in a Host State (SOMA)', endorsed by the Council on 18 September 2007

Council Doc 5705/15 of 28 January 2015, 'Civilian CSDP Best Practice Compilation' [EEAS document Ares(2014)4217483]

Council Doc 6877/18 of 7 March 2018, 'Upgraded Generic Standards of Behaviour for CSDP Missions and Operations', as endorsed by the Council on 22 January 2018

Council Doc 7106/02 of 8 March 2002, 'Civil-Military Co-operation (CIMIC) Concept for EU-Led Crisis Management Operations', endorsed by the EU Military Committee on 8 March 2002

Council Doc 7291/09 of 10 March 2009, 'Guidelines for allowances for seconded staff participating in EU civilian crisis management missions'

Council Doc 7790/17 of 29 March 2017, 'Ad hoc release of classified documents to the Court of Auditors'

Council Doc 8373/3/05 of 18 May 2005, 'Generic Standards of Behaviour for ESDP Operations'

Council Doc 8962/19 of 30 April 2019, 'Joint Action Plan Implementing the Civilian CSDP Compact', elaborated by the EEAS and the European Commission

Council Doc 9919/07 EXT2 of 1 February 2008, 'Draft Guidelines for Command and Control Structures for EU Civilian Operations in Crisis Management', Annex (partial declassification of document 9919/07 RESTREINT UE of 23 May 2007)

Council Doc 9919/07 of 1 February 2007, 'Draft Guidelines for Command and Control Structure for EU Civilian Operations in Crisis Management' RESTREINT EU

Decision of the Secretary-General of the Council/High Representative for the Common Foreign and Security Policy of 27 July 2000 on measures for the protection of classified information applicable to the General Secretariat of the Council [2000] OJ C239/1

Ministerial Declaration 'ESDP Ten Years—Challenges and Opportunities', 2974th External Relations Council meeting, Brussels, 17 November 2009

## European Commission

C(2009)9502/1 (30 November 2009) (Administrative Decision), 'Specific Rules for Special Advisers of the Commission entrusted with the implementation of operational CFSP actions and contracted international staff'

C(2012)4052 final (26 June 2012) (Administrative Decision), 'Rules for the Financial Management of the Common Foreign and Security Policy Missions'

COM(2001)428 final, 'European Governance—a White Paper', OJ [2001] C287/1

COM(2001) 647 final (29 November 2001), 'Financing of civilian crisis management operations'

COM(2014) 158 final (11 March 2014), 'A new EU Framework to strengthen the Rule of Law'

COM(2016) 950 final (30 November 2016), 'European Defence Action Plan'

COM(2019) 163 final, 'Further strengthening the Rule of Law within the Union—State of play and possible next steps'

Commission factsheet on the 'Partnership Framework' with third countries under the European Agenda on Migration dated 7 June 2016

Commission factsheet on the EU–Turkey Agreement of 18 March 2016 titled 'EU–Turkey Agreement: Questions and Answers'

## European Council

A Secure Europe in a Better World: European Security Strategy (ESS), endorsed by the European Council, Brussels, 11–12 December 2004

Action Plan for Civilian Aspects of ESDP, adopted by the European Council, Brussels, 17–18 June 2004

EU–Turkey European Council Statement of 18 March 2016 after the meeting of EU Heads of State or Government with Turkey

Presidency Conclusions of the Brussels European Council (11–12 December 2008), Annex 2: Declaration by the European Council on the enhancement of the European Security and Defence Policy (ESDP)

Presidency Conclusions of the Cologne European Council (2–4 June 1999), Annex III: Presidency Report on Strengthening of the common European policy on security and defence

Presidency Conclusions of the Helsinki European Council (10–11 December 1999), Annex 1 to Annex IV: Presidency progress report to the Helsinki European Council on strengthening the common European policy on security and defence

Presidency Conclusions of the Helsinki European Council (10–11 December 1999), Annex 2 to Annex IV: Presidency Report on Non-Military Crisis Management of the European Union (Action Plan)

Presidency Conclusions of the Laeken European Council (14–15 December 2001), Annex I: Laeken Declaration on the Future of the European Union

Presidency Conclusions of the Santa Maria da Feira European Council (19–20 June 2000), Annex I: Presidency Report on Strengthening the Common European Security and Defence Policy, Appendix 3: Study on concrete targets on civilian aspects of crisis management

Presidency Report to the Göteborg European Council (15–16 June 2001) on European Security and Defence policy, Annex I to the ANNEX: Police Action Plan, Council Doc 9526/1/01 REV 1 (11 June 2001)

Presidency Report to the Göteborg European Council (15–16 June 2001) on European Security and Defence policy, Annex III to the ANNEX: New Concrete Targets for Civilian Aspects of Crisis Management, Council Doc 9526/1/01 REV 1 (11 June 2001)

## European Court of Auditors

Avis n°1/1997 de la Cour des Comptes sur les conditions régissant l'exécution des dépenses dans le cadre de la politique étrangère et de sécurité commune (PESC)

Special report of the Court of Auditors No 2/1996 concerning the accounts of the Administrator and the European Union Administration, Mostar (EUAM) accompanied by the replies of the Commission and the Administrator of Mostar

Special report of the Court of Auditors No 13/2001 on the management of the common foreign and security policy (CFSP), together with the Council's replies and the Commission's replies [2001] OJ C338/01

Special report of the Court of Auditors No 18/2012, 'European Union assistance to Kosovo related to the rule of law'

Special report of the Court of Auditors No 9/2013, 'EU support for governance in the Democratic Republic of the Congo'.

Special report of the Court of Auditors No 7/2015, 'The EU police mission in Afghanistan: mixed results'

Special report of the Court of Auditors No 32/2016, 'EU assistance to Ukraine'

Special report of the Court of Auditors No 15/2018, 'Strengthening the capacity of the internal security forces in Niger and Mali: only limited and slow progress'

## European External Action Service

Civilian Operations Commander Instruction, 'Standard Operating Procedures on Whistleblowing', Ref Ares (2015)5643835 of 7 December 2015

Decision of the High Representative of the EU for Foreign Affairs and Security Policy of 19 September 2017 on the security rules for the European External Action Service ADMIN(2017) 10 OJ C126/1

EEAS Annual Activity Report 2018 (1 July 2019)

EEAS Annual Human Resources Report 2018 (July 2019)

EEAS, 'Organisation Chart of the EEAS' (July 2019) <https://eeas.europa.eu/headquarters/headquarters-homepage/3602/organisation-chart-of-the-eeas_en> [accessed 18 February 2020]

EEAS Review, European External Action Service 2013 1

Shared Vision, Common Action: A Stronger Europe. A Global Strategy for the European Union's Foreign and Security Policy (EUGS), presented by the High Representative Federica Mogherini on 28 June 2016

'The EU Integrated Approach to external conflicts and crises', EEAS/Commission services Issues Paper for PSC, dated 2 June 2017, Ref. Ares(2017)2821812

## European Ombudsman

European Ombudsman, 2009 Annual Report 2010

## European Parliament

European Parliament report on the implementation of the Common Security and Defence Policy (based on the Annual Report from the Council to the European Parliament on the Common Foreign and Security Policy), 3 November 2016 (A8-0317/2016)

European Parliament resolution of 12 December 2018 on the annual report on the implementation of the Common Foreign and Security Policy (2018/2097(INI))

European Parliament resolution of 21 May 2015 on financing the Common Security and Defence Policy (2014/2258(INI))

European Parliament resolution of 21 May 2015 on the implementation of the Common Security and Defence Policy (based on the Annual Report from the Council to the European Parliament on the Common Foreign and Security Policy) (2014/2220(INI))

European Parliament resolution of 7 May 2009 on the development of the relations between the European Parliament and national parliaments under the Treaty of Lisbon (2008/2120(INI))

European Parliament resolution on the European Ombudsman's Special Report to the European Parliament following the own-initiative inquiry into the existence and the public accessibility, in the different Community institutions and bodies, of a Code of Good Administrative Behaviour (C5-0438/2000—2000/2212 (COS)) [2002] OJ C72E/331

Minutes of the sitting of Friday 19 December 1997 [1998] OJ C14/409

Note by Elmar Brok and Roberto Gualtieri on parliamentary scrutiny of EU external action, including the common foreign security policy (CFSP) and the common security and defence policy (CSDP), following the entry into force of the Lisbon Treaty, draft version (7 November 2010)

Resolution on the proposal for an Interinstitutional Agreement between the European Parliament, the Council and the European Commission on provisions regarding financing of the Common Foreign and Security Policy (A4-0249/97), Annex: Interinstitutional Agreement between the European Parliament, the Council and the European

Commission on provisions regarding financing of the Common Foreign and Security Policy [1997] OJ C286/80

Rules of Procedure of the European Parliament, 8th parliamentary term, July 2016, ANNEX VII: Confidential and sensitive documents and information

## UN bodies

An Agenda for Peace. Preventive diplomacy, peacemaking and peace-keeping, A/47/277-S/24111 (17 June 1992), Report of the UN Secretary-General pursuant to the statement, adopted by the Summit Meeting of the Security Council on 31 January 1992

United Nations Peacekeeping Operations Principles and Guidelines (Capstone Doctrine, 2008), internal publication of the United Nations Department of Peacekeeping Operations and the Department of Field Support 2008

Towards an accountability system in the United Nations Secretariat, report of the Secretary-General of 29 January 2010, A /64/640

Approved resources for peacekeeping operations for the period from 1 July 2018 to 30 June 2019, note by the Secretary-General, A/C.5/72/2 (1 July 2018)

## Miscellaneous

Assembly of Western European Union, 'National parliamentary scrutiny of intervention abroad by armed forces engaged in international missions: the current position in law', Document A/1762 (2001) 2001 22.

Council of Europe (Venice Commission), 'Report on the Rule of Law', Study No 512/2009, CDL-AD(2011)003rev, Strasbourg, 4 April 2011

Council of Europe (Venice Commission), 'Rule of Law Checklist', CDL-AD(2016)007-e, Venice, 11–12 March 2016)

Final Report of Working Group IX on Simplification of 29 November 2002, CONV 424/02

International Law Association, Final Report on the Accountability of International Organisations, 2004

Joint Declaration on European Defence issued at the Franco-British Summit, Saint-Malo, 2–4 December 1998

Petersberg Declaration, issued by the Council of Ministers of the Western European Union, Bonn, 19 June 1992

Presidency Conclusions concerning the parliamentary scrutiny of the Common Foreign and Security Policy (CFSP) and Common Security and Defence Policy (CSDP), adopted at the Conference of the Speakers of the Parliaments of the EU, Brussels, 4–5 April 2011

Rules of procedure of the Inter-Parliamentary Conference for the Common Foreign and Security Policy and the Common Security and Defence Policy, adopted at its first meeting in Cyprus (9–10 September 2012), as amended at its meeting in Rome (5–7 November 2014)

State of the Union 2016—Towards a better Europe: a Europe that protects, empowers and defends, speech delivered by Jean-Claude Juncker on 14 September 2016

The Schuman Declaration (9 May 1950)

Unterrichtung durch die Kommission zur Überprüfung und Sicherung der Parlamentsrechte bei der Mandatierung von Auslandseinsätzen der Bundeswehr. Abschlussbericht der Kommission, Deutscher Bundestag, Drucksache 18/5000 (16 June 2015) 56

# Index

Note: *For the benefit of digital users, indexed terms that span two pages (eg 52–53) may, on occasion, appear on only one of those pages.*
Tables and figures are indicated by *t* and *f* following the page number.